17373EX_1 17373EX_4 © Westermann

CAMDEN TOWN

2

Erarbeitet von
Pamela Hanus
Kerstin Klemm
Christoph Reuter
Sylvia Wauer
sowie: Frauke Ibe, Peter Zocholl

Berater der Fachredaktion Gymnasium
Prof. Dr. Konrad Schröder

Fachliche Beratung
Helmut Bier
Roswitha Henseler
Ute Seemann
Ulrike Selz
Günther Sommerschuh
Prof. Dr. Karin Vogt

Diesterweg
westermann

CAMDEN TOWN 2

Materialien für Schülerinnen und Schüler

- Workbook 2 mit Lernsoftware und Audio-CD (ISBN 978-3-425-**73432**-3)
- Workbook 2 mit Audio-CD (ISBN 978-3-425-**73422**-4)
- Vocab Practice 2 (ISBN 978-3-425-**73442**-2)
- Klassenarbeitstrainer 2 (ISBN 978-3-425-**74121**-5)
- Lernsoftware 2
  - Einzelplatzlizenz (ISBN 978-3-425-**73482**-8)
  - Schullizenz (ISBN 978-3-425-**73492**-7)
- Camden Town Kit 1/2 (ISBN 978-3-425-**73452**-1)
- Vocab-App 2 – kostenfreier Download unter https://play.google.com/store, Stichwort: „Diesterweg"
- Grammar-App 2 (iPad) – Download über den Apple App Store, Stichwort: „Diesterweg"
- BiBox Digitale Unterrichtsmaterialien 2
  - Schüler-Einzellizenz (WEB-425-**30015**)
  - Basis-Einzellizenz (WEB-425-**30055**)

Materialien für Lehrkräfte

- Lehrerfassung zum Schülerband 2 (ISBN 978-3-425-**73502**-3)
- Workbook 2 mit Löser und Audio-CD (ISBN 978-3-425-**73512**-2)
- Teacher's Manual 2 (ISBN 978-3-425-**73522**-1)
- Differenzieren und Individualisieren 2 (ISBN 978-3-425-**71118**-8)
- Vorschläge für Lernerfolgskontrollen 2 (ISBN 978-3-425-**73532**-0)
- Audio-CD 2 mit DVD für Lehrkräfte (ISBN 978-3-425-**73572**-6)
- Interaktive Whiteboard-Software 2
  - Einzelplatzlizenz (ISBN 978-3-425-**73542**-9)
  - Schullizenz (ISBN 978-3-425-**73602**-0)
- BiBox Digitale Lehrermaterialien 2
  - Einzellizenz auf DVD-ROM (978-3-425-**73368**-5)
  - Einzellizenz (WEB-425-**73361**)
  - Schullizenz (WEB-425-**73375**)
- Kopiervorlagen 2 (ISBN 978-3-425-**73552**-8)
- Folien 2 (ISBN 978-3-425-**73562**-7)

westermann GRUPPE

Druck A⁶ / Jahr 2018
Alle Drucke der Serie A sind im Unterricht parallel verwendbar.

Redaktion: Lucas Mees und Dr. Heike Michaelis
Layout: Sandra Grünberg
Illustrationen: Ulf Marckwort, Kassel
Umschlaggestaltung: blum design und kommunikation GmbH, Hamburg
Druck und Bindung: westermann druck GmbH, Braunschweig

ISBN 978-3-425-**73402**-6

Wegweiser durch Camden Town

Kapitelteil

Aufbau der *Themes* 1–6

obligatorisch	A	Hier wird jeweils ein Unterthema des *Themes* behandelt.
	B	
	C	
fakultativ	Personal Trainer	Übungsteil zum Trainieren und Wiederholen
	Photo page	Fotos und landeskundliche Informationen (in *Theme* 1, 3 und 6)
	Optional	Literaturauszüge

Differenzierung und Individualisierung

❖ Extra — Fakultative zusätzliche Aufgabe
❖ Choose — Aufgabe mit Wahlmöglichkeiten
❖ Can you do it? — Aufgabe mit Hilfestellung
❖ B7 Target task — Offene Aufgabe, die differenzierte Ergebnisse hervorbringen kann

Die fakultativen Teile *Personal Trainer, Photo page* und *Optional* eignen sich für einen differenzierenden und individualisierenden Einsatz im Unterricht.

Kompetenzen

- Jedes Kapitel trainiert mehrere Kompetenzen (siehe Inhaltsverzeichnis).
- In den *target tasks* werden eine oder mehrere Kompetenzen intensiv trainiert. *Target tasks* sind umfangreichere Aufgaben, die Ergebnisse vorhergehender Übungen aufnehmen und einbinden.
- Auf den *Skills pages* befinden sich unterstützende Lern- und Arbeitstechniken zu allen Kompetenzen.
- Die Checklisten am Ende der Kapitel bieten eine Rückschau auf die Kompetenzen des jeweiligen Kapitels.

Anhang

Skills pages	Lern- und Arbeitstechniken
Language in Focus (LiF)	Grammatikanhang zum Nachschlagen
Words	Wortschatzanhang mit *Wordbanks* (thematischen Wortschatzsammlungen) und Wortlisten

Symbole

👥 / 👥	Partnerarbeit/Gruppenarbeit
🎧 *S 12, L 1/16*	Der Hörtext ist auf der Schüler-CD (Track 12) und auf der Lehrer-CD (CD1, Track 16).
🎥	Das Video zu der Aufgabe befindet sich auf der DVD.
● *P3*	Hierzu gibt es eine Übung (P3) auf den Personal-Trainer-Seiten.
📖 *WB A1, p. 3*	Hierzu gibt es eine Aufgabe im Workbook (Aufgabe A1 auf Seite 3).
● *Reading, p. 125*	Auf Seite 125 befinden sich Hilfen zum Lesen.
● *LiF 8: Present perfect, p. 140*	Auf Seite 140 befinden sich Hilfen zum Grammatikpensum *Present perfect*.
● *Wordbank People, p. 153*	Auf Seite 153 gibt es hilfreiche Wörter und Wendungen zum Thema *people*.
❖	Diese Aufgabe eignet sich besonders für Differenzierung/Individualisierung.
Need help? Look at pp. 20/21.	Um diese Aufgabe zu lösen, findest du Hilfen auf Seite 20 und 21.
Portfolio	Das Ergebnis kann im Portfolio-Ordner abgelegt werden.
✂ *Project*	Projekt
Support ·····	In dieser Box stehen Tipps und sprachliche Hilfen.

Back to Camden Town!

Emma Butler

- 12 years old
- brother: Jack
- hobbies: in-line skating, reading
- school: Camden School for Girls

George Lambraki

- 12 years old
- family: his father is from Greece
- twin sister: Caroline
- pet: dog (Patch)
- Manchester United fan
- school: William Ellis School

Gillian Collins
- 13 years old
- hobbies: football, animals
- family: she lives with her mum, but sees her dad at the weekend
- school: Camden School for Girls

Rajiv Khan
- 12 years old
- family: his family is from India
- sister: Sheree
- hobbies: music, football
- school: William Ellis School

Caroline Lambraki
- 12 years old
- family: her father is from Greece
- twin brother: George
- pet: cat (Socks)
- hobbies: in-line skating, music
- school: Camden School for Girls

Charlie Batson
- 12 years old
- family: his family is from Barbados
- two sisters: Josephine and Sharon
- Arsenal fan
- school: Acland Burghley School

Inhalt

Die gelb ausgezeichneten Teile sind als obligatorisch, die rot und grün ausgezeichneten Teile als fakultativ zu behandeln.
° Dieses Pensum befindet sich im Personal Trainer des Kapitels. • R = *revision*

Die Angebote in *Camden Town Gymnasium* sind nicht linear abzuarbeiten. Die Auswahl der Übungen und Übungsteile richtet sich nach den Schwerpunkten des schulinternen Curriculums.

Die gelb ausgezeichneten Teile sind als obligatorisch, die rot und grün ausgezeichneten Teile als fakultativ zu behandeln.
° Dieses Pensum befindet sich im Personal Trainer des Kapitels. • R = *revision*

Die Angebote in *Camden Town Gymnasium* sind nicht linear abzuarbeiten. Die Auswahl der Übungen und Übungsteile richtet sich nach den Schwerpunkten des schulinternen Curriculums.

1 After the holidays

Souvenirs, souvenirs

A1

a) Write down as many holiday words as you can.
You have got one minute. Who has got the most words?

b) Organize your words in a word web.
● P1 📖 WB A1, p. 4

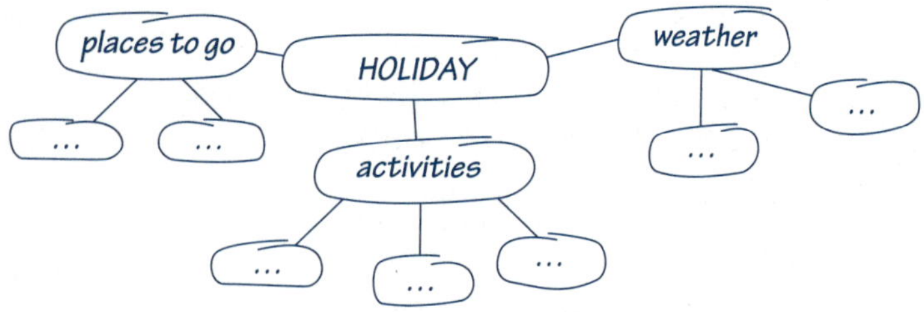

A2 🎧 L 1/1

a) The friends are back from holiday.
Look at their souvenirs. Say …
- … what they are
- … who brought them back
- … where they are from.

There is …/There are …

I think this is Rajiv's souvenir because he went to … /spent his holiday at/in …

b) Listen to the friends and complete the grid.
Were you right in a)?

souvenir	*whose?*	*where from?*
		Isle of Lewis
		Beam House
		Birmingham
		Thorpe Park
		…

c) Decide which of the friends' holidays you like best and say why.

I like Emma's holiday best because …

I think Caroline had a great time because …

A3 Target task ❖ ✂ *Project*

Need help? Look at pp. 20/21.

Prepare a collage about your holidays and present it.

Last year, your teacher asked you to collect souvenirs and/or write a postcard from your holidays (or your home town).

Did you have a good holiday?

That sounds great.

1 Work in groups of four.
Put all your souvenirs and postcards on a table. Every pupil says something about his/her holiday and souvenir. The others ask questions to find out more.

LiF 2R: Simple past, p. 136 · *P2-P5, P14* · *WB A2, A3, p. 4, 5*

had a wonderful/exciting holiday
went to Spain · stayed at home · went camping · …
stayed with my grandparents · went to the beach · …
It was warm/cold/sunny/rainy/cloudy/foggy/snowy/…
stayed for a week/two weeks/a weekend/…

Where did you stay?

Oh, that's too bad. Why didn't you like it?

What did you do?

How long did you stay?

Where did you find this souvenir?

I found/bought the souvenir …

2 Together prepare a collage about your holidays and present it to another group.

Speaking 1, p. 126 · *Wordbank Weather, p. 149*

Support

- Practise your presentation.
- Speak up.
- Look at page 126 for more tips.

3 Give the other group some feedback.
Don't forget to say something positive first.

Speaking 2, p. 127

Your presentation was easy to understand and you spoke clearly.

Your poster looks neat and tidy but you should speak up more.

Your presentation was fun to listen to/ really interesting.

Your poster looks attractive but it could be a bit more informative.

1 Holiday adventures

B1 L 1/2

a) Think of Caroline's holiday.
Where did she go? What did she do? What was her souvenir?

b) Close your books and listen to Gillian and Emma. What are they talking about?

c) Read the dialogue and answer the questions to get all the information about Emma and Caroline's holiday. Note down your answers.
- Where did they go?
- When did they go?
- What did they do/happened?

WB B1, p. 5

After the holidays Gillian and Emma meet at Westfield Shopping Centre.

Gillian: Hi Emma, where's Caroline? Isn't she coming?

Emma: Hi Gill. No, she's writing an email to Sophie, her friend from Manchester. She wants to tell her all about the pony camp in Wales.

Gillian: Oh, the pony camp. Did you like it?

Emma: Yes, it was great! I had the cutest pony! His name was Donald. He was as white as snow. He really was the prettiest pony of them all.

Gillian: So, what did you do at the pony camp?

Emma: We really had a lovely time: we cleaned the stables and went for rides. It was so much fun! We want to go again next year. Hey, why don't you come with us?

Gillian: Well, I really like animals but I don't think I'm a country person. There are no shops and no cinemas in the country. And London is much more exciting than Wales.

Emma: Well, there are some shops, but they're only small ones. The shops in London are bigger, of course. But it was nice to be in the country.

Gillian: But wasn't it a bit boring?

Emma: No, there was so much to do. One day we had a barbecue. And then there was the pony race.

Gillian: Caroline won the race, right?

Emma: Well … yes, you could say so. The funniest thing happened!

Gillian: Why was it funny?

Emma: Well, after the start Donald suddenly stopped and I fell off. It was terrible! I think a mouse scared him. Caroline rode Daisy. At first two other ponies, Lionheart and Princess, were faster than Daisy, but then they both went the wrong way. Nobody could stop them.

Gillian: No way!

Emma: Yes, and the story gets even funnier! Only Olivia and Caroline were left. Olivia was really better than Caroline. But her pony suddenly stopped, too, so Caroline came first.

Gillian: So, Caroline won the race because she was the only one left?

Emma: Yes, but don't tell anyone, please!

Gillian: OK.

Emma: Come on, let's go shopping – I think I missed shopping a bit after all.

B2

Gillian wants to tell her dad about the pony race. Complete her email and use these words and phrases to structure your text:

First … · Then … ·
Next … · In the end …

To: jfcollins@inter.net.co.uk

Hello!

Hi Dad,
How are you? I went to Westfield today and met Emma for some shopping. She went to a pony farm with her parents and Caroline in the holidays. She told me about a really funny pony race: first …
…

Love
Gillian xxx

B3

Gillian said, "I don't think I'm a country person". Are you a country or a city person? Why? Talk to a partner.

● *Wordbank In the country; city p. 149, 151*

B4 Grammar detective: comparison of adjectives

'small – smaller – smallest'
'exciting – more exciting – most exciting'
Can you solve this puzzle?

1 Copy the grid.
Look at B1 and fill in the grid.

adjective	comparative	superlative
cute	cuter	…
pretty	prettier	…
exciting	…	most exciting
big	…	biggest

2 Find more examples from B1. What is the rule?
When do you have to be careful with the spelling?

3 Look at LiF 3 on page 137 for help and write a grammar card.
Add the comparative and superlative forms of *good* and *bad* to your grammar card.

● *P11* *WB B2, p. 6*

B5

Emma and Gillian bought a lot of things at Westfield Shopping Centre. Look at them and compare them.

cheap · expensive · interesting · cool ·
big · delicious · cute · nice · good

Support

… as long as … / … as expensive as …
… longer than … / … more expensive than …
… the longest … / …the most expensive …

Example: ***The scarf is cheaper than the T-shirt.***

● *LiF 3: Steigerung von Adjektiven, p. 137/138* *WB B3, p. 6*

B6 ❖ Extra: Viewing: Adventure holidays

KG organizes adventure holidays for children.
George went on holiday with KG to Beam House.

a) Read the sentences. Then watch the advert and say which sentences are right and which are wrong.

1 At the summer camp there is a river where you can go kayaking.
2 You can go horse-riding on a KG holiday.
3 KG holidays are for boys only.
4 You can come to KG camps for a day, a week or a school holiday.
5 There are pupils from different countries, e.g. from Germany.
6 You can choose which activities you would like to do in the morning and in the afternoon.

b) Work with a partner. Are you interested in a KG holiday? Say why/why not.

B7 *L 1/3*

George told his friends everything about his holiday at Beam House – except one thing. Read the story and find out. *WB B4, p. 7*

George loved Beam House. He likes action and at Beam House you get a lot of that. On his first day he went surfing and abseiling. The next day, he went on the zip wire after breakfast. Later he also took some cool photos of the older kids doing motorsports on the quad bikes.

At five o'clock everyone at Beam House met to go orienteering. In George's group were Brady, Anna and Claire. The instructor gave them a map. They had to use a compass to find a treasure box and get back to Beam House as fast as possible. The girls were very excited.

First Claire took the compass and started to walk towards the woods while Anna, Brady and George followed.

"Walking around with a compass doesn't sound like a lot of fun," George thought, "but if I have to take part, I want to win."

After ten minutes of walking he asked Claire, "Are you sure you know where we're going?"

"Why?" she asked.

"I just wanted to check because I can see the river from here and the mark on the map is in the opposite direction."

"If you think you can do a better job, here you go!" Claire gave George the compass and looked at him angrily.

"Hey, calm down! We're a team, remember?" said Brady.

"OK then, let's go," George answered and turned round. The others followed him. However, while Anna and Brady talked and laughed, Claire didn't say a word.

They walked through the woods for twenty minutes. Everything seemed OK until George looked at the map again. Suddenly he wasn't sure about the right direction anymore and he became nervous.

"Do you need help?" Brady asked.

"No, no, it's OK," said George.

He didn't want to ask Brady for help in front of the girls. He almost started to run and the others followed.

"George, stop!" Anna finally shouted. "I can see a hill over there. I think we're lost!"

B8

What do you think happens next?
Use a grid to organize your ideas.
WB B5, p. 8

What?	*Who?*	*Where?*	*When?*
...	...	...	...

B9

It is easier to read a story that has a clear structure.
Read the story in B7 again and make a list of phrases or words you can use
- to structure a story (e.g. *on his first day, the next day*)
- to connect sentences (e.g. *and, but*) ● P6-P8 WB B6, p. 8

B10 Target task ❖ Portfolio

Need help? Look at pp. 21/22.

Finish the story from B7.
You can make it funny, scary or exciting.

1 Plan your story and use your ideas from B8.
Writing, p. 128

2 Structure your story and make it interesting.
LiF 2R: Simple past, p. 135; LiF 4: Connectives, p. 138

3 Swap your story with a partner's.
Use the checklist and give your partner feedback.
Speaking 2, p. 127

- ✓ *connectives (e.g. so, but, ...)*
- ✓ *structure words (e.g. first, then, ...)*
- ✓ *direct speech (e.g. "Why?" answered Claire.)*
- ✓ *adjectives, comparatives and superlatives (e.g. exciting, the scariest thing that ...)*

Your story is great but you need to add more direct speech to make it more interesting.

I like your story but you can use more words like 'because' or 'but' to connect your sentences.

Your story is really good but you can make it more interesting by using different adjectives.

4 Gallery walk: Hang up your stories in the classroom.
Choose three of your classmates' stories and read them.
Which one is your favourite and why?
Gallery walk, p. 130 WB B7, p. 9

1 Trouble at William Ellis

C1

a) It is the first day after the holidays at William Ellis School. Look at the picture and say why Mrs Brogden is angry.

Some boys are sitting …

b) Think – pair – share: What can make your teachers angry? Collect ideas and choose the top 5 things that can get you into trouble at school.

Think – pair – share, p. 130   *WB C1, C2, p. 10*

C2 *L 1/4*

a) On the first day of school Rajiv takes his new mobile phone with him. Listen to what he records with it. Find out what happens to him.

b) Speculate on what happens next to George and Rajiv.

I think they must …   *I guess they …*

c) Read how Mr Jackson, their teacher, and Mrs Edwards, the head teacher, talk to George and Rajiv. Were you right in b)? *P15*

Mrs Edwards: Rajiv, George, please sit down. Mr Jackson told me what you did in his history lesson. I'm really angry that you played with your mobile in Mr Jackson's class.

Rajiv: I'm really sorry, Mr Jackson. It was a stupid mistake.

Mrs Edwards: The school rules are very clear. Leave your mobiles at home or leave them in your bags. But you recorded parts of the lesson. I'm really disappointed in you.

Mr Jackson: You should learn about British history in my lessons, not about mobile phones. That was unacceptable. Why didn't you leave your mobile at home?

Rajiv: We're very sorry. It won't happen again. All the others talked about their exciting summer holidays, but I stayed at home all the time. So I thought, why not talk about my new mobile? But now I know it was wrong to bring it to school.

George: It was my mistake, really. I asked Rajiv to give me his mobile and I recorded the lesson. It was just a bit of fun.

Mr Jackson: I don't think so. Who knows what you wanted to do with those clips? Maybe you wanted to put them online.

Rajiv: No, really. We were a bit bored and it's the first day back at school. So we had that stupid idea. But it wasn't just George, it was my fault, too.

Mrs Edwards: It's good that you both see that you did something wrong. But I'm going to keep the mobile for the moment and I'm going to phone your parents. Mr Jackson and I agree that you should do something for history. As you didn't follow the history lesson, you must prepare a presentation on the Romans and the Celts.

George: The Romans and the Celts? Can't we choose another topic?

Mrs Edwards: No, you can't. Work hard on your presentation. You may go now.

C3

a) Look at C2 again and say how the people feel.

Mr Jackson *Mrs Edwards* *George* *Rajiv*	*feels* *is*	*sad* *disappointed* *angry* *happy* *very angry* *sorry* *...*	*that ...* *because ...*

b) Look at C2 again.
Start a grid and collect phrases that express that ...

- ... someone does not like something
- ... someone feels sorry for what he/she did
- ... someone knows that he/she did something wrong

P16, P12 WB C3–C5, p. 11, 12

c) ❖ Choose

- Write down how you can feel when your ...
  ... teacher gives you a lot of/no extra homework
  ... teacher asks you to write something on the board
  ... teacher talks to your parents
  ... teacher is late
  ... classmates are noisy

or

- Look at C2 again and complete the sentences.

1 The school rules say that pupils must ...
2 Mr Jackson wants to know why ...
3 George thinks it was just ...
4 Mrs Edwards is going to ...
5 George and Rajiv must ...
6 George wants to know if they can ...

C4

George calls his mother to tell her what happened.
Work with a partner. Complete the dialogue – one of you is Mrs Lambraki and the other one is George. Add phrases from C3b) where possible.

LiF 1R: Simple present, p. 133/134; 2R: Simple past, p. 135/136 WB C6, p. 13

George: Hi, Mum. I should tell you about what happened at school today.
Mrs Lambraki: Oh no, what did you ...?
George: I didn't do anything. It was Rajiv. He ... And then I ...
Mrs Lambraki: Why ...?
George: Because we were bored.
Mrs Lambraki: Oh George. Now what ... next?
George: Well, we had to go to Mrs Edwards. Mr Jackson was there, too. What ... when they called you?
Mrs Lambraki: ... And what ...?
George: Rajiv and I have to prepare a presentation about the Romans and Celts in Britain. ...
Mrs Lambraki: George, I'm really ...! ...

C5 ❖ Extra

a) Present your dialogues from C4 to another pair. Decide which of the two dialogues is better. Say why.

b) Present some good dialogues in class and discuss what makes them good dialogues. Think of what they are about and the language they use.

C6

A few days later George and Rajiv write notes to each other in their English lesson.

a) Put them in the right order. What are the notes about?

Reading, p. 125 WB C7, C8, p. 14

Hi, Rajiv. What do you think about what Mr Jackson said?

OK. Maybe we can make the presentation a little bit more interesting than a normal lesson. Maybe Charlie can help us.

You're right. Let's ask Charlie for help. He's good at history. We can talk about it at lunch.

No way, George. We should show him that we are not as stupid as he thinks we are.

Romans and Celts? I don't know anything about them. They both sound boring to me.

Good idea, but we could ask Mr Jackson for some ideas, too.

It was better than I thought. I think it was good that we said sorry again. He wasn't as angry as last lesson. But a presentation about Romans and Celts ... not so sure.

That's true. They sound really boring. Let's go to the library after lunch. Maybe we can find something that is more interesting than 'Roman cities in England'.

b) Look at the notes again and complete the sentences.

1 Rajiv thinks that Mr Jackson wasn't ...
2 The boys think that the Romans and Celts ...
3 They want to go to the library to ...
4 Rajiv doesn't want to ask Mr Jackson because ...
5 The boys think that Charlie ... because ...

c) Look at the notes again. Make a grid to collect phrases (how to agree/how to disagree). Then add more words/phrases to the grid.

P10

d) Look at your grid. Mark phrases you can only use with friends but not with teachers.

C7

L 1/5

a) Listen to Charlie's tips and note down the tip you like best. Say why. P13

Charlie's tip for/about… is my favourite because …

b) Listen again and complete the sentences with *as* ... *as* ... or ... *than* ... .

LiF 3: Steigerung von Adjektiven, p. 137/138 WB C9, p. 15

1 A presentation about Romans is ... one about Celts.
2 It is ... to find material on the Romans ... on the Celts.
3 The BBC websites often have ... information ... other websites and some books.
4 In the Horrible Histories books you can find pictures that are ... pictures from normal history books.
5 A presentation with those pictures is ... without the pictures.
6 But maybe Mr Jackson doesn't find it ... the pupils.

C8 L 1/6

George and Rajiv are in the library to prepare their history presentation when there is an announcement over the PA system.

a) Listen to the announcement.
What does the head teacher say?
Listening, p. 124

b) What do you think about what the pupils did?
P17 WB C10, p. 15

I think/don't think it's OK if you …

What they did was stupid/silly/clever/cool/… because …

C9 Target task

Project Portfolio P9

Write a dialogue between the two pupils from Year 8 and Mrs Edwards, the head teacher.

Need help? Look at pp. 22/23.

1 Work in groups of three. Choose one role and read your role card.
Think about your character:
- What kind of person is he/she?
- How does he/she feel?
- What does he/she say?

Wordbank People, p. 153

Mrs Edwards

- is very angry that the boys started their own business
- wants to find out about the details
- wants to punish them for what they did.

2 Plan your dialogue.
Use words and phrases from C3b) and C6.

Matt Hickman

- is not very clever or polite
- is always in trouble
- doesn't understand why the head teacher is angry
- thinks the sweets at school are too expensive so that pupils want to buy sweets from him.

Salman Amin

- is a good, polite pupil
- understands that he did something wrong but doesn't see why selling sweets is such a big problem
- saved the money for a new computer.

3 Present your dialogue to another group.
Give feedback.
- Were the characters convincing?
- Did the group use the language from C3b) and C6? Speaking 2, p. 127

Support

Giving feedback:
Patrick was very good as Salman/Matt because he …
I don't think Vanessa acted like the role card says because …
Jessica did not ask many questions as Mrs Edwards, but the role card says …
Lisa's questions as Mrs Edwards were very good because she asked about …
I liked Jens as Salman/Matt because he said that it was …'s fault, too.

Prepare your target task A3:

P1 Words: holidays

a) Find out the holiday words. Write them in your exercise book.

1 caebh	4 nnsuy
2 rdstpoca	5 ingghtsisee
3 caitsuse	6 nivesour

b) Choose five more holiday words and make a quiz for your partner like in a).

c) Find phrases to talk about holidays.

	at a hotel
	camping
	a fantastic holiday
stay	*on holiday*
go	*fun*
have	*sightseeing*
	for two weeks
	to Berlin

P2 Words: positive/neutral/negative adjectives

Complete the grid.

great · OK · fantastic · boring · alright · wonderful · exciting · really nice · terrible · good · so-so · brilliant

☺	😐	☹
great	*so-so*	…

P3 Revision: simple past

LiF 2R: Simple past, p. 135

Gillian did a lot of jobs in the holidays because her mum had to work.

a) Look at Gillian's list. Write down what she did.
Example:
Gillian … shopping.
She …

Gillian,
Please
- *go shopping (see shopping list)*
- *tidy up your room*
- *take out the rubbish*
- *phone Grandma*
- *bake a cake for the weekend*
- *clean the bathroom*

Thanks!
Mum

And don't forget to have some ice cream!

b) What did you do in your holidays? What didn't you do? Write down six sentences.
Example: *I went shopping but I didn't …*

P4 Revision: simple past (questions with question words)

LiF 2R: Simple past, p. 136

You are just back from your dream holiday.
Work with a partner.
He/She wants to know everything about it.

What did you do?
I went swimming/ had ice cream every day/ played beach volleyball/ met a film star/…

Where did you go for your holidays?
I went to New York/the North Pole/… I stayed with my cousin/… …

How long did you stay?
One day/week/… Ten weeks/…

Where did you stay?
I stayed in a five star hotel/ a holiday apartment/ with Mickey Mouse/…

What was the weather like?
It was sunny/ really cold/…

P5 Revision: simple past (questions and short answers) ● *LiF 2R: Simple past, p. 136*

a) Work with a partner.
Ask and answer questions about the friends from Camden.

make a cake for Charlie
see pickpockets at Camden Market
keep Oscar
have a birthday party
go to Portobello Road Market
buy a computer

Did the friends make a cake for Charlie?

Yes, they did.

...

b) Find five more questions for your partner.

Prepare your target task B10:

P6 Words: connectives ● *LiF 4: Verbindung von Sätzen, p. 138*

Use the connectives (e.g. *because, so, ...*) to link the sentences.

A holiday at Beam House is great for George		*he likes action.*
He took some cool photos	*because*	*some older kids did motorsports.*
At five o'clock everyone met	*after*	*they wanted to go orienteering.*
George doesn't like orienteering	*and*	*he wanted to win.*
They had to use a compass	*when*	*find a treasure box.*
Claire was angry	*but*	*George took the compass.*
George became nervous	*so*	*Brady wanted to help him.*
George almost started to run		*they were lost.*

P7 Words: writing a story *S 1, L 1/7*

Direct speech[1] makes stories more interesting.
But be careful – it's boring if you always use the word *say*.

a) What are these words?
You can use them instead of[2] *say*.

/ɑ:sk/ · /ˈʃaʊt/ ·
/ˈɑ:nsə/ · /kɔ:l/ ·
/lɑ:f/ · /əˈgri:/ · /tel/

b) Listen to the CD and check your words.

[1] direct speech – *direkte Rede*
[2] instead of – *statt*

P8 Words: adjectives

Nice is a nice word – but not if *nice* is the only adjective you use in your story!

a) Find other words for *nice*. You can use your dictionary.
Example: *pretty, amazing, lovely, …*

b) Caroline's classmate Hamida wrote a report about her holidays. Copy her text, but use other adjectives for *nice*.

In the summer holidays I went to Madagascar with my family. Madagascar is a nice island in the Indian Ocean. It was very hot. There were lots of nice white beaches and palm trees.
My sister and I went swimming in the sea every day while my mum and dad read their books on the beach. We saw many nice fish. There were pink ones, blue ones, green ones … all the colours of the rainbow!
The food there was nice. We ate coconuts and papayas.
The people of Madagascar are also very nice. They are always smiling.
One day we went walking around the island and I took lots of pictures with my new camera. There were so many nice things to see! Another day we went to a concert in the town. It was nice!
We also tried some Madagascan vanilla. It was very nice.
On the last day we were very sad to leave.
We had a nice holiday!

Prepare your target task C9:

P9 Words: giving feedback

Copy the grid and write down the statements in the right groups:

words	*grammar*	*structure*
…	…	…

1 It was good that you looked up some words in the dictionary.
2 It was easy to follow your dialogue because you connected the sentences with words like *because*.
3 I think there were some mistakes in your sentences. Don't forget the *-s* after *he, she, it*.
4 Sometimes you used pronouns like *it* or *they*, but it wasn't always clear who or what you were talking about.
5 You should check the word order of your dialogue again.
6 People don't just say *yes* or *no*, but they also explain why they think so. You should add that to your dialogue, too.
7 You tried to use a lot of different words and didn't use the same words again and again.
8 Some words were too difficult for me.

P10 Words: agreeing/disagreeing

a) Match the sentences that mean more or less the same[1].

1 I absolutely agree.
2 That's nonsense.
3 I can understand that point, but there are other things you should think about.

A That's really silly.
C I agree, but you shouldn't forget what other people might say.
B I think the same.

b) Read some rules from different British schools. Then say what you think of them. Say why you think so, too. You can use phrases from a), for example.

1. Pupils should wear school uniform.
2. Pupils should wait quietly in line[2] in front of the classroom.
3. All people at school should respect each other.
4. Pupils mustn't be late.
5. Pupils must eat food in the cafeteria and mustn't take any food out.
6. Pupils must keep their MP3 players and mobile phones in their bags during the school day.

[1] more or less the same – *mehr oder weniger das gleiche*
[2] quietly in line – *ruhig in einer Reihe*

Extra language training:

P11 Comparison of adjectives

LiF 3: Steigerung von Adjektiven, p. 137/138

Here are some activities you can do at Beam House. Compare[1] the activities. What are your favourite activities?

... is my favourite activity because ...

I think ... is ... than ...

[1] compare – *vergleichen*

dangerous · boring · exciting · interesting · silly · difficult · fascinating

archery

motorsport

body boarding

zip wire

P12 Revision: simple past (questions)

LiF 2R: Simple past, p. 136

❖ Can you do it?

1. Form the questions that go with these answers.

   I only saw Mr Jackson when it was too late to put the mobile phone away.
   → When ??? Mr Jackson?

   George and I had a meeting with the head teacher because Mr Jackson told her about the mobile phone. → Why ??? a meeting …?

2. **You can check your answers on page 221.**
3. **You need help?** → Do a), then b).
   You can do it? → Do b).

a) Rajiv's classmates want to find out more about his mobile. What are their questions?

1 Where … you get it? – I bought it in Oxford Street.
2 How much … it …? – It cost £50.
3 Why … you … that one? – I chose this one because it's cool!
4 Why … take it to school? – I took it to school because I thought you would like to see it.

b) George and Rajiv are not the only ones who got into trouble on the first day after the holidays. What did Mrs Edwards ask Dylan?

1 What … you …? – I drew a picture on my desk.
2 What …? – I drew a picture of Mrs Brogden.
3 You should take part in the lesson. Why …? – Because it was so boring.
4 What …? – I said sorry to Mrs Brogden and that I will clean the desk in the lunch break.

P13 Comparison of adjectives

LiF 3: Steigerung von Adjektiven, p. 137/138

Compare the two pictures of a village[1] in Roman Britain.
What is different?

[1] village – *Dorf*

big · colourful · dark · tall · happy · long

Extra skills training:

P14 Words: weather

S 2, L 1/8 ● Wordbank Weather, p. 149

Draw a picture of Great Britain like this:
Then listen to the weather report[1].
Use symbols to note down the information about the weather.
Add information on temperatures, too.

[1] weather report – *Wetterbericht*

P15 Reading

Reading p. 125

Read the dialogue in C2 (page 16) again. Are the statements true or false?
Correct the false sentences.

1 Pupils mustn't bring mobiles to William Ellis School.
2 Rajiv brought the mobile to be more interesting to the other pupils.
3 George says he didn't do anything wrong.
4 Mr Jackson is afraid that the boys could put the video clips on the Internet.
5 Both Rajiv and George had the idea about the mobile phone.
6 Mrs Edwards gives Rajiv the mobile phone back.

P16 Words: trouble at school

a) Look at the pictures. Write down what the pupils in Rajiv and George's class do wrong.

1

2

3

4

5

not wear · forget · take … to school · listen to … · not clean

b) What could the boys say to explain their mistakes? Use the words and phrases from C3b (page 17). Your ideas can be funny, too.

I'm really sorry. I don't wear my school tie because my dog ate it.

P17 Sounds

S 3, L 1/9

a) Listen to the words and repeat them. Then make a grid and put the words in groups like this:
b) Listen again and check your grid.

[t]	[d]	[ɪd]
liked	…	…

Holidays in Britain

Great Britain has miles and miles of coastline[1] with spectacular cliffs and long, sandy beaches. You can enjoy the fantastic scenery[2] and of course the seaside is a paradise for all watersports. Especially in Cornwall, where huge waves[3] roll in from the Atlantic, body boarding is a special sport that you might like to try.

Or maybe you are more interested in wildlife? There are many ideal places for birdwatching and you can see deer[4] or badgers[5] in the countryside. The islands north of the Scottish coast are not only famous for their ponies, but the Shetland Islands are also a fabulous place to see seals and even go whale spotting.

For those who love history, Great Britain has many special places of interest. Travel back in time and visit sights like Stonehenge, where druids[6] used to celebrate. Why not visit thermal spas[7] like Bath, where the ancient Romans[8] went to relax, or one of the many medieval[9] castles like Arundel in Sussex, and beautiful palaces like Hampton Court or Blenheim Palace?

Are you keen on futuristic places? Then visit Eden Project, where an artificial biosphere[10] makes it possible to walk through a man-made tropical jungle[11] in England.

Who wants to go to school in the holidays? Well, why not visit the places where famous people went to school, like playwright[12] William Shakespeare in Stratford-upon-Avon – or Oxford, where the Harry Potter films were filmed in the old university college of Christchurch.

1

3

5

1

a) Look at the pictures and read the texts. Which of the holiday ideas is most attractive to you? Say why.

b) Have a class survey. What are the top three in class?

2

Note down the places in a list and work with the map at the front of your book to find the places. Test your partner.

Where is Cornwall?

… is on/near the (south/west/…) coast.

It's in the north/ east/south/west.

[1] coastline – *Küstenlinie*
[2] scenery – *Landschaft*
[3] wave – *Welle*
[4] deer – *Rotwild*
[5] badger – *Dachs*
[6] druid – *Druide, Zauberer*
[7] thermal spa – *Thermalbad*
[8] ancient Romans – *(die) alten Römer*
[9] medieval – *mittelalterlich*
[10] artificial biosphere – *künstliche Biosphäre*
[11] jungle – *Dschungel*
[12] playwright – *Schriftsteller*

Kynance Cove, Cornwall

Hampton Court Palace, Surrey

2

Eden Project, Cornwall

4

Stonehenge

6

Seals on the coast of Shetland

7

Bodyboarder at Crooklets Beach, Cornwall

8

Romans and Celts

O1 ● Reading, p. 125

Rajiv and George are working on their history presentation for Mr Jackson's class.
Look at the comic about Romans and Celts on this page.
Choose the best title for the comic and explain your choice.

A How the Celts and the Romans changed Britain
B What the Romans built in Britain.
C The Romans in Britain

1

1. The Celts came to Britain in around 500 BC and took control of the country. They lived in tribes and often fought against others for land.

2

2. The Celts were not only good fighters, but also good farmers. They usually lived in round houses, often on the top of hills.

3

3. In 55 and 54 BC, Julius Caesar and his army landed in Britain. However, the Romans felt that the Celts and the British weather were too much for them and left.

4

4. In AD 43, the Romans invaded Britain again and this time they stayed in Britain and took control of the south of England. They hoped for better trade with the Celts.

5

5. The Romans brought a lot of new things with them: they built roads, temples, baths and stone houses and they brought new entertainment, such as gladiator fighting and wine.

6

6. Not all the Celts were happy with the Romans. The Celtic queen Boudicca and her men fought against the Romans in AD 60 and burned down some cities like London. In the end, however, the Romans won.

7

8

9

O2

a) Read the captions again and find the right words in the text:
- A a group of people who have the same language and religion and usually live in one area
- B to go to a country and fight
- C when people buy and sell goods

b) Start a timeline for Britain's early history.

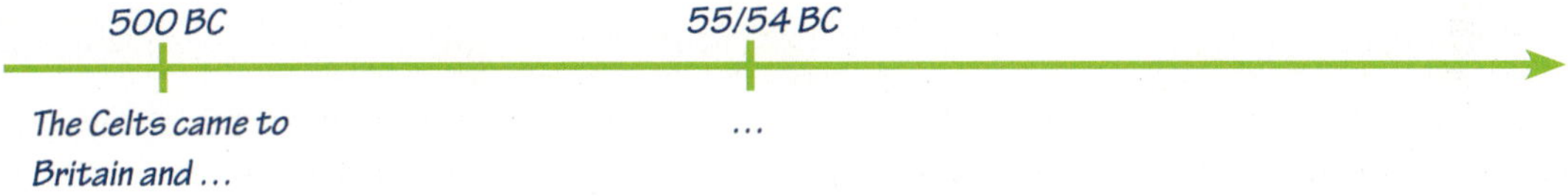

O3 S 4, L 1/10 Listening, p. 124

a) Follow the steps to write captions for pictures 7–9 in O1.

1 Look at the pictures 7–9 in the comic again.
2 Listen to a podcast about the Romans in Britain. Take notes for each picture.
3 Use your notes to write captions.

b) Add more information to your timeline from O2b.

Du kannst schon viel auf Englisch verstehen und ausdrücken. Du kannst ...
- ✓ über deine Ferien sprechen
- ✓ deinen Mitschülerinnen und Mitschülern Rückmeldung geben
- ✓ ein Ereignis nacherzählen
- ✓ Dinge vergleichen
- ✓ das Ende einer Geschichte verfassen
- ✓ Gefühle beschreiben
- ✓ Abneigungen und Missfallen äußern
- ✓ etwas vorschlagen, zustimmen und ablehnen

WB Portfolio-Fragebogen Theme 1

2 Let's get the party started

Festivals around the year

Chinese New Year

Gung Hei Fat Choi! That is 'Happy New Year!' in Chinese. Our New Year's Day is not on January 1st but in late January or in February. Then we clean our houses, decorate them with fruit and flowers and put up red and gold banners with short poems in the house because they bring good luck. Parents give their children red envelopes with money in them and we eat special food like dumplings or rice pudding. Many people watch the famous dragon dance because we Chinese believe that dragons are friendly. We also have fireworks that make a lot of noise to keep the monsters and bad luck away.

Diwali

In October or November Hindu people celebrate Diwali – the Festival of Lights. My family and I often go to Diwali in Trafalgar Square. Many groups dance there and perform stories about Diwali. Diwali is also a celebration for Lakshmi, the goddess of good luck and wealth. We put diyas – small lamps – and candles around our houses to help the goddess Lakshmi find her way into people's houses. We also give each other presents for Diwali, send cards and eat a lot of delicious sweets and cakes. But the best thing about Diwali is the fireworks!

A1

a) Think of three special days that you celebrate in your family (e.g. Christmas). Make notes on how you celebrate these days. Think about decorations, food, guests, clothes, …

Wordbank Festivals, p. 150

We always invite …

I don't wear my normal clothes, but …

b) Talk about these special days with a partner. *P1*

c) Make a list of the special days and celebrations in class. When do they take place over the year? *WB A1, p. 23*

d) ❖ **Extra:** Do you know any special celebrations in Britain or other English-speaking countries? Say what you know about them and add them to the list from c).

Bonfire Night

Remember, remember, the fifth of November! On November 5th 1605 Guy Fawkes and a group of men tried to blow up the Houses of Parliament in London to kill King James I. But their plan did not work. When people found out that the king was safe, they lit bonfires to celebrate. It is now a tradition to celebrate this event with fireworks and a bonfire.
In the past, children made dummies of Guy Fawkes to ask people for 'a penny for the Guy'. As it is usually cold in November, we have food that keeps us warm, like baked potatoes. But marshmallows and toffee apples are everyone's favourite food on Bonfire Night!

A2

The pupils at William Ellis present some celebrations for a school project.

a) Mini jigsaw: Work in groups of three. Each group member reads about one of the festivals. Copy the grid and fill it in for 'your' festival.

Mini jigsaw, p. 130 *Reading, p. 125*

	Chinese New Year	*Diwali*	*Bonfire Night*
When do people celebrate?			
What/Why do people celebrate?			
What do people do/wear/…?			

b) Present what you know about the celebrations to your group. Complete your grid with information about the other celebrations.

c) Imagine you have the chance to take part in one of these celebrations. Which one would you choose? Why?

P2, P3, P13 *WB A2–A4, p. 23-25*

Support

… is a holiday that … celebrate every year at …
The reason why they celebrate … is that …
It is a holiday that is famous for …
When you get the chance to go to these celebrations, you should try …
What is typical of that holiday is that …

A3 Target task *Project* *Portfolio*

Need help? Look at p. 40.

Work with a partner. Design a page for a 'special days' calendar.

Choose:

- a special day that you celebrate in your family or home town **or**
- a special day that British or other English-speaking people celebrate, e.g. Hogmanay, St Patrick's Day, Notting Hill Carnival. Find out as much as you can about your festival.

Wordbank Festivals, p. 150 *P8*

Support

- Plan your text so that your page answers the questions from the grid in A2a).
- If you use information from the Internet, make sure that your text is easy to read and understand.
- Include photos/pictures.

2 Party planners

B1 L 1/11

Caroline and Emma are watching a video.
It is of a celebration they had last year.
Listen to the sounds.
Which celebration is it? How did you find out?

Listening, p. 124 WB B1, p. 26

B2 L 1/12

a) Look at the card on Charlie's desk. What is it about?

b) There is a message on Charlie's mobile phone. Listen to it and find out what his problem is.

B3 L 1/13

a) What do you have to organize before you can have a party? Wordbank Festivals, p. 150

b) Close your books. Listen and find out what the girls are talking about. WB B2, p. 26

Caroline, Emma and Gillian are in Caroline's room.

Caroline: Let me just check our list. OK, I'm going to ask Mum and Dad to buy some fireworks for us. Some rockets and some bangers, of course. George is crazy about bangers – the noisier, the better. And we should get some sparklers for everyone. What do you think?

Emma: Well, it wouldn't be much fun without the boys ... so let them have their bangers.

Gillian: Really, Emma. I didn't know you were so interested in boys.

Emma: Well, some of them are quite OK, you know.

Gillian: Oh, are you thinking about anyone in particular?

Caroline: Just stop it, Gillian. We all know who that particular person is! Now, back to the list – we're going to have a party next weekend, remember?

Gillian: OK, Miss Bossyboots. So, what food are we going to have?

Caroline: Well, Emma is going to bring toffee apples. And I can ask Mum to make some of her delicious Greek snacks. What about you?

Gillian: I'm going to go shopping with Mum on Friday so I can bring whatever you like. Why don't we ask the others to bring some crisps and sweets, too?

Caroline: Great idea! But I already gave Charlie his invitation today. I know – we can text him about it. Now who else are we going to invite?

Gillian: Well, I don't want to have a party with people I don't like ...

Emma: And I don't want to have the same people all the time.

Gillian: I think the same people *and* that particular person Rick would be perfect!

Emma: Stop it, Gillian!

Mrs Lambraki: Caroline! Charlie's on the phone.

Caroline: Charlie? Are you sure he doesn't want to talk to George?

B4

Read the dialogue in B3 again.
Say how the girls feel and what they do. ● P9 WB B3, p. 27

Emma	*seems*	*angry*	*when*	*she thinks of …*
Caroline	*is*	*nervous*	*because*	*she tells …*
Gillian	*feels*	*annoyed*		*she remembers …*
		nosy		*the other girls …*
		funny		*Gillian …*
		surprised		*Caroline …*
		bossy		*…*

B5 L 1/14

a) Close your books.
Listen to Caroline and Charlie.
How does Caroline react to Charlie's news?

Caroline: Hi, Caroline speaking.
Charlie: Hi, Caroline, it's Charlie. Thanks again for the invitation. It's really great, but there's a bit of a problem. Rajiv just called and you'll never guess what – he is planning a Diwali party the same night as your bonfire party.
Caroline: Oh no! That's awful. I'm sure he'll invite the same people as us.
Charlie: Yeah, I think he'll invite George, you, of course, and Emma and Gillian. Maybe Rick and a few others. I think he wants to show his non-Hindu friends what Diwali is about.
Caroline: That's a great idea. I don't know much about Diwali. But we have just finished planning our party. What a mess!
Charlie: Yeah, well. I hope you'll sort that problem out. I'm sure both parties will be fantastic, but it won't be possible for me to go to both of them.
Caroline: Of course not. But maybe we can think of something. Emma and Gillian are here, so I'll talk to them first. Will you be at home later?
Charlie: Yeah, you can call me here.
Caroline: OK then. Let's talk later. Bye.

b) Complete the sentences.

1 Charlie hopes that Caroline will …
2 Charlie knows that he won't …
3 Caroline hopes that she and the other girls will …
4 Caroline says that she will …

WB B4, B5, p. 27, 28

Support

'll = will

B6 Grammar card: will future

You already know the *going to* future, but Caroline and Charlie use another tense to talk about the future – the *will future*.
Start a grammar card for the *will future*.

1 Look at B5 on page 33 again.
Note down examples of positive and negative sentences and questions.

2 How do you form the *will future*? Check LiF 6 on page 139.

3 Look at B5 again and find phrases that introduce sentences with the *will future*.
Example: ***I'm sure he'll invite the same people as us.***
Now check LiF 6 on page 139 again. When do you use the *will future*?
P10 *WB B6, p. 29*

B7

a) What will happen next?
Look at the pictures and write down if Caroline and Rajiv will do those things or not.
Example: ***I guess Caroline will be angry and disappointed.***
I think she'll ask Rajiv if …
LiF 6: will future, p. 139

I guess she/he/they won't … because …

I don't think she/he/they will … because …

Maybe she/he/they … because …

b) Round Robin: Work in groups. What will happen next? Write a short statement.
Round Robin, p. 130 *WB B7, B8, p. 30*

B8

a) Read Caroline's email to Rajiv. Were you right in B7b)?

Reading, p. 125

Hi Rajiv,

How are you?

I don't know if you already know, but we've got a problem. The girls and I are planning a party for November 5. We thought we could have a party at our house for Bonfire Night. But now Charlie tells me that you would like to have a Diwali party on the same night. I guess you'll probably invite the same people as us.

I talked to Emma and Gillian about it and we've got an idea, but I'm not sure that you'll like it. Don't you think it would be a good idea to have just one party on that night? Why don't we mix Bonfire Night and Diwali? There are fireworks for both festivals. What about one big party at our house? We've got enough room and Mum and Dad say it's no problem. Let's just celebrate in one place.

I hope you won't be upset about it. Please call or email back soon.

Bye,

Caroline

b) What are Caroline's arguments for a Diwali and Bonfire Night party? Note them down.

c) Look at the structure of Caroline's email. Where can you find the following parts?

1 Saying hello
2 Introducing the email with a friendly question/sentence
3 Explaining why you are writing the email
4 Making suggestions
5 Finishing the email with a friendly statement
6 Saying goodbye

P4, P5 *WB B9, p. 31*

d) Find words and phrases for each part of the email.
Example: *Hi; How…*
Then collect more words and phrases in class.

B9 Target task ❖ *Portfolio*

Need help? Look at p. 40/41.

Imagine you are Rajiv. Answer Caroline's email.

1 Before you start writing, decide how Rajiv feels about Caroline's idea. What would he like to do? Note down your ideas.

2 When you write the email, follow the structure from B8c).
- Use phrases from B8d) to write your email.
- Use the *will future* when necessary.

Wordbank Festivals, p. 150 *Writing, p. 128* *LiF 6: will future, p. 139*

2 The party

C1

What makes a good party?

There is good food.

…

C2 L 1/15

a) Read the dialogue between Caroline and George.
Find out what they and their friends expect of the party.

George: Do we know how many people are actually coming to the party?

Caroline: Well, Emma's coming, of course, and Gillian. And then some girls from my class, Sophie and Hamida. They're really looking forward to it because there'll be boys there! They haven't got any brothers, you see! If you like, I'll invite Denah, too. She's really nice and she thinks you're cool!

George: If you invite her, I'll never speak to you again! If she comes, she'll follow me around all the time and she always wants to talk about football. Rajiv thinks it's really funny, but it's just embarrassing.

Caroline: OK, OK, don't worry. I won't invite her. So which boys are coming?

George: Well, Rajiv, of course. It's his party, too. And Charlie will be there.They can't wait for the fireworks! I must tell Dad to buy more bangers. If we have lots of bangers, we can scare the girls.

Caroline: Very funny! But are only two boys coming, George? That's not many. Did Rajiv ask Rick?

George: Well, he asked him and Holden, but they're not sure. Maybe they'll go to Alexandra Palace to see the fireworks.

Caroline: But Rick must come! If he doesn't come, Emma will be so unhappy. She's got a big crush on him and she's so excited about the party.

George: So what do you want me to do? If I tell him about Emma, he'll probably be too embarrassed to come!

Caroline: That's true. But why don't you talk to Rick and Holden and tell them that they can come after the fireworks. If the party's good, there'll still be some people here. And it won't be much fun if we don't invite some more boys for my friends.

George: What do you mean – if the party's good? Of course it'll be good. There'll be a big bonfire and Mum says she'll make some souflaki for the barbecue, and there'll be hot dogs and …

Caroline: But that's only part of the fun, George. It's not so important how much food and drink we have. I'm really worried that not many boys will come. My friends can't wait to meet your friends. They'll be really disappointed if there aren't many boys! Please talk to Holden and Rick on Monday.

b) Say how …

- … George will feel if Denah comes to the party. Why?
- … Emma will feel if Rick doesn't come. Why?
- … Rajiv and Charlie will feel if there are not enough bangers.
- … Rick will feel if George tells him about Emma.
- … the girls will feel if the boys don't come.

● P11 WB C1, p. 32

C3 L 1/16

a) Listen to George's conversation with Rick and Holden. Will they come to the party?
Listening p. 124

b) Listen again and make a list of reasons for
- going to the fireworks at Alexandra Palace
- going to Rajiv and Caroline's party

c) ❖ **Extra:** What would you do? Say why.

C4 Grammar detective: conditional clauses, type 1

Will future or simple present? Can you solve the problem?

1 Look at this sentence:
If you invite her, I'll never speak to you again.

2 Find more examples from the dialogue in C2.

3 What is the rule?
How do you form conditional clauses, type 1?
Start a grammar card.
LiF 7: Bedingungssätze, Typ 1, p. 140 • P12 • WB C2, p. 33

C5

Mrs Lambraki is worried about the party preparations. So she talks to Caroline.
Work with a partner. Ask and answer Mrs Lambraki's questions. P7 • LiF 7: Bedingungssätze, Typ 1, p. 140

*help you · put up a tent · make some sandwiches · show them a film ·
run to the shop and buy more · ask our friends to be quiet · put him in George's room*

C6 ❖ **Extra**

Work in groups. Play the chain fantasy game:
LiF 7: Bedingungssätze, Typ 1, p. 140

If I win a lot of money, I'll travel around the world.

If I travel around the world, I'll go to …

If I go to …

…

C7

a) Look at the pictures and say what happens at the party.

b) Match the captions to the pictures.

A *George is really angry with Emma and so she starts to cry. This party is really horrible for Emma.*

B *The boys don't understand why Emma isn't having fun.*

C *Caroline isn't very pleased that Hamida seems to be too friendly towards Rajiv.*

D *The sparkler lands in the box of fireworks and they all start going off at once.*

E *Caroline feels very nervous because Emma is so unhappy. She hopes Rick will come soon.*

F *Emma is unhappy. She still hopes that Rick will come although it's getting quite late.*

G *The friends eat hot dogs and samosas around the bonfire. The boys can't wait to start the fireworks.*

H *Charlie and Rajiv try to cheer Emma up.*

I *The friends all bring things with them. The girls carry a guy.*

J *Emma, Gillian, Charlie and Rajiv come to the party together.*

C8

a) Now read the picture story. Compare the atmosphere at the beginning (picture 1) and the end (pictures 8–10).
Wordbank People p. 153

b) Dramatic reading: Read the story in groups of 8.
- Think about how your character feels.
- Try to learn your role by heart.
- Now read the story together.

Dramatic reading, p. 130 P6

C9

Look at the story again. Say what happens in the story.
Example: ***First, the doorbell rings. Emma, Gillian, … Then … After that … Later …*** P14

C10 Target task ❖ Project Portfolio
Write the end of the story. *Writing, p. 128*

Need help? Look at p. 41.

1 Work in groups.
Speculate on what happens next. *LiF 7: Bedingungssätze, Typ 1, p. 140*
Use a grid to organize your ideas.

I think the friends will …

If it's Rick, Emma will …

When?	Where?	What?	Who?
…	…	…	…

2 Agree on what happens.
3 Choose:
- Write a picture story. Draw pictures and write captions. or
- Write a story.

4 Find another group, present/read your stories and give feedback. *Speaking 2, p. 127* *WB C3, p. 33*

Support
Writing a picture story:
- Use connectives *(but, so, because, …)* for the captions.
- Add speech bubbles.

Support
Writing a story:
- Use connectives *(but, so, because, …)*.
- Add structure words *(first, then, after that, …)*.
- Use adjectives, comparatives and superlatives to make your story more interesting.

Prepare your target task A3:

New Year's Day is on …

P1 Words: festivals around the year

Match the dates to the calendar pages.

1 New Year's Day
2 Christmas Day[1]
3 Christmas Eve[2]
4 Halloween
5 Easter[3]
6 Valentine's Day[4]
7 Bonfire Night

[1] Christmas Day – *1. Weihnachtstag;*
[2] Christmas Eve – *Heiligabend;*
[3] Easter – *Ostern;* [4] Valentine's Day – *Valentinstag*

P2 Words: celebrations

Start word lists that help you talk about celebrations. You can find a lot of words and phrases in the texts on pages 30/31.

What you must do before a celebration
- *clean the house*
- …

What you do
- *give each other presents*
- …

P3 Listening

S 5, L 1/17 Listening, p. 124

a) Listen to Rajiv's classmate talk about Christmas. Copy the grid. Note down what is similar[1] to / different from Christmas in Germany.

Christmas in England and Germany

similar	*different*
…	…

[1] similar – *ähnlich*

b) Compare your notes with a partner's. Choose one thing about Christmas in England that you would like to have in Germany, too. Say why.

Prepare your target task B9:

P4 Say it in English

What do you say when …
… you like an idea?
… you're not sure?
… you don't like an idea?

Make a list.

It's a fantastic idea because …

Maybe it's a bit boring because …

I think it's cool because …

It's not perfect, but it's OK.

That's a great idea!

I think it's silly because …

I'm not sure about it because …

I'm afraid I don't like it because …

I don't know what to think about it because …

P5 Reading: Emma's email

Emma sent an email to her classmate Hamida. But there is something wrong. Puzzle out the missing words.

#&%$" Hamida,

+@!^ are you today? I'm very busy at the moment. Caroline, Gillian and I are preparing a &%$§§ =@>< party right now. But there's a problem. Rajiv wants to &!$%"=) a party on the same day as our party. But we have got an &%$"§!: We can all have one big /(„$" in one place. I hope that Rajiv ?="$§ say yes. Well, you MUST come to our party.

()"($)§%/%&, Emma

Prepare your target task C10:

P6 Words: connectives

Use connectives to make this text more interesting. ● *LiF 4: Connectives, p. 138*

after · then · so · suddenly · after that · finally · at first · when · later · because · and

Rick and Holden decide to go to Alexandra Palace. They want to see the fireworks. They watch the fireworks. They drink a coke. They get a text[1] from George. Rick suggests they go to George's party. They leave Alexandra Palace. They take the train to Camden Town. They ring the doorbell. George comes to the door. He tells them about the accident[2].

[1] text – *SMS;* [2] accident – *Unfall*

P7 Conditional clauses, type 1 (1) ● *LiF 7: Bedingungssätze, Typ 1, p. 140*

Gillian's mum has to work at the weekend.
Her mum wants Gillian to do some things. Write down sentences.
Example: ***If you clean the bathroom, I'll give you some extra pocket money[1].***

[1] pocket money – *Taschengeld*

1 clean bathroom/give you some extra pocket money
2 make beds/buy you a comic book
3 take you to the cinema/go shopping
4 do all your homework/clean the kitchen after dinner
5 bring you some sweets/don't play computer games

Extra language training:

P8 Sounds
S 6, L 1/18

a) Look at the following words with three syllables[1]. Copy the grid and fill in the words.

[1] syllable – *Silbe*

envelope · fireworks · festival · delicious · remember · potato · decorate

ˈ- (first syllable)	-ˈ- (second syllable)
envelope	delicious
…	…

b) Listen to the CD and check your answers. Repeat the words after the speaker.

P9 Revision: going to future
LiF 5R: going to future , p. 138

The Khans are preparing for Diwali.
Look at the pictures and write down what the Khans are going to do.

wear · decorate · prepare food · send · put · buy · give · make

Example: *1. Mr Khan is going to …*

1

Mr Khan

2

Mrs Khan

3

Sheree and Rajiv

4

Sheree

5

Mr and Mrs Khan

6

Mrs Khan

7

The Khans

8

Mr and Mrs Khan

P10 Will future
LiF 6: will future, p. 139

Oliver is George's classmate.
Look at the pictures of a Halloween party at his house.
What do you think the people will do? Write it down.

I think …
I'm sure …
Maybe …
I guess …

Example: *I guess the girl will eat …*

P11 **Revision: much, many, some, any, a lot of**

The Lambraki family are preparing for the party.
Read the dialogue and complete it. Use *much, many, some, any* or *a lot of*.

Mrs Lambraki: So, how 1 guests are coming to your party, Caroline?
Caroline: Well, I know that four of my friends are coming, but I don't know about Rajiv and George's friends.
George: Well, Charlie and Rajiv will be here but I'm not sure about the others.
Mrs Lambraki: So we don't know how 2 food and drink we need?
George: Just buy 3 everything. We'll eat it!
Caroline: What about chairs? Do we need to borrow[1] 4 chairs from Emma?
George: We don't need 5 chairs. We can stand. But what about the fireworks? Mum, Dad must buy 6 bangers.
Mrs Lambraki: George, we already have 7 bangers. Don't you think that's enough?
George: You can't have enough bangers!

[1] borrow – *ausleihen*

P12 **Conditional clauses, type 1 (2)** ● *LiF 7: Bedingungssätze, Typ 1, p. 140*

❖ **Can you do it?**

1. Complete the sentences.
   If Rick and Holden (not come) to the party, Emma (be) really upset.
   Rajiv (bring) some more food to the party if Caroline (ask) him.
2. **You can check your answers on page 221.**
3. **You need help?** → Do a), then b).
   You can do it? → Do b).

a) Match the sentence halves and write down the sentences.

if clause: simple present

1 If Mrs Lambraki (not make) enough snacks,
2 If George (not help) his mother with the preparations,
3 If it (rain) on the day of the party,
4 If Socks (get scared) because of the fireworks,
5 If the bonfire (go out),

main clause: will future

A Mrs Lambraki (be) angry.
B Caroline and George (be) disappointed.
C Caroline (put) her in her room.
D the guy (not burn[1]).
E the guests (be) hungry.

[1] burn – *(ver)brennen*

b) Look at the pictures and say what the friends will do on the Sunday after the party.
Example: ***If the weather is sunny, Caroline and Gillian will go to the park and have ice cream.***

1

sunny/park/ice cream

2

rainy/read a book

3

have some free time/play football

4

bored/phone

5

Gillian's mum/not there/watch TV

6

make more samosas/eat

Extra skills training:

P13 Viewing: Festivals

Leanne, Rebecca and Daniel talk about celebrations in their families.

Leanne

Rebecca

Daniel

a) Watch the beginning of the video (0:00–0:25).
Which special days does Rebecca's family celebrate?
Which special days does Daniel's family celebrate?

Halloween | Christmas | Valentine's Day | Bonfire Night | Easter | birthdays | New Year's Day | weddings[1] | Lent[2] | anniversaries[3]

Rebecca's family celebrates …

[1] weddings – *Hochzeiten;* [2] Lent – *Fastenzeit;* [3] anniversaries – *Geburts-/Jahrestage*

b) Watch the rest of the video. What are the teenagers' favourite celebrations? Note them down. Add information about why they like them and how they prepare for them.

	favourite celebration	*why?*	*how do they prepare?*
Leanne	*Christmas*	*no school, …*	*…*
…			

P14 Mediation

You spend Bonfire Night in England with your family. Your younger brother sees this poster and asks you what it means. Give him the main information in German.

Fame School: Trick or Treat

01

Do you like surprises? Tell your partner about a surprise you have had. Say what you liked/didn't like about it.

02 *Reading, p. 125*

Read the first part of the story and say why Danny does not want to go with Chloe.

Chloe, wearing her witch's[1] hat and with plastic talons[2] on her fingers, made her way out of the Rock Department and down the path. When she looked back, the ghost was bobbing[3] gently[4] at the door and her lantern flickered[5] with an orange glow[6] […]. She couldn't wait to see Danny's face once she got him to the Rock Department.

There were plenty of people eating in the dining room and, for a moment, Chloe had problems spotting Danny. Then she caught sight of him[7] at a table by the wall. He seemed very alone in the busy, noisy room, and her heart gave a little jump. She hurried over, so he wouldn't be on his own a moment longer.

"Hi!" He smiled when he saw her, and then his smile deepened.[8] "What *are* you wearing?"

Chloe grinned. "How do I look? Suitable[9] for Halloween?"

"Very cool … for a witch," Danny laughed.

"Hey, I'm sorry about Marmalade not turning up," she said. "I really thought he was going to be there."

"Don't worry," said Danny. "I've had a brilliant time. I want to tell you all about it … but how did you know he hadn't met me?"

"I just saw him," she explained. "In fact … a few of us, including Marmalade are over at the Rock Department waiting for you."

"Oh. Why's that?"

Chloe was already leading the way out of the dining room, and Danny hurried to keep up with her.

"It's difficult to explain," she told him, awkwardly.[10]

Halfway down the steps to the gravel drive Danny suddenly froze.[11] "Oh no you don't", he said. "You're not getting me like that. I'm not *that* stupid."

"What do you mean?" she said.

Danny gave her a triumphant laugh. "You … in your Halloween get up, all ready to give me a good scare on my birthday. Is Marmalade lurking[12] somewhere, with a bucket[13] of water to chuck over[14] me?"

"No!" said Chloe, earnestly. "It's not playing a trick, honestly. I need you to come with me. It's important."

"You'll have to do better than that," laughed Danny, turning to go back indoors. "I'm going to have my tea. I'm hungry."

"Danny?" Chloe felt desperate.[15] Everyone was waiting to greet[16] him and he was walking away. What could she do?

He turned back to her and she held out her hand.

"Please, Danny. We don't have time. You have to trust[17] me. Please."

He began to look a little bit uncertain[18]. Chloe took his hand and held it. She looked into his eyes. "You could call it a trick if you want," she admitted. "But it's a treat.[19] It's not scary, or horrible, or even silly. At least I hope you won't think so. It's a good thing, and it's especially for you."

---

[1] witch – *Hexe*
[2] talon – *Fingernagel, Kralle*
[3] bob – *schweben, dümpeln*
[4] gently – *sanft*
[5] flicker – *flackern*
[6] glow – *Lichtschein*
[7] catch sight of sb – *jmd erblicken*
[8] deepen – *vertiefen*
[9] suitable – *angemessen*
[10] awkward – *unbehaglich*
[11] freeze – *erstarren*
[12] lurk – *lauern*
[13] bucket – *Eimer*
[14] chuck over – *ausschütten über*
[15] desperate – *verzweifelt*
[16] greet – *begrüßen*
[17] trust – *vertrauen*
[18] uncertain – *unsicher*
[19] treat – *etwas Schönes*

O3

Which lines in the text show how Chloe feels about Danny? Describe/Speculate on her feelings for him.

O4

Read on and find out how the friends surprise Danny.

Chloe kept hold of Danny's hand[1] as they walked along the path to the Rock Department together. He was coming, though he still seemed a bit doubtful.[2] […]

First of all he caught sight of their pumpkin[3] lantern.

"It looks fantastic," he said. "But why did you bring it over here? And what's that blow-up ghost doing?"

Now, instead of her leading him Danny hurried up the path, pulling Chloe with him. "Is this what you were bringing me to see?"

"Yes," said Chloe. "Sort of."

"Well it's really cool," he told her pushing the ghost to make it bob about. "But you're not doing much to reassure[4] me. These all look more like Halloween tricks than treats!"

Chloe smiled. "Just wait until you see *this*!" She opened the door and suddenly there was light and noise and balloons and all his friends waiting.

"SURPRISE!"

"HAPPY BIRTHDAY!"

Everyone yelled as loudly as they could before dissolving[5] into excited giggles and laughter. Danny's friends surrounded him and several clapped him on his back.

He had dropped Chloe's hand in amazement,[6] but now he turned to her with a broad smile on his face.

"I never expected …" he gestured to the happy birthday banner, "all this … Why …? And how …?"

"Well, you were so unhappy," she explained. "And we wanted to do something to cheer you up." […]

"I'm gobsmacked[7] …," he said. "Wow. I can't believe you'd do all this … for me. It's amazing."

[1] keep hold of sth – *etw festhalten*
[2] doubtful – *skeptisch*
[3] pumpkin – *Kürbis*
[4] reassure – *beruhigen*
[5] dissolve – *auflösen*
[6] amazement – *Verwunderung*
[7] to be gobsmacked – *platt sein*

O5

What happens at the party? Write either Danny or Chloe's diary entry that day.

Du kannst schon viel auf Englisch verstehen und ausdrücken. Du kannst …

- ✓ über Feste und Feiertage sprechen
- ✓ ein Fest planen
- ✓ Hoffnungen und Erwartungen ausdrücken
- ✓ Bedingungen äußern
- ✓ auf eine E-Mail antworten
- ✓ eine Geschichte nacherzählen

WB Portfolio-Fragebogen Theme 2

3 London

Around London

A1

Round Robin: Collect ideas in class: 'When I think of London I think of …' *Round Robin, p. 130*

A2 *L 1/19*

a) Listen to the CD.
Note down the sights in the correct order.

b) Listen again and note down
what is special about the sights.

London Eye · Big Ben · Madame Tussauds · Trafalgar Square · Tower Bridge · Buckingham Palace · Covent Garden · Science Museum · Imperial War Museum · Sherlock Holmes Museum · Tate Modern · Emirates Stadium

c) Look at the photos. Can you name the sights?
Tell a partner what you know about them.
P1, P12 *WB A1, A2, p. 41*

I think this is …

This must be the …

1

Covent Garden

Just around the corner from the famous Royal Opera House is Covent Garden. This is a fantastic place to spend some time and watch acrobats and musicians. Covent Garden was once a fruit and vegetable market but now you can buy clothes and second-hand books here.

Have a snack and enjoy the fun. But watch out for pickpockets!

2

4

9

5
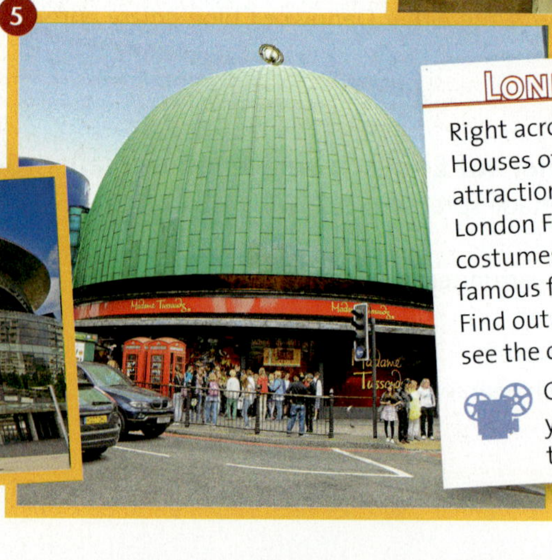

London Film Museum

Right across the Thames from the Houses of Parliament a special attraction is waiting for you. At the London Film Museum you can see costumes, props and film sets from famous films and TV programmes. Find out how films are made and see the cartoons.

Get into a car and see yourself in a film as you race through London.

A3

a) Which sights would you like to visit? Imagine what you can see or do there. ● P2

I'd like to visit Covent Garden because there are ...

b) Look at some tips on what to do in London at the bottom of these pages.
Read the texts and collect adjectives and phrases from the texts that make a place sound interesting.
Example: *It's worth a visit; a special attraction; ...* WB A3, p. 42

A4 Target task ❖ ✂ *Project*

Need help? Look at p. 58.

Write about a London tourist attraction and present it.

1. Choose a place in London you would like to visit and find out more about it. Try to find information that is interesting for young people.
2. Use your phrases from A3b) and the information you have collected to write a text about your tourist attraction. Include information about prices and things to see or do. Use adjectives (e.g. *the most exciting/ideal/perfect/best place to ...*).
3. Work in groups of six. Present your tourist attraction to the group. Each group chooses their top three attractions. Compare your results: What are the top three attractions in class?

● *Wordbank City, p. 151* ● *Speaking, p. 126/127* ● *LiF 3: Steigerung von Adjektiven, p. 137*

Arsenal Museum

Visit one of the world's greatest stadiums. This is the ideal place to visit if you're into football. The spectacular Arsenal Museum is open every day. But you can also do a fascinating tour of the stadium and the media centre.

Do the virtual tour on the Internet.

3

Science Museum

If you're into science, this museum is an absolute must.
See stunning science films in 3D, explore the universe and find out about how technology is changing our world. And the best thing is: it's for free.

Check the website to plan your visit.

6

7

8

Tate Modern

OK, so you're not interested in art, but you should still visit the Tate Modern. The building was a power station until 1981.
It's worth a visit just to see the building.

Go to the seventh floor to get an amazing view of London for free.

10

London – here we come!

B1

a) Read the chat messages to find out who wants to visit London.
What are the friends planning to do?

Caro: Hi Sophie + Rob. It's cool that you can come for the weekend. George and I have already made plans to show you around London! :-)

SOPHEE: Can't wait to see you again. A weekend in London is just so cool. You know I've never been to London before, so I'm really looking forward to it. Hope it's not only sightseeing though. ;-)

Caro: Don't worry. We haven't planned too much sightseeing although the Science Museum and the Natural History Museum are worth a visit. There are also some interesting places you haven't heard about, yet – like the Film Museum next to the London Eye. Is there anything you especially want to see?

SOPHEE: I'd love to go to Buckingham Palace. And what about Notting Hill, where all the film stars live?

Rob: No way! Sophie has read about all the film stars in London and she hasn't talked about anything else since. I don't want any more of that!!!

Caro: Hmm, we could do Buckingham Palace. But you can't go in. I've checked the Internet. It's only open to visitors in the summer … And if you're into film stars, then what about Madame Tussauds?

SOPHEE: Sounds great! I've always wanted to go there. My friend Cherry has just been there. She said there is a Chamber of Horrors.

Rob: Great idea! Anyway, I guess the London Eye is a must. And I think the Emirates Stadium sounds great.

Georgie: The Emirates Stadium? You must be joking! Have you turned into an Arsenal fan, Rob? ;-))
To be honest, it doesn't sound that exciting. If you want to do a stadium tour, I think the Wembley Stadium would be more interesting.

Rob: Don't worry – I haven't changed my mind about Manchester United!!! Wembley is OK with me, but it's not that high on my list. What I'd really like to do is to go to a big music store.

Caro: Buckingham Palace, Madame Tussauds, the London Eye … Cool! Sounds like a busy weekend. Why don't we go on a sightseeing tour? We'll find out more about it … Mum and Dad have offered to pay for tickets! :-) Looking forward to seeing you!!!

b) Read the chat again and complete the sentences.

1 ??? have made plans for Sophie and Rob.
2 ??? has never been to London before.
3 ??? has checked the Internet about Buckingham Palace.
4 ??? has always wanted to go to Madame Tussauds.
5 ??? hasn't changed his mind about Manchester United.
6 ??? have offered to pay for the tickets.

c) Read the chat again and collect phrases the friends use …

- … to make suggestions (e.g. *And what about …?*)
- … to say what they would like to do (e.g. *I'd love to go to …*)
- … to agree (e.g. *Sounds great!*)
- … to disagree (e.g. *You must be joking!*)

WB B1–B3, p. 43, 44

B2 Grammar card: present perfect (statements)

1 Look at these sentences from the chat: *George and I have already made plans …*
Sophie hasn't talked about anything else …
This is a new tense: the present perfect. Find more examples from B1.

2 How do you form the present perfect? When do you use it?
Check LiF 8 on page 140 and start a grammar card.
● P3, P8 WB B4, B5, p. 45

B3

Sophie and Rob have a lot to do before the weekend.
Look at their checklist and say what they have already done and what they haven't done yet. ● P9, P10
Example: *Sophie has already bought … Rob and Sophie haven't … yet.*

- *buy a present for Caroline (Sophie) ✓*
- *pack bags (Rob and Sophie)*
- *get a Manchester United T-shirt from fan shop (Rob)*
- *look up the train times on the Internet (Rob) ✓*
- *check batteries for cameras (Rob and Sophie) ✓*
- *think of present for Mrs Lambraki (Rob and Sophie)*
- *find photo CD from last school year (Rob) ✓*
- *email Caroline about tour (Sophie)*

B4

a) Look at the brochure about a London bus tour.
- Work with a partner. He/She closes his/her book.
- Now describe the brochure. He/She has to draw it.
- Compare the picture with the brochure.

at the top · in the middle · in big letters · at the bottom · below the heading

b) Do you want to go on the tour? Say why/why not.

B5

a) Read the brochure and try to puzzle out the meanings of these words and phrases.

live guide · commentary · fantastic offers wide choice · great value · river cruise

Support
- Can you puzzle it out from the context?
- Does it sound/look like a German/French/… word?
- Do you know a similar adjective or a similar word?

b) Now check a dictionary to see if you were right.
● How to work with a dictionary, p. 129

B6

a) Go through pages 48-51 and collect words to make a word web for 'city'. ● *Wordbank City, p. 151*

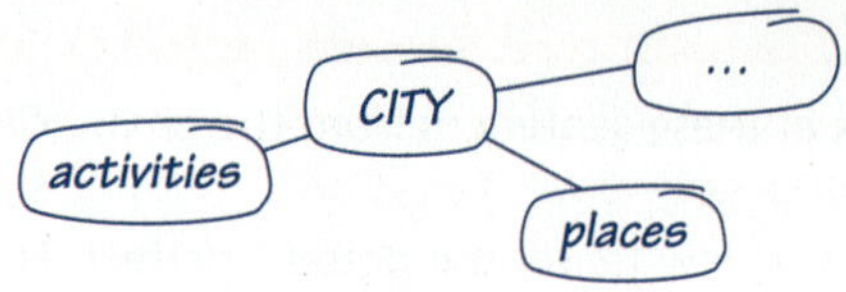

b) ❖ **Choose:**
- Write an acrostic about your favourite city. **or**
- Make a word search with city words for your partner.

B7 🎧 *L 1/20*

a) Close your books and listen to George and Rob.
Find out what the friends decide in the end. What are their reasons?

George: Hi Rob, how are you?

Rob: Well, we've packed our bags so we're almost ready.

George: Cool, I just need to know a few things before you come. Caroline and I have looked at different tours. She wants to do the Hop-on Hop-off tour. Have you ever done one of those tours?

Rob: You mean the open double-decker buses? Well, they're all over the place – even here in Manchester. Could be fun on a sunny day …

George: OK, then.

Rob: Hey, have you been to this famous battleship yet?

George: You mean the HMS Belfast? No, I haven't. But Caroline would hate it. It sounds OK to me, but it's not that high on my list.

Rob: I think the girls want to do their own little tour anyway. Shopping and Shakespeare's Globe …

George: Has Sophie already talked to Caroline about this?

Rob: I don't know, they text each other all the time … Have you booked anything yet?

George: Not yet. Why?

Rob: Well, it would be really cool to see the Emirates Stadium even if I'm not an Arsenal fan. I've just gone on a virtual tour on the Internet and I must admit I'd like to see the real thing … Hey, have you seen the new Sherlock Holmes film?

George: Yes, I have – it's fantastic!

Rob: I haven't seen it yet. But isn't there a Sherlock Holmes Museum in London? I know tickets can be quite expensive, but maybe we could …

George: Hasn't Mum phoned your mum?

Rob: I think she's talked to Dad. But I'm not sure what the phone call was about.

George: She wants to give us some money for our sightseeing …

Rob: Cool! Sounds great!

George: Right, see you at the weekend, then!

b) Read the dialogue.
Find the questions to the following answers in the dialogue. Who asks them and why? ● *P11*

1 No, I haven't. But Caroline would hate it.
2 I think she's talked to Dad.
3 You mean the open double-decker buses?
4 I don't know, they text each other all the time …
5 Not yet. Why?
6 Yes, I have – it's fantastic.

c) Read the dialogue between George and Rob again and add phrases to your list from B1c). ● *P5* 📖 *WB B6, B7, p. 46*

B8 Grammar card: present perfect (2) (questions)

1 Write down questions in the present perfect from the dialogue and use different colours like this:
Have you booked anything yet?
Has Caroline already talked to Sophie?

2 How do you form the questions?
Check LiF 8 on page 142 and add the rule to your grammar card. ● *P4* *WB B8, p. 47*

B9

- Look at the list and choose five activities.

  - *have tea with the Queen*
  - *go on a boat trip on the Thames*
  - *take photos of London from the London Eye*
  - *buy souvenirs in Covent Garden*
  - *climb the 199 steps up inside Tower Bridge*
  - *feed squirrels in Green Park*
  - *be on a double-decker bus*
  - *go shopping in Bond Street*
  - *visit Madame Tussauds*
  - *do a tour of the Emirates Stadium*

- Your partner asks questions to find out which activities you have chosen.
- If your answer is 'yes', your partner can go on. If your answer is 'no', it's your turn.
- The person who has found out all five activities first is the winner.

● *LiF 8: Present perfect, p. 142*

Have you had tea with the Queen?

Yes, I have.

No, I haven't.

B10 Target task

Portfolio

Need help? Look at pp. 58/59.

Write a dialogue between Caroline and George and act it out.
The friends want to see many different sights, but there isn't enough time.
George and Caroline have to decide what to do.

1 Work with a partner. Go through pages 50-52 and note down what sights/places Sophie, Rob, Caroline and George want to see.
● *Wordbank City, p. 151*

2 Sophie and Rob will arrive on Friday afternoon. They have to get back to Manchester on Sunday afternoon. Think about how many sights/places they could visit in that time.

3 Now plan a dialogue between Caroline and George. You have to agree on some sights and places. One of you is Caroline, one of you is George.

4 Write your dialogue. Use statements and questions in the present perfect when necessary. The phrases from B1c) and B7c) can help you.
● *LiF 8: Present perfect, pp. 141/142*

5 Practise your dialogue and present it to another pair. Then give feedback.
● *Speaking 2, p. 127*

Support
Have you seen/been to …? · I've never seen/been to …
I've already visited …, but I haven't …

Lost in London

C1

Have you ever been lost? Talk to a partner and tell him/her about your experiences.
- What happened?
- How did you feel?

Support

When I was small … · On a trip to … · Last year I got lost · I lost my way when … · I lost sight of … · I could not see/find … · I did not know where … · I was scared/worried/frightened/…

C2 L 1/21

a) Read the text and find out why George says: "We're not very well-organized today …".

A week later. Rob and Sophie are in London.

Sophie: It's past four o'clock. Where are the boys?

Caroline: It's only five past, Sophie. I'm sure they will be here soon.

Sophie: Well, Rob is always late.

Caroline: I'll phone George. … No answer. Let's just wait a few more minutes.

Five minutes later.

Caroline: Look, there's George. But where's Rob?

George: Hi girls, have you seen Rob? I've lost him.

Sophie: What do you mean, you've lost him? I thought you went to the HMS Belfast together.

George: Well, of course we did. Then we took the Tube to Baker Street. It was really full and when we got off I suddenly couldn't see Rob anymore.

Caroline: I don't believe it! It's only a short way from the station to here. How can anyone get lost?

Sophie: You don't know Rob! He's lost his way between his room and the bathroom before.

George: Sounds like Caroline! I'm surprised she found her way here!

Caroline: Very funny, George! Have you tried to phone Rob?

George: No, I haven't, my mobile's dead. I forgot to charge it.

Caroline: Oh great! That's why I couldn't phone you. What's Rob's number, Sophie?

Sophie: Erm … 0775 6488318. … And I've left my mobile at home.

George: We're not very well-organized today, are we? …

Rob: Hello!

Caroline: Hi Rob, it's Caroline!

Rob: Caroline, where are you all? I've rung George and Sophie again and again but they aren't answering.

Caroline: We'll explain that later. Where are you?

Rob: I don't really know. I came out of the Underground and started walking down the road …

Caroline: Have you seen any sights or road signs?

Rob: Well, I walked past a building on the left. There was a huge queue.

Caroline: That was Madame Tussauds. So you walked along Marylebone Road.

Rob: Yes, well, then I turned right because I thought I saw George, but it wasn't him. So I walked straight on to the next street and turned left.

Caroline: Can you see a street name? I've got a map here. I can tell you how to get to the museum then.

Rob: Well, I've just crossed a main street. Just a minute, it says Marylebone High Street and right in front of me is Nottingham Street …

b) Read the text again and collect information about Rob.
- Where and how did he lose George?
- Where is he now? Find the place on the map below.

● P13 WB C1, C2, p. 48

c) Find words and phrases in the text for giving/talking about directions and write them down in a list.

C3 L 1/22

a) Listen to Caroline's directions and follow them on the map. ● Listening, p. 124

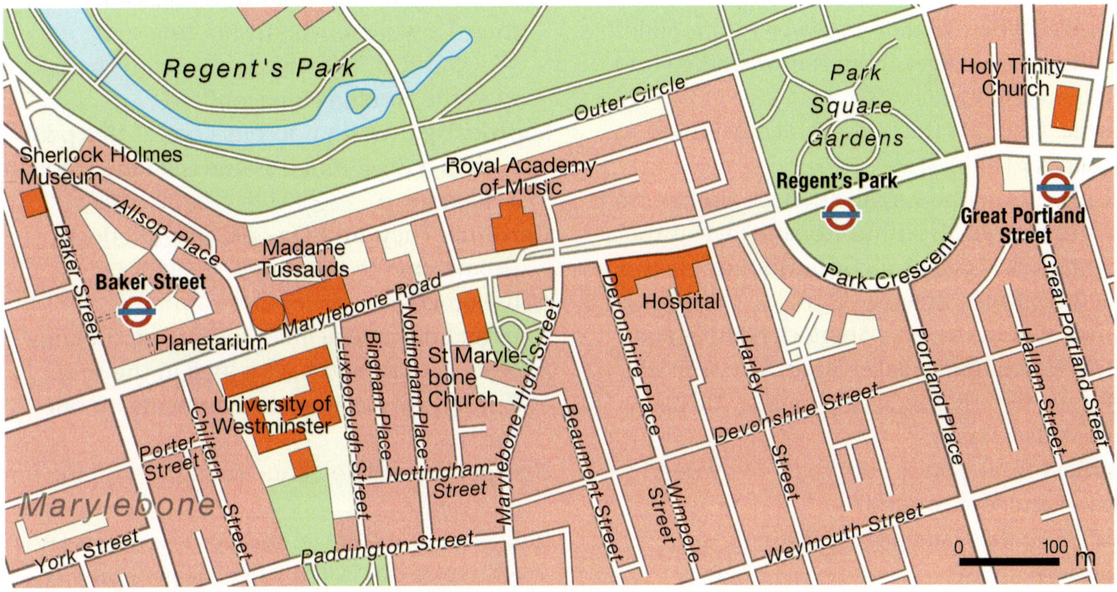

b) Listen again and add any new words or expressions to your list from C2c).

c) Match the expressions to the symbols. There are more symbols than you need. ● P6 WB C3, p. 49

1 walk straight on
2 turn left
3 turn right
4 walk past …
5 walk on till you get to …
6 on your right
7 on your left
8 cross the street

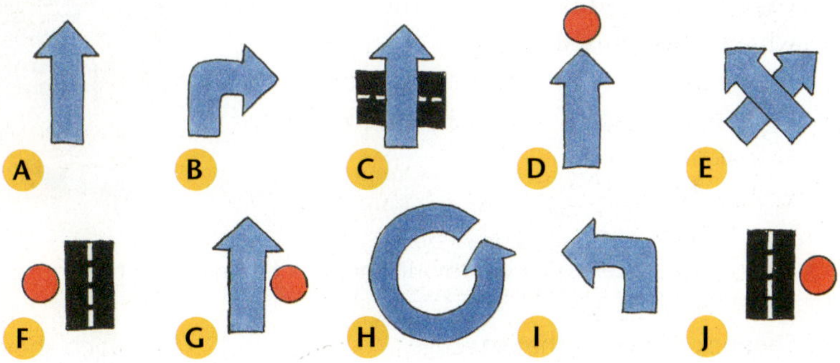

C4 ❖ Extra

Play a game:
Use the map and say where you are.
Your partner gives you directions, but he/she doesn't say where you are going.

● Wordbank City, p. 151

C5 L 1/23

a) Look at the picture and describe the man in it. What do you know about him? Note down your ideas. ● Wordbank People, p. 153

b) Read about the friends' visit to the Sherlock Holmes Museum and add any new information about Holmes to your notes from a).

Support

Mütze mit Ohrenklappen = deerstalker
Pfeife = pipe
Lupe = magnifying glass

George: Look, there he is. Hi Rob!
Sophie: So you've found us! Well done!
Rob: Well, you two didn't answer your mobiles!
Caroline: Let's forget about it now, and go into the museum.
George: So this is the house which belonged to Sherlock Holmes!
Caroline: Don't be stupid! Sherlock Holmes isn't a real person. Sir Arthur Conan Doyle is the writer who created Sherlock Holmes. He lived at 221b Baker Street.
George: But in the film, Sherlock Holmes and Dr Watson live in Baker Street. I've seen it! It's the film that Jude Law stars in. He plays Dr Watson and …
Sophie: I think you're both right. Why don't we go in and look around?
Rob: Wow, these stairs are really dark and narrow.
Sophie: The lights aren't very strong. They're like the gaslights that they had in the 19th century!
Rob: This looks like Sherlock Holmes' study.
George: Yeah – and this must be the medical bag which Watson used.
Caroline: And here's the bedroom. Look at all these photographs of the criminals who lived at that time!
Rob: Come upstairs! You must look at the man who has got a snake around his head. And there's a woman who is shooting someone. Wow! And all these weapons. This is better than the London Dungeon!
Sophie: Ugh! That's horrible. Look at this poor man in a cage! And this one is falling through a trapdoor.
Caroline: They are all people who Sherlock Holmes met in the stories. Look! It says so in the brochure.
George: I don't remember them from the film.
Sophie: Let's go and have a look in the shop. Perhaps we can find some presents for our parents.
George: Haven't you done enough shopping for one day?
Rob: Come on George! Perhaps I can get a DVD which we can watch when we get home.

c) Match the sentence halves about Sherlock Holmes and the museum.

1 Sherlock Holmes is the detective
2 The house in Baker Street is now a museum
3 There is a photo gallery
4 Jude Law is an actor
5 The lights are like the ones
6 On one of the photos there is a man

A which shows criminals from that time.
B who played Dr Watson in the film.
C that they had in the 19th century.
D which shows how Sherlock Holmes lived.
E who is falling through a trapdoor.
F that lived at 221b Baker Street.

C6 ❖ Extra: Grammar detective: relative clauses

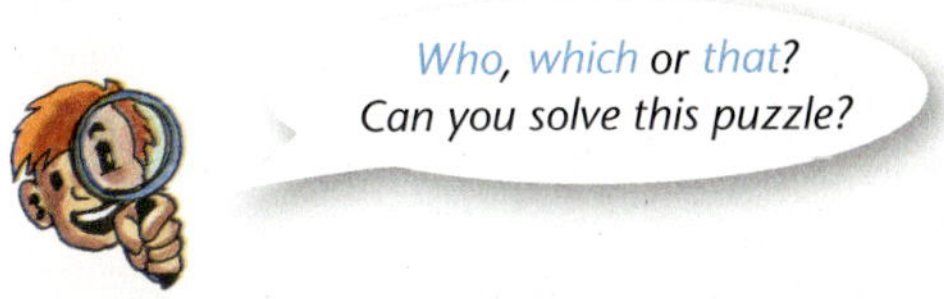

1 Find examples of relative clauses with who, which and that from C5 (e.g. *So this is the house which belonged to Sherlock Holmes.*).

2 When do you use *who*? When do you use *which*? When can you use *that*?
Look at LiF 9 on page 142 for help.
Write a grammar card for relative clauses.
P7 *WB C4, p. 50*

C7 ❖ Extra

a) Puzzle out the answers. You can find the answers in the dialogue from C5.

1 This is a person who writes stories.
2 This is the man who was Holmes' assistant and best friend.
3 This is something which a doctor often carries.
4 These are people that do bad things.
5 This is something that you can keep animals in.
6 This is something which you can buy for your friends.

b) Make five new puzzles for your partner. Use *who, which* and *that*.
Example: ***This is the boy in our class who … This is the room in our school that …***
LiF 9: Relativsätze, p. 142 *WB C5, p. 50*

C8 Target task ❖ Project Portfolio

Need help? Look at p. 60.

Write an English guidebook of your home town/area in class.

1 Collect places/sights/people that could be interesting for visitors.

2 Find out about the places/sights/people:
- Where are they? / Where did they live?
- What is special about them?

3 Choose one place/sight/person and write a paragraph for the guidebook. Describe the place/sight/person and note down directions, too.
Wordbank City, p. 151

Support
You can add pictures, too.

Extra: Gallery walk: Hang up your paragraphs and read them.
Choose the top three sights/places/people in your home town/area.
Gallery walk, p. 130 *P14, P15* *WB C6, p. 51*

Prepare your target task A4:

P1 Words: buildings and places

Wordbank City, p. 151

a) What are the words? You can find the buildings/places in a city.

tkemar · werto · rkpa · mseumu · lacepa · thetrea · idbrge · diustam

b) Now note down an example of each building/place in London.
Example: *tkemar = market: Camden Market, Covent Garden, …*

P2 Words: places

a) Match the parts to make correct phrases.
Sometimes there is more than one correct answer.

1 an amazing
2 the perfect way
3 a fantastic place
4 an absolute
5 a wonderful place
6 the ideal place
7 worth
8 one of the best places

A to see …
B to eat
C to visit if you're …
D to spend some time
E view
F a visit
G to go for a good time
H must

b) Use each phrase to write a sentence about the places in P1 or other sights in London.
Example: *Covent Garden is the ideal place in London to spend some time and watch acrobats and musicians.*

Prepare your target task B10:

P3 Present perfect (1)

LiF 8: Present perfect, p. 140

❖ **Can you do it?**

1. George ??? (want) to visit the London Dungeon for a long time.
   Most of his friends ??? (be) there before.
2. **You can check your answers on page 221.**
3. **You need help?** → Do a), then b).
   You can do it? → Do b).

a) Copy the grid. Find the present perfect forms.

infinitive	*present perfect*
plan	*have/has planned*
see	…
check	…
make	…
buy	…
eat	…

infinitive	*present perfect*
visit	…
meet	…
take	…
be	…
find	…
walk	…

b) Choose the correct form and write down the sentences about a school trip to London.

1 We (see already) a lot of London.
2 But we (not see) any film stars yet.
3 I (take already) photos of all the sights.
4 My friend (buy already) an "I love London" T-shirt.
5 I (not buy) a souvenir yet.
6 My friends and I (eat already) pizza at Piccadilly Circus.
7 We (not visit) any museums yet.
8 I (see) Big Ben before.

P4 Present perfect (2): questions

LiF 8: Present perfect, p. 142

Look at the words and write down eight questions. Ask a partner and note down his/her answers.

be · meet · eat · buy · read · climb · cook · do · drink · feed · find · fly · go · have · see · make · …

Have you ever bought a present for your teacher?

No, I haven't. Have you ever …?

…

P5 Words: suggesting, agreeing, disagreeing

Look at the pictures and write down what the other person could say in this situation. Try to use as many different phrases as possible.

I think … sounds so much cooler. · That's fantastic! · It would be cool to see the … · Could be fun. · I'm not sure. · I'm sure you would enjoy it, too. · I think it's a great idea! · I'd love to go to … · You must be joking. · What about …? · I must admit I'd like to see … · Well, why not? · Well, to be honest, I'd much rather … · I've always wanted to go … · Why don't we …?

Prepare your target task C8:

P6 Words: directions
S 7, L 1/24

a) Listen to the directions and follow them on the map. Where do you go?

b) Work with a partner and give him/her directions.

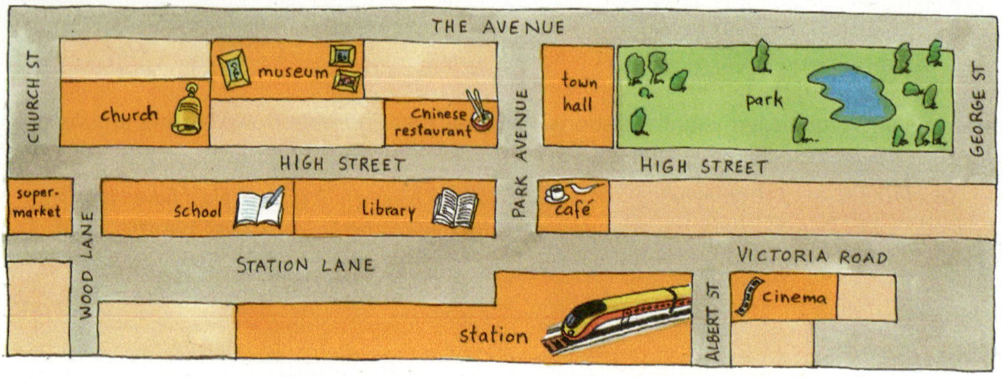

town hall – *Rathaus*

Extra language training:

P7 Relative clauses
LiF 9: relative clauses, p. 142

❖ Can you do it?

1. Write a short definition. Use relative pronouns (*who, which* or *that*).

Film star: actor/very famous

→ *A film star is an actor who …*

Covent Garden: place/was once a fruit market

→ …

2. You can check your answers on page 221.

3. You need help? → Do a), then b).

You can do it? → Do b).

a) What are the correct relative pronouns (*who, which* or *that*)?

1 A doctor is a person ??? looks after people when they are ill.
2 Mrs Dupuy is a woman ??? teaches French at my school.
3 Spaghetti bolognaise is a dish[1] ??? comes from Italy.
4 David Beckham is a footballer ??? played for Manchester United.
5 I love flowers ??? smell nice.

b) Write a short definition. Use relative pronouns (*who, which* or *that*).

1 Pickpocket: person/steals other people's money
2 Liverpool: English city/is the home of the Beatles
3 Clown: person/makes other people laugh
4 Madame Tussauds: wax[2] museum/is a tourist attraction in London
5 Thames: river/is more than 300 kilometres long

[1] dish – *Gericht*
[2] wax – *Wachs*

P8 Present perfect (3)

● LiF 8: Present perfect, p. 141

Look at the pictures. Write down what the pupils have already done or haven't done yet on their school trip to London. Example: ***We have already had tea.***

we/have/already

Johannes/be/Madame Tussauds/already

our group/not be/ to Tower Bridge

we/not do a bus tour

Kevin/just buy funny hat

Linda and Sara/not eat fish and chips/yet

we/check prices

we/not visit/the Tower/ yet

P9 Present perfect (4): word order

● LiF 8: Present perfect, p. 141

Write down the correct sentences. Then read the dialogue with a partner.

Linda: I'm really looking forward[1] to our trip to London!
ever / have / to London / you / been / ?
John: been / to Berlin, but / I / have / been / I / haven't / to London yet / .
Linda: packed / you / have / already / your things / ?
John: my bag / I / no, / haven't / packed / yet / .
put / I / but / have / on my bed / all the things / .
Linda: yet / a guidebook[2] / you / have / bought / ?
John: yet / haven't / I / no, / bought / a guidebook / .
looked up / I / but / have / all the sights / on the Internet / .
Linda: I'm so excited!

[1] I'm looking forward to – *Ich freue mich auf*
[2] guidebook – *Reiseführer*

P10 Present perfect (5)

Look at the tourists and the list of places. Say where they have or haven't been and what they have done. LiF 8: Present perfect, p. 141

be · London · visit · Paris · Rome · see · Texas · map · Hawaii · New York · Munich · Australia · kangaroo · buy

P11 Sounds *S 8, L 1/25*

a) Listen to the sentences and note down the words that are stressed[1] most.
Example: *1. But Caroline would hate it.*

1 But Caroline would hate it.
2 It seems OK with me, but it's not that high on my list.
3 Well, it would be cool to see the Emirates Stadium after all.
4 I must admit I'd like to see the real thing.
5 I know tickets can be quite expensive, but maybe we could ...
6 Sounds great!

b) Now say the sentences again and stress the right words.

[1] stress – *betonen*

Extra skills training:

P12 Listening *S 9, L 1/26*

Listen to the dialogues and match them to the sights.

London Eye · Tower · Tower Bridge · Big Ben · Shakespeare's Globe

P13 Reading Reading, p. 125

Read C2 on page 54 and answer the questions.

1 Why didn't George phone Rob?
2 Does Sophie phone her brother? Why/Why not?
3 What did Rob do after he lost George?
4 How can Caroline help?

P14 Mediation

Imagine you are in London with your parents. You want to visit the Sherlock Holmes Museum. Read its website and answer your parents' questions in German.

The Sherlock Holmes Museum

221b Baker Street London NW1 6XE England

Sherlock Holmes and Doctor John H. Watson

lived at **221b** Baker Street between 1881 and1904, according to the stories written by Sir Arthur Conan Doyle. The famous 1st floor study overlooking Baker Street still looks the same as it was in Victorian times.

Step back in time, and when you visit London, remember to visit **The World's Most Famous Address – 221b BAKER STREET –** the Official Home of Sherlock Holmes!

Open every day of the year (except Christmas Day) from 9.30am - 6pm
Admission: Adult **£6** Child **£4** (under 16 yrs)

1 Wann soll Sherlock Holmes in dem Haus gewohnt haben?
2 Schließt das Museum an bestimmten Tagen?
3 Wie sind die Öffnungszeiten?
4 Was müssen wir als Familie mit 3 Personen zahlen?

P15 Reading Reading, p. 125

FLORENCE NIGHTINGALE MUSEUM

OPENING TIMES
Monday-Sunday 10:00am – 5:00pm
(closed[1] Christmas Day)

ADMISSION PRICES
Adult £5.80
Child £4.80
Family £16.00
(two adults and up to five children)

Visitors can hear Florence's story in her own words through audio hot spots around the museum. There are two tours: one for 7–11 year olds and another for adults. The audio tour is included in the admission price.

The cost includes a free audio tour for adults and children.

Answer the following questions about the text.

1 What time does the museum open on Sundays?
2 How many days in the year is the museum closed?
3 How much does your mother have to pay to get into the museum?
4 How much does it cost a family of four to go to the museum?
5 How much does the audio guide cost?

[1] closed – *geschlossen*

Museums in London

1

The British Museum

Why not visit one of the world's finest collections[1] of ancient Egyptian mummies[2]? It is not only dead people that were mummified[3], but dead animals, too. You can also see cats and birds. Well worth a visit and entry is free.

The museums in Kensington

Three of the most popular museums in London are close together in Kensington: the Science Museum, the Natural History Museum and the Victoria and Albert Museum. At the Science Museum you can see, touch and experience the most important developments[4] in science in the last 300 years (including spaceships) – and don't forget the awesome IMAX cinema. Next door, in the Natural History Museum, you can find a moving model of Tyrannosaurus Rex – his eyes follow you around the room and he roars[5] very loudly when hungry! At the Victoria and Albert Museum you can see a fantastic fashion collection.

This is only a small selection of London museums. You might like to visit one of the more unusual museums, such as the Horniman Museum, where you will discover a brilliant aquarium and a rare collection of Asian and African masks. Or why not go to the London Transport Museum? Or to the Florence Nightingale Museum or …?

3

1

Look at the exhibits and put them in the right museum.

2

Choose the museum you find most interesting. Visit its website and write a short report about it:
- Where is it?
- What can you see/do there?
- What do you like best?

5

3

Think of the museums you have already visited.
Which is your favourite museum? Say why.

[1] collection – *Sammlung*
[2] mummy – *Mumie*
[3] mummified – *mumifiziert*
[4] development – *Entwicklung*
[5] roar – *brüllen*

2

4

6

7

The London Eye Mystery

O1

Imagine you were inside a London Eye capsule[1] high above the city.

- What can you see?
- How do you feel?

O2 Reading, p. 125

Read this excerpt from *The London Eye Mystery* and say what happens.

Before they move to New York, Aunt Gloria and her son, Salim, come to visit Ted and Kat and their parents. One day Ted and Kat take Salim on a trip to London.

My favourite thing to do in London is to fly the Eye.

On a clear day you can see for twenty-five miles in all directions because you are in the largest observation[2] wheel ever built. You are sealed into one of the thirty-two capsules with the strangers who were next to you in the queue, and when they close the doors, the sound of the city is cut off. You begin to rise.[3] The capsules are made of glass and steel and are hung from the rim[4] of the wheel. As the wheel turns, the capsules use the force of gravity[5] to stay upright. It takes thirty minutes to go a full circle.

From the top of the ride, Kat says London looks like toy-town and the cars on the roads below look like abacus beads[6] going left and right and stopping and starting. I think London looks like London and the cars like cars, only smaller.

The best thing to see from up there is the River Thames. You can see how it loops[7] and curves but when you are on the ground you think it is straight. […]

It is also interesting to watch the capsules on either side of yours. You see strangers looking out, just like you are doing. The capsule that is higher than yours becomes lower than yours and the capsule that is lower becomes higher. […]

And then your capsule goes lower and you are sad because you do not want the ride to end. You would like to go round one more time, but it is not allowed. So you get out feeling like an astronaut coming down from space, a little lighter than you were.

We took Salim to the Eye because he'd never been up before. A stranger came up to us in the queue, offering us a free ticket. We took it and gave it to Salim. We shouldn't have done this, but we did. He went up on his own at 11.32, 24 May, and was due to come down at 12.02 the same day. He turned and waved to Kat and me as he boarded,[8] but you couldn't see his face, just his shadow.[9] They sealed[10] him in with twenty other people whom we didn't know.

Kat and I tracked Salim's capsule as it made its orbit. When it reached its highest point, we both said "NOW!" at the same time. Kat laughed and I joined in. […]

Then the capsule landed. The doors opened and the passengers came out in twos and threes. They walked off in different directions. Their faces were smiling. Their paths probably never crossed again.

We waited for the next capsule and the next one and the one after that. He still didn't appear. Somewhere, somehow, in the thirty minutes of riding the Eye, in his sealed capsule, he had vanished[11] off the face of the earth.[12]

---

[1] capsule – *Kapsel*
[2] observation – *Beobachtung*
[3] rise – *aufsteigen*
[4] rim – *Rand*
[5] force of gravity – *Schwerkraft*
[6] abacus beads – *Kugeln auf einem Abakus*
[7] loop – *(sich) winden*
[8] board – *an Bord gehen*
[9] shadow – *Schatten*
[10] seal in – *einschließen in*
[11] vanish – *verschwinden*
[12] face of the earth - *Erdboden*

O3

a) Look up the London Eye on the Internet and find more information about
- ticket prices (standard tickets for adults and children)
- opening times (visitor information)
- how to get there (visitor information)

b) Design a tourist brochure for the London Eye.
- Use your information from a).
- Find pictures to make your brochure more attractive.
- Make the London Eye sound interesting.

brilliant · amazing · fantastic · stunning · you must go to … · don't miss … · it's the best sight/place … · it's worth a visit · you should …

O4 ❖ **Choose**

- Kat rings up her mother when Salim doesn't turn up. Write their telephone conversation. **or**
- Ted and Kat want to find out how Salim disappeared. Write a conversation between them in which they speculate about what might have happened.

O5 *S 10, L 1/27*

a) What do you think happened?

b) Now listen to the CD and find out what actually happened. Compare your ideas.

Du kannst schon viel auf Englisch verstehen und ausdrücken. Du kannst …

✓ über Sehenswürdigkeiten in London sprechen
✓ Vorschläge machen
✓ sagen, dass dir etwas gefällt/nicht gefällt
✓ ausdrücken, was du gerne tun möchtest
✓ über etwas berichten, das du schon einmal getan/erlebt hast
✓ jemandem den Weg beschreiben
✓ eine Person beschreiben
✓ einen Artikel für einen Reiseführer verfassen

WB Portfolio-Fragebogen Theme 3

Fun at school

A1

Look at the posters 1-3 at Camden School for Girls.
Which event would you like to go to?
Which one would you like to take part in?
Which one would you hate to go to? Say why.

WB A1, p. 59

A2

a) Make a list of events and activities that take place at your school.
Then compare the events and activities to the ones at Camden School for Girls.
Include places, prices, dates, classes/age groups.

At our school we also have/perform …

We organize … every year.

We don't have … There is no …

b) What is your favourite event/activity at your school? Say why.

Wordbank Entertainment, p. 152 · *P15, P16*

1

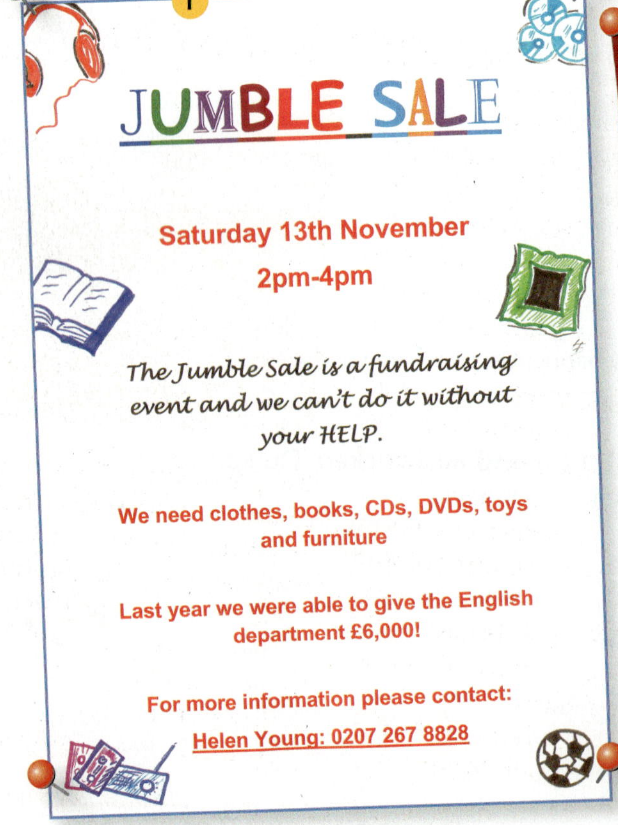

2

A3

a) Read the article from the Camden School Friday News below. Who gets a lot of praise?

b) Collect words and phrases you can use to praise someone. ● P1

A4 S 11, L 1/28

a) Listen to the friends and look at the posters to find out which event they are talking about. ● Listening, p. 124

b) Use the correct poster to note down information in a grid (*who, when, what, where?*). Then listen again and add more information to your grid. ● P2 WB A2, p. 59

A5 Target task ❖ Portfolio

Need help? Look at p. 78.

Write an article about the event from A4 for the Camden School Friday News.

1. Plan your article and think about
   - a title
   - an introduction: say what your article is about (*who, what, when, where?*).
   - the main part: describe the details and comment on them.
   - the ending: say something positive about the event.
2. Collect words and phrases for your article. Your list from A3b) can help you. ● Wordbank Festivals, p. 150
3. Write your article. ● Writing, p. 128
4. Give your article to a partner. Check your articles and give each other feedback. ● Speaking 2, p. 127 ● P9 ● LiF 2R: Simple past, p. 135 WB A3, p. 60

CAMDEN SCHOOL FRIDAY NEWS

CSG at Step Live! – a real success!

On Sunday, 110 girls from CSG performed in the *Step Live!* show at Sadler's Wells Theatre. *Step Live!* is the famous dance show for schools across London. As a reward for their hard work, the girls performed at Sadler's Wells – *the* dance theatre in London. The CSG Dance Company and Year 7 represented our school.

The CSG Dance Company performed in the first half with their 'Bad Romance' piece. They were the best act of the night, and received never-ending applause.

Almost all of Year 7 were on the stage with their 'Mamma Mia' piece.

The girls looked brilliant in their costumes and their dancing was excellent! So it was no surprise that they received the biggest applause of the night from the audience. It was the perfect end to the show.

Well done to everyone who took part – the show was a real success!

Time for talent

B1 L 1/29

a) Read these sentences from the dialogue below.
Speculate on what the girls are talking about.

1 "Don't you think we should do something totally different this year?"
2 "Don't worry, we can practise together."
3 "I just love auditions!"

b) Read the dialogue. What is it about? What are the girls' suggestions?
Say which one you like best and why.

Gillian: Hey, remember that Ms Walsh asked us to make suggestions for the next school play?

Emma: What about a Shakespeare comedy? We haven't had one for a while.

Caroline: Oh, yes. Let's do Shakespeare! I haven't had a big role for ages and I want to play Juliet!

Emma: 'Romeo and Juliet' isn't a comedy, silly ...

Gillian: Oh no, not another classic. We did 'A Christmas Carol' by Charles Dickens last year, remember? Don't you think we should do something totally different this year? Look, I've done some research on the Internet and I've found a comedy that sounds fantastic. It's called 'Invasion from Planet Zorgon'.

Emma: So it's about aliens? I'm not sure Ms Walsh would like that.

Gillian: But just think about it – it's really cool!

Caroline: Let me see. There are only six proper roles. That means not many people can take part.

Gillian: That's true. What do you suggest then?

Caroline: Hmm, I don't know. We haven't had a musical since 'The Lion King'. And that was two years ago! I loved 'The Lion King'. Maybe we could do 'Cats' or 'Starlight Express'?

Emma: Great idea! But the auditions ... I would be super-nervous. I haven't sung on stage since our last Christmas play.

Caroline: Don't worry, we can practise together. I love auditions!

Gillian: A musical? Oh no, not such boring, girly stuff again, please! Can't we find something that's more interesting than a story about cats or trains?

Emma: Like what?

Gillian: A really exciting story or an adventure maybe.

Emma: Like Sherlock Holmes?

Gillian: No, something like 'Twilight'! I've read all the books, and last weekend I watched the DVD 'New Moon' with Dad.

Emma: But that's not a play.

Gillian: I know. But it's just a first idea. Well, we could change it into a play. Why don't we try it?

Emma: OK, OK.

Caroline: A play about vampires? Great idea! Just think about the amazing costumes and the decoration for the stage. We could even have some music.

Gillian: Fantastic idea! Come on, girls, let's find Ms Walsh and ask her now!

c) Read the dialogue again and note down phrases to persuade someone about something (e.g. *Let's ...*). P3 WB B1, p. 61

B2

Write down five sentences. Some can be wrong. Then show them to a partner. He/She must say if they are right or wrong and correct the wrong sentences.

Gillian *Emma* *Caroline* *The girls*	*has* *hasn't* *have* *haven't*	*sung on a stage* *done a Shakespeare play* *read all the 'Twilight' books* *talked about their idea* *had a big role*	*since Christmas.* *for a while.* *for a short time only.* *for ages.*

B3 Grammar card: present perfect with *for/since*

1 Look at these sentences from B1:
I haven't had a big role for ages.
I haven't sung on stage since our last Christmas play.

2 In English you can use two words for the German word 'seit': *for* and *since*.
When do you use *since*? When do you use *for*?
Check LiF 10 on page 143 and add the information to your grammar card for the present perfect.

3 Think of four more sentences with *for* and *since* and add them, too.
P8 *WB B2, B3, p. 62*

B4

Work with a partner and talk about your hobby.
Say *since* when or *for* how long you …

- … have known the teacher/the other children in the group
- … have dreamed of a horse/boat/prize/…
- … have been interested in your hobby
- … have had/taken lessons
- … have wanted to …
- … have practised …

LiF 10: Present perfect: for/since, p. 143 *WB B4, B5, p. 63, 64*

B5 Target task

Portfolio

Need help? Look at p. 78.

Write a dialogue between Emma, Gillian, Caroline and Ms Walsh. The girls tell Ms Walsh about the vampire play, but she is not sure about it. So they try to persuade her. In the end, Ms Walsh says yes.

1 Work in groups of four.
- Collect ideas about why Ms Walsh doesn't like the idea of a vampire play.
- Find arguments to persuade Ms Walsh.

2 Write your dialogue. You can use the phrases from B1c).

3 Practise your dialogue and perform it in front of another group. Give feedback.
Wordbank Entertainment, p. 152 *Speaking 2, p. 127*

B6 ❖ Extra

Design a poster for the vampire play. You can look at the posters on pages 68/69 for help.

B7 Grammar card: present perfect or simple past?

1 Look at these sentences from the dialogue in B1:
*We haven't had a musical **since 'The Lion King'**. And that was **two years ago**!*

2 You can use the present perfect or the simple past for things that happened in the past.
But when do you use the present perfect?
When do you use the simple past?
Check LiF 11 on page 143 and write a grammar card.
Add four examples.
P10 *WB B6, p. 64*

B8

The girls have persuaded Ms Walsh, and she has written a play about vampires.
The next day there is an audition for pupils who want to take part in the play.
There are lots of things to do. *LiF 11: Present perfect or simple past, p. 143*

Caroline has got the to-do list and is checking with Ms Walsh to see if everything is ready.
Look at the checklist and write their dialogue. You can start like this:
Ms Walsh: "Caroline, has Emma ...?"
Caroline: "Yes, she has. She copied the script two weeks ago."
...

- *copy the script (Emma) ✓ (two weeks ago)*
- *buy vampire teeth (Gillian) ✓ (Friday)*
- *make posters for the auditions (Gillian) ✓ (last week)*
- *book assembly hall for the audition (secretary) ✓ (two days ago)*
- *make a list of the pupils who are interested (Emma) ✓ (yesterday)*
- *send the script to the pupils who are interested (Caroline) ✓ (yesterday afternoon)*
- *find music for the play (Caroline) (–)*

B9 L 1/30

Read Caroline's text message to Rajiv.
Then listen to the telephone conversation and find out what the text message is about. *Listening, p. 124*

B10

Look at these words and organize them in a word web.
In class find more words to describe music.

How to work with a dictionary, p. 129

melody · text/lyrics · happy · sad · quiet · rhythm · fast · slow · scary · cheerful · atmosphere · dark

B11

S 12, L 1/31

Three days later Caroline is at Rajiv's house.
He has written a vampire song.

a) Close your books and listen to the song.
What is it about?

b) Listen again and describe the music.
How does it make you feel?

c) ❖ **Choose:**
- Imagine you are the vampire.
  Write about a night in your life.

or
- Write a different last verse for the song.

Last week I couldn't get to sleep
The house was dark and eerie.
And I had the strangest feeling
something bad was near me.

I crept down to the basement
and guess what I found there?
A vampire lurking in the shadows!
It gave me such a scare.

He had ghostly skin and pointy teeth
but he didn't bite.
He said, 'Please, I just want a friend
to hang out with at night.'

Since then I haven't slept at all.
I can't wait for the day to end.
I just want to go down to the basement
to see my vampire friend.

B12 Target task ❖

Portfolio ● P4, P5

Present your favourite song.

Need help?
Look at p. 79.

1 Collect information about the singer/band.
Find out ...
- ... how long he or she has been a singer/they have been a band
- ... since when the singer/band has/have been famous
- ... since when they have been interested in music
- ... if they have won any prizes

Write a profile about the singer/band.

2 Makes notes about ...
- ... the kind of music (rock, pop, hip hop, ...)
- ... why you like the song
- ... how it makes you feel
- ... what you think of when you hear it

Support
The word web from B10 can help you.

3 Present your favourite song to your class.

Speaking 1, p. 126 WB B7, p. 65

It's show time!

C1 L 1/32

a) Read the story. What happens at the audition?

b) Write down two true sentences and one false sentence about the story.
Your partner must say which sentence is wrong and must correct it. WB C1, p. 65

It was the day of the audition and all the girls were very excited.
Caroline was happy, but she was nervous, too. She really wanted the leading role, but there were Anastasia and Moira, who also wanted the role.
"It would be OK for me if Anastasia got the role," Caroline said to Emma. "She's fascinating on stage, she speaks clearly and she acts convincingly – when she laughs, she laughs happily or nervously, just as the stage directions say."
"She's just a very good actress," Emma agreed admiringly.
"But Moira ...?" Caroline rolled her eyes and Emma pulled a face.

At the audition, Anastasia was first. When she went on the stage, her face was sad.
"OK, let's hear your part, then!" Ms Walsh said kindly. All the girls were quiet.
Anastasia started, but she spoke very slowly: "Will I have to ... stay in ... the shadows forever? ..."
"Come on, Anastasia! You know your words, don't you?"
"I do, Miss, but ..." Anastasia whispered and then she began to cry. Gillian ran to the stage and put her arms around her.
"What's wrong?" Ms Walsh asked worriedly, but Anastasia couldn't answer.

The girls went outside. "Tell me what's wrong," Gillian said quietly.
"I've mucked it up," Anastasia said sadly. "My mum had to go to hospital yesterday. And I'm so worried ..."
"Don't worry – if we tell Ms Walsh, you'll get another chance!" Gillian said cheerfully and smiled at her.
"I'm not sure I even want it now," Anastasia said and started to cry again.

Inside, Moira was next. There was loud applause from her friends when she went on stage. She turned around like a star.
"Can I begin, Miss?", she asked arrogantly, but didn't wait for an answer. She knew the words and spoke clearly: "Will I have to stay in the shadows forever? ..."
"Word, words, words," Emma said quietly, "but no emotion!" But Moira's friends clapped excitedly. Caroline watched them. "You're right," she answered nervously.

On stage Caroline wanted to be the best actress. She really liked the role and she knew she could be better than Moira.
"Will I ...," Caroline started loudly, but then she looked at Moira and her friends. They gave her the thumbs down behind Ms Walsh's back.
Caroline started to stammer. She tried to remember the words, but suddenly she couldn't remember anything.

C2

a) Copy the grid. Note down all the characters in the story, what they say/ask and how they say/ask it.

character	*what she says/asks*	*how she says/asks it*
Emma	*"She's just a very good actress."*	*admiringly*
Ms Walsh	*"OK, ..."*	...
...	...	...

b) Dramatic reading:

1 Practise reading the story:
- Read the story quietly twice.
- Remember how the characters feel. Use your notes from a) and show the feelings of the different characters.

2 Work in groups of four and have a reading competition. Find the best reader. You can use your grid from a) and a checklist to find out who read best.

Dramatic reading, p. 130

C3 Grammar detective: adverbs of manner

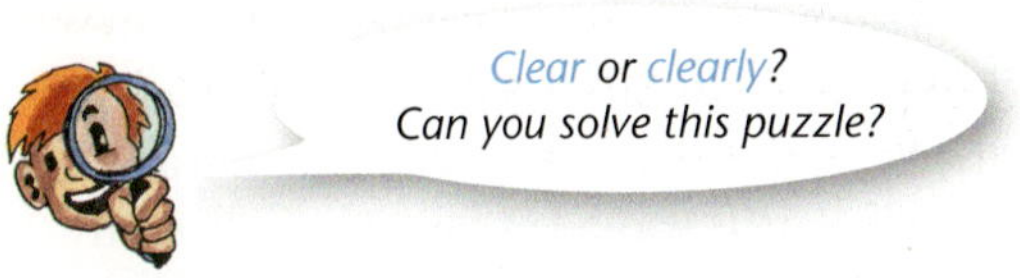

1 Look at these sentences from C1:

adjective	adverb
Caroline was happy.	*When she laughs, she laughs happily.*

2 Copy the grid and add more examples with *nervous/nervously, worried/worriedly, quiet/quietly, excited/excitedly* and *loud/loudly* from the story.

3 What do you describe with an adjective? What do you describe with an adverb? Look at LiF 12 on page 144 for help.

4 Start a grammar card. Look at LiF 12 on page 144 and find out about the spelling. When do you have to be careful? Add the information to your grammar card.

P11-P13 *WB C2, p. 66*

Support

There is an extra rule about *look* and *feel* and adjectives – read it on page 144!

C4

Work in groups and play this game:
- Write down these verbs on ten cards:

eat · walk · dance · sing · jump · talk · smile · move · laugh · play

- Now note down ten adverbs on ten different cards. Example: *angrily, happily, scarily ...*
- Make two piles (verbs and adverbs). Turn the cards upside down.
- Now one player takes a card from each pile and acts out what the cards say.
- The others must guess what the player is doing and how he/she is doing it.

LiF 12: Adverbien der Art und Weise, p. 144 *WB C3, C4, p. 66, 67*

C5 L 1/33

a) Think – pair – share: Speculate on how the story about the audition goes on.

Think – pair – share, p. 130

b) Read the story to find out if you were right. Reading, p. 125 WB C5, p. 68

1 Caroline was really upset. Emma tried to calm her down but Caroline didn't want to listen. "You know why I mucked it up?" she shouted angrily. "It was just because of Moira's friends – they pulled faces at me and now they've won." "We should talk to Ms Walsh," Emma suggested. "And tell her I was tricked out?", Caroline said. "No way! Then she'll think I'm just telling a sob story because I want to get the leading role. Anyway, Ms Walsh has offered me another job – she said I could be the prompter. That's OK." Caroline tried to sound cool, but Emma knew that her friend was hurt.

2 On Friday it was drama group again. That evening Caroline wrote in her diary:

Dear Diary,
I feel awful. At least I don't have to be on stage with Moira. The way she acts just makes me sick. She ruins everything!!!

3 All week Caroline was very gloomy. When George asked her what was wrong, she didn't answer. So George asked Emma.
"That audition was just so unfair," Emma said angrily. "The first night with Moira will be a nightmare for Caroline."
George felt sorry for his sister. He wasn't that interested in drama, but he still thought it was unfair.
"We must do something to cheer her up," he suggested. "Hey, there's a *Popsicles* concert on the day of the first performance. Maybe I can get some tickets for Caroline and me."
"What a great idea!" Emma answered. "But I don't think she can go. You know she's the prompter. She has to be there like everyone else."
"But her job is backstage, so anyone can do it. I'm sure someone else can do it for her."

4 A few days later, Caroline found an envelope in her room. Inside there were tickets for the *Popsicles* concert. Caroline couldn't believe it …

5 It was the last week before the play started. The girls tried on their costumes. The boys in the band were ready. Everything was prepared. But Ms Walsh was a bit worried. Moira wasn't very good. She spoke clearly and knew her words, but she didn't say them with feeling. But it wasn't only that. Moira was often difficult and the other girls on the stage were often tense when Moira was around. But it was too late now.
Finally, everyone was ready. But where was Moira? Ms Walsh was annoyed. She was really fed up with Moira, who always pretended to be a star. Finally, Moira arrived. "Oh, Ms Walsh," she whispered sweetly, "I need a microphone."
"What are you talking about?" Ms Walsh asked.
"Well, you can hear – I've lost my voice. But maybe I can act my part with a microphone."
"The drama group always works without microphones – and if you have one, everyone will need one. I'm afraid we can't do it."
Moira looked at Ms Walsh coldly. "Then we'll have to postpone the play."
"Postpone the play?" Ms Walsh was shocked. "We can't!"

C6

Choose a title for each part of the story and explain your choice. You can find different titles, too. ● P14 WB C6, p. 68

For part no. … I chose the title … because …

The idea · Keeping cool · Dear Diary · Hard times · Lost voice · Real friends · Moira wins · The surprise · A new chance? · Winners and losers · A difficult choice

C7

a) Say how Caroline feels …
- … when she talks to Emma after the audition
- … after the next meeting of the drama group
- … when she finds the tickets
- … when Moira can't act in the play

b) Caroline has got tickets for her favourite pop group – and she has the chance to take over Moira's role. What would you do if you were Caroline and why? ● P6 WB C7, p. 69

C8

Look at the story again. Collect different words for *say* and adjectives/adverbs that show how a character feels.

C9 Target task ❖ Project Portfolio ● P7

Need help? Look at p. 80.

Write your ending to the story from C5.

1 Look at the pictures and choose the ending you like best. Then write your ending to the story.

2 Plan your ending:
- What happens exactly? How will the characters in the story react? How will they feel? What will they say?
- Collect words and phrases for your story. ● *Wordbank Entertainment, p 152; People, p. 153*

3 Write the ending. Remember to …
- … use the simple past.
- … use direct speech (e.g. "OK, I can do it," Caroline said.).
- … include adjectives/adverbs to describe the characters' feelings and their actions. Your list from C8 can help you.
- … use different words for *say*. You can use your results from C8.

4 Work in groups and read your stories to your group. Then correct them and choose the one you like best. Present the story to the class. ● *Writing, p. 128* WB C8, p. 69

Prepare your target task A5:

P1 Words: adjectives

Look at the adjectives. Copy the grid and organize the words.

☺	☹
amazing	*disappointed*
…	…

amazing · bad · beautiful · awful · wonderful · boring · perfect · silly · lovely · terrible · exciting · fantastic · fascinating · stupid

P2 Listening S 11, L 1/28

Listen to the friends again and finish the sentences.

1 The music is …
2 The singers in the choir really …
3 They must put in …
4 Mr Gibson is …
5 He really has …
6 The audience …

Prepare your target task B5:

P3 Words: suggest, disagree, agree, persuade

a) Sort the phrases (suggest, disagree, agree, persuade).

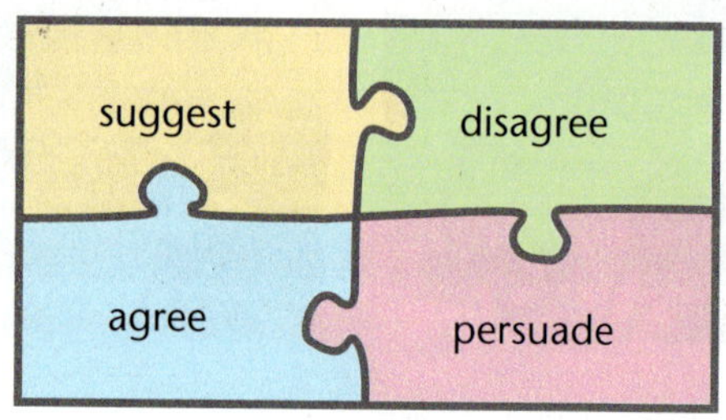

Let's …
Why not?
I'm not sure.
That sounds interesting, but …
You must be joking.
Maybe we could …
What about …?
To be honest, it doesn't sound that good.
It's important that …
Sounds great!
Can't we …?
Why don't we …?
Don't you think we should …?
But just think about it …
We could even …
No way!
You're right.
I don't think that this is a great idea.
That's a great idea.
Don't you think …?
OK, let's do it.
I completely agree.

b) Work with a partner. You are friends and want to spend Friday afternoon together. Make plans and try to persuade your friend to do what you have planned. Remember to be polite!

Prepare your target task B12:

P4 Writing

a) Read the article about Rihanna and note down facts about her.

Rihanna's birthday is on 20th February, 1988. When she was 16 she went to the USA to work with record producer[1] Evan Rogers.

She released[2] her first studio album, "Music of the Sun", in 2005. It featured[3] the top five single "Pon de Replay". Her second album, "A Girl Like Me" (2006), featured number one single "SOS". In 2007 she released her third album, "Good Girl Gone Bad". It featured the international hit singles "Umbrella", "Don't Stop the Music" and "Disturbia". The album won a Grammy. Since 2007 she has released many more albums, which were all an international success.

In 2006 Rihanna created the Believe Foundation[4] to help children. She is also the official face of tourism for Barbados.

In 2008 Rihanna appeared[5] in a Gucci advert for a special-edition handbag. She has also worked on a fragrance[6] called "Reb'l Fleur" with Jay-Z.

b) Use your notes from the article to create a profile.

Name: Rihanna *Date of birth: …*
Career: … *Famous songs: …*
Hobbies/Interested in: …
…

[1] record producer – *Schallplattenproduzent;*
[2] release – *veröffentlichen;*
[3] feature – *enthalten;* [4] foundation – *Stiftung;*
[5] appear – *auftreten;* [6] fragrance – *Parfum*

P5 Present perfect with for/since (1)

LiF 10: Present perfect (for/since), p. 143

Play this game with a partner.

1 Write something you have/haven't done on a piece of paper like this: *I haven't done my homework.*

2 Fold the paper so that your partner can't see what you have written.

3 Give the paper to your partner. Don't read what's on the paper!
Now write down a time with *since* or *for*.

4 Open the paper and read the sentence. *I haven't done my homework for three years.*

Prepare your target task C9:

P6 Reading

Reading, p. 125

a) Look at C5 on page 76 again.
Match the parts of the sentences.

Caroline was upset
Caroline didn't want to talk to Ms Walsh
George asked his sister
On the evening of the first night everything was ready
Finally, Moira arrived
Ms Walsh said no
Emma knew
George wanted to buy tickets for a pop concert
Caroline was very surprised

that
why
when
because
but
and

she didn't want to tell a sob story.
he wanted to cheer Caroline up.
said that she couldn't speak without a microphone.
Moira wasn't there.
Caroline was hurt.
she found the tickets.
of the audition.
she was sad.
Moira suggested they postpone the play.

b) Put the sentences in the correct order.

P7 Words: verbs and adverbs

To make a story interesting you should include direct speech.
Match the verbs to the adverbs, then make sentences.

Example: ***"Look, Roberta is talking to James," Myra whispered excitedly.***
"Oh no, Mr Grey is watching us," Rajiv whispered nervously.

whisper
shout
answer
ask
laugh
scream
stammer
cry

excitedly
nervously
happily
worriedly
angrily
disappointedly
arrogantly
seriously[1]

[1] seriously – *ernsthaft*

Extra language training:

P8 Present perfect with for/since (2)

LiF 10: Present perfect (for/since), p. 143

Look at the pictures and say what these people have/haven't done.
Use the verbs and *for/since*.
Example: ***He hasn't played football for three weeks.***

play · live · be · write · do · eat · have

football/three weeks

three words/4pm

this house/2009

karate/6 years

chocolate/three weeks

best friends/5 years

outside/2 days

dog/2005

P9 Revision: conditional clauses type I

LiF 7: Bedingungssätze, Typ 1, p. 140

Choose four of these sentences and write down what you will/won't do.

What if …

1 … I lose[1] my mobile phone?
2 … my favourite TV star sits next to me on the bus?
3 … they close the school?
4 … I find my diary on the Internet?
5 … I find €10,000?
6 … I see a pickpocket?

Example: *I will … if I lose my …*

[1] lose – *verlieren*

P10 Present perfect or simple past?

LiF 11: Present perfect or simple past, p. 143

Read the sentences and choose the correct form.

1 Mrs Carson lived/has lived in London since 2008.
2 She bought/has bought a small house in Camden in 2009.
3 She has got a sister, but she didn't see/hasn't seen her for a long time.
4 Her sister lived/has lived in India since 2010.
5 They were/have been very good friends when they were children.
6 Mrs Carson met/has met her husband five years ago.
7 At first she didn't talk/hasn't talked to him because she was/has been very shy[1].
8 But then they went/have gone to a party together. They were/have been together since then.

[1] shy – *schüchtern*

P11 Adjectives and adverbs of manner (1)

LiF 12: Adverbien der Art und Weise, p. 144

❖ **Can you do it?**
1. Caroline can read very ??? (quick).
   She is a ??? (quick) reader.
2. You can check your answers on page 221.
3. You need help? → Do a), then b).
   You can do it? → Do b).

a) Read the sentences and choose the correct form.

1 Caroline always learns her role (quick/quickly) and she acts very (good/well).
2 Everyone says she is a (good/well) actress.
3 At auditions she is sometimes a little (nervous/nervously).
4 But when she is on stage her performance is often (perfect/perfectly).
5 In the school play two years ago everyone clapped (wild/wildly).
6 The applause was (fantastic/fantastically).

b) Complete the sentences. Choose the correct form (adjective or adverb).

1 The boys in the band can sing very (good).
2 That's why their fans think the band is (amazing).
3 Ben has a (fantastic) voice.
4 Chris plays the guitar[1] (perfect).
5 Their friend Stephen has (great) ideas as a songwriter.
6 When he has an idea he can write a song (quick).

[1] guitar – *Gitarre*

P12 Adjectives and adverbs of manner: exceptions[1]

LiF 12: Adverbien der Art und Weise, p. 144

a) What are the missing adjectives/adverbs? Copy the grid and fill in the correct forms.

adjective	adverb	adjective	adverb
good			*high*
	fast	*late*	
hard			*near*

b) Write down six sentences and use the adjectives/adverbs from a).
Add two more sentences with *look* and *feel*.

[1] exception – *Ausnahme*

P13 Adjectives and adverbs of manner (2)

LiF 12: Adverbien der Art und Weise, p. 144

a) Choose adjectives or adverbs for the text about the audition.

worriedly · cool · clearly · quiet · dark · good · nervous · excitedly · excited · small · brilliant · sunny · worried · rainy · big · quietly · nervously · arrogantly · coolly · loudly · bored

It was a 1 day. Just before the audition, the girls felt a little 2 . Inside the 3 assembly hall a lot of girls were waiting. Some were talking to each other 4 , but some of them were 5 . Some watched the other girls 6 . First there were the auditions for the leading role. When Moira heard her name she turned around 7 and ran to the 8 stage. She thought she was really 9 and she began to speak 10 . She felt really 11 when the jury told her their result.

b) Find a partner who has chosen other adjectives/adverbs and read your texts to each other. Decide which fit better.

P14 Sounds S 13, L 1/34

Find the first letters of these words and say the words. Do you say /v/ or /w/? Then listen and check.

?egetable	?ery	?ideo
?atch	?isit	?ithout
?ater	?eather	?ay

Extra skills training:

P15 Reading Reading, p. 125

Work with a partner. One of you reads the sentences 1–5. The other chooses the correct phrase and reads the poster to answer the questions.

1 So quiz night is on Friday – that's what the poster says.
2 I'm babysitting from 9pm to 10pm. Is that OK for quiz night?
3 I'm always hungry in the evening. I hope there'll be some food.
4 £10 for a ticket – I don't have that much money.
5 I like quizzes, but the quizmaster is a bit boring, don't you think?

Pupils only have to pay … · That's OK. · Don't worry. · There's a new … · The quiz takes place … · I'm afraid not. · Quiz night is from … to … · The price includes … · That's right, but … · Well, …

P16 Say it in English

Look at Theme 4 again and find the answers.
Was sagst du auf Englisch, wenn du …

1 … etwas vorschlagen willst?
2 … wissen willst, was mit jemandem los ist?
3 … etwas toll findest?
4 … jemanden sagen willst, dass er sich keine Sorgen machen soll?

Monstroso

O1 Reading, p. 125

Monstroso by Charlie Higson is a story about Oscar, a boy who plays on his dad's computer although he is not allowed to do so.

Before you read the story, start a word web with computer words.
Which words do you also use in German?
Which are different?

O2

a) Look at this sentence from the story and speculate what the story is about:
"There on the desktop was the image of a clenched fist[1] with the words PROJECT X written across it in red."

b) Read the story and add more words to your word web from O1.

Oscar climbed[2] out of bed. He knew he shouldn't touch the computer. He'd promised Dad. He knew it was very special and important for Dad's work. He knew it was blah-di-blah-di-blah ...
It was a computer. A COMPUTER! And Oscar LOVED computers.
Before he even knew what he was doing, he found himself [...] pressing the power switch.
Oscar peered[3] at the computer screen. It looked exactly like the welcome screen on his own computer. There were various folders and documents and shortcuts he didn't recognize but his fingers danced across the keys and waggled[4] the little control stick and soon he was searching through the documents for anything that might be important and secret.
He couldn't find anything interesting. [...] Even the games on it would probably all be rubbish.
It was worth a look, though ...
He found the games folder and opened it. He scrolled down the list.
Just as he'd thought.
All the same boring games you got on any computer.
Solitaire, minesweeper, jacks – there was even a chess[5] game.
A chess game! Oscar groaned[6]. [...] He closed the folder. And then he spotted something. His eyes went wide, his heart started knocking against his ribs. There on the desktop was the image of a clenched fist with the words PROJECT X written across it in red.
It was a shortcut to a program ...
Why hadn't Oscar noticed it before? How could he have missed it? [...]
He was sure the icon hadn't been there before.
Had it somehow magically appeared?
Don't be stupid.
He must have triggered[7] some secret software on the laptop that had made the icon pop up.
Well, now that it had popped up, there was only one thing to do with it ...
Click on it.
That was what icons were for ...
PROJECT X.
What could it be? Oscar nervously moved the pointer over it, afraid to click. [...]
He took a deep breath and clicked. For a moment nothing happened. Then the screen went black. What had he done? [...]
Just as Oscar was beginning to think he must have killed the computer, the screen started to glow[8] with a strange green light and a throbbing[9] sound came from the speakers. [...]
Two words appeared on the screen.
ENTER USERNAME

---

[1] clenched fist – *geballte Faust*
[2] climb – *klettern*
[3] peer – *gucken*
[4] waggle – *wackeln (an)*
[5] chess – *Schach*
[6] groan – *stöhnen*
[7] trigger – *auslösen*
[8] glow – *leuchten*
[9] throb – *pochen*

Oscar typed in Dad's name. Dad wasn't clever or imaginative[10] enough to come up with a fancy code-name.

DO YOU WISH TO PROCEED, BRIAN?

Oscar clicked on YES. [...]

ENTER PASSWORD

Oscar knew the answer to that as well. Dad used the same password for everything and Oscar had found it out ages ago when he'd accidentally on purpose[11] overheard him telling it to Mum. [...]

Oscar typed in OSCAR1.

PROCEED, BRIAN.

Oscar pressed Enter and with a metallic clang the image of a great steel shutter[12] came on to the screen, slamming[13] shut. It immediately snapped open again to reveal[14] a new interface; designed to look like battle-scarred[15] metal, with panels and slots and buttons all over it. There were loads of instructions and options, the same as when you loaded any game. Oscar began to work his way through them. [...]

Screen after screen came up with a CLANG and Oscar kept on typing and clicking, his hands dancing over the keyboard like a crazy concert pianist. [...]

At last he reached the screen that asked him if he wanted to run the program. He clicked YES and it was done.

Another page of boxes appeared and Oscar's greedy[16] eyes quickly scanned the options. There were loads of them, most of which Oscar didn't understand, but there, in the lower right-hand corner, was one he was very familiar with:

CREATE YOUR WARRIOR[17]

Warrior!! Yes!!

[10] imaginative – *einfallsreich*
[11] accidentally on purpose – *aus Versehen mit Absicht*
[12] steel shutter – *Stahlklappe*
[13] slam shut – *zuknallen*
[14] reveal – *zeigen*
[15] battle-scarred – *vom Kampf gezeichnet*
[16] greedy – *gierig*
[17] warrior – *Krieger*

O3

a) Were you right in O2? Say why/why not.

b) Draw a picture of the warrior and describe him.

O4 *Writing, p. 128*

What might happen next? How could the story end?
Draw a comic or write the story down.
You can also use your computer words from O1.

Du kannst schon viel auf Englisch verstehen und ausdrücken. Du kannst ...

- ✓ über Veranstaltungen an deiner Schule sprechen
- ✓ einen Artikel über ein Ereignis schreiben
- ✓ einen Dialog verfassen und vorspielen
- ✓ deinen Lieblingssong vorstellen
- ✓ eine Geschichte vortragen
- ✓ erklären, wie jemand etwas macht
- ✓ das Ende einer Geschichte verfassen

WB Portfolio-Fragebogen Theme 4

5 Going green

Green Week or the Mill?

A1

In class talk about special events, trips and activities that take place at your school and note them down.

LiF 1R, p. 133, LiF 2R, p. 135, LiF 8, p. 140/141 WB A1, A2, p. 77

Every year we have a project week. Then we …

Last year we went to …/ organized …/ took part in …

I have already acted in the school play/played for the school team/…

There are always concerts/ music shows/dance shows/ … at our school in …

A2

a) Divide the class into two groups.
- Group A reads the report about Green Week.
- Group B reads the report about the Mill.
- Make notes on …
  - … who?
  - … what?
  - … where?
  - … when?
  - … why?

Reading, p. 125

b) Work with a partner who read the other report. Use your notes from a) to explain what your report is about.

c) Which report do you find more interesting? Say why.

Great success for the first Green Week at Camden School for Girls

"What's going on at CSG? Why are there so many people in green?" That is what many people asked when they walked past CSG last week in the first Green Week at our school. Although there were a lot of pupils in green clothes, Green Week was not about fashion. It was a very informative experience about the world that we live in and what we can do to save it.

Every day of the week, all the teachers and pupils did something different to learn more about the environment. Each day had a different motto. On Monday, for example, we all watched the excellent film "The Age of Stupid" to see what our planet will look like in 40 years. On Wednesday we talked about recycling waste. Some of our pupils collected four boxes of plastic bottles when they walked around Camden. On Friday, we used green handprints to form a tree. Teachers and

pupils made their green pledges for a better future – a future with more wind and solar energy! Thank you to everyone who took part in the projects. Please remember your green pledges. We still have great plans for the money that you and others donated to buy solar panels for our school. There is always more that we can do – but we have taken the first big step and the first Green Week at our school was a great success.

A3 🎧 L 1/35

a) The Lambrakis talk about George's trip to the Mill and Caroline's Green Week. Listen to them and find out what George and Caroline are going to do at the Mill/Green Week. Take notes.

Listening, p. 124

b) ❖ **Extra:** Would you like to have a Green Week at your school or go to the Mill?
Say why/why not.
Your notes from a) can help you.

A4

Look at the elements of a report below.
Read the reports again and find examples of them.

1. a headline
2. an entertaining beginning
3. a person's statement
4. details of an activity/event
5. a sentence that refers back to the title

Example: *details of an activity/event:*
On Monday, for example, we all watched …

WB A3, A4, p. 78, 79

A5 Target task ❖ ● *P1, P7* *Need help? Look at p. 96.*

Choose:

- Choose an event at your school and write a report about it for the English version of your school's website. **or**
- Prepare a school radio report in English about an event at your school. Present it to the class.

Support

- Look at your list from A1 and choose one event you want to write/talk about.
- Look at the reports in A2 again. Collect words and phrases that you can use with your report.
- To structure your report, you can use A4.
- Your report should answer the questions *who, what, where, when* and *why*.

The magic of the Mill

It is just one hour and a half on the motorway, but for many pupils it is like a fascinating trip into another world. Last week our Year 8 pupils spent a week at our field studies centre, the Mill, in Forest Green again.

"First I thought, 'Oh no, boring walks and lots of biology and geography exercises.' But it turned out to be lots of fun," Jeremy Fowler said when he came back.

Mr Scott, one of the teachers who organized

the stay at the Mill, agreed: "It's the combination of fieldwork and sport and adventures that makes it a fantastic trip."

The Mill is a great place for pupils to study birds and learn more about wildlife and plants. During the week, the pupils made posters about the birds which you can find at the Mill.

With football and other games, there was a lot of exciting entertainment – even if some boys were not happy that there were no supermarkets or shops nearby. But this is what makes the Mill so special. "I haven't really thought much about birds and other wild animals – we don't see them much in Camden. But it's almost magic to be away from the traffic and the noise of London for a few days," Manish Malik said about his experience.

B1

Think – pair – share: What can you do to protect the environment?

● Think – pair – share, p. 130 ● Wordbank Environment, p. 152

a) Write down as many ideas as you can.
You have got one minute.

recycle paper · turn off … when … · use …, not … · go by bike when …

b) Compare your list with a partner's and add new words.

c) Work in groups and share your ideas.

d) In class group your ideas like this:

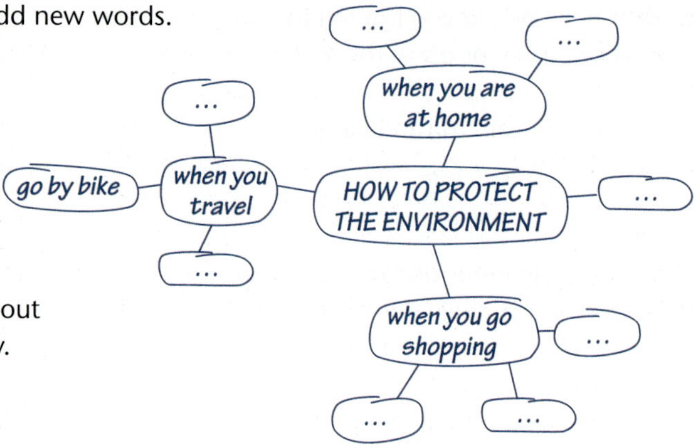

B2

L 1/36

a) Listen to Caroline and her mother and find out what the pupils do for Green Week that day.

● Listening, p. 124

b) Listen again and complete the sentences.

1 All pupils at Camden School for Girls have to …
2 Mrs Lambraki doesn't understand why Caroline doesn't …
3 When Caroline goes by bike, she can …
4 Mrs Lambraki doesn't know if Caroline's bike …
5 The bike doctor …
6 Caroline doesn't want to take Mrs Lambraki's bike because …

B3

a) In art class that morning, Caroline and her classmates design new signs that tell people how to protect the environment.
Look at the posters and write down the tips/rules.

turn off · recycle
leave on standby
go by … · throw away

Example: *You should turn off the lights when you leave the room.*
You mustn't/shouldn't …

b) Use your ideas from B1 to design your own poster. Show it to a partner.
He/She must say what your poster is about. ● Wordbank Environment, p. 152 ● P8 WB B1, p. 80

B4 L 1/37

a) Close your books and listen to Caroline and Emma and their teacher, Mrs Perry. Find out which two topics they are talking about. Listening, p. 124 WB B2, p. 80

b) Listen again and explain why …
- … Caroline feels angry
- … George is happy
- …the girls are excited

Caroline: I can't stand George these days. He can't stop telling me how fantastic his trip to the Mill will be. He thinks he'll be able to do whatever he wants there.

Emma: Really? That's just not fair! Yesterday we weren't even allowed to take a break until we finished our projects … and they can relax and enjoy their holiday!

Caroline: At the Mill they don't even have to do the washing-up after dinner. He's just so lazy!

Emma: Ssh, there's Mrs Perry.

Mrs Perry: Good morning, girls. Before we go on with our Green Week projects, there's something I have to tell you. You probably all know the TV station 'CamdenTV'. Well, they would like to interview some pupils about our Green Week for tomorrow's evening news.

Caroline: Wow, cool!

Emma: Will we all be allowed to talk to them?

Mrs Perry: I'm sorry, no. Just two of you will be able to talk to the reporter. So who wants to take part in the interview? … OK … There are six of you. So now we have to choose the two girls who'll represent the class. Let's have a vote.

A few minutes later:

Mrs Perry: OK, so it's you two, Caroline and Emma. Congratulations!

B5 Grammar card: modal verbs and their substitutes

1 You already know the modal verb *can*.
You can use *can* for the present tense and *could* for the past tense.
For other tenses, you need a substitute verb.
Look at line 3 in B4 and say what the substitute verb is.

2 Check LiF 13 on page 145 and find out about the substitute verbs of *must/mustn't, may* and *needn't*.
Write a grammar card.
P9 WB B3, p. 81

B6

The reporter gives Caroline and Emma some advice for the interview.

Look at the notes and say what
- they will be allowed to do/won't be allowed to do
- they will have to do/won't have to do

- *speak slowly and clearly*
- *use short sentences*
- *no "hello" to friends*
- *be polite*
- *no chewing gum*
- *no white or striped shirt*
- *normal clothes OK*

Example: *Caroline and Emma will have to speak slowly and clearly.*

LiF 13: Modal verbs, p. 145 P10 WB B4, B5, p. 81, 82

B7 L 1/38

After the lesson, Caroline calls her mother to tell her about the TV interview.

a) Read Caroline's answers and find out what Mrs Lambraki's questions are.

LiF 6: will future, p. 139, LiF 2R: Simple past, p. 135

Caroline: Hi, Mum! Guess what! I'll be on TV tomorrow!

Mrs Lambraki: Oh! What will you …?

Caroline: We will have to answer some questions.

Mrs Lambraki: …?

Caroline: The interview will be about Green Week.

Mrs Lambraki: …?

Caroline: The TV people didn't choose me. My class voted for me. But I won't be the only one.

Mrs Lambraki: …?

Caroline: Emma will be with me. Isn't that cool?

Mrs Lambraki: Yes, but …?

Caroline: We will have to answer some questions about Green Week – if we like it … erm, you know. We are super excited! We'll be on TV!!!

Mrs Lambraki: …?

Caroline: I'm not sure. I think it will be on at six o'clock. Oh, I have to go, Mum. Emma wants to talk to me now. Bye!

b) Now listen to the conversation and check if your questions are correct.

P2

B8 L 1/39

a) Read the interview. Who is more nervous – Caroline or Emma? Say why you think so.

Emma: Oh no, I'll make a fool of myself.

Caroline: Emma, you needn't worry. The TV people can cut out the bits where we say something wrong. It won't be live.

TV reporter: Ready, girls? Then let's start … We're here at Camden School for Girls today, where we will find out more about their Green Week. There are two girls from Year 8 with me – Caroline Lambraki and Emma Butler – who can tell us what is going on at their school at the moment. So, why is it called Green Week, Emma?

Emma: It's called Green Week … because we do a lot of projects about the environment.

Caroline: Yes, we cover topics like energy, wildlife, recycling, transport and much more. Every day has a different motto.

TV reporter: That sounds interesting. Can you give us an example of one of those days, Caroline?

Caroline: Today our topic is waste. We throw away so much … erm … plastic …erm … We throw away so much … erm … plastic and …

TV reporter: Do you mean paper and other materials, too?

Caroline: Yes, yes, so we produce a mountain of rubbish every year. So it's better if we collect paper and … paper … I mean, paper and …

Emma: … plastic and glass and other materials so that we can recycle them.

TV reporter: Are you trying to say that everything will be OK if we recycle as much as we can?

Emma: No, recycling isn't enough. We should buy products with less packaging and compost organic waste.

TV reporter: As you've mentioned organic waste, I've heard that some pupils have made something very special and delicious for you.

Caroline: That's right. Some Year 10 students went to the shops and supermarkets yesterday and collected all the fruit that the shops wanted to throw away. They used them to make smoothies for us in the lunch break.

TV reporter: It sounds as if you liked the smoothies, but how do you feel about Green Week as a whole?

Caroline: I wasn't sure at the end, I mean, at the beginning. We had a Green Week last year and it means a lot of work, but it's more fun than … erm … normal lessons.

Emma: Caroline's right. There are so many interesting activities this year that most of us really love it – and we also learn something about the environment.

TV reporter: You say Green Week is about learning. If I understood your head teacher correctly, Green Week is also about changing your behaviour. Do you agree?

Emma: That's true. Everyone had to walk to school or go by bike yesterday. A lot of pupils usually go by bus. I noticed that it's faster for me to go by bike. So I'll do it more often in the future.

TV reporter: Thank you very much, Emma and Caroline. That was it. You did a very good job.

b) Guess how Caroline and Emma feel after the interview.

c) Say what happened at Green Week. What do you think of the activities? How would you like them?

d) Note down words and phrases that show that you want to understand/are interested in/are listening to what the other person says. ● P3 WB B6, B7, p. 83
Example: *That sounds interesting; Do you mean …*

B9 Target task ❖ *Need help? Look at p. 97.*

Write an interview and act it out.
Work with a partner. One of you is a TV reporter and the other is a pupil at CSG.
The reporter interviews the pupil about Green Week.

1 Together think about what you are going to talk about. Here are some ideas:
- *wear warm pullovers to show that you can keep warm without central heating*
- *plant vegetables in the school garden*
- *go to a supermarket and find out where the fruit and vegetables come from*
- … ● *Wordbank Environment, p. 152*

2 Read your role cards and prepare your roles.

Role card: TV reporter
Ask about
- the activities
- the reason why pupils do them
- if the pupils like them and why

Role card: pupil at CSG
Talk about
- what you have done
- the reasons
- if you liked it and why

3 Take turns to write down your questions and answers.
The phrases from B8d) can help you.

4 Practise your interview, then act it out for another pair. Give feedback.
● *Speaking 2, p. 127* ● P13

5 At the Mill

C1

Remember your last class trip: what were you allowed/not allowed to do?
Write down the rules. WB C1, p. 84

C2

Before George's class go to the Mill, the parents get a letter from the school.
Read the letter and find out more about the Mill. P14

WILLIAM ELLIS SCHOOL

Highgate Road · London NW5 1RN
Head teacher: M. Edwards

Dear parents,

In two weeks Year 8 will be off to the Mill. I'm sure they'll have a great week.

Please make sure that your child brings camping things (a sleeping bag, a small rucksack, a plastic cup and plate, a knife, fork and spoon), enough clothes for a week, toothbrush/soap, a hat and an exercise book or diary. There are some games at the Mill, but pupils may also bring their own cards, games or books.

The children do not need to bring any extra food. There will be three meals a day. Pupils who are not able to eat certain foods or pupils who take medicine must bring a note with them and talk to Mr Glover before the trip.

The pupils are not allowed to bring radios, MP3 players, alcohol, computer games, mobile phones or pocket knives with them. If your child breaks the rules, we will ask you to come to the Mill and pick up your child immediately.

The pupils can walk to Forest Green, a small village near the Mill. There are no shops in Forest Green. As you know, teachers have already collected pocket money (£20/child), so pupils shouldn't bring any extra money. They will be able to buy food, drinks, pens, pencils, etc. at a small shop at the Mill.

Many thanks for your help.
Yours sincerely,

M. Edwards

C3

a) Make a list of rules for the trip and compare them to the rules for your class trips.

b) Work with a partner. Discuss which rules you find sensible, too strict or silly.
P12

C4 S 14, L 1/40

a) The boys are not very happy about the rules. Listen to them and note down their arguments.
Listening, p. 124 P15

b) The boys want to bring MP3 players with them. Write a short dialogue in which they try to convince Mr Glover. WB C2, p. 84

C5 L 2/1

a) Close your books and listen to the boys. Find out where they are.

Holden: Hey, George, give me back my MP3 player.
George: But this isn't yours.
Holden: But it looks like mine!
George: Well, it's Sam's.
Holden: It can't be his. He never gives his MP3 player away.
George: I know, but he brought his sister's.
Holden: What? He pinched his sister's player? It's hers? Oh, she'll go mad.
George: He says she won't miss it – she's on a class trip, too, and her teachers don't want any MP3 players on the trip.
Holden: OK, but the music must be awful.
George: It's not that bad. ... Hey, Rajiv, give us one of those bags of crisps. Whose are they anyway?
Rajiv: They're not mine. John and Leo are sitting here. The bags are theirs. They've gone to the front to talk to Stephen. ... Oh, there they are. Hey, Leo, those crisps – are they yours?
Leo: Yes, but we mustn't eat them on the coach. Let's have them later in the tents.

b) Read the dialogue. Find out which words the boys use for the following expressions:

your MP3 player · my MP3 player · Sam's MP3 player · his sister's MP3 player · my crisps · their bags · those crisps

c) Look at LiF 14 on page 146 and note down all the possessive pronouns and their German meanings.

LiF 14: Possessivpronomen, p. 146 · P11 · WB C3, p. 85

C6 L 2/2

a) Look at the pictures on this page and page 94. Speculate about what might happen at the Mill.

b) Read the story to find out if you were right.

P4

At the Mill

It was a quiet night at the Mill. The boys were all very tired after the long trip and a day full of activities. Rajiv was in a tent with George. There were two boys in every tent. Only Jason, who slept next to George and Rajiv, was alone in his tent. Rajiv and George didn't know Jason very well because he was very quiet.

Rajiv and George were asleep in their tent. Suddenly, they woke up. "Get off, get off!!" somebody screamed. It was Jason. Rajiv and George got up and looked out of their tent. Then they laughed. "Hey Jason, it's only the tent! It's fallen down." The boys started to put it up again. Then they heard an angry voice outside.

"What are you doing?" It was their teacher, Mr Glover. "Come on, Jason. You know the rules –

no fun and games after 10pm. We haven't been here for 24 hours and you're already breaking the rules!"

The next morning, Jason got up early. He wanted to do everything right that day. First he wanted to have a shower and then go to breakfast. He didn't want to be late.

Rajiv and George got up later. They didn't have time to take a shower and got dressed quickly. "Hurry up," Rajiv said to George.
They saw Jason a few metres away. "Come on, Jason. We'll be late for breakfast," George said. "Hey, where are your shoes?"
"I don't know," said Jason. "I can't find them."
"Oh, Jason. Here, you can wear my brown shoes," Rajiv said.

At breakfast, Mr Glover stood up. "This morning I found these shoes by the river," he said and held up a wet pair of shoes. "You all know you're not allowed to go down there without a teacher. The owner should come and see me after breakfast."
Everyone knew whose shoes they were and Jason felt terrible again. Rajiv and George felt sorry for him, but they saw a few boys laugh.

And the day only got worse for Jason. When the boys did a quiz, Jason lost. And he was late for lunch. Finally, he couldn't find his exercise book for his geography project. When one of the pupils found it and gave it to Mr Glover, it looked terrible. It was very dirty and Mr Glover said, "This looks like it has come straight from the bin." Jason went red in the face when all the other boys laughed.

Later, Jason sat near the tents. George saw him and said, "Hi Jason, I guess you've had quite a bad day."
"Yeah," said Jason. "Mr Glover is really angry with me. But you know what? I didn't really …"

Just then two other boys walked up to them. It was Michael and Matt. They were the class clowns. They often played tricks on other boys and were always in trouble. Matt had something small and red in his hands.
"Hey, Jason, are you having a bad day?" he said. "You should go home to your mum!"
"Why don't we help you go home?" Michael said with a strange laugh. Jason looked frightened. "Leave me alone," he said and ran away.

In the evening Jason and Mr Glover weren't at dinner. At about 7 o'clock Mr Glover came into the games room. He was upset.
"Now, you may have noticed that Jason isn't here," he said to the boys. "When we checked the tents, we found this red pocket knife under Jason's sleeping bag. We told you that you mustn't bring knives to the Mill. So we are going to send Jason home."

George looked at the red knife, then he looked at Matt and Michael. They were smiling. Suddenly George knew where he had seen the knife before – in Matt's hand that afternoon! George knew it wasn't Jason's knife and now he knew why Jason was so frightened and unhappy. "Matt and Michael are bullying him!" he thought. But George didn't know what to do. Should he tell Rajiv? Should he tell Mr Glover? But Jason's parents were on the way already. Should he talk to Matt and Michael? What was the right thing to do?

c) What should George do? What shouldn't he do?

I think he should/shouldn't …

d) Hot seat: Write down questions you would like to ask the different characters in the story. Choose pupils to be the characters and interview them. You can make up the answers.

Hot seat, p. 130 • P5

George, why didn't you …?

Mr Glover, did you notice …?

Matt and Michael, why…?

Jason, did you think you could …?

C7

Mr Glover has phoned Jason's parents. But before they arrive he talks to Jason. Read what he says to him. How does Jason react? Can you think of a reason?

Mr Glover: Jason, I'm really disappointed in you. I always thought you were a nice, quiet boy. But you were late for meals. The shoes I found at the river were yours … And the geography project you gave me was a mess – but you had done some work, so I thought I would give you another chance. But when we found the knife you hid in your tent – that was the limit, boy. You read the letter that explained the rules before the trip, didn't you?

Jason: Yes, sir.

Mr Glover: So you know this means you're going home.

Jason: Yes.

Mr Glover: Well, what do you have to say for yourself, boy?

Jason: I'm sorry, sir.

Mr Glover: Well, so am I. I've phoned your parents, who are very upset. And I'm sure your classmates will be very disappointed, too.

C8 ❖ Extra: Grammar card: contact clauses

1 You know relative clauses with the relative pronouns *who, which* and *that*. Here is an example from C7: *You read the letter that explained the rules before the trip.*

2 Now look at this sentence from C7: *The shoes I found at the river were yours.* This relative clause doesn't have a relative pronoun. It is called a *contact clause*. Look at C7 again and find more examples of contact clauses.

3 Check LiF 15 on page 147 to find out when you can leave out the relative pronoun. Write a grammar card for contact clauses. Add your examples. ● *P6* *WB C4, p. 85*

C9 ❖ Extra

a) How much do you remember about the story? Match the sentence halves.

1 The school sent a letter with rules	A that Michael and Matt threw in the river.
2 Matt and Michael are the boys	B which Michael and Matt put in Jason's tent.
3 Mr Glover found the shoes	C that everybody knew about.
4 Mr Glover found the knife	D which the others don't like.
5 Matt and Michael often play tricks	E that bullied Jason.
6 Mr Glover talked to Jason's parents,	F who were very upset.

b) Look at the sentences again. Where can you leave out the relative pronoun? Note down these sentences.

C10 Target task ❖ *Portfolio*

Need help? Look at pp. 98/99.

Write a letter.

George has decided to write a letter to Mr Glover.

1 Plan the letter. Think about
- what really happened at the Mill
- whose fault it was
- why George didn't say anything at the Mill
- what should happen to Jason, Matt, Michael

2 This is a letter to a teacher. Be polite. Start with *"Dear Mr Glover, …"* and finish with *"Yours sincerely, George Lambraki".* ● *Writing, p. 128* Then give your letter to a partner and read his/her letter. Give feedback.

● *Speaking 2, p. 127* *WB C5, C6, p. 86*

Prepare your target task A5:

P1 Writing

a) Match the parts of the report to their function.

1 A personal statement …
2 An entertaining beginning …
3 A sentence that refers back to the title …
4 Details …
5 A headline …

A … makes the readers more interested so that they read on.
B … is usually at the end of a report.
C … helps the readers to find out about the feelings of the people in the report.
D … tells the readers what the report is about.
E … can help the readers to imagine what happened.

b) Look at a) again and say which parts of a report you can see here.

1 *Year 7 at London Zoo*

2 *Who doesn't like looking at gorillas? Last week, Year 7 pupils took part in a programme at London Zoo. It was about how we put gorillas and many other animals in danger[1].*

3 *The pupils spent a day at London Zoo. They took part in a "Green Team Challenge" about the problems of gorillas today. They watched the gorillas, found out about the danger to them in Africa and learned what we can do to save them.*

4 *"I usually just look at the animals for fun, but I never thought about their situation in Africa," said Danny Mumbanga. "Now I know more about what we can do to help." His teacher, Mr Scott, agreed. "It isn't the same if we talk about animals in class and how you can save them. With London Zoo's programme, pupils understand better how much danger the gorillas are in."*

5 *Mr Scott and his class are now planning to collect[2] money to help London Zoo's programme to save gorillas in Africa. The gorillas' real kingdom in the African rainforest should survive[3]!*

[1] danger – *Gefahr*
[2] collect – *einsammeln*
[3] survive – *überleben*

Prepare your target task B9:

P2 Revision: simple present (questions)

Caroline and her classmates have prepared a quiz for Green Week, but now the questions are missing. Write down the questions. LiF 1Rc: Simple present, p. 134

Example: *Where should your food come from?*

Your food should come from your area so that you don't need much energy to transport it.

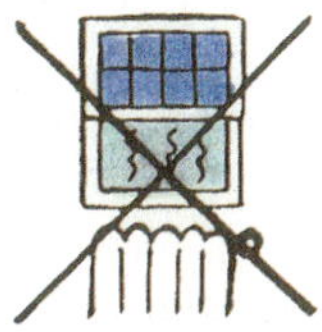

You should close the window when you leave the room or when you turn on the heating[2].

You can save energy if you turn off the lights, the computer, the TV etc. when you are not using them.

You should turn off the tap[3] while you are brushing your teeth.

You can find this sign on batteries because you shouldn't throw them into a normal rubbish bin[1].

This sign means that you can recycle this product.

[1] rubbish bin – *Mülltonne*
[2] heating – *Heizung*
[3] tap – *Wasserhahn*

P3 Words: an interview

A reporter in Camden wants to interview Karen, a pupil at CSG. Copy the interview and add some of the phrases from B8d) (page 91) to make the interview more interesting.

Example: *Reporter: That sounds interesting. What did you do?*

Reporter: I have heard about Green Week at your school. It seems to be a great event.
Karen: Yes. We do lots of projects. My friends and I have learnt a lot about the fact that the climate[1] is getting warmer and warmer.
Reporter: What did you do?
Karen: We watched a film and read some articles about the future of our planet.
Reporter: What do you think about it?
Karen: We must all start to change.
Reporter: What will you do in future?
Karen: I will walk to school or go by bike more often.
Reporter: So everything will be OK if we use our bikes more often?
Karen: No, there are lots of other things we can do, like saving water and energy.
Reporter: OK, thanks.

[1] climate – *Klima*

Prepare your target task C10:

P4 Connectives

Match the sentence halves and use connectives. LiF 4: Connectives, p. 138

Rajiv and George don't know Jason well
Jason feels scared
Mr Glover thinks Jason is having fun when he puts up the tent again
Jason doesn't say anything
Mr Glover is angry
Jason's exercise book looks terrible
Matt and Michael put a knife in Jason's tent
Mr Glover is upset
George knows what happened

because
so
when
although
but
and
so that

the tent falls down on him.
he finds Jason's shoes at the river.
all the boys laugh about it.
Jason is a very quiet boy.
he is angry with him.
Matt and Michael are bullying him.
doesn't tell Mr Glover that evening.
Jason has to go home.
phones Jason's parents.

P5 Words: feelings

Use these adjectives to say how Jason felt in the story on pages 93/94 …

- when he couldn't find his shoes.
- when Mr Glover held up his wet shoes.
- when he lost the quiz.
- when George talked to him.
- after Matt and Michael laughed at him.

scared · worried
surprised · happy
embarrassed · …

Extra language training:

P6 Contact clauses

LiF 15: Contact clauses, p. 147

❖ **Can you do it?**

1. Can you leave out the relative pronoun?
   Matt and Michael are the boys who are bullying Jason.
   George has seen the knife which Matt and Michael put in Jason's tent.
2. **You can check your answers on page 221.**
3. **You need help?** → Do a), then b).
   You can do it? → Do b).

a) Read the sentences and decide if you can leave out the relative pronoun.
Write down the sentences without the relative pronoun.

1 Mr Glover is the teacher who went to the Mill with his class.
2 Jason is a quiet boy who George and Rajiv don't know well.
3 Rajiv brings a brown bag to the Mill with all the things that he needs.
4 At the Mill the boys do a lot of projects which are very interesting.
5 They collect a lot of information which they have to write down in an exercise book.
6 There are dinner ladies[1] who are preparing the meals for the boys.

[1] dinner lady – *Kantinenmitarbeiterin*

b) Look at the pictures and write down a sentence for each picture with a relative or a contact clause.

Example: *These are the wet shoes that Mr Glover found at the river.*
These are the wet shoes Mr Glover found at the river.

1

2

3

4

5
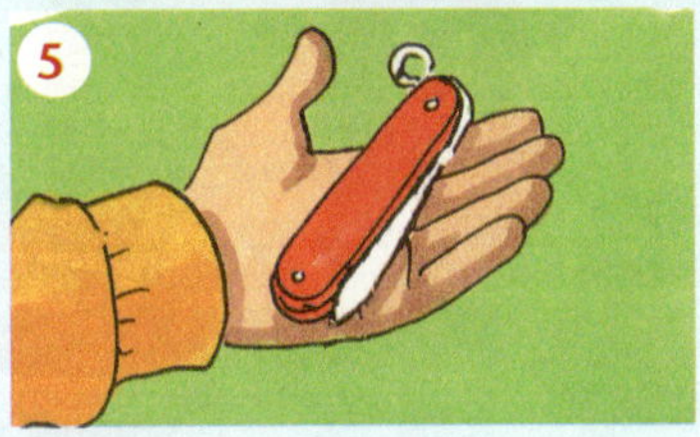
6

P7 Revision: relative clauses

LiF 9: Relative clauses, p. 142

Emma's brother Jack went to the Mill a few years ago. He shows Rajiv and George his photos. Write down what Jack might say.
Example: *This is the bed that I slept in. These are …*

bed/sleep

prepare/dinner

other boys/go to the Mill

sleep/my room

teacher/go with us

river/cold

P8 Revision: modal verbs

The Camden School for Girls' head teacher wants to write 'green rules' for the school. Look at his ideas and turn them into rules.
Use *must/mustn't, can, should/shouldn't, needn't.*

- *walk to school*
- *use recycled paper*
- *collect old paper and glass*
- *keep the school tidy*
- *leave the tap running*[1]
- *look after the school garden*
- *close the windows and doors to save energy*
- *waste*[2] *paper*

[1] leave the tap running – *den Wasserhahn laufen lassen*
[2] waste – *verschwenden*

P9 Modal verbs and their substitutes (1)

LiF 13: Modal verbs, p. 145/146

Sometimes Charlie and his mother have problems. Look at the picture and say what Mrs Batson might say to her son. Use *must, have to, mustn't, can't, not allowed to.*

P10 Modal verbs and their substitutes (2)

LiF 13: Modal verbs, p. 145/146

Think about when you were six years old.
What were/weren't you allowed to do?
What did/didn't you have to do?

Write down six sentences and read them to a partner.

P11 Possessive pronouns

LiF 14: Possessivpronomen, p. 146

The boys are at the Mill. Who do the things belong to?
Read the dialogue and write down the missing pronouns.

Mr Glover: Now, this bag is huge – whose is it? Is it [1], George?
George: No, sir, I think it belongs to Matt and Michael.
Rajiv: Yes, I'm sure it's [2]. They always pack their things together. And the brown bag is [3].
Mr Glover: Right, Rajiv, here you are. And this MP3 player – I think I saw Holden use it. So it must be [4].
Sam: Oh, no, that's my MP3 player.
George: But you said it isn't [5] – it's your sister's.
Sam: Well, yes, it's [6]. But she gave it to me for the trip, Mr Glover.
Mr Glover: Well, isn't your sister nice.
George: But Sam, you said that you pinched … ouch, Rajiv! Why are you kicking me?
Mr Glover: OK, Sam, so it's [7]. Here you are.

Extra skills training:

P12 Viewing: school rules

a) Watch the video clip to find out about the rules at Haverstock School. Note down five rules.

Example: *You have to …*
You are/aren't allowed to …

b) Work with a partner. Compare your results, then find out which of Haverstock School's rules are rules at your school, too. Which school rules are stricter – yours or Haverstock School's?

P13 Mediation

At the end of Green Week, the girls get a pledge card.
Tell your teacher in German what the pledge card is about.

PLEDGE CARD

Name:
School:

I promise
not to eat meat[1] all the time and have at least one meat-free day a week. ✓

I promise
to look for alternatives to international flights[2] and never fly within the UK. ✓

I promise
to recycle everything that is recyclable, including clothes and shoes. ✓

I promise
to turn off the TV and not leave it on standby when I am not using it. ✓

[1] meat – *Fleisch;* [2] flight – *Flug*

P14 Reading

Reading, p. 125

Right or wrong? Read the letter from William Ellis on page 92 again. Correct the wrong sentences.

1 The pupils must bring things to eat with them.
2 They mustn't bring knives.
3 They can buy extra food at the shops in Forest Green.
4 Pupils mustn't bring their mobile phones.
5 Pupils are not allowed to walk to the village.
6 The pupils should bring £ 20 for drinks, pens and pencils.

P15 Listening

S 14, L 1/40 *Listening, p. 124*

Listen to the boys again and finish the sentences.

1 George thinks that some rules for the trip to the Mill …
2 He can understand that computer games …
3 But he can't understand why the pupils mustn't …
4 Holden thinks computer games are OK because …
5 George doesn't want to take his MP3 player because …
6 George says that they could …

The Legend of Spud Murphy

01

a) Marty and his brother have to spend their holidays in the library while their mother is at work. Say how you would feel in their situation.

b) The two boys hate reading and they are scared of the strict librarian, Mrs Murphy. She says they must stay on a carpet in the children's corner and mustn't leave it. Speculate about what might happen. Then read the text to see if you were right. *Reading, p. 125*

Marty smiled. "The best way to mess with a librarian is to put things back in the wrong place. They hate that. It drives them nuts."
Marty was an expert on messing with librarians. There had been several notes home from the school library.
"So I'm just going to switch a few books for Mrs Spud Murphy. By the time she finds out, we'll be home watching cartoons." [...]
One book at a time, he switched almost every single book in the section. He put mysteries with romance, adventure with birdwatching and gardening with model aeroplanes. Spud would be furious[1]. [...]
Suddenly a shadow fell across my brother. [...]
Spud stood, slippered feet apart, with her hand hovering over the book stamps[2] on her belt.
It was too late to warn him. There was nothing I could do.
Spud's left hand moved with lightning speed, grabbing the book stamp and throwing it in one smooth precise motion[3]. [...] It was too late to move out of the way. All Marty could do was close his eyes and squeal like a kitten. [...]
"I knew it," said Spud slowly. "I can always tell a troublemaker." [...]
Marty stood slowly, no sudden moves. "I'm sorry, Spu– Mrs Murphy. I'll never leave the carpet again."
Spud slid across the floor on her slippers. "Too late for that. Since you're already off the carpet, you can fix the damage[4] you've done. [...] You get these in order by the time your mother comes to pick you up, and maybe I won't have to tell her how you set off the fire extinguishers[5]."
Marty's mouth flapped. "But ... I didn't."
Spud put her hands on her hips. "I know you didn't, and I'm sure your mother will believe that. Unless of course you've been in trouble before."
Marty thought about it for a moment, then began rearranging books as fast as he could. He knew when he'd met his match[6].
Two hours and fourteen papercuts later, Marty was finished. "That wasn't so bad," he said on the way to the exit. "I've had teachers meaner than her. [...] Do you think she'll really say I set off the fire extinguishers?" [...]
Marty had started to wander over towards Spud. [...] "Just one question, Mrs Murphy. You wouldn't really say I set off the fire extinguishers, would you?"
Spud smiled back at Marty. [...]
"Oh, wouldn't I?"
"I don't think so. Throwing a stamp is one thing. That was cool by the way."
"You liked that, did you Marty?"
"Sure did."
Spud opened the box on her desk. "I have a collection of stamps here. One came in last week you might like. It's in the shape of a pirate flag. A lot of the boys like me to stamp it on their forearms[7], like a temporary tattoo." She began to close the box. "But maybe you're too young."
Marty was already rolling up his sleeve. "No, I'd love that. On my arm. Wait until the lads in the swimming pool see this."
Spud selected a stamp, inking it on a blue pad. "Are you sure, Marty? This won't wash off for days."
"I'm sure. Stamp away."
"Well, if you're sure." Spud's smile widened.

"OK, then. Keep still." The librarian rolled the rubber stamp across Marty's forearm. Across and back, three times. When she removed the stamp, we leaned in to examine the pirate ship. Only it wasn't a pirate ship. It was a short sentence of three words. The words were: I LOVE BARBIE. "Oops," said Spud. "Wrong stamp. Sorry about that."

Marty couldn't speak. If anyone saw those words on his forearm, he'd be teased for all eternity[8]. [...] We walked to the door. Marty held his arm in front of him as though it belonged to someone else.
Spud called to him as he opened the door. "Oh, Marty," she said, "enjoy swimming."

---

[1] furious – *sehr wütend*
[2] stamp – *Stempel*
[3] in one smooth precise motion – *in einer flüssigen und präzisen Bewegung*
[4] fix the damage – *den Schaden beheben*
[5] fire extinguishers – *Feuerlöscher*
[6] he had met his match – *er hatte seinen Meister gefunden*
[7] forearm – *Unterarm*
[8] eternity – *Ewigkeit*

O2 *How to work with a dictionary, p. 129*

Find statements in the text that mean ...
- ... somebody is very angry about something
- ... very quickly
- ... cry like a baby cat
- ... go on and put the stamp on my arm

O3

Which of the following statements sums up the story best?
1. Mrs Murphy knows how to deal with difficult kids, so she teaches Marty a lesson.
2. Marty always wants to see what he can get away with but he has met his match in Mrs Murphy.
3. Marty often gets into trouble and that is why he sets off the fire extinguisher in the library.
4. Mrs Murphy is a librarian who hates children and does everything to keep them out of her library.

O4

Read the text again and collect phrases that are used to describe Mrs Murphy. Decide which of the following words fit her character and explain why.

cool · friendly · clever · strict · nasty · angry · helpful · scary

O5

a) With a partner take notes on Marty and his brother.

b) Imagine you could talk to Marty or his brother after what happened.
Write down questions you would like to ask them.

c) Hot seat: Put two people from the class in the hot seat as Marty and his brother and ask them about their experience in the library.
Hot seat, p. 130

Du kannst schon viel auf Englisch verstehen und ausdrücken. Du kannst ...
- ✓ über Umweltschutz sprechen
- ✓ deine Meinung ausdrücken
- ✓ Interesse an dem ausdrücken, was dein Gesprächspartner sagt
- ✓ ein Interview durchführen
- ✓ Personen zu ihren Handlungen befragen
- ✓ einen Brief verfassen

WB Portfolio-Fragebogen Theme 5

6 Fun and games

Are you fit?

A1 L 2/3

Listen to the CD. What are the different sports? Write them down. WB A1, p. 95

A2

Charles Cousins is a British rowing star. He is visiting William Ellis School to talk about fitness and health. To find out how fit the pupils are, they do a fitness test.

a) Are you fit? Do the fitness test with a partner. Note down your results on a piece of paper.

b) Check your results on page 105.

FITNESS TEST

1	Jump up and down for 30 seconds. Are you out of breath?
a	No, not at all.
b	A little bit.
c	Yes, I am!

2	Can you touch the floor like this?
a	Yes, I can.
b	I can, but it is difficult.
c	No, I can't. It's too hard.

3	Walk up and down 20 stairs quickly. Are you out of breath?
a	No, I'm not. That's easy.
b	Just a little.
c	Yes, I am!

4	Can you balance like this for 15 seconds?
a	Yes, I can.
b	Not quite.
c	Sorry, I can't do it.

5	Do press-ups. How many can you do?
a	More than 5.
b	2–5
c	I can hardly do one.

A3

Find words and phrases about sport and fitness in A2 and organize them in a word web.
You can add more words and phrases you know.
Wordbank Sport and health, p. 153 *P1* *WB A2, p. 95*

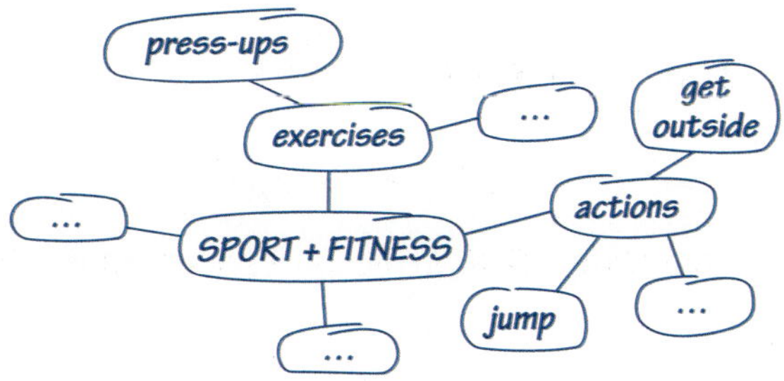

A4 ❖ **Extra: Viewing: Cha cha slide**

Dancing is a great way to get fit!
Watch the "Cha cha slide" and dance along. Have fun!

A5 *L 2/4*

a) Listen to Rajiv and George and find out what they are talking about. *Listening, p. 124*

b) Listen again and make notes. What did Rajiv/George like? What didn't they like? *WB A3, p. 96*

Rajiv	George

A6 Target task ❖ *Project* *Portfolio* *P2, P3*

Need help? Look at p. 114.

Write a dialogue between George and Caroline.
In the evening, George tells his sister about the day with Charles Cousins. *Writing, p. 124*

1 Plan your dialogue:
- What happened? What did George think about Charles Cousins? Collect words and ideas.
- What will Caroline say?

2 Write the dialogue, then show it to a partner. *Writing, p. 128*
Read his/her dialogue and give feedback. *Speaking 2, p. 127*

3 Choose one of your dialogues and act it out. *P9*

Support

The sports words from A3 and your notes from A5 can help you.

YOU HAVE ANSWERED MOSTLY ...

A	B	C
Congratulations! You're as fit as a fiddle! Keep up the good work! You can share your love for sport with your friends: you could organize a class football match, for example.	Not bad! You did quite well on most exercises but you can do better. If you get out of breath quickly, try to run or play tennis or football more often. If you are not very flexible, try stretching exercises every day.	Oh dear! You need to get off the couch! If you are in front of a computer or TV for more than an hour, turn it off and get outside. Cycling to school, playing football with friends or dancing are great fun!

The big match

B1

a) Read the two poems. Which poem do you like better? Say why.

I dreamt I played for England
I dreamt I scored each goal
I dreamt I left the players standing
as I took the team on whole
I dreamt the fans all cheered
I dreamt they called my name
before Mum pulled me out of bed
to end my greatest ever game.

Fifty thousand football fans shout
"Shoot, shoot, shoot!" –
all around the football ground –
"Shoot, shoot, shoot!"
Thirty yards out and I get set,
kick the ball straight in the net,
hear the roar I can't forget:
"Goal, goal, goal!"

b) Find titles for the poems and compare them in class. ● P10

c) **Extra:** Add more sport words to your word web from A3. ● Wordbank Sport and health, p. 153 WB B1, p. 96

B2

L 2/5

Last weekend, there was a football match between William Ellis School and Acland Burghley. On Monday, George meets Lewis, a boy from Acland Burghley.

a) Close your books and listen to them. Why are the boys arguing about the match?

George: You don't really think that Oliver played fairly, do you? Just look at my nose!

Lewis: Well, I can see your nose is hurt. But it wasn't Oliver's fault, was it? You pushed him and when he fell down, his elbow caught your nose. It was your own fault, wasn't it?

George: What??? The fact is that Oliver was pushing me! And while he was chasing the ball he hit me on the nose with his elbow. And it sure wasn't an accident!

Lewis: You are only saying that because your team lost the match.

George: Well, Oliver fell down while he was running. I didn't push him, did I?

Lewis: Well, I only know what I saw …

George: Then you know that Oliver also shouted at me while I was running towards the ball. And when I shouted back he pushed me.

Lewis: That's a great story, Georgie-boy.

George: Let's ask someone else, then. There's Gillian – hey Gill, can you tell Lewis here what happened to my nose during the match?

Gillian: Well, when the accident happened I was talking to Emma and we weren't really watching the game. But I have to go home now, sorry, George.

George: But – Gillian … ?

b) Read the dialogue and say what happened while … WB B2, B3, p. 97

- … Oliver was chasing the ball
- … Oliver was running
- … George was running towards the ball
- … Gillian was talking to Emma

While Oliver was chasing the ball, he hit George …

B3 Grammar card: past progressive

1 Look at B2 again and find examples like this:

While Oliver was chasing the ball he hit George on the nose.

past progressive — simple past

The past progressive is often used to describe past situations in sentences where one action takes place while something else is going on.

Oliver hit George on the nose

Oliver was chasing the ball

You form it with *was/were + infinitive + -ing.*

2 Check LiF 16 on page 147 and start a grammar card on the past progressive. ● *P4* *WB B4, p. 98*

B4

Work with a partner. Look at the pictures to find out what really happened at the match. Write the story. Use the past progressive when necessary.

● *LiF 16: Past progressive, p. 147* ● *Wordbank Sport and health, p. 153*

audience · stick out her tongue · flag · hold a sign · shout at · get angry · chase the ball · hit · bleed · fall to the ground · hurt

Example: *Oliver and George chased the ball.*
While George was running to … Oliver saw …

1 2 3 4 5 6 7

B5

George and Oliver went to the doctor's after the football match.
Look at the other patients in the waiting room.
What happened to them? ● Wordbank Sport and health, p. 153 ● LiF 16: Past progressive, p. 147 ● P13 WB B5, p. 99

The girl was playing hockey when she hurt her foot.

B6 L 2/6

On Sunday Gillian and Oliver speak to each other on the phone. Listen to them, then read these sentences. Are they right or wrong? Correct the wrong sentences. ● Listening, p. 124 ● P14 WB B6, p. 100

1 Oliver is calling Gillian.
2 Gillian wants to say sorry.
3 Oliver knows many girls who are interested in football.
4 Alex Scott is a man.
5 Oliver is still angry with Gillian.
6 Charlie is at Oliver's school.

B7 ❖ Extra L 2/6

a) Listen to the phone call again.
Note down useful words and phrases for a telephone conversation.
Example: ***Hello; Is that ...?; ...***

b) Write a telephone conversation between George and Oliver about the match.

B8 Grammar card: question tags

1 When George and Lewis were arguing about the match, they used some questions like these:
You don't really think that Oliver played fairly, do you?
But it wasn't Oliver's fault, was it?

The blue part of each sentence is called a *question tag*.
Look at B2 (page 106) again and find more examples.

2 Then check LiF 17 on page 148 and write a grammar card on question tags.
● P5 WB B7, p. 100

B9

How much do you remember about the match? Work with a partner and ask him/her about the match. Use question tags. *LiF 17: Question tags, p. 148*

George hit Oliver, didn't he?

No, he didn't.

B10 Target task

Project | Portfolio

Need help? Look at p. 115.

Write a mystery. Another group has to solve it later.

1 Work in groups of four. Choose a mystery or make up your own.

A After a football match, one player lies unconscious in the changing rooms. The only thing that is missing are his/her football boots.

B At a swimming competition one of the swimmers is locked in the toilets and misses the race.

C During a race a famous cyclist suddenly falls off his bike and breaks his right arm. The bike mechanic notices that someone must have done something to the bike before the race.

2 Now prepare role cards for each member of your group together:
- the victim
- witness 1
- witness 2
- the person who did it

Examples:

The victim
- man
- 20 years old
- the best football player in the team
- …

The person who did it
- man
- 22 years old
- he hurt the football player because …
- …

3 Read your role cards carefully. Discuss if there is anything that needs to be added/changed. Tip: Don't make it too easy for the police!

4 Get together with another group. They are the police and will ask each member of your group about the mystery.

What were you doing when …?

Where were you at 5:30?

How long have you known …?

You weren't at home last night, were you?

Is there anything you saw?

I was eating a sandwich when I heard a loud noise in …

I have known him for … years.

…

5 When "the police" have solved the mystery, it's your group's turn to ask questions about their mystery.

Wordbank Sport and health, p. 153 *Speaking 1, p. 126* *P15*

6 The Sports Day

C1

Think – pair – share: What do you like most about a sports competition? What do you dislike? Note down your ideas.

Think – pair – share, p. 130

I enjoy … most.

I can't stand …

I like … best.

The thing I dislike most about sports competitions is …

C2

Every year Camden School for Girls has a Sports Day. Each girl belongs to a house and the houses compete against each other.

a) Read about the Sports Day that took place last year and answer the questions in a few words.

1 Which years take part in the Sports Day?
2 What are the names of the Houses?
3 Who was most successful in the long jump?
4 Who won the 200m sprint?
5 Who won the House Cup?
6 What took place in the afternoon?

Battling to break the records

Last week Camden School for Girl's Sports Day took place at Finsbury Park. As always years 7-9 battled it out for the house cups.

The day started with the long jump. Meredith Lambert (Year 9) jumped the furthest. She broke the school record and put Red House in the lead. However, Rachel Cullen (Year 8) and Alex Eastman (Year 9) of Yellow House did fantastically well in the high jump. So the Yellows took the lead.

In the afternoon there were some really exciting races. Ronke Yussuf (Year 8) won the 100m and 200m sprints. Great running, Ronke! Alex Eastman was the fastest in Year 9. Both girls scored points for Yellow House.

In the relays it was neck and neck between the Yellows and the Reds. A lot depended on the result of the relay races. After the Year 7 relay, the Yellows were in the lead. After the Year 8 relay, the Blues overtook the Greens and gained third place. But it was clear that the winning house was going to be Red or Yellow.

The atmosphere in the stadium was tense. Finally, it was the Year 9 relay that decided everything. The Yellows came in first, and they won the House Cup! The audience cheered for ages.

In the afternoon everyone enjoyed the fun and games. As usual the fun relay against the teachers was a highlight. The teachers won narrowly. Well done to all!

b) Compare the Sports Day with the sports day at your school.

Example: *There are more events at CSG than at our school.*
We only … The girls at CSG are more competitive than …

exciting · boring · many · successful · competitive · funny · serious · outstanding

LiF 3: Steigerung von Adjektiven, p. 137/138 · P6 · WB C1, p. 101

C3 L 2/7

a) Caroline and Emma are both looking forward to this year's Sports Day. They are in Red House. Listen to them and find out why they are excited about Sports Day. Listening, p. 124

b) How will Caroline and Emma feel if they don't win the races? Say why.

c) Listen again and take notes. Find out what will happen if …

- … the Reds win the House Cup this year?
- … the Reds don't win the Cup?
- … the Reds come last in the House competition?
- … Emma trains a bit harder?
- … Caroline promises not to be so bossy?

C4 L 2/8

It's a week after Sports Day. Emma wrote a story about it for her English class.

a) Read the story and choose the best title for it. Give reasons.

- Victory for the Reds
- Emma's big day
- Friends forever

1 Caroline and I were really excited about Sports Day. The weeks before the big day we trained for at least half an hour after school every day. I took the race more seriously now. Thanks to Caroline I was running much more confidently and was getting so much better. Caroline wanted to come first in one of her races so she trained very hard and she ran faster from week to week.

2 Finally the big day arrived. We all met at Finsbury Park Stadium where the sports events were taking place. The stadium was full of us, all wearing our house colours. Of course, my classmates and I were all wearing red. We were chanting excitedly:

Nothing can stop the Reds!
Nothing can stop the Reds!
We'll never give up! We'll never give in!
We'll fight to the end, we've come here to win!

3 On the field Navina from our class was just doing the high jump. It was a fantastic jump and the Reds all cheered enthusiastically. Then a voice came over the loudspeaker: "The 200 metres will take place in 5 minutes!" Caroline looked rather pale and went to join the others at the starting line. Suddenly I had an idea. There was still time to send a message over the microphone. I ran to Mrs Shimmin, who was doing the "shout-outs" and wrote mine down quickly. Then I went back to my seat to watch the race. I crossed my fingers for luck. I knew how much Caroline wanted to win.

4 Now it was time for the race. Just then the loudspeaker came on: "This is a message for Caroline Lambraki from her friend, Emma: 'You can do it, Caroline! Go! Go! Go!'"

Caroline smiled at me. Then the race started: "On your marks, get set, go!" We all cheered madly. The girls just flew along the track. Caroline's main rival, Kadhija, was on her left. She ran faster than Caroline. I could see that Caroline was trying hard to keep up, but there was no way she could catch her. At the finishing line, Caroline fell on the ground dramatically.

5 "Great race, Caroline!" I said. "Well done!" "But I only came second," she answered. Typical Caroline. She hates to lose. "But your time was fantastic! Kadhija broke the school record, and you were just behind her!" But that didn't help much. Caroline was very disappointed.

6 Then it was time for my race. I was nervous, too. But I could only do my best. And in the end all that training helped – I came in third. Even Caroline felt better after my race. I hugged her. "That's all thanks to you, Caroline!" I said.

7 After the competitions there was an afternoon of fun. We all felt relaxed now and even Caroline joined in. At the end of the day we all waited impatiently to hear the results of the house competitions. When Mrs Shimmin announced the results, the Reds clapped more wildly than ever. For the first time in years we won the House Cup. What a day!

b) Find headings for the different paragraphs.
Example:
Paragraph 1 – Excited about Sports Day; paragraph 2 – …
● P7, P12

C5 L 2/9

a) Find examples of adverbs with *-ly* in Emma's story and write them down.
Example: *excitedly, …*

b) Do you know how to pronounce the words? Where is the stress? Check the CD to see if you were right.
● P8 WB C2, C3, p. 102, 103

C6 Grammar card: comparison of adverbs

1 Look at these sentences to find out about comparisons of adverbs:
I was running much more confidently.
She ran faster than Caroline.

2 Look at LiF 18 on page 148 and add the rules to your grammar card for adverbs.

3 Write down two sentences with *-er/-est*, two sentences with *more/most* and four sentences with a comparison of *well, badly* and *much*. P11 WB C4, p. 103

C7

Look at these verbs and adverbs and write down five sentences about your classmates.
Example: *Leon swims faster than Ben.*
LiF 18: Steigerung von Adverbien, p. 148 WB C5, p. 104

swim/fast · run/quickly · sing/well · write/clearly · draw/beautifully ·

C8 ❖ Choose

Wordbank Sports and health, p. 153 WB C6, p. 104

- Write your own class chant.
  - Use rhyming words.
  - Repeat words or sounds.

We're cool! We're crazy!
We're never ever lazy!
We'll beat you! Defeat you!
We'll even try to eat you!
Gooooo (put the name of your class here)!

or

- Write your sports profile.
  Describe your hobby and use the words and phrases from A3.

Support

I love basketball because …
My favourite sport/team is …
I'm really good at … / I could improve my …
I play in a team/at a club/…
I have been training since … / I started when I was …
I (don't) take it very seriously.

C9 Target task ❖ Portfolio

Write Caroline's story about Sports Day.

Need help? Look at p. 116.

1 Look at Emma's story in C4 again.
What are her thoughts, feelings and opinions?

2 Compare Caroline to Emma.
What do you think Caroline's thoughts, feelings and opinions might be?

Support

These words can help you:
nervous, excited, upset, disappointed, ambitious, confident, frustrated, angry, determined, relaxed, jealous, emotional

3 Now write Caroline's story. Describe what happens from her point of view.
- Include Caroline's thoughts, feelings and opinions.
- Add direct speech.
- Use adjectives and adverbs (and comparisons when necessary) to make the story more interesting.
- Add connectives (e.g. *and, but*) and structure words (e.g. *first, then*).

LiF 18: Steigerung von Adverbien, p. 148 Writing, p. 128 WB C7, p. 105

Prepare your target task A6:

P1 Words: sport and health

Find the odd one out and give a reason.

'Football' isn't a verb.

1 swim · football · do press-ups · run · jump
2 chips · coke · fruit · hamburger · pizza
3 hockey · basketball · tennis · volleyball · football
4 watch TV · cycle · go by bus · play computer games · go by car

P2 Words: positive and negative adjectives

What are the words? Note them down and sort them into positive and negative adjectives.

1 /greɪt/
2 /ˈbɔːrɪŋ/
3 /ˈterəb(ə)l/
4 /ˈɪntrəstɪŋ/
5 /ˈfæsɪneɪtɪŋ/
6 /ˈɔːf(ə)l/
7 /bæd/
8 /fænˈtæstɪk/
9 /ˈwʌndəf(ə)l/
10 /ˈlʌvli/
11 /ɪkˈsaɪtɪŋ/
12 /ˈbɒsi/
13 /ɪmˈbærəsɪŋ/
14 /ˈhɒrəb(ə)l/

P3 Words: expressing opinion

Read the dialogue between George and Rajiv about Charles Cousins.
Note down all the words and phrases you can use to express your opinion.
Example: *Charles Cousins is a great guy, isn't he?; …*

Rajiv: Phew, I'm exhausted[1]. Charles Cousins is a great guy, isn't he? It's so exciting to have such a famous person come to our school!
George: Pfff …
Rajiv: What do you mean?
George: He made us run for 20 minutes round the football field … boring. What's the point really?
Rajiv: Err, what do you think? Charles explained how important it is to be fit. Plus, if your muscles[2] are not warm before a competition or match you can get hurt. And come on, 20 minutes is nothing. We sometimes run more than half an hour before we start our football training.
George: Why didn't they get a footballer to come to our school? That would have been cool!
Rajiv: I think it was really interesting what Charles told us about his training and his career. I would love to try rowing too!
George: But a fitness test? Please! Why did he give us a test to do? Does he think he's a teacher?
Rajiv: I think the fitness test was fun. At least a lot more fun than science with Mr Basildon.
George: You're right. But balancing on one foot is silly. That's something for girls.
Rajiv: You didn't listen to anything he said, did you? Balance and coordination is important for football too, you know.
George: But what does he know about football? He is a rower. And why did he talk about eating fruit and vegetables and wholemeal[3] bread and pasta for such a long time? Who is interested in that?
Rajiv: Well, he's a famous rower. So he must know a thing or two about sports and health.
George: OK …
Rajiv: Come on grumpy, let's get lunch. Maybe you'll be in a better mood[4] after you've had some food.

[1] exhausted – *erschöpft, aufgebraucht;* [2] muscle – *Muskel, Stärke;* [3] wholemeal – *Vollkornmehl, Vollkorn-;* [4] mood – *Laune, Stimmung*

Prepare your target task B10:

P4 Past progressive

LiF 16: Past progressive, p. 147

Lionel had a terrible day. Look at the pictures and describe his day.
Example: *Lionel was eating his breakfast when …*

eat breakfast/fly away

look for/walk into

look for/park/start to rain

arrive/sit

P5 Question tags

LiF 17: Question tags, p. 148

Nathan is from New Zealand. He is at William Ellis School for one year.
Read his conversation with Rajiv and note down the correct question tags.

Rajiv: So you're from New Zealand, 1 ?
Nathan: Yes, I'm from Auckland, I miss it a bit.
Rajiv: But you like it here, 2 ?
Nathan: Yes, I do. Everyone has been very nice to me.
Rajiv: But I guess you haven't seen much of the city yet, 3 ?
Nathan: No, not really. But my host family[1], the Bakers, want to show me all the sights. Do you know Colin Baker?
Rajiv: Yes, I do. He's in the football team, 4 ?
Nathan: Yeah, he's a great player, 5 ?
Rajiv: Yes, he is. I know his parents, too. They're really friendly, 6 ?
Nathan: Yes, they're all very nice. Listen, maybe we can do something together soon. You don't have time tonight, 7 ?
Rajiv: No, I don't, sorry. But what about Friday? Look at this flyer for the open-air concert with the Electric Girls near Camden Lock Market. Looks good, 8 ?
Nathan: Oh yes, I know some of their songs. We can walk there, 9 ?
Rajiv: Yes, we can walk there. Let's meet at the corner of Parkway and Camden High Street at seven.
Nathan: OK, great. See you then.

[1] host family – *Gastfamilie*

Prepare your target task C9:

P6 Revision: comparison of adjectives

Look at the Sports Day results and compare them.
Example: *Harriet's jump was high, but Rachel's was higher than Harriet's and Alexandra's jump was the highest.* ● LiF 3: Steigerung von Adjektiven, p. 137/138

1	2	3	4
jump/high	jump/long	time/fast	result/good
Alexandra: 1.40 metres	Meredith: 4.35 metres	Ronke: 13.1 seconds	Yellows: 174 points
Rachel: 1.25 metres	Gloria: 4.32 metres	Nadine: 13.5 seconds	Reds: 167 points
Harriet: 1.1 metres	Amber 4.1 metres	Natalie: 13.7 seconds	Blues: 150 points

P7 Words: competition

Look at the following sentences and complete them.
Be careful: Some of the words are irregular verbs!

be in the lead · battle it out · win · beat · fight hard · start · overtake

1 Caroline hoped to [1] the Year 7 sprint on Sports Day.
2 She trained every day and [2] to improve her time.
3 Before the race [3] , the girls went to the starting line.
4 When the race started, Caroline and Kadhija [4] on the track.
5 Kadhija [5] and Caroline couldn't [6] her.
6 It was Caroline's best time, but Kadhija still [7] her.

P8 Revision: adverbs of manner

● LiF 12: Adverbien der Art und Weise, p. 144

Look at the pictures and describe what the people did at the football match and how they did it.
Example: *Before the match many people waited impatiently outside the stadium.*

impatient · enthusiastic · excited · nervous · loud

Extra language training:

P9 Revision: adverbs of frequency

Write down these sentences in the correct order. Be careful where you put the adverb (e.g. *sometimes, often, …*).

1 with his father / plays basketball / Oliver / sometimes / .
2 Perfect Peter / never / eats / fast food / .
3 after the football training / is / Sarah / very tired / often / .
4 takes / Karen / usually / the bus / to school / .
5 to bed / often / on school days/ Hugo / goes / at nine o'clock / .
6 always / Sam / and sweets / after school / eats ice cream / .

P10 Revision: will future

LiF 6: will future, p. 139

What will the friends do in 20 years? Think about them and write two sentences about each friend.
Example: *I think George will be a famous film star. He won't have a boring job or children.*

film star · doctor · teacher · banker · lawyer[1] · housewife[2] · nurse[3] · stewardess · model · mechanic

[1] lawyer – *Rechtsanwalt/Rechtsanwältin;* [2] housewife – *Hausfrau;* [3] nurse – *Krankenschwester/Pfleger*

P11 Comparison of adverbs

LiF 18: Steigerung von Adverbien, p. 148

❖ **Can you do it?**

1. Emma can run two kilometres quite easily. But Caroline can run two kilometres ??? (fast). Charlie is a terrible dancer, but George dances even ??? (terrible).
2. **You can check your answers on page 221.**
3. **You need help?** → Do a), then b).
   You can do it? → Do b).

a) Complete the sentences.

1 Gillian runs quite fast. But Caroline runs even …
2 Emma trained quite seriously for her race but Caroline trained even …
3 Mrs Lambraki plays golf well but her husband plays even …
4 Charlie plays football well. But Phil Jones from Manchester United plays football …
5 Emma sometimes reacts emotionally but when Caroline loses she reacts …

b) Mr Wilson is a sports teacher at CSG. He is talking to some girls before Sports Day. Fill in adverbs and decide when you have to use comparative or superlative forms.

"Becky, please try to run 1 (fast) than you normally do at the beginning of the race. You always start off quite 2 (slow)."
"Katrina, you must train 3 (hard) to beat Thomasina from the green team in the 110 metre hurdles[1]. She moves 4 (quick) than you."
"Georgia, today you've done a lot 5 (good) than yesterday. Well done!"
"Joanna, you know that you run 6 (fast) of all of you, but you should still take the competition 7 (serious). Che Chon from the Blue team did really 8 (good) yesterday and Dana didn't do 9 (bad), either."

[1] hurdles – *Hürdenlauf*

Extra skills training:

P12 Say it in English

Look at Theme 6 again and find the answers.

Was sagst du auf Englisch, wenn …

1 du sagen willst, dass jemand selber schuld hat?
2 wenn eine Mannschaft die Führung übernimmt?
3 wenn zwei Mannschaften nur haarscharf auseinander liegen?
4 du jemanden anfeuern willst?
5 du „auf die Plätze, fertig, los!" sagen willst?

P13 Words: body parts

a) Draw a person, but use the hand you don't usually write with. Then label as many body parts as you can in two minutes.

b) Compare your results with a partner and add any new words.

P14 Viewing: Karate with Jessica

a) Watch the film clip and say where it was filmed.

b) Watch the clip again. Right or wrong?

1 Jessica usually trains four times a week.
2 The training sometimes starts with a warm-up.
3 Stretching different parts of your body is important.
4 Jessica's team uses punchbags[1] in their training.
5 Jessica loves karate because her team are all her friends.

[1] punchbag – *Sandsack*

P15 **Writing** Reading, p. 125

Look at the pictures and write a story about Robin Hood.

You can start like this: ***One day the Sheriff … The farmer called for help. He was very …***

[1] recognize – *erkennen*

Sports in London

In 2012, billions of people from all over the world watched their athletes when they competed for[1] medals at the 30th Summer Olympic Games. The sports events took place in many new sports facilities[2], the Olympic Stadium for example. Now Londoners can use the facilities and have moved into[3] the Olympic Village.
This does not mean, however, that there is no more world-class sport, because London is the home of many top sports events:
In late March or early April, there is the famous University Boat Race on the River Thames. Students from the University of Cambridge and the University of Oxford have competed against each other in rowing boats every spring for more than 150 years. In April, thousands of runners come to London for the London Marathon, one of the biggest marathons in the world. On the first weekend in July, the best tennis players in the world fight for glory[4] in the Wimbledon finals. In the summer months, cricket is one of the most popular sports because you need good weather and a lot of sunshine as matches can last a few days.
All year round, you can go and see football and rugby matches. There are a number of Premier League football teams in London – Arsenal and Chelsea are just two of them. Many matches of England's national team are played at Wembley Stadium as well as the English cup final. Twickenham Stadium is sometimes called the home of English rugby. In spring, it is here that matches of the Six Nations rugby tournament[5] take place – a competition between the six best European rugby teams.

1

Look at the photos and identify the kinds of sports you can see.
Example: *cricket – rowing – ...*

2 *S 15, L 2/10*

Listen to the radio commentaries for sports events. Find out which sports or sport event they are about.

3

Choose one topic and prepare a presentation or poster:
a) One of the sports and its rules, e.g. rugby, cricket
b) One of the stadiums
c) One of the sports events

4 *S 16, L 2/11*

a) Listen to the official song of the 2012 Summer Olympics in London, "Survival"[6] by Muse. Note down words from the song that tell you it is a song for a sports event.
b) Listen again and explain your reaction to the song.

I think of ... when I listen to that song.

The song makes me feel happy/aggressive/relaxed/...

I wouldn't normally listen to a song like that because ...

This is the kind of music that I like because ...

c) Many sportmen and sportswomen listen to music before an important competition. Choose a song that makes you feel good and ready to take part in a competition. Explain why that song is so special to you.

---
[1] compete for – *antreten gegen*
[2] sports facility – *Sportstätte*
[3] move into – *umziehen in*
[4] glory – *Ehre*
[5] tournament – *Turnier*
[6] survival – *Überleben*

1

2

3

4

5

6

7

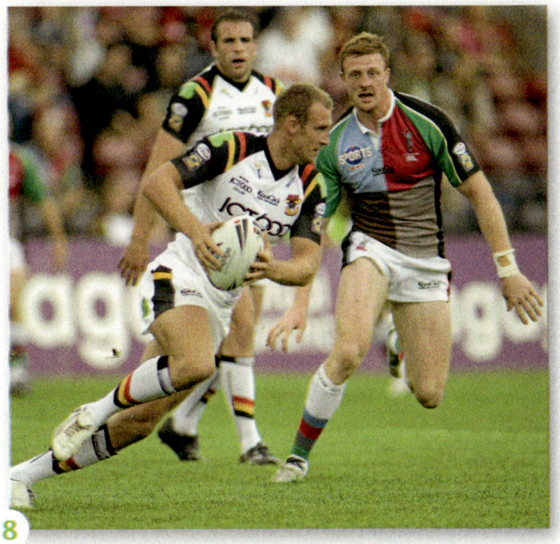

8

The Boy in the Dress

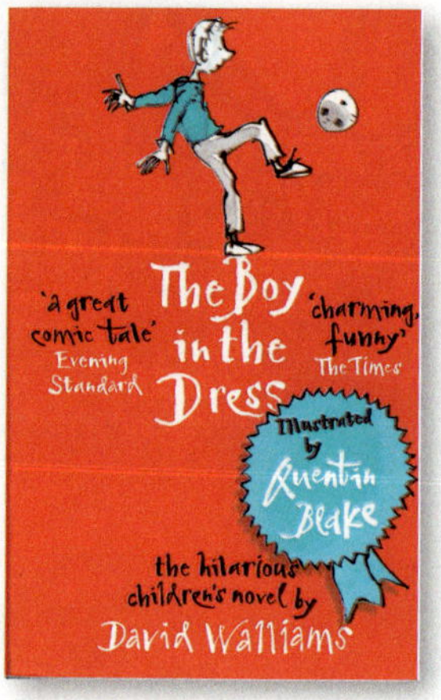

01

a) Look at these clothes. Are there any that are for boys only or for girls only?

shoes · trousers · tie · skirt · socks · suit · dress · shirt · T-shirt · gloves · boots · jacket · coat · football boots · scarf · hat · shorts

b) Can you think of any situations when girls might wear boys' clothes or boys girls' clothes?

02 Reading, p. 125

Read the first part of the story and say why the boys wear dresses.

Dennis lives with his dad and brother. His mother left the family some time ago and Dennis misses her very much. He misses her clothes, too, and he becomes interested in fashion. His father is not very happy about this, but Dennis shares his love of beautiful dresses with his new friend, Lisa.
One day Lisa persuades him to wear a dress to school. The headmaster, Mr Hawtrey, expels him.
Dennis is the best football player in the school and that means that the school team are much weaker without him. When they play against Maudlin Street School in the cup final, they are losing 6-0 at half time, but still the headmaster refuses to let Dennis play.

The second half was about to begin, and Maudlin Street were all waiting on the pitch[1], eager to[2] finish off their demolition job[3]. The school's team was nowhere to be seen. Had they run away?
Then, suddenly, Lisa stepped out of the changing room[4] and held the door open.
First Gareth ran out wearing a gold lamé ball gown[5] ... Then Darvesh followed in a yellow polka dot frock[6] ... Then the defenders were right behind in matching red cocktail dresses ... The rest of the team followed in a variety of outfits from Lisa's wardrobe ... And finally Dennis came out of the dressing room – in a pink bridesmaid's[7] dress.
There was a huge cheer from the crowd. [...]
As they ran onto the pitch, Mr Hawtrey bellowed[8] at Gareth.
"WHAT ON EARTH DO YOU THINK YOU ARE DOING, BOY?"
"You expelled[9] Dennis for wearing a dress. But you can't expel us all, Sir!" he shouted back triumphantly.
All the boys in the team lined up [...] behind their captain, striking poses[10] like they were dancers in a Madonna video. The crowd went wild.
"THIS IS A DISGRACE[11]!" bellowed Mr Hawtrey.
He stormed off. [...] Gareth smiled at Dennis.
"Come on boys. Let's do it!" said Gareth. [...]
Within seconds Dennis had scored a goal. The Maudlin Street team were still in shock. They were still 6-1 down, but Dennis and his team-mates were back in the game.
"Woo!" shouted Darvesh, as he hitched up[12] his skirt and weaved[13] round a defender. Laughing, Dennis scored again. He was on his way to a hat-trick and he was a hundred times happier than he had ever been. He was doing the two things he loved most at once: playing football and wearing a dress. Then Darvesh scored [...] 6-3.
"My boy! My boy in the yellow polka-dot dress

[1] pitch – *Spielfeld*
[2] eager to – *erpicht sein auf*
[3] demolition job – *Zerstörung*
[4] changing room – *Umkleidekabine*
[5] gold lamé ball gown – *Ballkleid aus schimmerndem, goldenen Stoff*
[6] polka dot frock – *Kleid mit Punkten*
[7] bridesmaid – *Brautjungfer*
[8] bellow – *bellen*
[9] expel – *von der Schule verweisen*
[10] strike a pose – *sich in Positur werfen*
[11] disgrace – *Schande*
[12] hitch up – *hochziehen*
[13] weave – *schlängeln*

has scored!" shouted Darvesh's Mum. They were on fire. Dennis set up a fantastic cross for Gareth, who just had to tap[14] it into the net. 6-4. […] The crowd laughed and cheered.
Then another goal followed and another. 6-6.
Now there were only a few more minutes of the game to play. One more to go. And they'd have done it. […]
But, at that moment Dennis fell to the ground in pain[15]. The crowd gasped[16]. […]

[14] tap – *anticken*
[15] in pain – *voller Schmerzen*
[16] gasp – *Luft anhalten*

03

What do you think will happen? Read on and find out if you were right.

"OI!" WHAT'S GOING ON HERE?"
Dad.
Dennis couldn't believe it. Dad had never come to see him play for the school before, and now here Dennis was, lying on the ground with tears in his eyes wearing a dress. He was going to be in so much trouble … But Dad looked at Dennis and smiled.
"OI! REF!" he shouted. "That kid kicked my son!"
Dennis rose to his feet, his leg still glowing[1] with pain but a warm feeling spreading[2] through him. He steadied[3] himself. Then he smiled back over at Dad.
"You OK?" asked Darvesh.
"Yeah," said Dennis.
"COME ON, SON!" shouted Dennis's Dad, really getting into it now. "YOU CAN DO IT!"
"I called him at half-time," said Darvesh. "After what you said about your Dad never seeing you play a match, I thought he wouldn't want to miss this."
"Thanks, mate" said Dennis. Whenever he thought Darvesh couldn't surprise him any more, couldn't be a better friend, he went ahead and did it.
Gareth tackled the ball off one of the Maudlin Street boys. Darvesh ran up the outside, and Gareth passed it to him. Maudlin Street charged towards[4] Darvesh and he passed back to Gareth. Gareth panicked for a moment, then passed to Dennis, who weaved straight past the defence before booting it right over the goalie's[5] head and into the back of the net. The keeper didn't stand a chance. 6-7! The final whistle[6] blew. It was all over.

[1] glow – *glühen*
[2] spread – *sich verbreiten*
[3] steady – *(sich) aufrichten*
[4] charge towards – *auf jmd. zurennen*
[5] goalie – *Torwart*
[6] final whistle – *Schlusspfiff*

04

Describe Dennis's feelings towards his father. Explain why you think it is so important to Dennis that he watches the match.

05

At the end of the game Mr Hawtrey comes back and tells Dennis that he is still expelled from school. Write a dialogue between the headmaster and Dennis's father.

Du kannst schon viel auf Englisch verstehen und ausdrücken. Du kannst …

- ✓ über verschiedene Sportarten sprechen
- ✓ eine Geschichte anhand von Bildern verfassen
- ✓ über Krankheiten und Verletzungen sprechen
- ✓ ein Telefongespräch führen
- ✓ beschreiben, wie jemand etwas tut

WB Portfolio-Fragebogen Theme 6

Listening

Du kennst ja schon einige Tricks, wie du einen Hörtext besser verstehen kannst:

1. Vor dem Hören
Bevor du einen Text hörst, kannst du dir folgende Fragen stellen:
- Was ist das für ein Text?
- Wie lautet das Thema?
- Gibt es Bilder? Was ist zu sehen?

2. Beim Hören
Um einen Hörtext besser zu verstehen, ist es sinnvoll, sich Notizen zu machen.
Du kannst wichtige Wörter (*keywords*) in einer Liste notieren.

Manchmal ist es aber auch hilfreich, eine Tabelle auszufüllen.
- Lies dir die Überschriften der Tabelle genau durch, bevor du den Text anhörst.
- Höre dir den Text zwei- bis dreimal an, sodass du die Tabelle nach und nach ausfüllen kannst.

souvenir	*whose?*	*where from?*
photo	*Emma's*	*pony camp*
...	...	...

Du kannst auch ein Schema mit *wh*-Fragen erstellen und es beim Hören ausfüllen.
Die Fragen *who, what, where, when* und *why* helfen dir dabei genau zu verstehen, worum es geht.

who	*what*	*where*	*when*	*why*
...	...	...	...	...

3. Nach dem Hören
Vergleiche deine Ergebnisse mit denen eines Mitschülers.

Bei manchen Höraufgaben musst du Sätze vervollständigen.
- Lies dir die Satzanfänge genau durch, bevor du den Text zum ersten Mal hörst.
- Notiere dir dann die Antworten.
- Höre den Text zwei- oder dreimal und vervollständige die Sätze nach und nach.

1 All pupils at Camden School for Girls have to ...
2 Mrs Lambraki doesn't understand why Caroline doesn't ...
3 When Caroline goes by bike, she can ...

Skills: Reading

Du weißt bereits, wie du englische Texte leichter verstehen kannst:

- Lies dir die Überschrift durch und überlege, worum es gehen könnte.
- Schau dir die Bilder an.

Es gibt verschiedene Techniken, um einen Text zu lesen.

1. Einen Text überfliegen (skimming)

Lies den Text zügig durch, um herauszufinden, was passiert und wer beteiligt ist.

Who?

What?

Sherlock Holmes – The World's Most Famous Detective Sherlock Holmes is the world's most famous detective. Dr. Watson assisted him. Sherlock Holmes and Dr. Watson lived at 221b Baker Street, London, between 1881-1904. There the two friends discussed the terrible crimes, which only a logically brilliant mind like Holmes' could solve. Watson, like the reader, was fascinated by Holmes because he was able to solve mysteries largely from within the safety of his Baker Street domicile.

2. Einen Text genau lesen (reading for detail)

- Um einen Text genau zu lesen und alle Details zu verstehen, ist es sinnvoll, den Text mehrmals durchzulesen.
- Versuche die Fragen *who, what, where* und *when* zu beantworten.
- Übrigens: Du musst nicht jedes Wort verstehen – versuche unbekannte Wörter aus dem Zusammenhang zu erschließen.

Who?

Where?

When?

What?

Sherlock Holmes – The World's Most Famous Detective Sherlock Holmes is the world's most famous detective. Dr. Watson assisted him. Sherlock Holmes and Dr Watson lived at 221b Baker Street, London, between 1881-1904. There the two friends discussed the terrible crimes, which only a logically brilliant mind like Holmes' could solve. Watson, like the reader, was fascinated by Holmes because he was able to solve mysteries largely from within the safety of his Baker Street domicile.

assist = Dt.: *assistieren, unterstützen*

logically = Dt.: *logisch*

fascinated = Dt.: *fasziniert*

safety (Nomen von safe) = Dt.: *Sicherheit*

domicile = Dt.: *Domizil, Wohnung*

Tipp: Wenn du ein Wort nicht selbst erschließen kannst, kannst du es in deinem *dictionary* ab Seite 186 oder in einem Wörterbuch nachschlagen. Wie das geht, wird auf Seite 129 beschrieben.

S

Skills: Speaking

1 Einen Vortrag halten

Wenn du einen Vortrag halten willst oder Arbeitsergebnisse präsentieren möchtest, können dir folgende Tipps dabei helfen:

1. Plane deinen Vortrag

- Worüber möchtest du sprechen? Mache dir Notizen.
- In welcher Reihenfolge möchtest du das, was du sagen willst, präsentieren? Ordne deine Notizen.

Ein Vortrag ist in folgende Teile gegliedert:
A Einleitung *(introduction)*
B Hauptteil *(middle)*
C Schluss *(end)*

2. Übe deinen Vortrag

- Lege dir Sätze zurecht, die dir dabei helfen, deinen Vortrag zu gliedern.

A Einleitung *(introduction)*:
- *I'm going to tell you about ...*
- *My topic is ...*
- *What I'd like to talk about is that ...*
- *First, I'm going to talk about ...*
- *I'd like to begin with ...*
- *First of all, I must say that ...*

B Hauptteil *(middle)*
- *There are a number of points that are important.*
- *First of all, ... Secondly ...*
- *That's why ...*

C Schluss *(end)*
- *Finally, let me tell you about ...*
- *All in all ...*
- *In short ...*

- Für deine Zuhörer ist es interessanter, wenn du nicht alles abliest, sondern frei sprichst. Lerne einige Sätze auswendig, aber nicht alles. Notiere dir die wichtigsten Punkte auf Kärtchen.
- Übe die Aussprache von schwierigen Wörtern. Sprich sie mehrmals laut vor dich hin.
- Übe deinen Vortrag vorher. Du kannst ihn deinen Eltern, Geschwistern oder Freunden vortragen.

3. Halte deinen Vortrag

- Schau deine Zuhörer beim Sprechen an.
- Achte darauf, dass du nicht zu schnell sprichst.
- Sprich laut und deutlich.

Tipp
Wenn du mal den Faden verlierst:
Bleibe ruhig und versuche, dich an deinen Text zu erinnern.
Du kannst dann sagen:
"Just a moment, please" oder "Wait a second".

Skills: Speaking

2 Bei der Partner- oder Gruppenarbeit Englisch sprechen

Im Englischunterricht arbeitest du oft mit einem Partner oder in einer Gruppe zusammen. Auch wenn es dir vielleicht komisch vorkommt, solltest du mit deinen Mitschülern Englisch sprechen – du lernst so besser Englisch und kannst deine Arbeitsergebnisse leichter vorstellen.

Hier findest du einige Tipps zur Partner- und Gruppenarbeit:
- Präge dir bestimmte Ausdrücke und Sätze ein. Dann kannst du dich besser mit deinen Mitschülern unterhalten.

Mit jemandem zusammenarbeiten:
- *Do you want to work with me?*
- *Whose turn is it?*
- *Can I be …?*
- *Can you explain that, please?*

Wenn du etwas sagen möchtest:
- *Excuse me, I think it's my turn to say something now.*
- *I'd like to say something if you don't mind.*
- *Sorry, have you finished? Can I say something now?*

Wenn du einen Vorschlag machen möchtest:
- *Let's do it this way/like this.*
- *You/We could write something different here.*
- *Why don't you/we change this?*

Wenn du Rückmeldung/Feedback geben möchtest:
- *Your presentation was easy to understand/ fun to listen to/really interesting and you spoke clearly.*
- *I really like your story because it is … . Well done!*
- *Your poster looks attractive/interesting/neat and tidy but you should speak up more.*
- *Your report is very well-structured but it could be a bit more informative.*
- *I don't think Vanessa really acted like the role card says because …*
- *Patrick was very good as Salman/Matt because he …*

- Auch im Gespräch mit deinen Mitschülern solltest du immer höflich und freundlich sein. Verwende *sorry, please* und *thank you.*

Tipp: Weitere nützliche Ausdrücke für die Partner- und Gruppenarbeit findest du auf dem Einleger.

Skills: Writing

1 Einen Text verfassen

Du kennst bereits die drei wichtigen Schritte, die dir beim Verfassen eines Textes helfen:

1. Planen → **2. Schreiben** → **3. Überarbeiten**

Schau dir diese Geschichte an. Sophie aus Manchester hat sie geschrieben und sie dann überarbeitet.

You'll never believe what happened to me last week! I usually visit my grandma on Sunday afternoon. **Well**, this Sunday was very different. **When** I rang the doorbell, no one opened the door. So I went round to the back of the house and looked through the window. There was Gran in her chair. **"Gran, Gran! It's me, Sophie. Wake up!"** I shouted **nervously**, but she didn't move. "Something must be wrong," I thought and decided to act. I took a **huge** stone from the garden and threw it at the window. The window broke, of course, and then Gran finally woke up! **Luckily**, she wasn't angry when she heard my story. **In the end she just laughed and laughed.**

Tipp 1: Ein guter Anfang macht neugierig!

Tipp 2: Verwende abwechslungsreiche Satzanfänge.

Tipp 3: Direkte Rede macht die Geschichte lebendiger.

Tipp 4: Adjektive und Adverbien machen die Geschichte interessanter.

Tipp 5: Der letzte Satz rundet die Geschichte ab.

2 Checkliste: Einen Brief/eine E-Mail schreiben

Dos ✓
- Schreib oben rechts deine Adresse auf (bei einer E-Mail nicht notwendig).
- Fang den Brief/die E-Mail mit „Dear ..." an. Eine E-Mail an einen Freund/eine Freundin kannst du auch mit „Hi ..." beginnen.
- Im ersten Absatz beschreibst du kurz, warum du den Brief/die E-Mail schreibst.
- Beende deinen Brief/deine E-Mail mit „Best wishes" oder „Love" (für Freunde).
- Unterschreib den Brief/die E-Mail.

Don'ts ✗
- Vergiss nicht, dass das erste Wort nach der Anrede großgeschrieben wird.
- Fall nicht gleich mit der Tür ins Haus – beginn mit einem höflichen Satz (z. B. "Thank you so much for your letter!"/"It was so nice to hear from you.").

3 Checkliste: Das Ende einer Geschichte schreiben

Dos ✓
- Lies dir den Anfang der Geschichte genau durch.
- Überlege, wie die Geschichte geschrieben ist und versuche, den Stil der Geschichte beizubehalten.

Don'ts ✗
- Wechsle nicht die Perspektive – wenn z.B. George den Anfang der Geschichte erzählt, sollte auch das Ende aus seiner Sicht erzählt werden.

Skills: How to work with a dictionary

Inzwischen weißt du ja, dass du Wörter in deinem *dictionary* ab Seite 186 nachschlagen kannst. Dort findest du alle Wörter, die in diesem Buch vorkommen, sowie die wichtigsten Wörter aus Band 5.

Wenn du ein englisches Wort nicht verstehst, kannst du es im *English-German dictionary* ab Seite 186 nachschlagen.

Wenn du etwas auf Englisch sagen willst und du ein Wort brauchst, das du nicht kennst, kann dir das *German-English dictionary* ab Seite 205 helfen.

Manchmal suchst du aber vielleicht auch ein Wort, das nicht im *dictionary* steht. Dann kannst du ein zweisprachiges Wörterbuch benutzen. Das geht so: Schlage das Wort im Wörterbuch nach. Zu vielen Wörtern gibt es mehrere Informationen:

Anhand der Lautschrift kannst du erkennen, wie das Wort ausgesprochen wird.

Hier findest du die verschiedenen deutschen Bedeutungen von *record*.

record [ˈrekɔ:d]
N.
1. Aufzeichnungen, Unterlagen, Akte, Protokoll.
This summer has been the hottest on record.
Dieser Sommer war der heißeste seit der (Wetter-)Aufzeichnung.
2. Schallplatte
He has got a lot of ABBA records.
Er hat viele Schallplatten von ABBA.
3. Rekord
She broke the world record.
Sie hat den Weltrekord gebrochen.

record [rɪˈkɔ:d]
V.
1. etw. aufnehmen
Can you record "Grey's Anatomy" for me?
Kannst du "Grey's Anatomy" für mich aufnehmen?
2. etw. aufzeichnen, festhalten
He recorded the event in the minutes of the meeting.
Er hielt den Vorfall in dem Sitzungsprotokoll fest.

Die Abkürzung zeigt dir an, um welche Wortart es sich handelt. Das Wort *record* kann sowohl ein Nomen als auch ein Verb sein.

Anhand der Beispielsätze kannst du herausfinden, in welchem Zusammenhang das Wort verwendet werden kann.

Skills: Methods

1 Think – pair – share

Diese Methode kannst du zusammen mit deinen Mitschülern nutzen, um dich einem Thema zu nähern:

1 *Think*: Sammle deine Gedanken und mache dir Notizen.
2 *Pair*: Tausche dich mit einem Partner aus. Ergänze deine Notizen.
3 *Share*: Teilt eure Gedanken dann mit einem anderen Paar.

2 Mini jigsaw (Mini-Gruppenpuzzle)

Diese Methode kennst du schon aus Klasse 5:

1 Ihr teilt den Text/die Texte untereinander auf. Jede/r liest einen Teil.
2 Dann tauscht ihr euch aus, sodass jede/r über jeden Text oder alle Textteile Bescheid weiß.

3 Round Robin

Mit dieser Methode könnt ihr euch vor der ganzen Klasse kurz zu einem Thema äußern.

1 Überlege dir eine kurze Stellungnahme aus ein bis zwei Sätzen zu dem vorgegebenen Thema.
2 Reihum äußert sich jeder in der Klasse. Dabei sind keine Kommentare und direkte Reaktionen erlaubt.
3 Wenn jemand bereits dasselbe gesagt hat, was du sagen wolltest, überlege, ob dir nicht noch ein weiterer Punkt einfällt oder ob du deine Stellungnahme zumindest etwas anders formulieren kannst.

4 Dramatic reading

Auch diese Methode kennst du schon – du verwendest sie, um einen Text lebendig vorzutragen.

1 *Buzz reading*: Du liest den Text mit leiser Stimme mehrmals durch.
2 *Read and look up*: Du schaust dir jeden Satz einzeln an und prägst ihn dir ein. Sieh dann hoch und sprich den Satz möglichst natürlich. Arbeite den ganzen Text auf diese Weise durch.
3 Überlege, wie sich die Person gerade fühlt, deren Rolle du liest. Versuche, die Sätze entsprechend zu lesen und zu betonen.

5 Gallery walk

Du weißt bereits, wie ein *gallery walk* funktioniert:

1 Ihr hängt euer Ergebnis im Klassenraum auf.
2 Einer von euch stellt es euren Mitschülern vor. Dabei sollte jeder aus eurer Gruppe einmal das Ergebnis vorstellen, aber auch die anderen Ergebnisse anschauen.

6 Hot seat

Auch diese Methode kennst du schon aus Klasse 5:

1 Lies den Text durch.
2 Eine/r von euch stellt sich vor, dass er/sie eine Figur aus dem Text ist.
3 Die anderen überlegen sich Fragen an die Figur, die diese beantworten muss. Sie kann sich die Antworten auch ausdenken.

Language in Focus

LiF steht für *Language in Focus*. Das ist der Grammatikteil von Camden Town, in dem die englische Sprache genauer unter die Lupe genommen wird. Du findest in LiF die grammatischen Regeln. Wenn vorne im Buch zum Beispiel ● *LiF 1R: Simple present, p. 133* steht, kannst du in LiF unter Nummer 1R die passenden Regeln nachschlagen. Das „R" hinter der Nummer steht für *revision* (Wiederholung). So gekennzeichnete Regeln kennst du bereits aus dem letzten Jahr.
Auf dieser Seite findest du die grammatischen Begriffe auf Englisch und auf Deutsch.

Grammatical terms

Englisch	LiF	Deutsch	Beispiel
adjective	3	Adjektiv	a perfect day, a big house
adverb		Adverb	
adverb of frequency		Häufigkeitsadverb	George sometimes helps at home.
adverb of manner	12, 18	Adverb der Art und Weise	Simon sings badly.
article		Artikel	
definite article		bestimmter Artikel	the
indefinite article		unbestimmter Artikel	a / an
clause of comparison	3	Vergleichssatz	Sarah is as tall as Anne.
comparison		Vergleich	
comparative	3	Komparativ (1. Steigerungsform)	Jill is taller than Tom. The film was more interesting than the book.
superlative	3	Superlativ (Höchststufe bei Vergleichen)	Karen is the oldest girl in our class.
comparison of adjectives	3	Steigerung von Adjektiven	London is bigger than Berlin.
comparison of adverbs	18	Steigerung von Adverbien	Greg runs faster than his brother.
conditional clause	7	Bedingungssatz	If you miss the bus, you will be late.
conjunction	4	Konjunktion	Charlie is happy because he can play football.
connective	4	Verbindungswort	We have enough food so we don't need to go shopping.
contact clause	15	Relativsatz ohne Relativpronomen	He is the boy I met on holiday.
future		Futur (Zukunft)	
going to future	5R	Futur mit *going to*	She's going to buy a CD.
will future	6	Futur mit *will*	I'm sure she will be a pop star.
genitive		Genitiv	
genitive with *of* / *s*-genitive		Genitiv mit *of* / *s*-Genitiv	the name of the ship / Dan's dog
imperative		Imperativ	Please sit down! Don't shout!
infinitive		Infinitiv (Grundform)	(to) walk, (to) go, (to) read, …
long form		Langform	Charlie is not from Germany.
modal verb	13	Modalverb	can, must, need, should, …
noun		Nomen (Hauptwort, Substantiv)	song, child, car, dog, …
object		Objekt	We've got a car.
past participle	8c	Partizip Perfekt	eaten, gone, started, …
past tense		Vergangenheitsform	
simple past	2R	einfache Vergangenheit	They played football yesterday.
past progressive	16	Verlaufsform der Vergangenheit	Emma was reading a book.

personal pronoun		Personalpronomen (persönliches Fürwort)	
object pronoun		Objektpronomen	me, you, him, her, it, them
subject pronoun		Subjektpronomen	I, you, he, she, it, we, they
plural		Plural (Mehrzahl)	cars, numbers, … /
regular / irregular		regelmäßig / unregelmäßig	children, women, …
possessive determiner	14	Possessivbegleiter	my, your, his, her, its, our, their
possessive pronoun	14	Possessivpronomen	His dog is so cute! – It's not his.
present perfect	8	Perfekt	David has cleaned the kitchen.
present tense		Präsens (Gegenwart)	
present progressive		Verlaufsform der Gegenwart	It's raining.
simple present	1R	einfache Gegenwart	I often walk to school.
question		Frage	
question tag	17	Bestätigungsfrage	The book is great, isn't it?
question word	1Rc	Fragewort	who, where, what, when, why, how, …
relative clause	9	Relativsatz	This is the man who helped Sherlock Holmes.
relative pronoun	9	Relativpronomen	The DVD that she gave me was great.
short answer		Kurzantwort	Yes, I am. / No, I'm not.
short form		Kurzform	he's, they're, …
singular		Singular (Einzahl)	dog, friend, house, …
statement		Aussagesatz	She's from Camden. /
positive / negative		bejaht / verneint	I don't like football.
subject		Subjekt	Our school is great. / Jo and I like football.
substitute form	13	Ersatzform	They won't be able to come.
verb		Verb	
regular / irregular		regelmäßig / unregelmäßig	(to) look, (to) walk / (to) meet, (to) see
word order		Satzstellung	Sarah (s) is reading (v) a book (o).
s-v-o (subject-verb-object)		S–V–O (Subjekt–Verb–Objekt)	

LiF 1R Die einfache Gegenwart (The simple present)

a) Simple present: Aussagesätze (Statements)

Das *simple present* verwendest du, …
- … um über Gewohnheiten oder regelmäßige Handlungen zu sprechen:
  *They **play** football every Tuesday.*
- … um über aufeinander folgende Handlungen zu sprechen:
  *First Caroline **makes** her bed. Then she **loads** the dishwasher. After that she **phones** Emma.*
- … um über Zustände zu sprechen, die längere Zeit andauern:
  *Emma and Gillian **live** in London.*

	Simple present: Aussagesätze		
Singular	I often	play	football in the park.
	You sometimes	play	tennis.
	He never	plays	hockey.
	She	plays	volleyball on Tuesdays.
	It always	plays	with other dogs.
Plural	We	play	basketball every Monday.
	You always	play	hockey.
	They	play	games at the weekend.

! Achte auf Besonderheiten in der 3. Person Singular:

1. Person Singular	3. Person Singular
I wash	he/she/it washes
I tidy	he/she/it tidies
I go	he/she/it goes
I do	he/she/it does

He tidies his room every week.

! Anders als im Deutschen stehen Häufigkeitsadverbien wie *never, sometimes* oder *always* im Englischen meist zwischen Subjekt und Verb:

Subjekt	Häufigkeitsadverb	Verb		
I	sometimes	help	at home.	Ich helfe manchmal zu Hause.
Charlie	never	walks	to school.	Charlie läuft nie zur Schule.

b) Simple present: Verneinung (Negation)

Sätze im *simple present* kannst du mit ***don't/doesn't (do not/does not)*** verneinen:

Simple present: Verneinung
I don't play football.
He doesn't work in London.

! Denk daran, dass du *don't/doesn't* nicht immer verwenden kannst.
Beispiel:
Bei *be* sagst du *I'm not / he's not* usw.
Bei *have* got sagst du *I haven't got / he hasn't got* usw.
Bei *can* sagst du *I can't / he can't* usw.

c) Simple present: Fragen (Questions)

Wenn du Entscheidungsfragen im *simple present* stellen möchtest, verwendest du einfach ***do*** oder ***does*** am Satzanfang:

Entscheidungsfragen und Kurzantworten mit *do* + Verb		
	+	–
Do you play volleyball?	Yes, I do.	No, I don't.
Do they like pizza?	Yes, they do.	No, they don't.
Does Jack know Gillian?	Yes, he does.	No, he doesn't.

! Entscheidungsfragen mit ***be, can*** und ***have got*** bildest du ohne *do/does* am Satzanfang:

Entscheidungsfragen und Kurzantworten mit *be, can, have got*		
	+	–
Are you eleven?	Yes, I am.	No, I'm not.
Can you play an instrument?	Yes, I can.	No, I can't.
Has Emma got a new book?	Yes, she has.	No, she hasn't.

Bei Fragen mit Fragewörtern steht das Fragewort am Satzanfang:

Simple present: Fragen mit Fragewörtern		
What	do	you usually do after school?
Where	does	Caroline live?
How	do	you spell 'juice'?
Where	is	George?
What	can	we eat?
Who	has got	an idea?

LiF 2R Die einfache Vergangenheit (The simple past)

a) Simple past: Regelmäßige Formen (Regular forms)

Das *simple past* verwendest du, wenn du über etwas sprechen willst, das in der Vergangenheit liegt und abgeschlossen ist. Deshalb steht es oft mit Zeitangaben wie *last week, last year* oder *yesterday*, die ausdrücken, dass etwas vorbei ist.

Das *simple past* der regelmäßigen Verben bildest du, indem du die Endung *-ed* an den Infinitiv anhängst:
watch + ed → *watched*

Simple past: regelmäßige Formen
Yesterday I watched a great film about elephants.
Last week Sarah helped John with his maths homework.

! Besonderheiten:

to like	→	liked	He liked the rabbit in the window.
to stop	→	stopped	The man stopped and looked at Greg.
to try	→	tried	I tried to help him.

b) Simple past: Unregelmäßige Formen (Irregular forms)

Die unregelmäßigen Verben haben im *simple past* eine eigene Form, die du lernen musst, z. B.:

Infinitiv	simple past	
to have	had	Sarah had a great holiday.
to go	went	She went to France with her family.
to find	found	She and her sister found new friends during their holiday.
to do	did	They did lots of interesting things together.
to feel	felt	Sarah felt sad when the holiday was over.
to say	said	Her parents said: "We can come back next year."

! Viele unregelmäßige Verben kommen sehr häufig vor – deshalb lohnt es sich, ihre Formen zu lernen. Eine Liste mit unregelmäßigen Verben, die in diesem Buch vorkommen, findest du auf Seite 219.

Be hat als einziges englisches Verb zwei Formen im *simple past*, ***was*** und ***were***:
I / he / she / it ***was*** *– you / we / they* ***were***

Simple past von *be*		
I	was	very hungry after school.
They	were	in London yesterday.
It	wasn't	cold yesterday.
We	weren't	at the party.

They were in Glasgow together last year.

c) Simple past: Verneinung (Negation)

Sätze im *simple past* kannst du mit ***didn't (did not)*** verneinen. ***Didn't*** ist in allen Personen gleich.

Simple past: Verneinung
George didn't talk to Emma yesterday.
I didn't go to London last year.

d) Simple past: Fragen (Questions)

Entscheidungsfragen im *simple past* kannst du mit ***did*** stellen:

Simple past: Entscheidungsfragen und Kurzantworten		
	+	–
Did you go on holiday?	Yes, we did.	No, we didn't.
Did Rajiv buy a new football yesterday?	Yes, he did.	No, he didn't.

Did Rajiv buy a new football yesterday? – Yes, he did.

! Entscheidungsfragen mit *was* und *were* stellst du ohne *did:*
Were *you in Manchester last week? – Yes, we were. / No, we weren't.*
Was *it interesting? – Yes, it was. / No, it wasn't.*

Wenn du eine Frage mit ***what, when, where, why*** oder ***how*** stellen möchtest, stellst du das Fragewort an den Satzanfang:

Simple past: Fragen mit Fragewort	
What did Charlie buy?	– He bought a football.
When did you go to France?	– I went there last summer.
Where did you stay?	– We stayed at a hotel.
Why did Sarah laugh?	– I don't know.
How did you like the book?	– It was great.
What was in Caroline's school bag?	– A pencil case and five books.
Where were you yesterday?	– I was at home.

What did you do? – I was at the beach all the time.

LiF 3 Die Steigerung von Adjektiven (The comparison of adjectives)

Mit Adjektiven lassen sich Personen oder Sachen näher beschreiben. Wenn du mehrere Personen oder Sachen miteinander vergleichen möchtest, kannst du ein Adjektiv steigern. Die Steigerungsformen heißen ***comparative*** (Komparativ) und ***superlative*** (Superlativ).
Tom is very tall. Jill is even ***taller****.* – Tom ist sehr groß. Jill ist sogar noch größer.
Karen is the ***oldest*** *girl in our class.* – Karen ist das älteste Mädchen in unserer Klasse.

a) Regelmäßige Steigerung (Regular comparative/superlative forms)

adjective	comparative	superlative	
cheap *billig* old *alt*	cheaper *billiger* older *älter*	(the) cheapest *(am) billigsten* (the) oldest *(am) ältesten*	Einsilbige Adjektive steigerst du, indem du *-er* oder *-est* anhängst.
pretty *hübsch* easy *leicht*	prettier *hübscher* easier *leichter*	(the) prettiest *(am) hübschesten* (the) easiest *(am) leichtesten*	Bei zweisilbigen Adjektiven, die auf -y enden, wird aus dem *-y* ein *-i.*
nice *nett* big *groß* hot *heiß*	nicer *netter* bigger *größer* hotter *heißer*	(the) nicest *(am) nettesten* (the) biggest *(am) größten* (the) hottest *(am) heißesten*	**!** Bei manchen Adjektiven ändert sich die Schreibweise.

b) Unregelmäßige Steigerungsformen (Irregular comparative/superlative forms)

Es gibt auch unregelmäßige Steigerungsformen der Adjektive, die du wie Vokabeln lernen musst:

adjective	comparative	superlative
good *gut*	better *besser*	(the) best *(am) besten*
bad *schlecht*	worse *schlechter*	(the) worst *(am) schlechtesten*

c) Steigerung mit *more* und *most* (Comparison with *more* and *most*)

Die Steigerungsform von Adjektiven mit mehr als zwei Silben bildest du mit *more* und *most:*
The green T-shirt is ***more expensive*** *than the blue one.* – Das grüne T-Shirt ist teurer als das blaue.

adjective	comparative	superlative
interesting *interessant*	more interesting *interessanter*	(the) most interesting *(am) interessantesten*
difficult *schwierig*	more difficult *schwieriger*	(the) most difficult *(am) schwierigsten*

d) Vergleichssätze (Clauses of comparison)

Vergleichssätze	
The blue T-shirt is cheaper than the green one. *Das blaue T-shirt ist billiger als das grüne.*	Für den Vergleich von Dingen und Personen verwendest du ***than*** und den Komparativ.
Sarah is as tall as Anne. *Sarah ist so groß wie Anne.*	Sind die Eigenschaften gleich, verwendest du ***as … as***.

LiF 4 Verbindung von Sätzen: *connectives* (Linking sentences: connectives)

Connectives sind Wörter, mit denen du Sätze verbinden kannst. Mit ihnen kannst du einen Text gut strukturieren.
Zu den *connectives* gehören auch die Konjunktionen. Du kennst bereits eine Reihe von Konjunktionen, mit denen du zwei Hauptsätze oder einen Hauptsatz und einen Nebensatz verbinden kannst, z. B. *and, but, because.*

Connectives	
Mr Brown is our French teacher and Mrs Thompson is our English teacher.	*… und …*
Carol likes ice cream but she doesn't like chocolate.	*… aber …*
Charlie is happy because he can play football.	*… weil …*
Carl went into the house when it started to rain.	*… als …*
We have enough food so we don't need to go shopping.	*… also …*
Zoe didn't know that her mother could hear her.	*… dass …*
The boys played football although the weather was bad.	*… obwohl …*
After they played football, they went home.	*Nachdem …*

LiF 5R Das Futur mit *going to* (The *going to* future)

Das **Futur mit *going to*** verwendest du, um über Pläne oder Absichten zu sprechen.
Du kannst mit dem ***going to*** aber auch ausdrücken, dass du glaubst, dass etwas gleich passieren wird.

Futur mit *going to*
I'm going to watch a film this evening.
Are you going to go to the party?
What are you going to do?
It's going to rain this afternoon.

LiF 6 Das Futur mit *will* (The *will* future)

Das ***will future*** verwendest du, um darüber zu sprechen, was in der Zukunft passiert.
Mit dem *will future* kannst du Vorhersagen oder Vermutungen ausdrücken.

Du bildest das *will future* mit ***will*** und dem Infinitiv des Verbs.
will ist in allen Personen gleich. Die Kurzform lautet *'ll*, z. B. in *I'll, we'll.*

will future	
I **will** help you with your homework.	*Ich werde dir mit deinen Hausaufgaben helfen.*
You**'ll** find new friends.	*Du wirst neue Freunde finden.*
The weather **will** be great tomorrow.	*Das Wetter wird morgen großartig sein.*

Wenn du eine Vermutung ausdrücken willst, kannst du den Satz mit *I think, I'm sure, I hope* oder *maybe* beginnen:
I think *England* ***will win*** *the match.* – Ich denke, dass England das Spiel gewinnen wird.

! Im Deutschen verwenden wir oft die Gegenwart, um über zukünftige Dinge zu sprechen. Das ist im Englischen in der Regel nicht möglich:
I'll talk *to Sarah tomorrow.* – Ich spreche morgen mit Sarah.

Die Verneinung bildest du mit ***will not*** oder der Kurzform ***won't***:

will future: **Verneinung**	
I **won't** live in London.	*Ich werde nicht in London leben.*
There **won't** be any rain tomorrow.	*Morgen wird es nicht regnen.*

Entscheidungsfragen bildest du, indem du *will* an den Satzanfang stellst.
Bei Fragen mit Fragewörtern steht das Fragewort am Satzanfang:

will future: **Fragen und Kurzantworten**	
Will I be rich? – Yes, you **will**. / No, you **won't**.	*Werde ich reich sein? – Ja. / Nein.*
What will you be when you grow up?	*Was wirst du, wenn du erwachsen bist?*
Who will win the next football match?	*Wer wird das nächste Fußballspiel gewinnen?*

! Nicht verwechseln:
I ***will*** *go to London.* – Ich **werde** nach London gehen.
I ***want to*** *go to London.* – Ich **will** nach London gehen.

LiF 7 Bedingungssätze, Typ 1 (Conditional clauses, type 1)

Ein Bedingungssatz besteht aus einem *if*-Satz *(if-clause)* und einem Hauptsatz *(main clause)*:

- Der *if*-Satz nennt eine Bedingung. Der Hauptsatz drückt aus, was passiert, wenn die Bedingung erfüllt ist. Die Bedingung kann jederzeit eintreten.
- Im *if*-Satz steht das *simple present,* im Hauptsatz das *will future.*

***if*-Satz** (Bedingung: *Wenn …*)	**Hauptsatz** (Folge: *dann …*)	
If you **miss** the bus,	you **will be** late.	*Wenn du den Bus verpasst, kommst du zu spät.*
If it **rains**,	they **won't go** to the beach.	*Wenn es regnet, werden sie nicht zum Strand gehen.*

Der Hauptsatz kann auch am Anfang des Satzes stehen.
Dann steht kein Komma vor dem *if*-Satz:
They won't go to the beach if it rains.

Im Hauptsatz kannst du auch Modalverben (z. B. *can, must*) oder den Imperativ verwenden:
*If it rains, we **can go** inside.* – Wenn es regnet, können wir reingehen.
*If you like her, you **must call** her.* – Wenn du sie magst, musst du sie anrufen.
*If you need help, **ask** Lisa.* – Wenn du Hilfe brauchst, frag Lisa.

! *If* und *when* kannst du im Deutschen mit „wenn" übersetzen. Im Englischen werden sie aber unterschiedlich verwendet:

- ***If** I see Ben on Monday, I'll give him the book.*
  Der Sprecher verwendet *if*, weil er nicht sicher ist, ob er Ben am Montag sieht.
  Du kannst *if* hier mit „wenn" oder „falls" übersetzen.
- ***When** I see Ben on Monday, I'll give him the book.*
  Der Sprecher hat fest vor, Ben am Montag zu sehen.
  Du kannst *when* hier mit „wenn" übersetzen, aber nicht mit „falls".

LiF 8 Das Perfekt (The present perfect)

a) Present perfect: Verwendung (Use)

Das *present perfect* verwendest du, …

- … wenn Handlungen oder Ereignisse schon beendet sind, aber noch Auswirkungen in die Gegenwart haben:
  *David **has cleaned** the kitchen.*
  David hat die Küche geputzt (sie ist noch sauber).
- … wenn ein Vorgang in der Vergangenheit begonnen hat und bis in die Gegenwart andauert:
  *Claire **has** never **been** to the Tower of London.* –
  Claire ist (bis heute) noch nie im Tower of London gewesen.

She **has bought** new clothes.

b) Present perfect: Aussagesätze (Statements)

Das *present perfect* bildest du mit *have/has* + **Partizip Perfekt *(past participle)*.**
Die Verneinung bildest du mit *haven't/hasn't* + **Partizip Perfekt**.

Present perfect			
	have/has	Partizip Perfekt	
I	have	**cleaned**	the kitchen.
He	has	**gone**	to London.
We	have	**seen**	the Queen.
They	haven't	**helped.**	

The boys have tidied their room.

Das *present perfect* kannst du mit Adverbien der unbestimmten Zeit verwenden, z. B. mit *already, just, ever, never*. Die Adverbien stehen dann direkt vor dem Partizip Perfekt:
I have ***never*** *been to London.* – Ich war noch nie in London.
Angela has ***just*** *seen the Queen.* – Angela hat eben gerade die Königin gesehen.
! Beachte die Ausnahme: *yet* steht am Satzende:
I haven't been to London ***yet****.* – Ich war noch nicht in London.

! Beachte bei den Kurzformen:
he's ***gone*** = *he has* ***gone***
he's ***going*** = *he is* ***going***

c) Das Partizip Perfekt (The past participle)

Bei regelmäßigen Verben bildest du das Partizip Perfekt mit dem **Infinitiv** + *-ed*.

Infinitiv	Partizip Perfekt
clean	cleaned
help	helped
play	played

Unregelmäßige Verben haben unregelmäßige Formen.
Diese Formen solltest du wie Vokabeln lernen, z. B.:

Infinitiv	simple past	past participle
be	was/were	been
do	did	done
have	had	had
buy	bought	bought
catch	caught	caught
find	found	found
give	gave	given

He has bought a new football.

! Eine Liste mit unregelmäßigen Verben, die im Buch vorkommen, findest du auf Seite 219.

d) Present perfect: Fragen und Kurzantworten (Questions and short answers)

Entscheidungsfragen im *present perfect* bildest du, indem du das Subjekt und *have/has* vertauschst. Bei Fragen mit Fragewörtern steht das Fragewort am Satzanfang:

Present perfect: Fragen und Kurzantworten				
Have	you	finished	your homework?	Yes, I have. / No, I haven't.
Has	Jill	bought	a new book?	Yes, she has. / No, she hasn't.

Present perfect: Fragen mit Fragewort			
What	have	you	done?
Why	hasn't	she	come?

LiF 9 Relativsätze (Relative clauses)

a) *who, which* und *that*

Mit Relativsätzen kannst du eine Person oder eine Sache genauer beschreiben.
Ein Relativsatz beginnt in der Regel mit einem Relativpronomen, z. B. mit *who, which* oder *that:*

	Relativsatz		
This is the man	who helped Sherlock Holmes.		*Das ist der Mann, der Sherlock Holmes geholfen hat.*
The book	which I bought yesterday	is really good.	*Das Buch, das ich gestern gekauft habe, ist wirklich gut.*
The team	that won the game	had a big party.	*Das Team, das das Spiel gewann, feierte eine große Party.*
The DVD	that she gave me	was great!	*Die DVD, die sie mir gegeben hat, war großartig!*

Die Relativpronomen *who, which* und *that* verwendet man im Singular und im Plural. Dabei verwendet man *who* für Personen, *which* für Dinge und *that* sowohl für Personen als auch für Dinge.

! Die Wortstellung ist in englischen Relativsätzen anders als im Deutschen:
That's the man who helped my father. Das ist der Mann, der meinem Vater geholfen hat.

b) *whose*

Relativsätze können auch mit *whose* („dessen/deren") + Nomen beginnen:

	Relativsatz	
I know a man	whose grandmother is 100 years old.	*Ich kenne einen Mann, dessen Großmutter 100 Jahre alt ist.*

! ***whose*** = dessen/deren ***who's*** *(who is)* = wer ist

LiF 10 Das Perfekt mit *for* und *since* (The present perfect with *for* and *since*)

Wenn du sagen möchtest, **wie lange** etwas andauert, verwendest du das *present perfect* mit ***for*** (*for* + Zeitraum).
Wenn du sagen möchtest, **seit wann** etwas andauert, verwendest du das *present perfect* mit ***since*** (*since* + Zeitpunkt):

	for +	**Zeitraum**		***since*** +	**Zeitpunkt**
I have been angry	for	an hour.	I have been angry	since	12 o'clock.
I haven't seen her	for	three days.	I haven't seen her	since	Sunday.
We've been friends	for	a long time.	We've been friends	since	2009.

LiF 11 Perfekt oder einfache Vergangenheit? (Present perfect or simple past?)

Das *present perfect* und das *simple past* werden unterschiedlich verwendet:

present perfect		
Vergangenheit	**Gegenwart**	
David **has** already **cleaned** the kitchen.	It is clean now.	Die Handlung ist beendet, hat aber noch Auswirkungen auf die Gegenwart.
They **have been** friends since 2009.		Der Vorgang hat in der Vergangenheit begonnen und dauert bis in die Gegenwart an.

Das *present perfect* kannst du mit Adverbien der unbestimmten Zeit verwenden wie *already, just, ever, never, not yet.*

simple past		
Vergangenheit	**Gegenwart**	
Karen **bought** a book **yesterday**. We **went** to Scotland **in 2011**. I **saw** Jane **when she left school.**		Der Vorgang liegt in der Vergangenheit und ist abgeschlossen – er ist vorbei.

Das *simple past* steht oft mit Zeitangaben wie *last week, last year, yesterday, in 2009.*

LiF 12 Adverbien der Art und Weise (Adverbs of manner)

Adjektive beschreiben ein Nomen näher:
Wie ist eine Person oder Sache?

Adverbien der Art und Weise beschreiben ein Verb näher:
Wie tut jemand etwas oder **wie geschieht** etwas?

Im Deutschen sind Adjektive und Adverbien in der Regel äußerlich nicht zu unterscheiden. Im Englischen haben sie meist verschiedene Formen. Die meisten Adverbien der Art und Weise bildest du, indem du an das Adjektiv die Endung *-ly* anhängst:

Adjektiv	Adverb		
loud slow bad	loud**ly** slow**ly** bad**ly**	The boys speak **loudly**. Mr Glover drives **slowly**. Simon sings **badly**.	
happy terrible	happ**ily** terrib**ly**	She laughed **happily**. Simon sings **terribly**.	Achte auf die Schreibung: *-y* wird zu *-ily* *-le* wird zu *-ly*

Einige Adverbien haben Sonderformen, die du wie Vokabeln lernen solltest:

Adjektiv	Adverb	
good	**well**	Rajiv is a good guitar player. He plays the guitar **well**.
fast	**fast**	Kemi is a fast runner. She runs **fast**.
hard	**hard**	Mr Khan is a hard worker. He works **hard**.

Adverbien der Art und Weise stehen nach dem Verb.
In Sätzen mit Objekt stehen sie nach dem Objekt:

Subjekt	Verb	Objekt	Adverb
She	runs		**fast**.
He	plays	the guitar	**well**.

He dances very **well**.

! Nach einigen Verben der Sinneswahrnehmung (z. B. *look, feel*) verwendet man kein Adverb, sondern das Adjektiv:
*She **looks beautiful**.*
*Leo **feels terrible**.*

LiF 13 Modalverben und ihre Ersatzformen (Modal verbs and their substitute forms)

Du kennst bereits einige Modalverben wie *can, must* oder *need*. Die meisten Modalverben haben nur Formen für das *simple present*. Im *present perfect, simple past* und *will future* verwendest du deshalb die **Ersatzformen *(substitute forms)***.

Wenn du sagen willst, dass jemand in der Lage oder fähig ist, etwas zu tun, verwendest du *can* und die Ersatzform *be able to*:

***can – be able to* (können)**		
simple present	can	I can swim.
simple past	was able to	She was able to answer all the questions.
present perfect	has/have been able to	He has been able to find a new piano teacher.
will future	will be able to	They won't be able to come to the party.

! Im *simple past* kannst du auch *could/couldn't* verwenden:
I couldn't go to London because I was ill.

Mit *may, can* und der Ersatzform *be allowed to* kannst du ausdrücken, dass etwas erlaubt ist:

***may, can – be allowed to* (dürfen)**		
simple present	may/can	May/Can I open the window?
simple past	was allowed to	Ben was allowed to go to the football match.
present perfect	has/have been allowed to	Kemi has been allowed to go to the concert.
will future	will be allowed to	Jo will be allowed to go to the party next week.

Mit *may not, can't* und der Ersatzform *not be allowed to* kannst du ein Verbot ausdrücken:

***may not, can't – not be allowed to* (nicht dürfen)**		
simple present	may not/can't	Sorry, but you may not/can't leave your bike here.
simple past	wasn't allowed to	He wasn't allowed to watch TV yesterday.
present perfect	hasn't/haven't been allowed to	Lynn hasn't been allowed to go to the concert.
will future	won't be allowed to	Jo won't be allowed to stay until 1 am.

Mit *must* und der Ersatzform *have to* kannst du ausdrücken, dass etwas getan werden muss:

must – have to **(müssen)**		
simple present	must	You must drive on the left in Britain.
simple past	had to	It was very late so she had to go.
present perfect	has/have had to	Jo has had to go home. She didn't feel well.
will future	will have to	I will have to eat less chocolate.

Mit *needn't* und der Ersatzform *don't have to* kannst du ausdrücken, dass etwas nicht notwendig ist:

needn't – don't have to **(nicht müssen)**		
simple present	needn't	We needn't buy milk. There's enough in the fridge.
simple past	didn't have to	You didn't have to buy me a present.
present perfect	hasn't/haven't had to	Tom hasn't had to get up early for years.
will future	won't have to	We won't have to go to school tomorrow. It's a holiday.

LiF 14 Possessivpronomen (Possessive pronouns)

Du kennst bereits die Possessivbegleiter, z. B. *my* und *your*. Mit Possessivbegleitern kannst du sagen, wem etwas gehört oder zu wem etwas gehört. Du verwendest die Possessivbegleiter immer zusammen mit einem Nomen.
Anders ist es bei den Possessivpronomen. Wie alle Pronomen verwendest du sie statt eines Nomens. Auch mit den Possessivpronomen kannst du sagen, wem etwas gehört oder zu wem etwas gehört:

Possessivbegleiter + Nomen	Possessivpronomen	
my shoes	mine	Whose shoes are these? – They're mine.
your mobile	yours	I can't find my mobile. Can I use yours?
his dog	his	His dog is so cute! – It's not his. It's Helen's dog.
her car	hers	Is this Tom's or Helen's car? – It's hers.
your tickets	yours	We have our tickets, but where are yours?
our house	ours	Their house is much bigger than ours.
their cat	theirs	Zoe and Jill have a cat. Our cat is younger than theirs.

LiF 15 Relativsätze ohne Relativpronomen (Contact clauses)

Relativsätze, bei denen du das Relativpronomen weglassen kannst, heißen *contact clauses*. Hauptsatz und Relativsatz stehen dann in direktem „Kontakt", weil kein Relativpronomen zwischen ihnen steht. Das Relativpronomen kannst du nur dann weglassen, wenn es das Objekt eines Relativsatzes ist:

	Relativsatz mit Relativpronomen als Objekt	Contact clause
I liked the shoes *... die Schuhe,*	which we saw in the shop. *die ...*	I liked the shoes we saw in the shop.
He is the boy *... der Junge,*	who I met on holiday last year. *den ...*	He is the boy I met on holiday.

Ist das Relativpronomen dagegen Subjekt des Relativsatzes, kannst du es nicht weglassen:

	Relativsatz mit Relativpronomen als Subjekt		
That is the boy	**who**	plays football for England.	*... der Junge, der ...*
There is a photo	**which**	shows Kate and Sam at the beach.	*... ein Foto, das ...*

LiF 16 Die Verlaufsform der Vergangenheit (The past progressive)

Im Englischen gibt es anders als im Deutschen zu allen Zeiten zwei verschiedene Formen, die unterschiedlich verwendet werden: eine *simple form* und eine *progressive form.* Das *present progressive* kennst du bereits: Du verwendest es, wenn du sagen möchtest, was jemand gerade tut oder was gerade passiert: *Emma is reading a book.*

Es gibt auch für die Vergangenheit eine *progressive form,* das ***past progressive***. Du verwendest es, um auszudrücken, **was jemand gerade tat** oder **was gerade passierte**. So bildest du das *past progressive:*

Simple past-Form von *be (was/were)* + *-ing*-Form

Past progressive	Simple past
Emma **was reading** a book *Emma las gerade ein Buch,*	when Rajiv **called**. *als Rajiv anrief.*
The pupils **were running** around *Die Schüler rannten herum,*	when the teacher **came**. *als der Lehrer kam.*
was gerade passiert: *past progressive*	neues Ereignis: *simple past*

Emma was reading a book when her father came to say goodnight.

LiF 17 Bestätigungsfragen (Question tags)

Wenn du erwartest, dass ein Gesprächspartner dir zustimmt, kannst du eine Bestätigungsfrage stellen. Im Englischen verwendest du dafür *question tags*. Du kannst sie mit „... oder?", „... nicht wahr?" übersetzen. *Question tags* werden an den Hauptsatz angehängt:

Bejahter Aussagesatz ⊕	question tag ⊖	Verneinter Aussagesatz ⊖	question tag ⊕
The book is great,	isn't it?	This film isn't interesting,	is it?
We have a lot of time,	haven't we?	You haven't got time,	have you?
Alex can come with us,	can't he?	He can't see us,	can he?
Rajiv likes music,	doesn't he?	Tom doesn't like apples,	does he?

! Ein Teil des Satzes muss positiv, der andere negativ sein:
*The T-shirt **is** cool, **isn't** it?*
*George **doesn't** like dancing, **does** he?*

Bei Sätzen mit Hilfsverben bestehen die *question tags* aus Hilfsverb und Personalpronomen:
*We **can** stay in London, **can't** we?*
Bei Sätzen ohne Hilfsverb verwendest du eine Form von *do*: *Sarah helped Kim, **didn't she?***

LiF 18 Die Steigerung von Adverbien (Comparison of adverbs)

Du weißt bereits, wie Adjektive gesteigert werden (→ LiF 3).
Für die Steigerung von Adverbien gelten die gleichen Regeln.

*Greg runs **faster** than his brother.*
Greg rennt schneller als sein Bruder.
*Sophie plays the guitar **more beautifully** than Karen.*
Sophie spielt schöner Gitarre als Karen.

He runs the fastest.

adverb	comparative	superlative	
hard fast	harder faster	hardest fastest	Einsilbige Adverbien steigerst du, indem du *-er* und *-est* anhängst.
beautifully delightedly	more beautifully more delightedly	most beautifully most delightedly	Adverbien, die auf *-ly* enden, steigerst du mit *more* und *most*.

Es gibt auch unregelmäßige Steigerungsformen der Adverbien, die du wie Vokabeln lernen musst:

adverb	comparative	superlative
well	better	best
badly	worse	worst
much	more	most

In den Wordbanks findest du die wichtigsten Wörter zu einem Thema zusammengefasst. Wenn vorne im Buch zum Beispiel ● *Wordbank City p. 151* steht, findest du in der *Wordbank City* auf Seite 151 zu diesem Thema passende Wörter.

Wordbank
In the country

Animals and plants

cow · horse · pony · pig · chicken · bird · fox · rabbit · hedgehog · frog · dog · cat · mouse · rat · flower · tree · plant

Places

forest · woods · river · hill · village · farm · mountain

Wordbank Weather

Talking about the weather

sunny · rainy · cloudy · foggy · snowy · wet · hot · warm · cold

W Wordbank Festivals

Festivals and celebrations

birthday · Christmas · New Year · Chinese New Year · Halloween · Diwali · Bonfire Night · Hogmanay · St. Patrick's Day · Valentine's Day · Easter · Lent

You can …

celebrate Diwali/St. Patrick's Day/…
invite/meet friends
write cards
buy decorations
decorate the house
have a party
let off fireworks/rockets/sparklers/bangers
watch fireworks
have a barbecue
buy presents
prepare food
make a cake
have a special meal
wear special clothes
play music

Talking about festivals and celebrations

Happy birthday!

Do we know how many people are coming to the party?

What will we do if we don't have enough drinks?

Merry Christmas!

Congratulations!

When can we start the fireworks?

What about a big party at our house?

Happy New Year!

Come on, let's light some sparklers.

These samosas are great. Did you make them?

Party food and drinks

snacks · cake · pizza · muffins · crisps · baked potato · toffee apple · samosa · souflaki · chocolate · ice cream · juice · fruit · sweets · hamburgers

Wordbank City

Streets, places and buildings

street · road · building · park · stadium · church · hospital · university · station · tower · shop · store · cinema · centre

Giving directions

Walk on till you get to the hospital.

Turn around and cross the street.

Walk straight on.

Excuse me, can you tell me the way to …, please?

Turn left/right.

Walk past Madame Tussauds.

On your left/right there's a big store.

Stop at the corner.

You can …

visit a museum
see attractions
show somebody around
go on a tour
take a double-decker bus
book tickets
take the Tube/the Underground
go by bus/bike/train
get lost/lose your way/ask for the way

Sights and attractions

London Eye · Madame Tussauds · Tate Modern · Covent Garden · Tower Bridge · Big Ben · Science Museum · Film Museum · Trafalgar Square · Buckingham Palace · Imperial War Museum · Sherlock Holmes Museum · Emirates Stadium

I'd love to go to Buckingham Palace.

It would be cool to see the Emirates Stadium.

Why don't we go on a sightseeing tour?

I've never been to London before.

The London Eye is a must!

W

Wordbank Entertainment

Fun and entertainment

fundraising · jumble sale · quiz night · concert · play · cinema · circus

You can …

hold a jumble sale · give a concert · sing in a choir · perform on stage · receive applause · go to an audition · perform a play · watch a comedy · write a script · go to a premiere · watch a film at the cinema · go to the circus · be an actor/actress · be a prompter

Wordbank Environment

Environment

planet · solar energy · solar panel · transport · waste · glass · plastic · paper · bottle · organic waste

You can …

save the environment
use solar energy
donate money
buy solar panels
protect the planet
turn off the light
leave the TV on standby
save energy
go by bike
recycle glass
compost organic waste
plant flowers
collect glass

Talking about the environment

What can we do to save the environment?

We should buy products with less packaging.

We produce a mountain of rubbish every day.

Recycling isn't enough. We should save energy, too.

We should compost organic waste.

There is always more that we can do.

You could go by bike when it's not raining.

Let's protect our planet!

Wordbank Sport and health

Sport

basketball · tennis · football · volleyball · dancing · rowing · karate · judo · horse-riding · swimming · cycling · long jump · high jump · running

You can ...

go for a ride · win a prize · do stretching exercises · score a goal · chase the ball · be successful · win the House Cup · break the record · be in the lead · overtake a rival · fight for the ball · keep up with your rival · improve your time · beat the others · sing a chant · go surfing · organize a football match

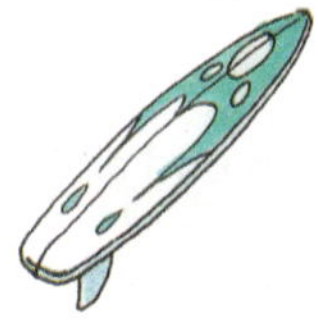

Health

You can ...

be out of breath
balance on one leg
be as fit as a fiddle
hurt your leg
break your arm
eat fast food
be a couch potato
continue being active
keep up the good work
be flexible
do exercise

Wordbank People

Describing people

strong · cute · pretty · honest · boring · stunning · poor · silent · sensible · strict · successful · attractive

You can be ...

bored · nervous · confident polite · embarrassed · angry · famous · busy · delighted · annoyed · popular · disappointed · nosy · brilliant · excited · bossy · silly · arrogant · kind · tidy · cheerful · careful · gloomy · upset · serious · determined

You can feel ...

bored
nervous
fabulous
tense
frustrated
jealous
awful
bad
fantastic

You can do something ...

carefully · nervously · arrogantly · fast · confidently · quietly · noisily

So funktionieren die Wortlisten

Es gibt Wortlisten nach *Themes* und alphabetische Wortlisten *(Dictionaries)*.

Wortlisten nach *Themes*

In den Wortlisten nach *Themes* ab Seite 155 findest du die Wörter in der Reihenfolge, in der sie in den *Themes* vorkommen.
Am Ende der Wortliste zu jedem *Theme* steht *Say it in English*, eine Liste mit nützlichen Redewendungen.

Dictionaries

Camden Town hat zwei *dictionaries*:

1 Im *English-German dictionary* ab Seite 186 kannst du nachschlagen, wenn du die Bedeutung von einem englischen Wort aus dem Buch wissen möchtest.
2 Im *German-English dictionary* ab Seite 205 kannst du nachschlagen, wenn dir mal ein englisches Wort nicht einfällt.

So kannst du die Wortlisten nach *Themes* und die *dictionaries* benutzen:

Fett gedruckte Wörter solltest du dir merken.	**different** / ˈdɪfrənt /
Die / Lautschrift / zeigt an, wie man ein Wort ausspricht.	**busy** / ˈbɪzi /
! weist auf wichtige Besonderheiten hin.	**!** Englisch *sensible* = Deutsch „vernünftig“
↔ bedeutet „ist das Gegenteil von“.	to remember ↔ to forget
In den gelb hinterlegten Kästen stehen Wörter, die du dir merken solltest, Tipps und Hinweise.	**Verben und Präpositionen zusammen lernen** Folgt einem Verb eine Präposition, dann verändert sich dadurch die Bedeutung des Verbs, z. B. bei *to look:* *to **look up*** (nachschlagen)
(informal) bedeutet: Dieses Wort ist umgangssprachlich.	No way! *(informal)* / ˌnəʊ ˈweɪ /
(*pl* **knives**) bedeutet: Dieses Wort hat einen unregelmäßigen Plural *(knives)*.	**knife** (*pl* **knives**) / naɪf, naɪvz /
(no pl) bedeutet: Dieses Wort hat keinen Plural.	**medicine** *(no pl)* / ˈmed(ə)s(ə)n /
(only pl) bedeutet: Dieses Wort wird nur oder gewöhnlich im Plural benutzt.	**news** *(only pl)* / nju:z /
° bedeutet: Dieses Wort ist nur für einen bestimmten Text wichtig. Du brauchst es nicht zu lernen.	° coastline / ˈkəʊstˌlaɪn /
(irr) bedeutet: Dieses Verb ist unregelmäßig. Auf Seite 219 kannst du *irregular verbs* nachschlagen.	to **come** *(irr)* / kʌm /
Folgende Abkürzungen werden noch verwendet:	sb = somebody sth = something etw = etwas jdm / jdn = jemandem / jemanden

Word lists

Theme 1: After the holidays

	English	German	Example	
	souvenir /ˌsuːvəˈnɪə/	Andenken, Souvenir		
A1	**as ... as** /æz æz/	so ... wie	John is **as** tall **as** Mark.	p. 10
	most /məʊst/	(die) meisten	**Most** children like chocolate.	
	to **organize** /ˈɔːɡənaɪz/	organisieren; *hier:* ordnen	You can **organize** your words in a word web.	
A2	**back** /bæk/	(wieder) zurück	It's September. The pupils are **back** from holiday.	
	to **complete** /kəmˈpliːt/	vervollständigen, ausfüllen	**Complete** the **grid**.	
	grid /ɡrɪd/	Gitter(netz); *hier:* Tabelle		
	whose /huːz/	wessen		

	English	German	Example	
	which /wɪtʃ/	welche(r, s)		
	best /best/	am liebsten/am meisten	I like a holiday by the sea **best**.	
A3	to **prepare** /prɪˈpeə/	vorbereiten, erstellen	At the weekend, Lynn **prepares** breakfast for her parents.	p. 11
	to **ask (for sth)** /ˈɑːsk fə ˌsʌmθɪŋ/	(um etw) bitten	You can **ask** Sarah **for** help.	
	to **collect** /kəˈlekt/	sammeln; *hier:* aufheben	The teacher **collected** the pupils' homework.	
	home town /ˈhəʊm ˌtaʊn/	Heimatstadt		
	to **find out** /ˌfaɪnd‿ˈaʊt/ *simple past:* **found out** /ˌfaʊnd‿ˈaʊt/	herausfinden	Look on the Internet to **find out** more about the Isle of Lewis.	
	(too) bad /tuː ˈbæd/	(zu) schade		
	rainy /ˈreɪni/	regnerisch		
	cloudy /ˈklaʊdi/	bewölkt, bedeckt		
	foggy /ˈfɒɡi/	neblig		
	snowy /ˈsnəʊi/	schneereich		
	presentation /ˌprez(ə)nˈteɪʃ(ə)n/	Präsentation	Jill's **presentation** was very good.	
	to speak up /ˌspiːk‿ˈʌp/ *simple past:* spoke up /ˌspəʊk‿ˈʌp/	lauter sprechen		
	clearly /ˈklɪə(r)li/	klar, deutlich		
	neat /niːt/	ordentlich, sauber		
	tidy /ˈtaɪdi/	ordentlich		
	a bit /ə ˈbɪt/	ein bisschen, ein wenig	Could you speak up **a bit**, please? I can't hear you.	
	informative /ɪnˈfɔː(r)mətɪv/	informativ		
B1	to **note down** /ˌnəʊt‿ˈdaʊn/	(sich) notieren	to **note down** = to write down	p. 12
	pony camp /ˈpəʊni ˌkæmp/	Reiterferienlager		
	cute /kjuːt/	süß, niedlich		
	snow *(no pl)* /snəʊ/	Schnee	Last winter, there was a lot of **snow**.	
	pretty /ˈprɪti/	hübsch, nett	very **pretty** = beautiful	
	stable /ˈsteɪb(ə)l/	Stall, Box		
	to go for a ride /ˌɡəʊ fər‿ə ˈraɪd/	eine Fahrt machen; *hier:* ausreiten		
	ride /raɪd/	Fahrt		

	so /səʊ/	so; *hier:* sehr	There was **so** much to do at the pony camp.
	country /ˈkʌntri/	Land	Germany is a **country.**
	than /ðæn/	als	More **than** 60 million people live in the UK.

one/ones

1. What about these T-shirts? Do you like the green **one**? Was ist mit diesen T-Shirts? Magst du das grüne?
2. There are a lot of shops, but only small **ones.** Es gibt viele Geschäfte, aber nur kleine.

	boring /ˈbɔːrɪŋ/	langweilig	**boring** ↔ exciting, interesting
	barbecue /ˈbɑːbɪˌkjuː/	Grill, Grillparty	The weather is great. Let's have a **barbecue**!
	race /reɪs/	Rennen	Geoff won the **race.** 
	start /stɑːt/	Anfang, Beginn	**start** ↔ end
	suddenly /ˈsʌd(ə)nli/	plötzlich	**Suddenly** he started to cry. I was very surprised.
	to fall off /ˌfɔːl‿ˈɒf/ *simple past:* fell off /ˌfel‿ˈɒf/	(hinunter)fallen	
	fast /fɑːst/	schnell	It's late. Let's get back as **fast** as possible.
	both /bəʊθ/	beide	They are **both** from London. 
	No way! *(informal)* /ˌnəʊ ˈweɪ/	Ausgeschlossen! *hier:* Jetzt echt, oder?	
	better /ˈbetə/	besser	good → **better** → best
	the only one /ðiˌˈəʊnli ˌwʌn/	der/die/das Einzige	
	to be left *(irr)* /ˌbiː ˈleft/	übrig bleiben	
	anyone /ˈeniˌwʌn/	(irgend)jemand	What's 13 x 23? Does **anyone** know the answer?
	to **miss** /mɪs/	vermissen	When I'm on holiday, I always **miss** my cat.
	after all /ˌɑːftər‿ˈɔːl/	schließlich; *hier:* zumindest	
B2	**phrase** /freɪz/	Satz, Ausdruck	*p. 13*
	to **structure** /ˈstrʌktʃə/	strukturieren	
	first /fɜːst/	zuerst, als Erstes	**First** we went to the cinema, then we went to a party.
	love /lʌv/	Liebe; *hier:* alles Liebe *(Briefschlussformel)*	
B3	**city** /ˈsɪti/	(Groß)stadt(-), städtisch	**city** ↔ country
B4	to **fill in** /ˌfɪl‿ˈɪn/	(aus)füllen, eintragen	**Fill in** the grid.
	careful /ˈkeəf(ə)l/	vorsichtig	
B5	to **compare** /kəmˈpeə/	vergleichen	**Compare** them. The girl is taller than the boy.
	delicious /dɪˈlɪʃəs/	köstlich, lecker	This cake is **delicious.** Can I have the recipe?
	support /səˈpɔːt/	Unterstützung; *hier:* Hilfestellung	
	scarf /skɑːf/	Schal	This **scarf** is £14.99.
B7	except /ɪkˈsept/	außer	*p. 14*
	abseiling *(no pl)* /ˈæbseɪlɪŋ/	Abseilen	

	the next day / ðə ˈnekst‿deɪ /	am nächsten Tag		
	zip wire / ˈzɪp ˌwaɪə /	Seilrutsche		
	everyone / ˈevriˌwʌn /	jede/r	**everyone** = everybody	
	around / əˈraʊnd /	umher; um; rund um; um … herum		
	compass / ˈkʌmpəs /	Kompass		
	instructor / ɪnˈstrʌktə /	*hier:* Betreuer/in		
	treasure *(no pl)* / ˈtreʒə /	Schatz		
	woods *(only pl)* / wʊdz /	Wald		
	if / ɪf /	wenn, falls, ob	Please bring me the book **if** you can find it.	
	river / ˈrɪvə /	Fluss	The Thames is a **river**.	
	mark / mɑːk /	Fleck, (Kenn)zeichen; *hier:* Markierung		
	opposite / ˈɒpəzɪt /	gegenüberliegend		
	direction / dɪˈrekʃ(ə)n /	Richtung		
	here you go / ˌhɪə ju ˈgəʊ /	Hier, bitte!, Bitte schön!		
	angrily / ˈæŋgrɪli /	verärgert, zornig, wütend	"Stop it!" he shouted angrily.	
	to **remember** / rɪˈmembə /	sich erinnern	to **remember** ↔ to forget	
	to turn (a)round / ˌtɜːn‿əˈraʊnd /	sich umdrehen		
	the others / ði‿ˈʌðəz /	die anderen		
	however / haʊˈevə /	jedoch		
	while / waɪl /	während	Tom didn't say a word **while** the others laughed.	
	through / θruː /	durch	Let's walk **through** the park.	
	until / ʌnˈtɪl /	bis		
	to **become** / bɪˈkʌm / *simple past:* **became** / bɪˈkeɪm /	werden	**!** *to* ***become*** bedeutet „werden". *to get* bedeutet „bekommen".	
	nervous / ˈnɜːvəs /	nervös	Lucy gets very **nervous** during exams.	
	it's OK *(informal)* / ɪts‿əʊˈkeɪ /	es geht schon		
	almost / ˈɔːlməʊst /	fast, beinahe	It's **almost** one o'clock. 	
	hill / hɪl /	Hügel, Berg		
	to be lost *(irr)* / ˌbiː ˈlɒst /	sich verirrt haben, sich verlaufen haben		
B9	clear / klɪə /	klar, deutlich		p. 15
	structure / ˈstrʌktʃə /	Struktur, Aufbau		
	e.g. / ˌiː ˈdʒiː /	z. B. *(zum Beispiel)*	**e.g.** = for example	
	to connect / kəˈnekt /	verbinden, anschließen		
B10	direct speech / dɪˌrekt ˈspiːtʃ /	direkte Rede		
	different / ˈdɪfrənt /	anders, andere(r, s); *hier:* verschieden	At London Zoo you can see lots of **different** animals.	
	which one / ˈwɪtʃ wʌn /	welche(r, s)		
C1	trouble *(no pl)* / ˈtrʌb(ə)l /	Schwierigkeiten, Ärger		p. 16
	to make sb angry *(irr)* / ˌmeɪk ˌsʌmbədi‿ˈæŋgri /	jdn wütend machen		
	to get into trouble *(irr)* / ˌget‿ɪntʊ ˈtrʌb(ə)l /	in Schwierigkeiten geraten		
C2	to record / rɪˈkɔːd /	aufzeichnen, aufnehmen		
	to **guess** / ges /	(er)raten; *hier:* annehmen	Where's Jill? – I **guess** she's in the cafeteria.	
	head teacher / ˌhed‿ˈtiːtʃə /	Schulleiter/in, Direktor/in		

that /ðæt/	dass	Everybody knows **that** London is in England.
mistake /mɪˈsteɪk/	Fehler, Irrtum, Versehen	
clear /klɪə/	klar, deutlich; *hier:* eindeutig	The school rules about mobile phones are very **clear**.
British /ˈbrɪtɪʃ/	britisch	
unacceptable /ˌʌnəkˈseptəb(ə)l/	inakzeptabel, nicht hinnehmbar	
It won't happen again.	Es wird nicht wieder vorkommen.	
I don't think so.	Das glaube ich nicht.	
maybe /ˈmeɪbi/	vielleicht, möglicherweise	**maybe** = perhaps
bored /bɔːd/	gelangweilt	
fault /fɔːlt/	Schuld, Fehler	
to **phone** /fəʊn/	anrufen, telefonieren	Let's **phone** Lisa. Do you have her phone number?
as /æz/	weil, da	**as** = because
on /ɒn/	*hier:* über; zu	
the Romans /ðə ˈrəʊmənz/	die Römer	
the Celts /ðə ˈkelts/	die Kelten	
C3 to **feel** /fiːl/	(sich) fühlen	Mr Blake **feels** very angry. p. 17
simple past: **felt** /felt/		
to feel sorry *(irr)* /ˌfiːl ˈsɒri/	bedauern, leidtun	
to express /ɪkˈspres/	ausdrücken, aussprechen	
someone /ˈsʌmwʌn/	(irgend)jemand, irgendwer	**someone** = somebody
C4 **anything** /ˈeniθɪŋ/	(irgend)etwas, (irgend)was	The music is too loud. I can't hear **anything**.
C6 **a few** /ə ˈfjuː/	einige, wenige	**a few** ↔ a lot of p. 18
note /nəʊt/	Notiz, Mitteilung	She is writing a **note** during her history lesson. 
each other /ˌiːtʃ‿ˈʌðə/	einander, gegenseitig	
help /help/	Hilfe	If you need **help**, just call me.
to **show** /ʃəʊ/	zeigen	
simple past: **showed** /ʃəʊd/		
Roman /ˈrəʊmən/	Römer/in, römisch	
Celt /kelt/	Kelte/Keltin	
how to /ˈhaʊ tə/	wie man	
to **disagree** /ˌdɪsəˈgriː/	nicht übereinstimmen, nicht einverstanden sein	My friend thinks "Twilight" is the best book ever, but I **disagree**.
to mark /mɑːk/	markieren, kennzeichnen	
C7 favourite /ˈfeɪv(ə)rət/	Liebling, Favorit/in	
material /məˈtɪəriəl/	Material, Stoff	
on /ɒn/	auf; *hier:* zu	For our history project, we need material **on** the Celts.
the BBC (= British Broadcasting Corporation) /ðə ˌbiː biː ˈsiː, ˌbrɪtɪʃ ˈbrɔːdkɑːstɪŋ ˌkɔːpəˌreɪʃ(ə)n/	*britische Rundfunkanstalt*	
without /wɪðˈaʊt/	ohne	**without** ↔ with

C8 announcement /əˈnaʊnsmənt/	Bekanntmachung, Mitteilung, Durchsage	p. 19
over /ˈəʊvə/	über	The head teacher made an announcement **over** the PA system.
PA (= public address) system /ˌpiː‿ˈeɪ ˌsɪstəm, ˌpʌblɪk‿əˈdres‿ˌsɪstəm/	Lautsprecheranlage	
C9 **role** /rəʊl/	Rolle	Lynn is playing the **role** of Cleopatra.
to **think about sb/sth** *(irr)* /ˈθɪŋk‿əˌbaʊt ˌsʌmbədi/ ˌsʌmθɪŋ/	an jdn/etw denken, über jdn/etw nachdenken	That's very difficult. I'll have to **think about it**.
character /ˈkærɪktə/	Charakter, Figur	
what /wɒt/	welche(r, s)	Can you tell me **what** kind of person he is?
kind /kaɪnd/	Art, Sorte	
to **plan** /plæn/	planen	We **are planning** to have a party tomorrow. – Great!
polite /pəˈlaɪt/	höflich	It's not very **polite** to shout in a library.
to start a business /ˌstɑːt‿ə ˈbɪznəs/	ein Unternehmen gründen; *hier:* Handel treiben	
to punish /ˈpʌnɪʃ/	(be)strafen	
to **see** /siː/ *simple past:* **saw** /sɔː/	sehen; *hier:* verstehen	I **see** why you're angry.
such /sʌtʃ/	solch(er/es)	I don't think it's **such** a big problem.
to **save money** /ˌseɪv ˈmʌni/	Geld sparen	He's **saving** his **money** for a new bike. 
convincing /kənˈvɪnsɪŋ/	überzeugend	
language /ˈlæŋgwɪdʒ/	Sprache	French, English and German are **languages**.
to **act** /ækt/	handeln, vorgehen; *hier:* schauspielern	Philip **is acting** in a play.
as /æz/	als	

Say it in English – Theme 1

So kannst du …

nach dem Urlaub fragen	Did you have a good holiday? / How long did you stay? Where did you stay? / What did you do?
sagen, was du in deinen Ferien gemacht hast	I went to Spain. / I went camping. / I stayed at home. I stayed with my grandparents. I stayed for a week/two weeks/a weekend.
sagen, wie dein Urlaub war	I had a wonderful/exciting holiday. It was warm/cold/sunny/rainy. It was cloudy/foggy/snowy.
Vergleiche anstellen	The scarf is cheaper than the T-shirt. The shops in London are bigger than in Wales. It was better than I thought.
über etwas spekulieren	I think they must … / I guess they …
sagen, wie sich jemand fühlt	Mr Jackson feels sad/disappointed/angry. Mrs Edwards feels happy/very angry.
dich für etwas entschuldigen	I'm really sorry.
zugeben, dass du etwas falsch gemacht hast	It was all a stupid mistake. It was wrong to bring the mobile to school.
etwas vorschlagen	Let's ask Charlie for help. / We could ask Mr Jackson for some ideas. / Maybe we can make the presentation a little bit funnier than a normal lesson.
sagen, wie du die Handlungen anderer findest	What they did was stupid/silly/clever/cool because … I think it's OK/not OK/not a big problem if you …
Rückmeldung zu einer Präsentation und einem Poster geben	Your presentation was easy to understand and you spoke clearly. / Your presentation was fun to listen to/was really interesting. Your poster looks neat and tidy but you should speak up more. / Your poster looks attractive but it could be a bit more informative.
Rückmeldung zu einer Geschichte geben	Your story is really interesting but you can make it more exciting by using different adjectives. Your story is great but you need to add more direct speech to make it more interesting. I like your story but you can use more words like 'because' or 'but' to connect some sentences.
Rückmeldung zu einer gespielten Szene geben	Patrick was very good as Salman because he … / Lisa's questions as Mrs Edwards were very good because she asked about … / I liked Jens as Matt because he said …

Theme 2: Let's get the party started

	to get sth started *(irr)* /ˌget ˌsʌmθɪŋ ˈstɑːtɪd/	etw ins Laufen bringen		p. 30
A1	**special** /ˈspeʃ(ə)l/	besondere(r, s)	My birthday is a **special** day for me.	
	Christmas /ˈkrɪsməs/	Weihnachten		
	to **celebrate** /ˈseləˌbreɪt/	feiern	It's your birthday. Let's **celebrate**!	
	decoration /ˌdekəˈreɪʃ(ə)n/	Dekoration, (Christbaum)schmuck		

normal / ˈnɔːm(ə)l /	normal, üblich	
celebration / ˌseləˈbreɪʃ(ə)n /	Feier	
A2 **member** / ˈmembə /	Mitglied	David is a **member** of a football club. p.30/31
reason / ˈriːz(ə)n /	Grund	Why don't you like Jo? What's the **reason**?
Chinese New Year / ˌtʃaɪˌniːz ˌnjuː ˈjɪə /	*Chinesisches Neujahrsfest*	
New Year / ˌnjuː ˈjɪə /	Neujahr	1st January = **New Year**
to **decorate** / ˈdekəreɪt /	dekorieren	to **decorate** – decoration
to put up *(irr)* / ˌpʊt‿ˈʌp /	aufhängen, hochheben	
banner / ˈbænə /	Transparent, Banner, Fahne	
to bring good/bad luck *(irr)* / ˌbrɪŋ‿ˌɡʊd/ˌbæd ˈlʌk /	Glück/Unglück bringen	
luck *(no pl)* / lʌk /	Glück	Good **luck**!
envelope / ˈenvələʊp /	Briefumschlag	
dumpling / ˈdʌmplɪŋ /	Teigtasche	
rice pudding / ˌraɪs ˈpʊdɪŋ /	Milchreis	
famous / ˈfeɪməs /	berühmt	Elvis Presley was a **famous** singer.
dragon / ˈdræɡən /	Drache	
dance *(no pl)* / dɑːns /	Tanz	
noise *(no pl)* / nɔɪz /	Lärm, Krach	There's a lot of **noise** on our street. 
fireworks *(only pl)* / ˈfaɪəˌwɜːks /	Feuerwerk	**fireworks** 
to keep away *(irr)* / ˌkiːp‿əˈweɪ /	fernhalten	
bad luck / ˌbæd ˈlʌk /	Pech, Unglück	
Diwali / dɪˈwɑːli /	*hinduistisches Lichterfest*	
Hindu / ˈhɪnduː /	Hindu, hinduistisch, Hindu-	
festival / ˈfestɪv(ə)l /	Fest	There are many music **festivals** in summer.
to **perform** / pəˈfɔːm /	vorführen, aufführen	They **performed** a fantastic circus show.
goddess / ˈɡɒdes /	Göttin	
wealth / welθ /	Reichtum, Vermögen, Fülle	
candle / ˈkænd(ə)l /	Kerze	
into / ˈɪntuː /	in	
each other / ˌiːtʃ‿ˈʌðə /	einander, gegenseitig	Jo and Tom are talking to **each other**.
the best thing (about) / ðə ˈbest ˌθɪŋ‿əˌbaʊt /	das Beste (an)	
bonfire / ˈbɒnˌfaɪə /	Freudenfeuer, Scheiterhaufen	
to blow up *(irr)* / ˌbləʊ‿ˈʌp /	aufblasen, *hier:* in die Luft sprengen	
Houses of Parliament / ˌhaʊzɪz‿əv ˈpɑː(r)ləmənt /	das Parlament *(von Großbritannien)*	
to **kill** / kɪl /	töten, umbringen	Tigers can **kill** other animals and eat them.
king / kɪŋ /	König	Henry VIII was a famous **king**.
to light / laɪt / *simple past:* lit / lɪt /	anzünden	
past / pɑːst /	Vergangenheit	In the **past**, people didn't have computers.

	dummy /ˈdʌmi/	Puppe	
	penny /ˈpeni/	Penny *(Untereinheit des brit. Pfunds)*	
	baked potato /ˌbeɪkt pəˈteɪtəʊ/	Ofenkartoffel	
	toffee apple /ˈtɒfi‿æp(ə)l/	*kandierter Apfel*	
	to **imagine** /ɪˈmædʒɪn/	sich vorstellen	
	would /wʊd/	würde(n/st/t)	
A3	**English-speaking** /ˈɪŋglɪʃˌspiːkɪŋ/	englischsprachig	England and the USA are **English-speaking** countries.
	Hogmanay /ˈhɒgmənеɪ/	*traditionelles schottisches Neujahrsfest*	
	St Patrick's Day /sənt ˈpætrɪks ˌdeɪ/	*irischer Nationalfeiertag*	
	to **include** /ɪnˈkluːd/	beinhalten, *hier:* mit einschließen	

Beim Vokabellernen

Nicht nur für das Vokabellernen gilt: Du solltest dich an dem Ort, an dem du arbeitest, wohlfühlen und durch nichts abgelenkt sein! Eine gewisse Ordnung erleichtert das Arbeiten. Mache regelmäßig Pausen, in denen du z. B. das Fenster öffnest, etwas trinkst und dich bewegst. So kannst du dich besser konzentrieren.

B1	planner /ˈplænə/	Planer/in	p. 32
B2	**What is ... about?** /ˌwɒt‿ɪz əˈbaʊt/	Worum geht es in/bei ...?	**What is** the film **about?** – It's about a boy who wants to be famous.
	in style /ɪn ˈstaɪl/	stilvoll	
	would like to /wʊd ˈlaɪk tʊ/	würde(n/st/t) gern	Jane **would like to** be famous.
	fabulous /ˈfæbjʊləs/	fabelhaft, sagenhaft	How was your holiday? – It was **fabulous**.
	himself /hɪmˈself/	sich, selbst, *hier:* persönlich	
	message /ˈmesɪdʒ/	Nachricht, Botschaft	James is not here. Would you like to leave a **message**?
B3	**before** /bɪˈfɔː/	bevor, ehe	Let's go home **before** it starts to rain.
	to **close** /kləʊz/	schließen, zumachen	to **close** ↔ to open
	rocket /ˈrɒkɪt/	Rakete	**rocket** 
	banger /ˈbæŋə/	Knaller, Kracher	
	to be crazy about sb/sth /ˌbiː ˈkreɪzi‿əˌbaʊt ˌsʌmbədi/ˌsʌmθɪŋ/	nach jdm/etw verrückt sein	
	noisy /ˈnɔɪzi/	laut	**noisy** ↔ quiet
	the ... the /ðə ðə/	je ..., desto ...	George likes bangers. **The** noisier **the** better!
	sparkler /ˈspɑːklə/	Wunderkerze	
	wouldn't (= **would not**) /ˈwʊd(ə)nt, wʊd ˈnɒt/	würde(n/st/t) nicht	I **wouldn't** like to go to the party.
	quite /kwaɪt/	ziemlich, ganz	Jill can sing and play the piano. She's **quite** good at music.
	anyone in particular /ˌeniˌwʌn‿ɪn pəˈtɪkjʊlə/	jemand Bestimmtes	
	Stop it! /ˈstɒp‿ɪt/	Hör auf!, Hört auf!	
	bossy-boots *(informal)* /ˈbɒsibuːts/	*rechthaberische, belehrende Person*	
	Greek /griːk/	Grieche/Griechin, griechisch	
	whatever /wɒtˈevə/	was auch immer, egal was	

	crisps *(only pl)* / krɪsps /	Chips		
	to **text (sb)** / ˈtekst ˌsʌmbədi /	(jdm) eine SMS senden	Steve **texts** his friends every day.	

crisps

	else / els /	sonst (noch)	Who **else** is coming to the party?	
	the same / ðə ˈseɪm /	der-/die-/dasselbe		
B4	**annoyed** / əˈnɔɪd /	verärgert	My teacher is **annoyed** because I didn't do my homework.	p. 33
	nosy / ˈnəʊzi /	neugierig	Anna is very **nosy**. She likes to know everything about people.	
	bossy / ˈbɒsi /	herrschsüchtig, herrisch	John is **bossy**. He always tells me what to do.	
B5	to **react (to sb / sth)** / riˈækt‿tə ˌsʌmbədi / ˌsʌmθɪŋ /	(auf jdn/etw) reagieren	How did Alex **react to** the bad **news**? – He was very sad.	
	news *(only pl)* / nju:z /	Neuigkeit, Nachricht		
	speaking / ˈspi:kɪŋ /	sprechend, *hier:* am Apparat		
	it's (= it is) / ɪts, ˈɪt‿ɪz /	es ist, *hier:* hier spricht		
	just / dʒʌst /	nur, bloß, einfach, *hier:* gerade	Helen **just** called – What did she say?	
	will / wɪl /	werden		
	guess what / ˌges ˈwɒt /	stell dir vor!, rate mal!		
	as / æz /	als, *hier:* wie		
	us *(informal)* / ʌs /	uns, *hier:* wir		
	What a / an ...! / ˈwɒt‿ə /	Was für ein(e) ... !		
	mess / mes /	Unordnung, Durcheinander		
	to sort out / ˌsɔ:t‿ˈaʊt /	klären/regeln		
	won't (= will not) / ˈwəʊnt, wɪl ˈnɒt /	nicht werden		
B6	**tense** / tens /	Zeitform, Tempus	The simple present and the simple past are **tenses**.	p. 34
	future / ˈfju:tʃə /	Zukunft		
	positive / ˈpɒzətɪv /	positiv, *hier:* bejahend		
	negative / ˈnegətɪv /	negativ, ablehnend, *hier:* verneinend		
	to **form** / fɔ:m /	formen, bilden	Can you **form** a sentence in French?	
	to introduce / ˌɪntrəˈdju:s /	vorstellen, *hier:* einleiten		
B8	**probably** / ˈprɒbəbli /	wahrscheinlich	I can **probably** come to your party, but I am not 100% sure.	p. 35
	to **be upset (about sth)** *(irr)* / ˌbi‿ʌpˈset‿əˌbaʊt ˌsʌmθɪŋ /	(über etw) traurig/aufgebracht sein	Karen's cat is ill. She **is** very **upset about** it.	
	soon / su:n /	bald	When is your birthday? – It's **soon**. It's next week.	
	part / pɑ:t /	Teil	Which **part** of the story did you like best?	
B9	to **feel** / fi:l /	(sich) fühlen, *hier:* halten von	How do you **feel** about my idea?	
	necessary / ˈnesəs(ə)ri /	nötig, notwendig, erforderlich		
C1	to **make** / meɪk / *simple past:* **made** / meɪd /	machen, *hier:* ausmachen	What **makes** a great party?	p. 36
C2	to **expect** / ɪkˈspekt /	erwarten, rechnen		
	actually / ˈæktʃuəli /	eigentlich, wirklich, *hier:* tatsächlich		

to **speak to sb** *(irr)* / ˈspiːk tʊ ˌsʌmbədi /	mit jdm reden	Tom is very sad. I must **speak to** him.
to follow sb around / ˌfɒləʊ ˌsʌmbədi‿əˈraʊnd /	jdm überallhin folgen	
embarrassing / ɪmˈbærəsɪŋ /	peinlich, unangenehm	I forgot your birthday. How **embarrassing**!
to have a crush on sb *(irr)* / ˌhæv‿ə ˈkrʌʃ‿ɒn ˌsʌmbədi /	in jdn verknallt sein	
to **want sb to do sth** / ˌwɒnt ˌsʌmbədi tə ˈduː ˌsʌmθɪŋ /	wollen, dass jd etw tut	
embarrassed / ɪmˈbærəst /	verlegen, peinlich berührt	
still / stɪl /	(immer) noch, noch immer	Zoe is **still** in bed at 11 o'clock.
important / ɪmˈpɔːt(ə)nt /	wichtig, wesentlich, bedeutend	Don't forget it. It's **important**.
C3 **conversation** / ˌkɒnvəˈseɪʃ(ə)n /	Gespräch, Unterhaltung	I had a **conversation** with my brother. We talked for hours. *p. 37*
C5 **about** / əˈbaʊt /	über, *hier:* wegen	My parents are worried **about** my exam results.
preparation / ˌprepəˈreɪʃ(ə)n /	Vorbereitung, Zubereitung	There is lots of **preparation** to do for the party.
bored / bɔːd /	gelangweilt	I have nothing to do. I am **bored**.
to **get scared** *(irr)* / ˌget ˈskeəd /	sich (anfangen zu) fürchten	My dog **gets scared** when it's noisy.
C7 **everyone** / ˈevriˌwʌn /	jede/r, *hier:* alle zusammen	Hello **everyone**! *p. 38*
guy / gaɪ /	Kerl, Typ, *hier:* Guy-Fawkes-Puppe	
might / maɪt /	vielleicht	
samosa / səˈməʊsə /	*indische Teigtasche*	
to **die (of)** / ˈdaɪ‿əv /	sterben (an)	to **die** ↔ to live

Gegensätze

Inzwischen kennst du schon sehr viele englische Wörter. Von vielen Wörtern gibt es Gegensätze. Um dir Wörter leichter zu merken, kannst du dir Gegensätze notieren, z. B.:

to remember ↔ to forget
start ↔ end
a few ↔ a lot of

inside / ˈɪnˌsaɪd /	innen, drinnen, *hier:* nach drinnen	Let's go **inside**, it's starting to rain.
to spoil / spɔɪl /	verderben, ruinieren	
doorbell / ˈdɔːbel /	Türklingel	
caption / ˈkæpʃ(ə)n /	Überschrift, Titel, Bildunterschrift	
toward(s) / təˈwɔːdz /	in Richtung, *hier:* gegenüber	
to land / lænd /	landen	
to go off *(irr)* / ˌgəʊ‿ˈɒf /	hochgehen, explodieren	
at once / æt ˈwʌns /	sofort	
so / səʊ /	so, *hier:* sehr	I'm **so** happy. = I'm very happy.
although / ɔːlˈðəʊ /	obwohl	
to **get** / get / *simple past:* **got** / gɒt /	erhalten, bekommen, *hier:* werden	It's **getting** late. I must go now.
around / əˈraʊnd /	um ... herum	
to **cheer up** / ˌtʃɪər‿ˈʌp /	aufmuntern	She's so sad. We must **cheer** her **up**.
to **carry** / ˈkæri /	tragen	She's **carrying** five bags. 

C8	atmosphere /ˈætməsˌfɪə/	Atmosphäre, Stimmung		p. 39
	beginning /bɪˈɡɪnɪŋ/	Anfang, Beginn	**beginning** ↔ end	
	by heart /ˌbaɪ ˈhɑːt/	auswendig	Did you learn the poem **by heart**?	
C9	to **ring (up)** /ˌrɪŋ‿ˈʌp/ *simple past:* **rang (up)** /ˌræŋ‿ˈʌp/	anrufen, klingeln, läuten	Sophie **rings** her grandmother every weekend to talk to her.	
C10	to **speculate (on)** /ˈspekjuleɪt‿ɒn/	spekulieren, Vermutungen anstellen (über)	We don't know why. We can only **speculate**.	
	to **organize** /ˈɔːɡənaɪz/	organisieren	Let's **organize** a party!	
	to **agree (on)** /əˈɡriː‿ɒn/	zustimmen, *hier:* sich einigen (auf)	Do you want to meet tomorrow or on Friday? We need to **agree on** a day.	
	speech bubble /ˈspiːtʃˌbʌb(ə)l/	Sprechblase		

Say it in English – Theme 2

So kannst du …

über Feste sprechen	Diwali is a holiday that Hindus celebrate every year in October or November. Diwali is a holiday that is famous for its fireworks. For Diwali people give each other presents, send cards and eat sweets. The reason why people celebrate Bonfire Night is that they want to remember November 5th 1605, when the plan to kill King James I did not work.
sagen, wie jemand sich fühlt	Alex feels angry/annoyed. Kate is nervous/surprised.
Vermutungen äußern	Maybe they will celebrate together because … I guess they won't celebrate together because … I don't think she will like the idea because …
sagen, was du erwartest	I expect the food will be good.
Vorschläge machen	Don't you think it would be a good idea to have just one party? Why don't we mix Bonfire Night and Diwali? What about one big party at our house? Let's just celebrate in one place.
Bedingungen ausdrücken	If you like, I'll invite Denah, too. If you invite her, I'll never speak to you again!

Theme 3: London

A2	**sight** /saɪt/	Sehenswürdigkeit	Big Ben and the London Eye are famous London **sights**.	p. 48
	order /ˈɔːdə/	Ordnung, Reihenfolge		
	about /əˈbaʊt/	über, *hier:* an	What is special **about** London?	
A3	bottom /ˈbɒtəm/	Boden, (unteres) Ende		p. 49
	page /peɪdʒ/	Seite	Look at **page** 48 of your book.	
	to make sb do sth *(irr)* /ˌmeɪk ˌsʌmbədi ˈduː ˌsʌmθɪŋ/	jdn zu etwas bringen, jdn etwas tun lassen		
	to be worth sth /ˌbiː ˈwɜːθ ˌsʌmθɪŋ/	etw wert sein		
	visit /ˈvɪzɪt/	Besuch		

attraction / əˈtrækʃ(ə)n /	(Touristen)attraktion	Vicky thinks the best **attraction** in London is Big Ben.
I'd like to (= I would like to) / aɪd ˈlaɪk tʊ, aɪ ˌwʊd ˈlaɪk tʊ /	ich würde gern	
A4 **corner** / ˈkɔːnə /	Ecke	The house is on the **corner** of New Street. 
acrobat / ˈækrəˌbæt /	Akrobat/in	
musician / mjuˈzɪʃ(ə)n /	Musiker/in	
once / wʌns /	früher, einst	
vegetable / ˈvedʒtəb(ə)l /	Gemüse	**vegetables** 
to watch out (for) / ˌwɒtʃ‿ˈaʊt fɔː /	aufpassen (auf)	
right / raɪt /	gleich, direkt	
across / əˈkrɒs /	über, *hier:* jenseits; gegenüberliegend	My house is **across** the road. Over there!
costume / ˈkɒstjuːm /	Kostüm	At Halloween, people wear **costumes**.
prop / prɒp /	Requisite	
programme / ˈprəʊɡræm /	Programm, Sendung	
to **get into** *(irr)* / ˈget‿ˌɪntʊ /	einsteigen in	**Get into** the car! We have to leave now.
yourself (*pl* yourselves) / jəˈself, jəˈselvz /	dich, dir, selbst	
to race / reɪs /	rennen, *hier:* rasen	
to be into sb/sth *(irr) (informal)* / ˌbi‿ˈɪntuː ˌsʌmbədi / ˌsʌmθɪŋ /	an jdm/etw interessiert sein	
spectacular / spekˈtækjʊlə /	atemberaubend, fantastisch	The holiday was **spectacular**. Everyone really enjoyed it.
stadium / ˈsteɪdiəm /	Stadion	**stadium** 
virtual / ˈvɜːtʃʊəl /	virtuell	
(a) must *(no pl)* / ə ˈmʌst /	(ein) Muss	
stunning / ˈstʌnɪŋ /	toll, fantastisch, umwerfend	It was a **stunning** film. We all liked it.
to **explore** / ɪkˈsplɔː /	erforschen, untersuchen	We have only one day to **explore** the city.
the universe / ðə ˈjuːnɪˌvɜːs /	das Universum	
to **change** / ˈtʃeɪndʒ /	(ver)ändern	Some things never **change**.
for free *(informal)* / fə ˈfriː /	gratis, umsonst	You can get into the Science Museum **for free**.
still / stɪl /	trotzdem	You don't like art? You should **still** visit the Tate Modern just to see the **building**.
building / ˈbɪldɪŋ /	Gebäude	
power station / ˈpaʊə ˌsteɪʃ(ə)n /	Kraftwerk	
floor / flɔː /	Boden, *hier:* Stock(werk)	Sarah lives on the 7th **floor**.
view / vjuː /	(Aus)sicht, (Aus)blick	He is enjoying the spectacular **view**. 
B1 **to show sb (a)round** *(irr)* / ˌʃəʊ ˌsʌmbədi‿əˈraʊnd /	jdn herumführen	When you come to visit, I will **show you around** the city. p. 50
to **wait** / weɪt /	warten, *hier:* erwarten	It's my birthday soon. I can't **wait**!
before / bɪˈfɔː /	zuvor, vorher	Have you been to London **before**?
though / ðəʊ /	trotzdem, *hier:* aber	I like warm weather. I hope it's not too hot, **though**.
natural history *(no pl)* / ˌnætʃ(ə)rəl ˈhɪst(ə)ri /	Naturkunde	
yet / jet /	bis jetzt, schon, noch	Have you met our new teacher **yet**?
especially / ɪˈspeʃ(ə)li /	besonders, insbesondere	

I'd (= I would) /aɪd, aɪ ˈwʊd/	ich würde	
not ... anything else /nɒt ˌeniθɪŋ‿ˈels/	gar nichts anderes	
since /sɪns/	seitdem, seither	Daniel has won tickets for the football match. He hasn't talked about anything else **since**.
there /ðeə/	dahin, dorthin	
Chamber of Horrors /ˈtʃeɪmbər‿əv ˈhɒrəz/	Horrorkabinett	
anyway /ˈeniˌweɪ/	sowieso, jedenfalls, *hier:* na ja	
You must be joking! *(informal)* /juː məs bi ˈdʒəʊkɪŋ/	Das meinst du doch nicht im Ernst!	
to turn /tɜːn/	(sich) umdrehen, *hier:* werden	
honest /ˈɒnɪst/	ehrlich	What about the Tate Modern? – To be **honest**, I'm not into art.
to **change one's mind** /ˌtʃeɪndʒ wʌnz ˈmaɪnd/	es sich anders überlegen, *hier:* seine Meinung ändern	Michael won't come to the party. He **has changed his mind**.
store /stɔː/	Laden, Geschäft, Kaufhaus	
busy /ˈbɪzi/	beschäftigt, arbeitsreich, *hier:* ereignisreich	We're going to have a **busy** weekend: London Zoo, Madame Tussauds, the London Eye ...
to **go on a tour** *(irr)* /ˌgəʊ‿ɒn‿ə ˈtʊə/	eine Tour machen	Let's **go on a** sightseeing **tour**!
to **pay** /peɪ/	(be)zahlen	My parents have offered to **pay** for tickets.
suggestion /səˈdʒestʃ(ə)n/	Vorschlag	 He's making a **suggestion**.

B2

Unregelmäßige Verben

Unregelmäßige Verben haben unregelmäßige Formen: für das *simple past* und auch für das Partizip Perfekt. Diese Formen solltest du wie Vokabeln lernen, z. B. für *to do*: *did (simple past)* und *done* (Partizip Perfekt). Du findest die Formen in der Liste der unregelmäßigen Verben (S. 219).
Sie werden immer so angegeben: *to do, did, done*.

Infinitiv — *simple past* — Partizip Perfekt

B3 **before** /bɪˈfɔː/	vor	**before** ↔ after p. 51
to **pack one's bags** /ˌpæk wʌnz ˈbægz/	die Koffer packen	Jason had one hour to **pack his bags** for his holiday.
to **look up sth** /ˌlʊk‿ˈʌp ˌsʌmθɪŋ/	etw nachschlagen, etw heraussuchen	When does the show begin? – I don't know. I must **look it up**.

Verben und Präpositionen zusammen lernen

Folgt einem Verb eine Präposition, dann verändert sich dadurch die Bedeutung des Verbs, z. B. bei *to look*:

*to **look up*** (nachschlagen)	*You can **look up** the word in the dictionary.*
*to **look at*** (ansehen)	***Look at** that picture.*
*to **look for*** (suchen)	*Kemi is **looking for** her pencil.*
*to **look after*** (sich kümmern um)	*Gillian wants to **look after** a dog.*
*to **look forward to*** (sich freuen auf)	*Charlie is **looking forward to** the party.*

Daher ist es wichtig, dass du dir nicht nur das Verb, sondern auch die dazugehörigen Präpositionen notierst. Mithilfe von Beispielsätzen kannst du dir die unterschiedlichen Bedeutungen leichter merken.

	train /treɪn/	Zug	**train**
	battery /ˈbæt(ə)ri/	Batterie	
	to email /ˈiːmeɪl/	e-mailen, eine E-Mail schreiben	
B4	**top** /tɒp/	oberes Ende, Spitze	
	middle /ˈmɪd(ə)l/	Mitte	
	letter /ˈletə/	Brief, *hier:* Buchstabe	
	below /bɪˈləʊ/	unter, unterhalb	
	heading /ˈhedɪŋ/	Überschrift, Titel	
	choice /tʃɔɪs/	Wahl	
B5	meaning /ˈmiːnɪŋ/	Bedeutung	
	similar /ˈsɪmɪlə/	ähnlich	Tom and Greg are brothers. They look **similar**.
	dictionary /ˈdɪkʃən(ə)ri/	Wörterbuch	Look the word up in a **dictionary**!

Wortfelder

Inzwischen weißt du ja schon, wie man Wortfelder zusammenstellt. Du lernst immer mehr neue Wörter – und da sind sicherlich einige dabei, die in Wortfelder passen, die du früher schon mal angelegt hast. Ergänze deine alten Listen und schau dir die alten Wörter noch einmal an.

B6	search /sɜːtʃ/	Suche, *hier:* Suchaufgabe	
B7	to hop on/off /ˌhɒp‿ˈɒn, ˌhɒp‿ˈɒf/	schnell ein-/aussteigen	p. 52
	ever /ˈevə(r)/	jemals	Have you **ever** been to London?
	double-decker /ˌdʌb(ə)l ˈdekə/	Doppeldecker	
	all over the place /ˌɔːl‿ˈəʊvə ðə ˌpleɪs/	überall	
	battleship /ˈbæt(ə)lʃɪp/	Schlachtschiff	
	not that high on my list	nicht so weit oben auf meiner Liste	
	anyway /ˈeniˌweɪ/	sowieso, jedenfalls, *hier:* ohnehin	The teacher explained the task to us again but we knew it **anyway**.
	to **book** /bʊk/	reservieren, buchen	We should **book** the hotel soon.
	even if /ˈiːv(ə)n‿ɪf/	selbst wenn	
	to **admit** /ədˈmɪt/	zugeben	Helen did not want to **admit** her mistake.
	the real thing /ðə ˈrɪəl ˌθɪŋ/	das Echte, das Wahre	
	phone call (= **telephone call**) /ˈfəʊn ˌkɔːl, ˈtelɪˌfəʊn ˌkɔːl/	Anruf, Telefongespräch	Anna has just called. – What was the **phone call** about?
B8	like this /ˌlaɪk ˈðɪs/	so, auf diese Weise	p. 53
B9	**winner** /ˈwɪnə/	Gewinner/in, Sieger/in	No. 19 is the **winner**.
	queen /kwiːn/	Königin	
	to **go on a trip** *(irr)* /ˌgəʊ‿ˈɒn‿ə ˈtrɪp/	einen Ausflug/eine Reise machen	The weather is great. Let's **go on a trip** to the seaside!
	step /step/	Schritt, *hier:* (Treppen)stufe	
	inside /ˈɪnˌsaɪd/	innen, drinnen, im Inneren	It was very warm **inside** the house.

	squirrel /ˈskwɪrəl/	Eichhörnchen		
C1	to **lose one's way** *(irr)* /ˌluːz wʌnz ˈweɪ/	sich verirren	I don't know where I am. **I've lost my way.**	p. 54
	to lose sight of *(irr)* /ˌluːz‿ˈsaɪt‿əv/	aus den Augen verlieren		
	frightened /ˈfraɪt(ə)nd/	verängstigt	William was very **frightened** when he lost his way.	
C2	well-organized /ˌwel‿ˈɔːgənaɪzd/	gut organisiert		
	only /ˈəʊnli/	nur, *hier:* erst	It's **only** 3 o'clock and I'm already hungry!	
	to **lose, lost, lost** /luːz, lɒst, lɒst/	verlieren, *hier:* aus den Augen verlieren		
	Tube /tjuːb/	*hier:* die (Londoner) U-Bahn		
	full /fʊl/	voll, *hier:* überfüllt	The Tube is usually very **full**.	
	to **get off** /ˌget‿ˈɒf/	aussteigen	Let's **get off** the train at Baker Street.	
	not ... anymore /nɒt‿ˌeniˈmɔː/	nicht mehr	I **don't** talk to him **anymore**.	
	station /ˈsteɪʃ(ə)n/	Bahnhof, Haltestelle, Station	Baker Street is one of the biggest Underground **stations** in London.	
	to **get lost** *(irr)*/ˌget ˈlɒst/	sich verirren, sich verlaufen	to **get lost** = to lose one's way	
	bathroom /ˈbɑːθˌruːm/	Bad(ezimmer)		
	here /hɪə/	hierher		
	dead /ded/	tot		
	to charge /tʃɑːdʒ/	aufladen		
	that's why /ˈðæts ˌwaɪ/	deshalb, darum, deswegen	Ryan is ill. **That's why** he can't come.	
	the Underground *(no pl)* /ði‿ˈʌndəˌgraʊnd/	U-Bahn	Let's take **the Underground**. It's faster than the bus.	
	road /rəʊd/	Straße	**road** 	
	sign /saɪn/	Zeichen, (Straßen-/Verkehrs)schild	**sign** 	
	huge /hjuːdʒ/	riesig, riesengroß		
	queue /kjuː/	Schlange, Reihe		

Giving directions

directions *(only pl)* /dɪˈrekʃ(ə)nz/	Anweisungen, Instruktionen, *hier:* Wegbeschreibung	
past /pɑːst/	an ... vorbei, hinter, nach	Walk **past** the hotel.
along /əˈlɒŋ/	entlang	Walk **along** the road.
to **turn right/left** /ˌtɜːn ˈraɪt/ˈleft/	rechts/links abbiegen	**Turn left/right** at the hotel.
to walk (straight) on /ˌwɔːk‿ˈɒn, ˌwɔːk ˌstreɪt‿ˈɒn/	(immer geradeaus) weiterlaufen	**Walk straight on.**
to **cross** /krɒs/	überqueren	**Cross** the **main street** when you see a big, red building.
main /meɪn/	Haupt-	

	it says /ɪt ˈsez/	darauf steht		
C3	**church** /tʃɜːtʃ/	Kirche	**church** 	p. 55
	hospital /ˈhɒspɪt(ə)l/	Krankenhaus	Olivia's dad is in **hospital**. He's very ill.	
	university /ˌjuːnɪˈvɜːsəti/	Universität(-s)		

	till (= **until**) / tɪl, ʌn'tɪl /	bis	Walk on **until** you see a big, green building.
C5	to **describe** / dɪ'skraɪb /	beschreiben	
	which / wɪtʃ /	der/die/das	This is the house **which** my parents bought in 1995.
	to **belong to sb** / bɪ'lɒŋ tə ˌsʌmbədi /	jdm gehören	This isn't my car. It **belongs to** my sister.
	Sir / sɜː /	*engl. Adelstitel*	
	writer / 'raɪtə /	Verfasser/in, Autor/in	Charles Dickens was a famous **writer**.
	who / huː /	der/die/das	Sir Arthur Conan Doyle is the writer **who** created Sherlock Holmes.
	to create / kri'eɪt /	erschaffen	
	to star in a film/play / ˌstɑːr‿ɪn‿ə 'fɪlm/'pleɪ /	in einem Film/Theaterstück die Hauptrolle spielen	
	to **look around** / ˌlʊk‿ə'raʊnd /	sich umsehen	**Look around.** What can you see?
	narrow / 'nærəʊ /	eng, schmal	
	light / laɪt /	Licht, Lichtquelle, Lampe	The **light** went out. It was dark.
	strong / strɒŋ /	stark, kräftig, fest	He's very **strong**.
	gaslight / 'gæsˌlaɪt /	Gaslampe	
	century / 'sentʃəri /	Jahrhundert	a **century** = 100 years
	study / 'stʌdi /	Arbeitszimmer	
	medical bag / 'medɪk(ə)l ˌbæg /	Arztkoffer	
	bedroom / 'bedruːm /	Schlafzimmer	I sleep in my **bedroom**.
	criminal / 'krɪmɪn(ə)l /	Verbrecher/in	
	upstairs / ʌp'steəz /	(nach) oben	
	to shoot sb, shot sb, shot sb / 'ʃuːt, ʃɒt, ʃɒt ˌsʌmbədi /	jdn anschießen, jdn erschießen	
	weapon / 'wepən /	Waffe	
	°London Dungeon / ˌlʌndən 'dʌndʒ(ə)n /	*Londoner Gruselmuseum*	
	horrible / 'hɒrəb(ə)l /	schrecklich	**horrible** = terrible
	poor / pɔː /	arm	Oh, **poor** Socks! She looks cold.
	trapdoor / 'træpˌdɔː /	Falltür	
	it says so / ɪt 'sez‿səʊ /	es steht da	
	to **have a look** *(irr)* / ˌhæv‿ə 'lʊk /	nachsehen, nachschauen	I need a T-shirt. Let's **have a look** in the shop.
	to get home *(irr)* / ˌget 'həʊm /	nach Hause kommen	
	gallery / 'gæləri /	Galerie	
	actor / 'æktə /	Schauspieler	Brad Pitt and George Clooney are famous **actors**.
C8	guidebook / 'gaɪdˌbʊk /	Reiseführer	
	area / 'eəriə /	Gebiet, Region, Gegend	What **area** of London do you live in?
	paragraph / 'pærəˌgrɑːf /	Absatz, Abschnitt	

p. 57

Wordbanks p. 149 | **Word lists p. 154** | English-German dictionary p. 186

Say it in English – Theme 3

So kannst du ...

über Sehenswürdigkeiten reden	This is a fantastic place to spend some time. This is the ideal place to visit if you're into football. You can do a fascinating tour of the stadium. The Tate Modern is worth a visit just to see the building. If you're into science, the Science Museum is an absolute must. And the best thing is: it's for free.
Vorschläge machen	We could do Buckingham Palace. And what about Notting Hill? If you're into stars, what about Madam Tussauds? Why don't we go on a sightseeing tour?
sagen, was du gerne ansehen würdest	I'd love to go to Buckingham Palace. I've always wanted to go to Madame Tussauds. I think the Emirates Stadium sounds great. I'd really like to go to a big music store.
Zustimmung ausdrücken	Sounds great! Great idea! Could be fun on a sunny day.
Ablehnung ausdrücken	You must be joking! It's not that high on my list.
eine Broschüre beschreiben	At the top/At the bottom there is ... In the middle there are ... Below the heading there is ...
sagen, wo du schon/noch nicht warst	I've never been to ... I've visited ..., but I haven't ...
fragen, ob jemand etwas schon gesehen hat	Have you seen ...?
eine Wegbeschreibung geben	Walk straight on. Turn left/right. Walk past the park. / Walk on till you get to the church. Cross the street. On your left/right there is a ...

Theme 4: School life

A1	to **hate to do** / ˌheɪt‿tə ˈduː /	etw äußerst ungern tun		p. 68
	jumble sale / ˈdʒʌmb(ə)l seɪl /	Flohmarkt, Wohltätigkeitsbasar		
	fundraising / ˈfʌndreɪzɪŋ /	Geldbeschaffung, Wohltätigkeits-/Benefiz-		
	toy / tɔɪ /	Spielzeug(-)	Caroline collects **toy** elephants.	
	be able to do sth *(irr)* / ˌbi‿ˌeɪbl tə ˈduː ˌsʌmθɪŋ /	etw tun können	I'm ill. I'**m not able to** go to school.	
	department / dɪˈpɑːtmənt /	Institut, Abteilung		
	to contact sb / ˈkɒntækt ˌsʌmbədi /	sich mit jdm in Verbindung setzen		
	pre- / priː /	Vor-		
	concert / ˈkɒnsət /	Konzert	The band played for three hours. It was a great **concert**!	
	choir / ˈkwaɪə /	Chor		

symphony orchestra /ˈsɪmfəni‿ɔːkɪstrə/	Sinfonieorchester	
selection /sɪˈlekʃ(ə)n/	Auswahl	
popular /ˈpɒpjʊlə/	beliebt, populär	Football is the most **popular** sport in England.
main hall /ˌmeɪn ˈhɔːl/	Hauptsaal	
included /ɪnˈkluːdɪd/	inklusive	
drink /drɪŋk/	Getränk	**drink** ↔ food
prize /praɪz/	(Sieg)preis, Gewinn	
winning team /ˌwɪnɪŋ ˈtiːm/	Siegermannschaft	
A2 to **include** /ɪnˈkluːd/	beinhalten, *hier:* aufnehmen	
age /eɪdʒ/	Alter	What's your **age**? – I'm twelve years old.
A3 article /ɑːtɪk(ə)l/	Artikel	p. 69
praise *(no pl)* /preɪz/	Lob	
to praise /preɪz/	loben	
success *(no pl)* /səkˈses/	Erfolg	Everybody is cheering. The show is a real **success**.
to **perform** /pəˈfɔːm/	vorführen, aufführen, *hier:* auftreten	The pupils **performed** in the assembly hall.
hard /hɑːd/	hart, schwer, schwierig	All the pupils worked **hard** for the exam.
across /əˈkrɒs/	über, *hier:* in ganz	
reward /rɪˈwɔːd/	Belohnung, Anerkennung	
year /jɪə/	Jahr; *hier:* (Schul-)Jahrgang	Every pupil in **Year** 8 can take part in the school project.
to represent sb/sth /ˌreprɪˈzent ˌsʌmbədi/ˌsʌmθɪŋ/	jdn/etw repräsentieren, jdn vertreten	
company /ˈkʌmp(ə)ni/	Firma, *hier:* Truppe, Ensemble	
half (*pl* halves) /hɑːf, hɑːvz/	Hälfte	
piece /piːs/	Stück	
act /ækt/	Akt, (Show)nummer	
to **receive** /rɪˈsiːv/	erhalten, bekommen	**Have** you **received** my email?
never-ending /ˌnevərˈendɪŋ/	endlos, unaufhörlich	
applause *(no pl)* /əˈplɔːz/	Applaus, Beifall	
stage /steɪdʒ/	Bühne	All of Year 7 were on the **stage** and performed a fantastic show.
brilliant *(informal)* /ˈbrɪljənt/	*hier:* toll, klasse	The girls looked **brilliant** in their costumes.
excellent /ˈeksələnt/	ausgezeichnet	He's very good at playing the guitar. He's an **excellent** musician.
audience /ˈɔːdiəns/	Publikum, Besucher, Zuschauer	After the concert, the **audience** cheered for ten minutes.
A5 **title** /ˈtaɪt(ə)l/	Titel	What's the **title** of your favourite book?
introduction /ˌɪntrəˈdʌkʃ(ə)n/	Vorstellung, *hier:* Einleitung	
detail /ˈdiːteɪl/	Detail, Einzelheit	
to **comment (on)** /ˈkɒment‿ɒn/	kommentieren	
ending /ˈendɪŋ/	Ende, Schluss	
B1 talent /ˈtælənt/	Talent, Begabung	p. 70
audition /ɔːˈdɪʃ(ə)n/	Vorsprechen, Vorsingen, Vorspielen	
Ms /məz/	Fr., Frau *(Alternativbezeichnung zu Mrs und Miss, die sowohl für verheiratete wie unverheiratete Frauen zutrifft)*	

play /pleɪ/	Spiel, *hier:* (Theater)stück	The actors performed a fantastic **play**.
comedy /ˈkɒmədi/	Komödie	
for a while /fər‿ə ˈwaɪl/	eine ganze Weile, *hier:* schon länger	
for /fər/	seit	
ages /eɪdʒɪz/	eine Ewigkeit, Ewigkeiten	
silly /ˈsɪli/	Dussel, Dummerchen	
classic /ˈklæsɪk/	Klassiker	
by /baɪ/	von	*Romeo and Juliet* is a play **by** William Shakespeare.
totally /ˈtəʊt(ə)li/	völlig, total	
to **do research** *(irr)* /ˌduː ˈriːsɜːtʃ/	(er)forschen, recherchieren	They **did** some **research** on the Internet for their project.
invasion /ɪnˈveɪʒ(ə)n/	Invasion, Eindringen	
let me see /ˌlet mi ˈsiː/	Moment (mal), also	
proper /ˈprɒpə/	echt, richtig	Karen always starts the day with a **proper** breakfast.
to **suggest** /səˈdʒest/	vorschlagen	Let's play a game. – What game do you **suggest**?
ago /əˈgəʊ/	vor	They moved to London two years **ago**.

for /fɔː/ und *since* /sɪns/

For und *since* kannst du mit *seit* übersetzen. Sie werden unterschiedlich verwendet:

for verwendest du mit einem Zeitraum: *They have been neighbours **for five years**.*
since verwendest du mit einem Zeitpunkt: *I haven't seen her **since Sunday**.*

For und *since* werden mit dem *present perfect* verwendet.

girly /ˈgɜːli/	mädchenhaft	
stuff *(no pl, informal)* /stʌf/	Zeug, Sachen	
twilight /ˈtwaɪlaɪt/	Dämmerung, Zwielicht	
vampire /ˈvæmpaɪə/	Vampir/in	**vampire** 
to **persuade** /pəˈsweɪd/	überreden, überzeugen	We couldn't **persuade** him to change his mind.
B4 for how long /fə ˈhaʊ ˌlɒŋ/	wie lange (schon)	p. 71
to dream (of), dreamt/dreamed, dreamt/dreamed /ˈdriːm‿əv, ˈdremt/ˈdriːmd/	träumen (von)	
B5 **argument** /ˈɑːgjʊmənt/	Auseinandersetzung; Argument	Caroline and George had an **argument** about their party.
B8 to **copy** /ˈkɒpi/	abschreiben, niederschreiben, *hier:* kopieren	John always **copies** Anne's maths homework.
script /skrɪpt/	Drehbuch, Skript, Regiebuch	
secretary /ˈsekrətri/	Sekretär/in	
assembly hall /əˈsembli ˌhɔːl/	(Versammlungs)saal, Aula	
B9 **text message** /ˈtekst ˌmesɪdʒ/	SMS	Steve is writing a **text message**. 
B10 **melody** /ˈmelədi/	Melodie	This song has a nice **melody** and great **lyrics**. p. 73
lyrics *(only pl)* /ˈlɪrɪks/	(Lied)text	
slow /sləʊ/	langsam	**slow** ↔ fast
cheerful /ˈtʃɪəf(ə)l/	fröhlich, vergnügt, heiter	
B11 **eerie** /ˈɪəri/	unheimlich	She was scared because there was an **eerie** noise.
to creep, crept, crept /kriːp, krept, krept/	kriechen, steigen	

	basement /ˈbeɪsmənt/	Untergeschoss, Keller	
	to lurk /lɜːk/	lauern, sich verborgen halten	
	shadow /ˈʃædəʊ/	Schatten	
	to give sb a scare *(irr)* /ˌɡɪv ˌsʌmbədi‿ə ˈskeə/	jdm einen Schreck einjagen	
	such /sʌtʃ/	so	
	ghostly /ˈɡəʊstli/	geisterhaft	
	skin *(no pl)* /skɪn/	Haut	Her **skin** was very red because of the sun.
	pointy /ˈpɔɪnti/	spitz	
	to **bite, bit, bitten** /baɪt, bɪt, bɪt(ə)n/	beißen	Yesterday a dog **bit** me.
	to hang out with sb *(irr)* /ˌhæŋ‿ˈaʊt wɪð ˌsʌmbədi/	Zeit mit jdm verbringen	
	at all /æt‿ˈɔːl/	überhaupt	Do you like dancing? – No. Not **at all**.
	verse /vɜːs/	Strophe	The first **verse** of the song is the best.
B12	**singer** /ˈsɪŋə/	Sänger/in	My favourite **singer** is Adele.
	profile /ˈprəʊfaɪl/	Profil, Porträt	
C1	leading role /ˌliːdɪŋ ˈrəʊl/	Hauptrolle	p. 74
	convincing /kənˈvɪnsɪŋ/	überzeugend	Dan was very **convincing**. Everybody believed him.
	just /dʒʌst/	genau	
	actress /ˈæktrəs/	Schauspielerin	Angelina Jolie is Katy's favourite **actress**.
	admiring /ədˈmaɪərɪŋ/	bewundernd	
	to roll one's eyes /ˌrəʊl wʌnz‿ˈaɪz/	die Augen verdrehen	
	to pull a face /ˌpʊl‿ə ˈfeɪs/	das Gesicht verziehen	
	kind /kaɪnd/	nett, freundlich, liebenswürdig	Billy was very **kind**. He helped the old lady.
	forever /fərˈevə/	ewig, ständig	He said, "I will love you **forever**."
	Miss /mɪs/	*hier:* Frau Lehrerin *(Anrede)*	
	to **whisper** /ˈwɪspə/	flüstern	to **whisper** ↔ to shout
	What's wrong? /ˌwɒts‿ˈrɒŋ/	Was ist los?	
	outside /ˌaʊtˈsaɪd/	außen, außerhalb, *hier:* nach draußen	**outside** ↔ inside
	to muck sth up *(informal)* /ˌmʌk ˌsʌmθɪŋ‿ˈʌp/	etw vermasseln	
	to **smile (at)** /ˈsmaɪl‿æt/	(an)lächeln	
	arrogant /ˈærəɡənt/	arrogant	Matt is very **arrogant**. He always thinks he is the best.
	emotion /ɪˈməʊʃ(ə)n/	Gefühl, Emotion	
	to clap /klæp/	klatschen	
	to give sb the thumbs down *(irr)* /ˌɡɪv ˌsʌmbədi ðə ˌθʌmz ˈdaʊn/	*jemandem den Daumen nach unten zeigen*	
	back /bæk/	Rücken, Rückseite	Jo hit Sam behind the teacher's **back**.
	to stammer /ˈstæmə/	stottern, stammeln	
C2	twice /twaɪs/	zweimal	p. 75
	to **remember** /rɪˈmembə/	sich erinnern, *hier:* daran denken	Please **remember** to buy milk.
	competition /ˌkɒmpəˈtɪʃ(ə)n/	Wettbewerb	The Olympics is a big sports **competition**.
C3	spelling *(no pl)* /ˈspelɪŋ/	Rechtschreibung, *hier:* Schreibweise	
C4	card /kɑːd/	Karte	
	to **move** /muːv/	(sich) bewegen	The boat **is moving** very slowly.

	pile / paɪl /	Stapel, Haufen	
	to turn sth upside down / ˌtɜːn ˌsʌmθɪŋ‿ˌʌpsaɪd‿ˈdaʊn /	etw auf den Kopf stellen, *hier:* umdrehen	
	player / pleɪə /	Spieler/in	
C5	to trick sb (out of sth) / ˌtrɪk ˌsʌmbədi‿ˈaʊt‿ɒv ˌsʌmθɪŋ /	jdn (um etw) betrügen	*p. 76*
	to tell a sob story *(irr) (informal)* / ˌtel‿ə ˈsɒb ˌstɔːri /	mit einer Mitleid heischenden Ausrede daherkommen	
	prompter / ˈprɒmptə /	Souffleur/Souffleuse *(jd, der den Text flüsternd vorspricht)*	
	drama group / ˈdrɑːmə ˌgruːp /	Theatergruppe, Schauspielgruppe	
	at least / æt ˈliːst /	mindestens, wenigstens, *hier:* zumindest	It's cold. **At least** it isn't raining.
	to ruin / ˈruːɪn /	zerstören, verderben, kaputtmachen	
	gloomy / ˈgluːmi /	trostlos, düster, *hier:* betrübt	
	first night / ˌfɜːst ˈnaɪt /	Premiere	
	nightmare / ˈnaɪtˌmeə /	Albtraum	The first night was a **nightmare**. Everything went wrong.
	everyone else / ˌevriˌwʌn‿ˈels /	jede/r andere	
	someone else / ˌsʌmwʌn‿ˈels /	jemand anders	
	tense / tens /	angespannt	
	to be around *(irr)* / ˌbi‿əˈraʊnd /	in der Nähe sein	
	to be fed up with sb/sth *(irr) (informal)* / ˌbiː ˌfed‿ˈʌp wɪð /	jdn/etw satthaben	
	to **pretend** / prɪˈtend /	vorgeben, vortäuschen	Lara isn't asleep. She's only **pretending** to be asleep.
	sweetly / ˈswiːtli /	süß(lich)	
	microphone / ˈmaɪkrəˌfəʊn /	Mikrofon	
	voice / vɔɪs /	Stimme	Lynn can't speak. She has lost her **voice**.
	to postpone / pəʊsˈpəʊn /	verschieben	
C6	to keep cool *(irr)* / ˌkiːp ˈkuːl /	ruhig bleiben, cool bleiben	*p. 77*
	loser / ˈluːzə /	Verlierer/in	**loser** ↔ winner
C7	to take over, took, taken / ˌteɪk‿ˈəʊvə, ˌtʊk, ˌteɪkən /	übernehmen	
C9	**the one** / ðə ˈwʌn /	der-/die-/dasjenige	Read the stories. Then choose **the one** you like best.

Say it in English – Theme 4

So kannst du …

dich positiv über eine Aufführung äußern	They were the best act of the night, and received never-ending applause. The girls looked brilliant in their costumes and their dancing was excellent! It was the perfect end to the show.
sagen, seit wann etwas andauert	I haven't had a big role for ages. I haven't performed on stage since our last Christmas play.
sagen, wie jemand etwas tut	She speaks clearly and she acts convincingly.
sagen, wie sich jemand fühlt	Caroline was really upset. She felt horrible. Ms Walsh was a bit worried/was annoyed. Ms Walsh was shocked.

Theme 5: Going green

	Going green /ˌgəʊɪŋ‿ˈgriːn/	*sich immer umweltbewusster verhalten*		*p. 86*
	mill /mɪl/	Mühle		
A2	to divide into /dɪˈvaɪd‿ˌɪntʊ/	(auf)teilen in		
	report /rɪˈpɔːt/	(Zeitungs-)Bericht, (Zeitungs-) Meldung	Did you read the **report** about Sports Day?	
	fashion /ˈfæʃ(ə)n/	Mode		
	to **save** /seɪv/	retten, schützen, (be)wahren	We should **save** the **environment** for our children and grandchildren.	
	environment *(no pl)* /ɪnˈvaɪrənmənt/	Umwelt		
	planet /ˈplænɪt/	Planet	our **planet** 	
	handprint /ˈhændˌprɪnt/	Handabdruck		
	plastic /ˈplæstɪk/	Plastik(-), Kunststoff(-)		
	to make a pledge *(irr)* /ˌmeɪk‿ə ˈpledʒ/	geloben		
	solar /ˈsəʊlə/	Solar-, Sonnen-		
	energy *(no pl)* /ˈenədʒi/	Energie, Kraft	It's good for the environment to use solar **energy**.	
	to donate /dəʊˈneɪt/	spenden		
	solar panel /ˈsəʊlə ˌpæn(ə)l/	Sonnenkollektor		
	to take a step *(irr)* /ˌteɪk‿ə ˈstep/	einen Schritt machen		
	magic *(no pl)* /ˈmædʒɪk/	Magie, Zauber		
	motorway /ˈməʊtəˌweɪ/	Autobahn		
	another /əˈnʌðə/	noch eine(r, s), *hier:* ein(e) andere(r)	Have you got **another** pencil?	
	field study /ˈfiːld ˌstʌdi/	Feldstudie *(systematische wiss. Beobachtung außerhalb des Labors)*		
	forest /ˈfɒrɪst/	Wald	**forest**	
	walk /wɔːk/	Spaziergang		
	biology *(no pl)* /baɪˈɒlədʒi/	Biologie		
	exercise /ˈeksəsaɪz/	Übung, Aufgabe		
	to turn out /ˌtɜːn‿ˈaʊt/	sich herausstellen		
	stay /steɪ/	Aufenthalt		
	combination /ˌkɒmbɪˈneɪʃ(ə)n/	Kombination, Verbindung		
	fieldwork /ˈfiːldˌwɜːk/	Feldarbeit, Feldforschung		
	to **study** /ˈstʌdi/	studieren, sich befassen mit, erforschen	Let's **study** the wildlife here to find out more about animals and plants.	
	wildlife *(no pl)* /ˈwaɪldˌlaɪf/	*die (natürliche) Tier- und Pflanzenwelt*		
	plant /plɑːnt/	Pflanze	A flower is a **plant**.	
	entertainment /ˌentəˈteɪnmənt/	Unterhaltung	There's a lot of **entertainment**: football, games and other activities.	
	nearby /ˌnɪəˈbaɪ/	in der Nähe gelegen, nahe gelegen		
	magic /ˈmædʒɪk/	magisch, zauberhaft, wundervoll		
	traffic *(no pl)* /ˈtræfɪk/	Verkehr	There's a lot of **traffic** in the morning. 	
A3	to **take notes** *(irr)* /ˌteɪk ˈnəʊts/	sich Notizen machen	Listen and **take notes**.	*p. 87*

A4	**headline** / ˈhedˌlaɪn /	Schlagzeile	**headline** = title	
	entertaining / ˌentəˈteɪnɪŋ /	unterhaltsam	**entertaining** ↔ boring	
	to refer (back) to / rɪˌfɜː ˈbæk tʊ /	(zurück)verweisen auf, sich beziehen auf		
B1	to **protect** / prəˈtekt /	(be)schützen	How can we **protect** the environment?	p. 88
	to **turn off** / ˌtɜːn‿ˈɒf /	abschalten, ausmachen	Please **turn off** the TV.	
	to **recycle** / riːˈsaɪk(ə)l /	wiederverwenden	It's a good idea to **recycle** paper.	
	by bike / ˌbaɪ ˈbaɪk /	mit dem (Fahr)rad	Let's go **by bike**.	
B2	that day / ˌðæt ˈdeɪ /	an diesem Tag		
	bike doctor / ˈbaɪk ˌdɒktə /	*jemand, der Fahrräder repariert*		
B3	to leave on standby *(irr)* / ˌliːv‿ɒn ˈstændbaɪ /	im Stand-by-Betrieb lassen		
	to **throw, threw, thrown (away)** / ˌθrəʊ, θruː, θrəʊn‿əˈweɪ /	(weg)werfen		
B4	to **stand, stood, stood** / stænd, stʊd /	stehen, *hier:* ertragen, aushalten		p. 89
	be allowed to do sth *(irr)* / ˌbi‿əˌlaʊd‿tə ˈduː ˌsʌmθɪŋ /	etw tun dürfen	I'm sorry. I **wasn't allowed to go** to your party.	
	to take a break *(irr)* / ˌteɪk‿ə ˈbreɪk /	eine Pause machen		
	to **finish** / ˈfɪnɪʃ /	(be)enden, aufhören, *hier:* abschließen	He **hasn't finished** his maths homework. 	
	to do the washing up *(irr)* / ˌduː ðə ˌwɒʃɪŋˈʌp /	abspülen, abwaschen		
	lazy / ˈleɪzi /	faul, träge	Don't be **lazy**! Help me with the cooking.	
	TV station / ˌtiː ˈviː ˌsteɪʃ(ə)n /	Fernsehsender		
	to **interview** / ˈɪntəˌvjuː /	interviewen, befragen		
	news *(only pl)* / njuːz /	Neuigkeit, Nachricht, *hier:* Nachrichtensendung		
	reporter / rɪˈpɔːtə /	Reporter/in	The **reporter is interviewing** a famous actor for the evening **news**.	
	to have a vote *(irr)* / ˌhæv‿ə ˈvəʊt /	abstimmen		
	Congratulations! / kənˌɡrætʃʊˈleɪʃ(ə)nz /	Gratuliere!, Glückwunsch!	Well done! **Congratulations!**	
B5	**may** / meɪ /	können, dürfen	**May** I open the window?	
B6	**advice** *(no pl)* / ədˈvaɪs /	Rat, *hier:* Tipp		
	chewing gum *(no pl)* / ˈtʃuːɪŋ‿ˌɡʌm /	Kaugummi		
	striped / straɪpt /	gestreift		
	shirt / ʃɜːt /	Hemd	He's wearing a **shirt**. 	
B7	to vote for sb/sth / ˈvəʊt fə ˌsʌmbədi / ˌsʌmθɪŋ /	für jdn/etw stimmen		p. 90
	super *(informal)* / ˈsuːpə /	besonders		
	to be on *(irr)* / ˌbi‿ˈɒn /	auf dem Programm stehen, laufen		
B8	to make a fool of sb/oneself *(irr)* / ˌmeɪk‿ə ˈfuːl‿əv ˌsʌmbədi / wʌnˌself /	jdn/sich lächerlich machen		

to cut out, cut out, cut out /ˌkʌt‿ˈaʊt/	(her)ausschneiden	
bit /bɪt/	Stück, Teil	I think this film is great. I liked the **bit** about snakes best.
to **go on, went on, gone on** /ˌɡəʊ‿ˈɒn, ˌwent‿ˈɒn, ˌɡɒn‿ˈɒn/	weitergehen, *hier:* passieren	What's **going on** at the moment?
to cover /ˈkʌvə/	bedecken, *hier:* sich befassen mit, behandeln	
topic /ˈtɒpɪk/	Thema	What are we going to talk about? What's the **topic**?
transport *(no pl)* /ˈtrænspɔːt/	Transport, Beförderung	
waste *(no pl)* /weɪst/	Verschwendung, Vergeudung; *hier:* Abfall	We are **producing** too much **waste**.
to **produce** /prəˈdjuːs/	herstellen, produzieren	
glass *(no pl)* /ɡlɑːs/	Glas	
product /ˈprɒdʌkt/	Produkt, Erzeugnis	We should buy **products** with **less** packaging.
less /les/	weniger	
packaging *(no pl)* /ˈpækɪdʒɪŋ/	Verpackungsmaterial	
to compost /ˈkɒmpɒst/	kompostieren	
organic waste /ɔːˌɡænɪk ˈweɪst/	Biomüll	
to **mention** /ˈmenʃ(ə)n/	erwähnen	I talked to Alex yesterday. He didn't **mention** his trip to London.
lunch break /ˈlʌntʃ breɪk/	Mittagspause	
as a whole /æz‿ə ˈhəʊl/	als Ganzes (betrachtet)	
behaviour *(no pl)* /bɪˈheɪvjə/	Benehmen, Verhalten, Betragen	Leaving rubbish in the forest is bad **behaviour**.
by bus /ˌbaɪ ˈbʌs/	mit dem Bus	How did you get to the cinema? – We went **by bus**.
B9 to keep warm *(irr)* /ˌkiːp ˈwɔːm/	warm halten, nicht frieren	p. 91
central heating *(no pl)* /ˌsentrəl ˈhiːtɪŋ/	Zentralheizung	
to plant /plɑːnt/	pflanzen	
C2 to be off *(irr)* /ˌbi‿ˈɒf/	(weg)gehen	p. 92
to **make sure (that)** *(irr)* /ˌmeɪk ˈʃɔː ðæt/	darauf achten, (dass)	Please **make sure that** you bring enough food for the trip.
sleeping bag /ˈsliːpɪŋ ˌbæɡ/	Schlafsack	
cup /kʌp/	Tasse, Becher	
plate /pleɪt/	Teller	
knife (*pl* **knives**) /naɪf, naɪvz/	Messer	
fork /fɔːk/	Gabel	
spoon /spuːn/	Löffel	
toothbrush /ˈtuːθˌbrʌʃ/	Zahnbürste	**toothbrush**
soap /səʊp/	Seife	piece of **soap**
meal /miːl/	Mahlzeit, Essen	There will be three **meals**: breakfast, lunch and dinner.
certain /ˈsɜːt(ə)n/	sicher, gewiss, bestimmt	How old is she? – I think she's 14 but I'm not **certain**.
medicine *(no pl)* /ˈmed(ə)s(ə)n/	Medizin, Medikamente	
alcohol *(no pl)* /ˈælkəˌhɒl/	Alkohol	
pocket knife /ˈpɒkɪt ˌnaɪf/	Taschenmesser	**pocket knife**

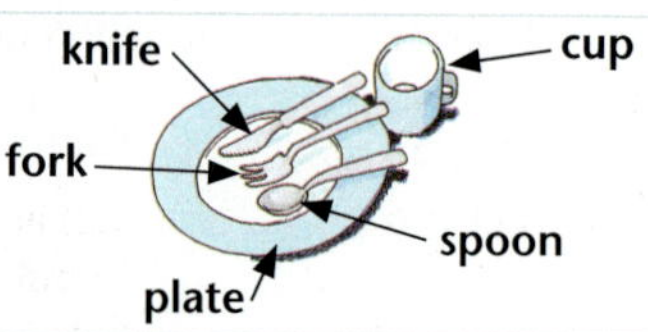

to **break, broke, broken** /breɪk, brəʊk, ˈbrəʊkən/	(zer)brechen; *hier:* verstoßen gegen	Try not to **break** the rules.
to **pick up** /ˌpɪk‿ˈʌp/	aufheben, *hier:* abholen	Peter has missed the bus. His father is coming to **pick** him **up**.
immediately /ɪˈmiːdiətli/	sofort, gleich, direkt	**immediately** ↔ later
village /ˈvɪlɪdʒ/	Dorf	**village** ↔ city
to **collect** /kəˈlekt/	einsammeln	
pocket money /ˈpɒkɪt ˌmʌni/	Taschengeld	My parents give me £5 **pocket money** every week.
Yours sincerely /jɔːz‿sɪnˈsɪəli/	Mit freundlichen Grüßen	
C3 **sensible** /ˈsensəb(ə)l/	vernünftig, angemessen	**sensible** ↔ silly **!** Englisch *sensible* = Deutsch „vernünftig"
strict /strɪkt/	streng, strikt, genau	Our school rules are very **strict**.
C4 to **convince** /kənˈvɪns/	überzeugen	He had a very good argument so he was able to **convince** me.

C5

Possessive pronouns

p. 93

Die Wörter ***mine, yours, his/hers/its, ours*** und ***theirs*** nennt man Possessivpronomen *(possessive pronouns)*. Wie alle Pronomen verwendet man sie statt eines Nomens: *This is not your mobile. It's* ***mine.*** (→ LiF 14, Seite 146)

to give away, gave away, given away /ˌɡɪv‿əˈweɪ, ˌɡeɪv‿əˈweɪ, ˌɡɪvən‿əˈweɪ/	verschenken, hergeben	
to pinch /pɪntʃ/	kneifen, *hier:* klauen	
to go mad *(irr)* /ˌɡəʊ ˈmæd/	verrückt werden; ausflippen	
bag /bæɡ/	Tasche, *hier:* Tüte	She's carrying five **bags**. 
anyway /ˈeniˌweɪ/	sowieso, jedenfalls, *hier:* überhaupt	
front *(no pl)* /frʌnt/	vorderer Bereich	
coach /kəʊtʃ/	(Omni)bus, Reisebus	**coach** 
following /ˈfɒləʊɪŋ/	folgende(r, s)	
C6 to **wake up, woke up, woken up** /ˌweɪk‿ˈʌp, ˌwəʊk‿ˈʌp, ˌwəʊkən‿ˈʌp/	aufwecken, aufwachen	He **has** just **woken up**. 
Get off!	Geh weg!	
to fall down, fell down, fallen down /ˌfɔːl ˈdaʊn, ˌfel ˈdaʊn, ˌfɔːlən ˈdaʊn/	hin(unter)fallen, (ein)stürzen, *hier:* zusammenfallen	
to **put up, put up, put up** /ˌpʊt‿ˈʌp/	aufhängen, hochheben, *hier:* aufstellen	It's time to **put up** our tent.
early /ˈɜːli/	früh, zeitig	During the holidays I never get up **early**.
to **have/take a shower** *(irr)* /ˌhæv/ˌteɪk‿ə ˈʃaʊə/	sich duschen	He**'s taking a shower**. 
Hurry up! /ˌhʌri‿ˈʌp/	Beeil dich!, Beeilt euch!	
metre /ˈmiːtə/	Meter	
to **stand up, stood up, stood up** /ˌstænd‿ˈʌp, ˌstʊd‿ˈʌp/	aufstehen	to **stand up** ↔ to sit down

to hold up, held up, held up /ˌhəʊld‿ˈʌp, ˌheld‿ˈʌp/	hochhalten	
wet /wet/	nass	It's raining. My shoes are **wet**.
owner /ˈəʊnə/	Besitzer/in, Eigentümer/in	
dirty /ˈdɜːti/	dreckig, schmutzig	
straight /streɪt/	gerade(aus), direkt	
bin /bɪn/	Mülleimer, Mülltonne	
to go red *(irr)* /ˌɡəʊ ˈred/	rot werden	
to walk up to sb /ˌwɔːk‿ˈʌp tə ˌsʌmbədi/	auf jdn zugehen	
to play a trick on sb /ˌpleɪ‿ə ˈtrɪk‿ɒn ˌsʌmbədi/	jdm einen Streich spielen	
to leave sb alone *(irr)* /ˌliːv ˌsʌmbədi‿əˈləʊn/	jdn in Ruhe lassen	
may /meɪ/	können, dürfen, *hier:* vielleicht	
to **bully** /ˈbʊli/	tyrannisieren, mobben	Jo and Alicia are **bullying** Janet. It's awful for her.

Say it in English – Theme 5

So kannst du ...

über Aktivitäten an deiner Schule sprechen	Last year we went to .../we organized ... Last year we took part in ... I have already acted in the school play/played for the school team. Every year we have a project week. There are always concerts/music shows/dance shows at our school.
über Umweltschutzmaßnahmen reden	You should recycle paper/turn off the lights. You can go by bike.
fragen, ob etwas erlaubt sein wird	Will we be allowed to talk to them?
über ein Verbot sprechen	Yesterday we weren't even allowed to take a break until we had finished our projects.
in einem Interview Interesse zeigen	That sounds interesting. Do you mean paper and other materials, too? Are you trying to say that everything will be OK if we recycle as much as we can? As you've mentioned organic waste, I've heard that some pupils have made something very special. It sounds as if you liked the smoothies, but how do you feel about Green Week as a whole?
eine andere Person befragen	Mr Glover, did you notice ...? George, why didn't you ...? Jason, did you think you could ...?

Theme 6: Fun and games

A2	rowing *(no pl)* / ˈrəʊɪŋ /	Rudern		p. 104
	health *(no pl)* / helθ /	Gesundheit	Nina has **health** problems. She's often ill.	
	up and down / ˌʌp‿ən ˈdaʊn /	auf und ab		
	second / ˈsekənd /	Sekunde		
	to be out of/short of breath *(irr)* / ˌbi‿ˌaʊt‿əv / ʃɔːt‿əv ˈbreθ /	atemlos sein, außer Atem sein		
	to **touch** / tʌtʃ /	berühren	Don't **touch** it. It's hot.	
	stairs / steəz /	Treppe, *hier:* Treppenstufe		
	a little / ə ˈlɪt(ə)l /	(ein) wenig, ein bisschen		
	to balance / ˈbæləns /	balancieren		
	press-up / ˈpresʌp /	Liegestütz		
	hardly / ˈhɑːdli /	kaum	She is ill. She can **hardly** speak.	
	mostly / ˈməʊstli /	meistens, größtenteils, hauptsächlich		
	as fit as a fiddle (informal) / æz ˌfɪt‿æz‿ə ˈfɪd(ə)l /	fit wie ein Turnschuh		
	to keep up *(irr)* / ˌkiːp‿ˈʌp /	hochhalten, *hier:* weiterhin tun		
	to share / ʃeə /	teilen		
	to **get, got, got/gotten** / get, gɒt, gɒt/ˈgɒtən /	erhalten, bekommen, *hier:* werden, geraten	The boys **got** into trouble.	
	to **run (away)** / ˌrʌn(‿əˈweɪ) /	(weg)rennen, *hier:* laufen		
	flexible / fleksəb(ə)l /	flexibel, biegsam, gelenkig		
	to **cycle** / ˈsaɪk(ə)l /	Rad fahren, radeln	to **cycle** = to ride a bike	
	stretching exercise / ˈstretʃɪŋ‿ˌeksəsaɪz /	Dehnungsübung		
	Oh dear! *(informal)* / əʊ ˈdɪə /	Du meine Güte!		
	to **get off** *(irr)* / ˌget‿ˈɒf /	aussteigen, *hier:* runterkommen		
A3	**about** / əˈbaʊt /	über, *hier:* zu		p. 105
A6	sports *(only pl)* / spɔːts /	Sport, Sportart		
B1	to **score (a goal)** / ˌskɔːr‿ə ˈgəʊl /	(ein Tor) schießen	Alex **scored** a fantastic goal.	p. 106
	to **leave, left, left** / liːv, left, left /	verlassen, weggehen, *hier:* lassen	She **left** him waiting outside.	
	to **stand, stood, stood** / stænd, stʊd, stʊd /	stehen	Jack had to **stand** in the corner.	
	I took the team on whole. / aɪ ˌtʊk ðə ˌtiːm‿ɒn ˈhəʊl /	Ich nahm es mit der ganzen Mannschaft auf.		
	to **pull** / pʊl /	ziehen		
	to **end** / end /	beenden, zu Ende bringen; enden		
	to **shoot, shot, shot** / ʃuːt, ʃɒt /	schießen		
	all around / ˌɔːl‿əˈraʊnd /	überall		
	ground / graʊnd /	(Erd)boden, Erde, *hier:* Platz		
	yard / jɑːd /	*Längenmaß (91,44 cm)*		
	to get set *(irr)* / ˌget ˈset /	vorbereiten, bereit machen		
	net / net /	Netz		
	roar *(no pl)* / rɔː /	Brüllen, Dröhnen, *hier:* Tosen		
B2	to **argue (about)** / ˈɑːgju‿əˌbaʊt /	sich streiten (wegen)	Caroline and George **are** always **arguing about** jobs around the house.	
	to **push** / pʊʃ /	stoßen, schieben	to **push** ↔ to pull	
	to **fall down, fell down, fallen down** / ˌfɔːl ˈdaʊn, ˌfel ˈdaʊn, ˌfɔːlən ˈdaʊn /	hin(unter)fallen, (ein)stürzen		

	elbow /ˈelbəʊ/	Ell(en)bogen	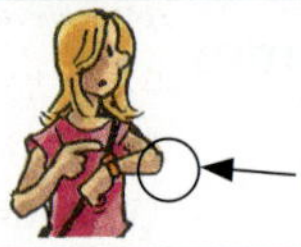	
	to **catch, caught, caught** /kætʃ, kɔːt, kɔːt/	fangen, *hier:* treffen		
	fact /fækt/	Wirklichkeit, Tatsache		
	while /waɪl/	während, als	**While** you were sleeping, the dog ate the cake.	
	to chase /tʃeɪs/	hinterherlaufen, verfolgen		
	to **hit, hit, hit** /hɪt/	schlagen, treffen, stoßen (gegen)		
	accident /ˈæksɪd(ə)nt/	Unfall	Ben had a car **accident** last year.	
	toward(s) /təˈwɔːdz/	in Richtung		
	during /ˈdjʊərɪŋ/	während	**During** the holidays you can sleep late.	
B3	something else /ˌsʌmθɪŋ‿ˈels/	etwas anderes		p. 107
B4	to stick out, stuck out, stuck out /ˌstɪk‿ˈaʊt, ˌstʌk‿ˈaʊt/	ausstrecken, *hier:* herausstrecken		
	tongue /tʌŋ/	Zunge		
	flag /flæg/	Fahne, Flagge		
	to **hold, held, held** /həʊld, held/	halten	Rajiv **is holding** an MP3 player in his hand.	
	to bleed, bled, bled /bliːd, bled/	bluten		
	ground /graʊnd/	(Erd)boden, Erde		
B5	waiting room /ˈweɪtɪŋ ˌruːm/	Wartezimmer		p. 108
	to **hurt, hurt, hurt (sb)** /hɜːt, hɜːt, hɜːt ˌsʌmbədi/	(jdm) wehtun, (jdn) verletzen	Oliver didn't want to **hurt** George.	
B10	mystery /ˈmɪst(ə)ri/	Geheimnis, Rätsel, *hier:* mysteriöse Geschichte		p. 109
	to solve /sɒlv/	lösen, *hier:* aufklären		
	to make up *(irr)* /ˌmeɪk‿ˈʌp/	erfinden, (sich) ausdenken		
	unconscious /ʌnˈkɒnʃəs/	bewusstlos	After the accident Sue was **unconscious** for ten minutes.	
	changing room /ˈtʃeɪndʒɪŋ ˌruːm/	(Umkleide)kabine		
	to **lock** /lɒk/	(ab)schließen, *hier:* einschließen		
	to **miss** /mɪs/	verfehlen, versäumen, verpassen		
	cyclist /ˈsaɪklɪst/	Radfahrer/in		
	to **break one's arm** *(irr)* /ˌbreɪk wʌnz‿ˈɑːm/	sich den Arm brechen		
	victim /ˈvɪktɪm/	Opfer		
	witness /ˈwɪtnəs/	Zeuge/Zeugin	Two **witnesses** saw the accident.	
C1	to **dislike** /dɪsˈlaɪk/	nicht mögen	to **like** ↔ to dislike	p. 110
	most /məʊst/	am meisten		
C2	to compete /kəmˈpiːt/	wetteifern, antreten, kämpfen		
	against /əˈgenst/	gegen	Manchester United are playing **against** Arsenal.	
	successful /səkˈsesf(ə)l/	erfolgreich	She has won every match. She's very **successful**.	
	long jump *(no pl)* /ˈlɒŋ dʒʌmp/	Weitsprung		
	cup /kʌp/	Tasse, Becher, *hier:* Pokal		
	to battle (out) /ˌbæt(ə)l‿ˈaʊt/	(aus)kämpfen		
	to **break, broke, broken** /breɪk, brəʊk, ˈbrəʊkən/	(zer)brechen, *hier:* neu aufstellen	He was the fastest. He even broke the school record.	
	record /ˈrekɔːd/	Rekord		

the furthest / ðə 'fɜ:ðɪst /	am weitesten	
to **put, put, put** / pʊt, pʊt, pʊt /	setzen, legen, *hier:* bringen	
lead / li:d /	Leine, *hier:* Führung	
high jump *(no pl)* / 'haɪ dʒʌmp /	Hochsprung	
relay (race) / 'ri:leɪ reɪs /	Staffellauf	
neck and neck / ˌnek‿ən‿'nek /	Kopf an Kopf	
to **depend (on)** / dɪ'pend‿ɒn /	abhängen (von)	Why not go swimming tomorrow? – Hmm, it **depends on** the weather.
to be in the lead *(irr)* / ˌbi‿ɪn ðə 'li:d /	in Führung sein	
to **overtake, overtook, overtaken** / ˌəʊvə'teɪk, ˌəʊvə'tʊk, ˌəʊvəˌteɪkən, /	überholen, einholen	Lisa ran faster so she **overtook** the other girls.
to gain / geɪn /	bekommen, erreichen, gewinnen	
as usual / æz 'ju:ʒʊəl /	wie üblich	
competitive / kəm'petətɪv /	konkurrierend, kampfbereit	Gina is very **competitive**. She always wants to win.
serious / 'sɪəriəs /	ernst	
outstanding / aʊt'stændɪŋ /	außergewöhnlich, bemerkenswert, hervorragend	Their performance was **outstanding**.
C3 to **come, came, come** / kʌm, keɪm, kʌm /	kommen, *hier:* werden	p. 111
to **train** / treɪn /	trainieren	Alex **trains** three days a week.
to **promise** / 'prɒmɪs /	versprechen	
C4 **victory** / 'vɪkt(ə)ri /	Sieg	They won the match. It was a great **victory**!
at least / æt 'li:st /	mindestens, wenigstens	It's raining. **At least** it's not cold.
confident / 'kɒnfɪd(ə)nt /	zuversichtlich, selbstsicher, selbstbewusst	
to chant / tʃɑ:nt /	singen, im Sprechchor rufen	
nothing / 'nʌθɪŋ /	nichts	Lisa really wants to run the 100m. **Nothing** can stop her.
to **give up, gave up, given up** / ˌgɪv‿'ʌp, ˌgeɪv‿'ʌp, ˌgɪvən‿'ʌp /	aufgeben, resignieren	After 3000m she was really tired but she didn't **give up**.
to give in, gave in, given in / ˌgɪv‿'ɪn, ˌgeɪv‿'ɪn, ˌgɪvən‿'ɪn /	nachgeben, aufgeben	
to **fight, fought, fought** / faɪt, fɔ:t /	(be)kämpfen	Four teams **are fighting** to gain first place.
field / fi:ld /	Wiese, Feld, *hier:* Spielfeld	
jump / dʒʌmp /	Sprung, Satz	
enthusiastic / ɪnˌθju:zi'æstɪk /	enthusiastisch, begeistert	All the fans were **enthusiastic**.
loudspeaker / 'laʊdˌspi:kə /	Lautsprecher	
rather / 'rɑ:ðə /	ziemlich, recht	Carla looked **rather** pale.
pale / peɪl /	blass, bleich	
to **join** / dʒɔɪn /	verbinden, *hier:* sich gesellen	Let's **join** the others.
starting line / stɑ:tɪŋ laɪn /	Startlinie	
seat / si:t /	(Sitz)platz	
to cross one's fingers for luck / ˌkrɒs wʌnz ˌfɪŋgəz fə 'lʌk /	die Daumen drücken	
to come on *(irr)* / ˌkʌm‿'ɒn /	anfangen, beginnen, angehen	

On your marks, get set, go! /ˌɒn jə ˈmɑːks, ˌget ˈset, ˈgəʊ/	Auf die Plätze, fertig, los!	
mad /mæd/	wahnsinnig, verrückt	
track /træk/	Weg, Pfad, (Lauf)bahn	
rival /ˈraɪv(ə)l/	Rivale/Rivalin, Konkurrent/in	Sue was Sandra's main **rival**.
to keep up *(irr)* /ˌkiːp‿ˈʌp/	hochhalten, *hier:* dranbleiben	
way /weɪ/	Weg, *hier:* Möglichkeit	
finishing line /ˈfɪnɪʃɪŋ laɪn/	Ziellinie	
dramatic /drəˈmætɪk/	dramatisch, *hier:* theatralisch	
Typical! *(informal)* /ˈtɪpɪk(ə)l/	Typisch!	
to come in *(irr)* /ˌkʌm‿ˈɪn/	hereinkommen, *hier:* ins Ziel einlaufen	
to hug /hʌg/	umarmen	
impatient /ɪmˈpeɪʃ(ə)nt/	ungeduldig	Hurry up! – Don't be so **impatient**.
to announce /əˈnaʊns/	bekanntgeben, verkünden	
than ever /ðæn‿ˈevə/	als jemals zuvor	
C5 to **pronounce** /prəˈnaʊns/	aussprechen	Some names are difficult to **pronounce**. p. 112
stress /stres/	Betonung	
C7 to **swim, swam, swum** /swɪm, swæm, swʌm/	schwimmen	She is **swimming** very fast. 
C8 chant /tʃɑːnt/	(Sprech)gesang Sprechchor	
rhyming /ˈraɪmɪŋ/	Reim-	
to **repeat** /rɪˈpiːt/	wiederholen, *hier:* nachsprechen	The pupils carefully **repeated** the words.
never ever /ˌnevər‿ˈevə/	nie im Leben, niemals	
to **beat, beat, beaten** /biːt, biːt, ˈbiːtən/	schlagen, übertreffen	Arsenal **has beaten** Liverpool 2-1.
to defeat /dɪˈfiːt/	besiegen, schlagen	
to **improve** /ɪmˈpruːv/	(sich) verbessern, besser werden	to **improve** = to get better
C9 **thought** /θɔːt/	Gedanke	What are your **thoughts** on this topic?
opinion /əˈpɪnjən/	Meinung, Ansicht, Standpunkt	
point of view /ˌpɔɪnt‿əv‿ˈvjuː/	Ansicht, Einstellung, Perspektive	
ambitious /æmˈbɪʃəs/	ehrgeizig	Lisa wants to win every race. She's very **ambitious**.
frustrated /frʌˈstreɪtɪd/	frustriert	Caroline came in second. She was very **frustrated**.
determined /dɪˈtɜːmɪnd/	entschlossen	
relaxed /rɪˈlækst/	entspannt, locker	She was rather nervous. She wasn't **relaxed** at all.
jealous /ˈdʒeləs/	eifersüchtig, neidisch	
emotional /ɪˈməʊʃ(ə)nəl/	emotional, gefühlvoll	

Lerntipps

- Ergänze deine Vokabelkartei, deine *word webs* usw. immer wieder, wenn du neue Wörter lernst.
- Weniger ist mehr! Um Vokabeln langfristig zu behalten, ist es wichtig, dass du sie regelmäßig wiederholst. Es bringt dir mehr, wenn du jeden Tag 5–10 Minuten und pro Tag nicht mehr als 8–12 neue Vokabeln lernst, als wenn du dir angewöhnst, seltener und dafür mehr Vokabeln auf einmal zu lernen.

Say it in English – Theme 6

So kannst du …

über Sport und Fitness reden	Are you out of breath?
	How many press-ups can you do?
	You're as fit as a fiddle.
	Keep up the good work and continue being active.
	If you get out of breath quickly, try to run, cycle or play tennis or football regularly.
	If you are not very flexible, try doing stretching exercises every day.
	Try to do more exercise every day.
über deine sportlichen Aktivitäten sprechen	My favourite sport …
	I'm really good at …
	I could improve my …
	I play in a team/at a club/…
	I (don't) take it very seriously.
eine Bestätigungsfrage stellen	You don't really think that Oliver played fairly, do you?
	But it wasn't Oliver's fault, was it?
eine Person befragen	What were you doing when …?
	Where were you at 5:30?
	How long have you known …?
	You weren't at home last night, were you?
sagen, was dir am meisten Spaß macht	I like … best.
	I enjoy … most.
sagen, was du nicht magst	I can't stand …
	The thing I dislike most about sports competitions is …
Vergleiche anstellen	Leon is swimming faster than Ben.
	The Reds clapped more wildly than ever.

English-German dictionary

Hier findest du die Wörter, die in deinem Buch vorkommen.
- Die **fett gedruckten** Wörter solltest du dir merken.
- Wörter mit einem ° sind nur für einen bestimmten Text wichtig. Du brauchst sie nicht zu lernen.
- 1B1 bedeutet: Dieses Wort kommt in *Theme* 1, Aufgabe B1 vor.
- I bedeutet: Dieses Wort kommt in Band I (5. Klasse) vor.
- Folgende Abkürzungen werden noch verwendet:
  P = *Personal Trainer* PP = *Photo page* O = *Optional*

A

a/an /ə, ən/ ein(e) I
a bit /ə ˈbɪt/ ein bisschen, ein wenig 1A3
a few /ə ˈfjuː/ einige, wenige 1C6
a little /ə ˈlɪt(ə)l/ (ein) wenig, (ein) bisschen 6A2
a lot (of) /ə ˈlɒt‿əv/ viel(e), eine Menge I
(a) must *(no pl)* /ə ˈmʌst/ (ein) Muss 3A4
° a week /ə ˈwiːk/ in der Woche 6P14
about /əˈbaʊt/ über, von I; an 3A2; wegen 2C5; zu 6A3
abseiling *(no pl)* /ˈæbseɪlɪŋ/ Abseilen 1B7
accident /ˈæksɪd(ə)nt/ Unfall 6B2
acrobat /ˈækrəˌbæt/ Akrobat/in 3A4
across /əˈkrɒs/ über I; jenseits; gegenüberliegend 3A4
across London: in ganz London 4A3
to **act** /ækt/ handeln, vorgehen; schauspielern 1C9
act /ækt/ Akt, (Show)nummer 4A3
activity /ækˈtɪvəti/ Aktivität, Tätigkeit I
actor /ˈæktə/ Schauspieler 3C5
actress /ˈæktrəs/ Schauspielerin 4C1
actually /ˈæktʃuəli/ eigentlich, wirklich; tatsächlich 2C2
° AD (= Anno Domini) /ˌeɪ ˈdiː, ˌænəʊ ˈdɒmɪnaɪ/ nach Christus 1O1
to **add (sth to sth)** /ˈæd/ (etw etw) hinzufügen I
address /əˈdres/ Adresse, Anschrift I
admiring /ədˈmaɪərɪŋ/ bewundernd 4C1
to **admit** /ədˈmɪt/ zugeben 3B7
adult /ˈædʌlt/ Erwachsene/r I
adventure /ədˈventʃə/ Abenteuer, Erlebnis I
adverb /ˈædvɜːb/ Adverb 6C5
° adverb of frequency /ˌædvɜːb‿əv‿ˈfriːkwənsi/ Häufigkeitsadverb 6P9
adverb of manner /ˌædvɜːb‿əv‿ˈmænə/ Adverb der Art und Weise 6C6
° advert (= advertisement) /ˈædvɜːt, ədˈvɜːtɪsmənt/ Anzeige, Inserat; Werbespot 1B6
advice *(no pl)* /ədˈvaɪs/ Rat; Tipp 5B6
to **be afraid (of)** /ˌbi‿əˈfreɪd‿əv/ Angst haben/sich fürchten (vor) I
I'm afraid /ˌaɪm‿əˈfreɪd/ leider I
after /ˈɑːftə/ nach I
after all /ˌɑːftər‿ˈɔːl/ schließlich; zumindest 1B1
after that /ˌɑːftə ˈðæt/ danach I
afternoon /ˌɑːftəˈnuːn/ Nachmittag I
in the afternoon /ˌɪn ði‿ˈɑːftəˌnuːn/ am Nachmittag I
again /əˈgen/ wieder, noch einmal I
against /əˈgenst/ gegen 6C2
age /eɪdʒ/ Alter 4A2
ages /eɪdʒɪs/ eine Ewigkeit, Ewigkeiten 4B1
ago /əˈgəʊ/ vor 4B1
to **agree (on)** /əˈgriː‿ɒn/ zustimmen I; sich einigen (auf) 3B10
alcohol *(no pl)* /ˈælkəˌhɒl/ Alkohol 5C2
all /ɔːl/ alle(s) I
all around /ˌɔːl‿əˈraʊnd/ überall 6B1
all over the place /ˌɔːl‿ˈəʊvə ðə ˌpleɪs/ überall 3B7
all summer /ˌɔːl ˈsʌmə/ den ganzen Sommer I
all the time /ˌɔːl ðə ˈtaɪm/ die ganze Zeit I
almost /ˈɔːlməʊst/ fast 1B7, beinahe 3B7
alone /əˈləʊn/ allein I
° alone verlassen 2O2
along /əˈlɒŋ/ entlang 3C2
° along /əˈlɒŋ/ dazu 6A4
already /ɔːlˈredi/ schon, bereits I
° alright (= all right) /ɔːlˈraɪt/ in Ordnung 1P2
also /ˈɔːlsəʊ/ auch I
although /ɔːlˈðəʊ/ obwohl 2C7
always /ˈɔːlweɪz/ immer I
am (= ante meridiem) /ˌeɪ‿ˈem, ˌænti məˈrɪdiəm/ morgens, vormittags (nur hinter Uhrzeit zwischen Mitternacht und 12 Uhr mittags) I
° amazement *(no pl)* /əˈmeɪzmənt/ Erstaunen, Verwunderung 2O4
amazing /əˈmeɪzɪŋ/ erstaunlich, toll I
ambitious /æmˈbɪʃəs/ ehrgeizig 6C9
° ancient /ˈeɪnʃ(ə)nt/ alt, antik 1PP
and /ænd/ und I
angrily /ˈæŋgrɪli/ verärgert, zornig, wütend *(Adverb)* 1B7
angry /ˈæŋgri/ verärgert, zornig, wütend I
animal /ˈænɪm(ə)l/ Tier I
° anniversary /ˌænɪˈvɜːs(ə)ri/ Jubiläum, Jahrestag 2P13
to announce /əˈnaʊns/ bekanntgeben, verkünden 6C4
announcement /əˈnaʊnsmənt/ Bekanntmachung, Mitteilung, Durchsage 1C8
annoyed /əˈnɔɪd/ verärgert 2B4
another /əˈnʌðə/ noch eine(r, s) I; ein(e) andere(r) 5A2
answer /ˈɑːnsə/ Antwort I
to **answer** /ˈɑːnsə/ (be)antworten I
to **answer the phone** /ˌɑːnsə ðə ˈfəʊn/ ans Telefon gehen I
any /ˈeni/ (irgend)ein(e), jede(r, s) I
anyone /ˈeniˌwʌn/ (irgend)jemand 1B1
anyone in particular /ˌeniˌwʌn‿ɪn pəˈtɪkjʊlə/ jemand Bestimmter 2B3
anything /ˈeniθɪŋ/ (irgend)etwas, (irgend)was 1C4
not ... anything else /nɒt ˌeniθɪŋ‿ˈels/ gar nichts anderes 3B1
anyway /ˈeniˌweɪ/ sowieso, jedenfalls, ohnehin 3B7
anyway /ˈeniˌweɪ/ na ja 3B1, überhaupt 5C5
applause *(no pl)* /əˈplɔːz/ Applaus, Beifall 4A3
apple /ˈæp(ə)l/ Apfel I
toffee apple /ˈtɒfi‿ˌæp(ə)l/ *kandierter Apfel* 2A2
April /ˈeɪprəl/ April I
° archery *(no pl)* /ˈɑːtʃəri/ Bogenschießen 1P11
area /ˈeəriə/ Gebiet, Region, Gegend 3C8
to **argue (about)** /ˈɑːgju‿əˌbaʊt/ sich streiten (wegen) 6B2

argument /ˈɑːgjʊmənt/ Auseinandersetzung, Argument 4B5
arm /ɑːm/ Arm I
to break one's arm /ˌbreɪk wʌnz‿ˈɑːm/ sich den Arm brechen 6B10
◦ army /ˈɑːmi/ Armee, Heer 1O1
around /əˈraʊnd/ umher; um; rund um; um … herum 1B7
to **arrive** /əˈraɪv/ ankommen; da sein I
arrogant /ˈærəgənt/ arrogant 4C1
◦ arrogantly /ˈærəgəntli/ arrogant *(Adverb)* 4P13
art /ɑːt/ Kunst(unterricht) I
article /ɑːtɪk(ə)l/ Artikel 4A3
◦ artificial /ˌɑːtɪˈfɪʃ(ə)l/ künstlich 1PP
as /æz/ weil, da 1C2, als, wie 2B5
as … as /æz æz/ so … wie 1A1
as a whole /æz‿ə ˈhəʊl/ als Ganzes (betrachtet) 5B8
as fit as a fiddle *(informal)* /æz ˌfɪt‿æz‿ə ˈfɪd(ə)l/ fit wie ein Turnschuh 6A2
as usual /æz ˈjuːʒʊəl/ wie üblich 6C2
to **ask** /ɑːsk/ fragen I
to **ask (for sth)**: (um etw) bitten 1A3
assembly hall /əˈsembli ˌhɔːl/ (Versammlungs)saal, Aula 4B8
at /æt/ auf, an, in, bei, um I
at all /æt‿ˈɔːl/ überhaupt 4B11
at first /æt ˈfɜːst/ zuerst I
at home /æt ˈhəʊm/ zu Hause I
at least /æt ˈliːst/ mindestens, wenigstens; zumindest 4C5
at night /æt ˈnaɪt/ nachts I
at once /æt ˈwʌns/ sofort 2C7
at the moment /ˌæt ðə ˈməʊmənt/ im Moment I
atmosphere /ˈætməsˌfɪə/ Atmosphäre, Stimmung 2C8
attraction /əˈtrækʃ(ə)n/ (Touristen)attraktion 3A3
attractive /əˈtræktɪv/ attraktiv, verlockend I
audience /ˈɔːdiəns/ Publikum, Besucher, Zuschauer 4A3
audition /ɔːˈdɪʃ(ə)n/ Vorsprechen, Vorsingen, Vorspielen 4B1
August /ˈɔːgəst/ August I
aunt /ɑːnt/ Tante I
autumn /ˈɔːtəm/ Herbst I
away /əˈweɪ/ weg I
awful /ˈɔːf(ə)l/ furchtbar, schrecklich I
◦ awkwardly /ˈɔːkwə(r)dli/ unbeholfen; verlegen 2O2

B

back /bæk/ Rücken, Rückseite 4C1
back /bæk/ (wieder) zurück I
bad /bæd/ schlecht; schlimm I
◦ badger /ˈbædʒə/ Dachs 1PP
bag /bæg/ Tasche I; Tüte 5C5
to **pack one's bags** /ˌpæk wʌnz ˈbægz/ die Koffer packen 3B3
to **bake** /ˈbeɪk/ backen I
baked potato /ˌbeɪkt pəˈteɪtəʊ/ Ofenkartoffel 2A2
to balance /ˈbæləns/ balancieren 6A2
ball /bɔːl/ Ball 6B1
◦ balloon /bəˈluːn/ (Luft)ballon 2O4
banana /bəˈnɑːnə/ Banane I
banger /ˈbæŋə/ Knaller, Kracher 2B3
banner /ˈbænə/ Transparent, Banner, Fahne 2A2
barbecue /ˈbɑːbɪˌkjuː/ Grill, Grillparty 1B1
basement /ˈbeɪsmənt/ Untergeschoss, Keller 4B11
bathroom /ˈbɑːθˌruːm/ Bad(ezimmer) 3C2
◦ baths *(only pl)* /bɑːθs/ Bäder, Heilbad 1O1
battery /ˈbæt(ə)ri/ Batterie 3B3
to battle (out) /ˌbæt(ə)l‿ˈaʊt/ (aus) kämpfen 6C2
battleship /ˈbæt(ə)lʃɪp/ Schlachtschiff 3B7
◦ BC (= before Christ) /ˌbiː ˈsiː, bɪˌfɔː ˈkraɪst/ vor Christus 1O1
to **be** *(irr)* /biː/ sein I
to **be able** to **do sth** /ˌbi‿ˌeɪbl tə ˈduː/ etw tun können 4A1
to **be afraid (of)** /ˌbi‿əˈfreɪd‿əv/ Angst haben/sich fürchten (vor) I
to **be allowed** to **do sth** /ˌbi‿əˌlaʊd‿tə ˈduː/ etw tun dürfen 5B4
to **be angry with sb** /ˌbi‿ˈæŋgri wɪð/ sich über jdn ärgern I
to be around /ˌbi‿əˈraʊnd/ in der Nähe sein 4C5
to **be asleep** /ˌbi‿əˈsliːp/ schlafen I
to **be called** /ˌbiː ˈkɔːld/ genannt werden, heißen I
to be crazy about sb/sth /ˌbiː ˈkreɪzi‿əˌbaʊt/ nach jdm/etw verrückt sein 2B3
to be fed up with sb/sth *(informal)* /ˌbiː ˌfed‿ˈʌp wɪð/ jdn/etw satthaben 4C5
to **be free** /ˌbiː ˈfriː/ frei haben/sein, Zeit für etw haben I
to **be fun** /ˌbiː ˈfʌn/ Spaß machen I
to **be good at** /ˌbiː ˈgʊd‿ət/ gut in … sein I
to be in the lead /ˌbi‿ɪn ðə ˈliːd/ in Führung sein 6C2
to be into sb/sth *(informal)* /ˌbi‿ˈɪntuː/ an jdm/etw interessiert sein 3A4
to **be interested (in)** /ˌbi‿ˈɪntrəstɪd‿ɪn/ sich interessieren (für), interessiert sein (an) I
to be left /ˌbiː ˈleft/ übrig bleiben 1B1
to be lost /ˌbiː ˈlɒst/ sich verirrt haben, sich verlaufen haben 1B7
to **be lucky** /ˌbiː ˈlʌki/ Glück haben I
to **be missing** /ˌbiː ˈmɪsɪŋ/ fehlen I
to be off /ˌbi‿ˈɒf/ (weg)gehen 5C2
to be on /ˌbi‿ˈɒn/ auf dem Programm stehen, laufen 5B7
to be out of/short of breath /ˌbi‿ˌaʊt‿əv/ʃɔːt‿əv ˈbreθ/ atemlos sein, außer Atem sein 6A2
to **be over** /ˌbi ˈəʊvə/ vorbei sein I
to **be right** /ˌbiː ˈraɪt/ recht haben I
to **be sure** /ˌbiː ˈʃɔː/ sicher sein I
to **be upset (about sth)** /ˌbi‿ʌpˈset/ (über etw) traurig/aufgebracht sein 2B8
to be worth sth /ˌbiː ˈwɜːθ/ etw wert sein 3A3
to **be wrong** /ˌbiː ˈrɒŋ/ nicht stimmen; sich irren I
◦ to be keen on sb/sth *(informal)* /ˌbiː ˈkiːn‿ɒn/ auf jdn/etw scharf sein 1PP
◦ to be similar (to sb/sth) /ˌbiː ˈsɪmɪlə tə/ (jdm/etw) ähnlich sein 2P3
beach /biːtʃ/ Strand I
to beat *(irr)* /biːt/ schlagen, übertreffen 6C8
beautiful /ˈbjuːtəf(ə)l/ schön I
because /bɪˈkɒz/ weil, da I
to **become** *(irr)* /bɪˈkʌm/ werden 1B7
bed /bed/ Bett I
to **go to bed** /ˌgəʊ tə ˈbed/ ins Bett gehen I
bedroom /ˈbedruːm/ Schlafzimmer 3C5
before /bɪˈfɔː/ bevor, ehe 2B3; zuvor, vorher 3B1; vor 3B3
beginning /bɪˈgɪnɪŋ/ Anfang, Beginn 2C8
to **begin** /bɪˈgɪn/ anfangen, beginnen I
behaviour *(no pl)* /bɪˈheɪvjə/ Benehmen, Verhalten, Betragen 5B8
behind /bɪˈhaɪnd/ hinter I

to **believe** /bɪˈliːv/ glauben I
to **belong to sb** /bɪˈlɒŋ tə/ jdm gehören 3C5
below /bɪˈləʊ/ unter, unterhalb 3B4
best /best/ beste(r, s) I
best /best/ am liebsten/am meisten 1A2
better /ˈbetə/ besser 1B1; lieber 6B1
between /bɪˈtwiːn/ zwischen I
big /bɪg/ groß I
bike *(informal)* /baɪk/ (Fahr)rad I
bike doctor /ˈbaɪk ˌdɒktə/ *jemand, der Fahrräder repariert* 5B2
bin /bɪn/ Mülleimer, Mülltonne 5C6
biology *(no pl)* /baɪˈɒlədʒi/ Biologie 5A2
◦ biosphere /ˈbaɪəʊˌsfɪə/ Biosphäre (irdischer Lebensraum) 1PP
bird /bɜːd/ Vogel I
◦ bird-watching *(no pl)* /ˈbɜːd ˌwɒtʃɪŋ/ *Beobachten von Vögeln* 1PP
birthday /ˈbɜːθdeɪ/ Geburtstag I
bit /bɪt/ Stück, Teil 5B8
to **bite** *(irr)* /baɪt/ beißen 4B11
black /blæk/ schwarz I
to bleed /bliːd/ bluten 6B4
blond(e) /blɒnd/ blond I
to blow up *(irr)* /ˌbləʊ‿ˈʌp/ aufblasen; in die Luft sprengen 2A2
◦ blow-up /ˈbləʊ‿ʌp/ aufblasbar 2O4
blue /bluː/ blau I
board /bɔːd/ Brett, Tafel I
boat /bəʊt/ Boot, Schiff I
◦ to bob /bɒb/ sich bewegen, hüpfen 2O2
◦ body /ˈbɒdi/ Körper 6P14
◦ body part /ˈbɒdi ˌpɑːt/ Körperteil 6P13
◦ body boarding /ˈbɒdi ˌbɔːdɪŋ/ *im Liegen surfen* 1PP
bonfire /ˈbɒnˌfaɪə/ Freudenfeuer, Scheiterhaufen 2A2
book /bʊk/ Buch I
to **book** /bʊk/ reservieren, buchen 3B7
boot /buːt/ Stiefel I
bored /bɔːd/ gelangweilt 2C5
boring /ˈbɔːrɪŋ/ langweilig 1B1
◦ born /bɔːn/ geboren 4P4
bossy /ˈbɒsi/ herrschsüchtig, herrisch 2B4
bossy-boots *(informal)* /ˈbɒsibuːts/ *rechthaberische, belehrende Person* 2B3
both /bəʊθ/ beide 1B1
bottle /ˈbɒt(ə)l/ Flasche I
bottom /ˈbɒtəm/ Boden, (unteres) Ende 3A3
box /bɒks/ Kiste, Schachtel I
boy /bɔɪ/ Junge I
to take a break /ˌteɪk‿ə ˈbreɪk/ eine Pause machen 5B4

to **break** *(irr)* /breɪk/ (zer)brechen; verstoßen gegen 5C2; neu aufstellen 6C2
to **break a rule**: gegen eine Regel verstoßen 5C2
to **break one's arm** /ˌbreɪk wʌnz‿ˈɑːm/ sich den Arm brechen 6B10
breakfast /ˈbrekfəst/ Frühstück I
to **have breakfast** /ˌhæv ˈbrekfəst/ frühstücken I
to be out of/short of breath /ˌbiˌaʊt‿əv/ʃɔːt‿əv ˈbreθ/ atemlos sein, außer Atem sein 6A2
brilliant *(informal)* /ˈbrɪljənt/ toll, klasse 4A3
to **bring** *(irr)* /brɪŋ/ (mit)bringen I
to bring good/bad luck /ˌbrɪŋ‿ˌgʊd/ˌbæd ˈlʌk/ Glück bringen/Unglück bringen 2A2
Britain /ˈbrɪt(ə)n/ Großbritannien I
British /ˈbrɪtɪʃ/ britisch 1C2
◦ broad /brɔːd/ breit 2O4
brochure /ˈbrəʊʃə/ Broschüre, Katalog I
brother /ˈbrʌðə/ Bruder I
brown /braʊn/ braun I
◦ bucket /ˈbʌkɪt/ Eimer, Kübel 2O2
building /ˈbɪldɪŋ/ Gebäude 3A4
◦ to build *(irr)* /bɪld/ bauen 1O1
to **bully** /ˈbʊli/ tyrannisieren, mobben 5C6
◦ to burn down *(irr)* /ˌbɜːn ˈdaʊn/ abbrennen, niederbrennen 1O1
◦ bus stop /ˈbʌs‿ˌstɒp/ Bushaltestelle 6P5
to start a business /ˌstɑːt‿ə ˈbɪznəs/ ein Unternehmen gründen; Handel treiben 1C9
busy /ˈbɪzi/ beschäftigt, arbeitsreich; ereignisreich 3B1
◦ busy /ˈbɪzi/ bewegt 2O2
but /bʌt/ aber I
butter /ˈbʌtə/ Butter I
to **buy** *(irr)* /baɪ/ kaufen I
by /baɪ/ von 4B1
by bike: mit dem (Fahr)rad 5B1
by bus: mit dem Bus 5B8
by heart /ˌbaɪ ˈhɑːt/ auswendig 2C8
◦ by car /ˌbaɪ ˈkɑː/ mit dem Auto 6P1
bye *(informal)*/**goodbye** /baɪ, gʊdˈbaɪ/ tschüss I

C

◦ c (= circa) /ˈsɜːkə/ circa, zirka 1O1
cage /keɪdʒ/ Käfig I
cake /keɪk/ Kuchen I
calendar /ˈkælɪndə/ Kalender I
to **call** /kɔːl/ rufen, nennen, anrufen I
◦ to call for help /ˌkɔːl fə ˈhelp/ um Hilfe rufen 6P15
to **calm down** /ˌkɑːm ˈdaʊn/ sich beruhigen I
camera /ˈkæm(ə)rə/ Kamera, Fotoapparat I
◦ camp /kæmp/ (Zelt)lager 1B6
camping *(no pl)* /ˈkæmpɪŋ/ Camping, Zelten 1A3
can /kæn/ können I
candle /kænd(ə)l/ Kerze 2A2
caption /ˈkæpʃ(ə)n/ Überschrift, Titel, Bildunterschrift 2C7
car /kɑː/ Auto I
card /kɑːd/ Karte I
to **care (about)** /ˈkeə‿əˌbaʊt/ sich etw machen (aus) I
◦ career /kəˈrɪə/ Beruf, Karriere, Werdegang 4P4
careful /ˈkeəf(ə)l/ vorsichtig 1B4
carpet /ˈkɑːpɪt/ Teppich I
to **carry** /ˈkæri/ tragen 2C7
◦ castle /ˈkɑːs(ə)l/ Burg, Schloss 1PP
cat /kæt/ Katze I
◦ to catch sight of /ˌkætʃ ˈsaɪt‿əv/ jdn/etw erblicken 2O2
to **catch** *(irr)* /kætʃ/ fangen I; treffen 6B2
to **celebrate** /ˈseləˌbreɪt/ feiern 2A1
celebration /ˌseləˈbreɪʃ(ə)n/ Feier 2A1
Celt /kelt/ Kelte/Keltin 1C6
◦ Celtic /ˈkeltɪk/ keltisch 1O1
central heating *(no pl)* /ˌsentrəl ˈhiːtɪŋ/ Zentralheizung 5B9
centre /ˈsentə/ Zentrum, Mitte I
century /ˈsentʃəri/ Jahrhundert 3C5
certain /ˈsɜːt(ə)n/ sicher, gewiss, bestimmt 5C2
chain /tʃeɪn/ Kette 2C6
chair /tʃeə/ Stuhl I
Chamber of Horrors /ˈtʃeɪmbər‿əv ˈhɒrəz/ Horrorkabinett 3B1
to **change** /ˈtʃeɪndʒ/ (ver)ändern 3A4
to **change one's mind** /ˌtʃeɪndʒ wʌnz ˈmaɪnd/ es sich anders überlegen; seine Meinung ändern 3B1
changing room /ˈtʃeɪndʒɪŋ ˌruːm/ (Umkleide)kabine 6B10
chant /tʃɑːnt/ (Sprech)gesang, Sprechchor 6C8
to chant /tʃɑːnt/ singen, im Sprechchor rufen 6C4
character /ˈkærɪktə/ Charakter, Figur 1C9
to charge /tʃɑːdʒ/ aufladen 3C2
to chase /tʃeɪs/ hinterherlaufen, verfolgen 6B2
cheap /tʃiːp/ billig, preiswert I

to **cheer** /tʃɪə/ jubeln I
to **cheer up** /ˌtʃɪər‿ˈʌp/ aufmuntern 2C7
cheerful /ˈtʃɪəf(ə)l/ fröhlich, vergnügt, heiter 4B10
cheese /tʃiːz/ Käse I
◦ chess *(no pl)* /tʃes/ Schach(spiel) 5P1
chewing gum *(no pl)* /ˈtʃuːɪŋ‿ˌɡʌm/ Kaugummi 5B6
chicken /ˈtʃɪkɪn/ Huhn I
child (*pl* **children**) /tʃaɪld, ˈtʃɪldrən/ Kind I
◦ Chinese /ˌtʃaɪˈniːz/ Chinese/Chinesin, chinesisch 5P1
Chinese New Year /ˌtʃaɪˌniːz ˌnjuː ˈjɪə/ *Chinesisches Neujahrsfest* 2A2
◦ chips *(only pl)* /tʃɪps/ Pommes frites 6P1
chocolate *(no pl)* /ˈtʃɒklət/ Schokolade I
choice /tʃɔɪs/ Wahl 3B4
choir /ˈkwaɪə/ Chor 4A1
to **choose** *(irr)* /tʃuːz/ (aus)wählen I
Christmas /ˈkrɪsməs/ Weihnachten 2A1
◦ to chuck *(informal)* /tʃʌk/ schmeißen; kippen 2O2
church /tʃɜːtʃ/ Kirche 3C3
cinema /ˈsɪnəmə/ Kino I
circus /ˈsɜːkəs/ Zirkus I
city /ˈsɪti/ (Groß)stadt(-), städtisch 1B3
to clap /klæp/ klatschen 4C1
◦ to clap sb on the back /ˌklæp ˌsʌmbədi‿ɒn ðə ˈbæk/ jdm auf die Schulter klopfen 2O4
class /klɑːs/ (Schul)klasse I
classic /ˈklæsɪk/ Klassiker 4B1
classmate /ˈklɑːsˌmeɪt/ Klassenkamerad/in, Mitschüler/in I
classroom /ˈklɑːsˌruːm/ Klassenzimmer I
to **clean** /kliːn/ sauber machen, reinigen, putzen I
clear /klɪə/ klar, deutlich; eindeutig 1C2
◦ cliff /klɪf/ Klippe, Kliff 1PP
to **climb (up)** /ˌklaɪm‿ˈʌp/ (hinauf) steigen, klettern (auf), besteigen I
clock /klɒk/ Uhr I
to **close** /kləʊz/ schließen, zumachen 2B3
clothes *(only pl)* /kləʊðz/ Kleider, Kleidung I
cloud /klaʊd/ Wolke I
cloudy /ˈklaʊdi/ bewölkt, bedeckt 1A3
club /klʌb/ Klub, Verein 6C8
coach /kəʊtʃ/ Trainer/in I; (Omni)bus, Reisebus 5C5
◦ to coach /kəʊtʃ/ trainieren 6P11
coast /kəʊst/ Küste I
◦ coastline /ˈkəʊstˌlaɪn/ Küste(nlinie) 1PP
coat /kəʊt/ Mantel I
cold /kəʊld/ kalt I
to **collect** /kəˈlekt/ sammeln, einsammeln; aufheben 1A3
◦ college /ˈkɒlɪdʒ/ Gymnasium, Hochschule; Fachbereich 1PP
colour /ˈkʌlə/ Farbe I
◦ colourful /ˈkʌləf(ə)l/ farbenfroh 1P13
combination /ˌkɒmbɪˈneɪʃ(ə)n/ Kombination, Verbindung 5A2
to **come** *(irr)* /kʌm/ kommen I; werden 6C3
to come in /ˌkʌm‿ˈɪn/ hereinkommen, ins Ziel einlaufen 6C4
to come on /ˌkʌm‿ɒn/ anfangen, beginnen, angehen 6C4
Come on! *(informal)* /ˌkʌm‿ˈɒn/ Komm(t) jetzt!, Mach(t) schon! I
comedy /ˈkɒmədi/ Komödie 4B1
◦ comic book /ˈkɒmɪk bʊk/ Comicbuch 2P7
to **comment (on)** /ˈkɒment‿ɒn/ kommentieren 4A5
company /ˈkʌmp(ə)ni/ Firma; Truppe, Ensemble 4A3
to **compare** /kəmˈpeə/ vergleichen 1B5
compass /ˈkʌmpəs/ Kompass 1B7
to compete /kəmˈpiːt/ wetteifern, antreten, kämpfen 6C2
competition /ˌkɒmpəˈtɪʃ(ə)n/ Wettbewerb 4C2
competitive /kəmˈpetətɪv/ konkurrierend, kampfbereit 6C2
to **complete** /kəmˈpliːt/ vervollständigen, ausfüllen 1A2
◦ completely /kəmˈpliːtli/ völlig 4P3
to compost /ˈkɒmpɒst/ kompostieren 5B8
concert /ˈkɒnsət/ Konzert 4A1
confident /ˈkɒnfɪd(ə)nt/ zuversichtlich, selbstsicher, selbstbewusst 6C4
Congratulations! /kənˌɡrætʃʊˈleɪʃ(ə)nz/ Gratuliere!, Glückwunsch! 5B4
to connect /kəˈnekt/ verbinden, anschließen 1B9
connective /kəˈnektɪv/ Bindeglied, Bindewort 1B10
to contact sb /ˈkɒntækt/ sich mit jdm in Verbindung setzen 4A1
◦ control *(no pl)* /kənˈtrəʊl/ Kontrolle; Herrschaft 1O1
conversation /ˌkɒnvəˈseɪʃ(ə)n/ Gespräch, Unterhaltung 2C3
to **convince** /kənˈvɪns/ überzeugen 5C4
convincing /kənˈvɪnsɪŋ/ überzeugend 4C1
to **cook** /kʊk/ kochen I
cooking /ˈkʊkɪŋ/ Kochen
to **copy** /ˈkɒpi/ abschreiben, niederschreiben; kopieren 4B8
corner /ˈkɔːnə/ Ecke 3A4
to correct /kəˈrekt/ korrigieren 6B6
costume /ˈkɒstjuːm/ Kostüm 3A4
◦ to cost *(irr)* /kɒst/ kosten 1B6
couldn't (= **could not**) /ˈkʊdnt, kʊd ˈnɒt/ *Vergangenheitsform von „can't"* I
country /ˈkʌntri/ Land 1B1
◦ countryside *(no pl)* /ˈkʌntriˌsaɪd/ Land, Landschaft 1PP
◦ in the countryside /ˌɪn ðə ˈkʌntriˌsaɪd/ auf dem Land 1PP
of course /əv ˈkɔːs/ natürlich I
cousin /ˈkʌz(ə)n/ Cousin, Cousine I
to cover /ˈkʌvə/ bedecken; sich befassen mit, behandeln 5B8
cow /kaʊ/ Kuh I
crazy /ˈkreɪzi/ verrückt I
to be crazy about sb/sth /ˌbiː ˈkreɪzi‿əˌbaʊt/ nach jdm/etw verrückt sein 2B3
to create /kriˈeɪt/ erschaffen 3C5
◦ creative /kriˈeɪtɪv/ kreativ, schöpferisch 5P1
to creep *(irr)* /kriːp/ kriechen, steigen 4B11
criminal /ˈkrɪmɪn(ə)l/ Verbrecher/in 3C5
crisps *(only pl)* /krɪsps/ Chips 2B3
◦ Croatia /krəʊˈeɪʃə/ Kroatien 4A1
to **cross** /krɒs/ überqueren 3C2
to cross one's fingers for luck /ˌkrɒs wʌnz ˌfɪŋɡəz fə ˈlʌk/ die Daumen drücken 6C4
to **cry** /kraɪ/ weinen, schreien I
cup /kʌp/ Tasse, Becher 5C2; Pokal 6C2
cupboard /ˈkʌbəd/ Schrank I
customer /ˈkʌstəmə/ Kunde/Kundin I
to cut out *(irr)* /ˌkʌt‿ˈaʊt/ (her) ausschneiden 5B8
cute /kjuːt/ süß, niedlich 1B1
to **cut** *(irr)* /kʌt/ schneiden I
to **cycle** /ˈsaɪk(ə)l/ Rad fahren, radeln 6A2
cyclist /ˈsaɪklɪst/ Radfahrer/in 6B10

D

dad *(informal)* /dæd/ Papa, Vati I
to **dance** /dɑːns/ tanzen I
dance *(no pl)* /dɑːns/ Tanz 2A2
◦ dancer /ˈdɑːnsə/ Tänzer/in 6P11

dangerous /ˈdeɪndʒərəs/ gefährlich I
dark /dɑːk/ dunkel I
date /deɪt/ Datum I
daughter /ˈdɔːtə/ Tochter I
day /deɪ/ Tag I
the next day /ðə ˈnekst‿deɪ/ am nächsten Tag 1B10
dead /ded/ tot 3C2
Dear ..., /dɪə/ Sehr geehrte(r) ...; Liebe(r, s) ... I
December /dɪˈsembə/ Dezember I
to **decide** /dɪˈsaɪd/ entscheiden, bestimmen I
to **decorate** /ˈdekəreɪt/ dekorieren 2A2
decoration /ˌdekəˈreɪʃ(ə)n/ Dekoration, (Christbaum)schmuck 2A1
◦ to deepen /ˈdiːpən/ (sich) vertiefen, verstärken; intensiver werden 2O2
◦ deer /dɪə/ Hirsch 1PP
◦ deerstalker /ˈdɪəˌstɔːkə/ *Mütze mit Ohrenklappen* 3C5
to defeat /dɪˈfiːt/ besiegen, schlagen 6C8
delicious /dɪˈlɪʃəs/ köstlich, lecker 1B5
delighted /dɪˈlaɪtɪd/ hocherfreut, begeistert I
department /dɪˈpɑːtmənt/ Institut, Abteilung 4A1
to **depend (on)** /dɪˈpend‿ɒn/ abhängen (von) 6C2
to **describe** /dɪˈskraɪb/ beschreiben 3C5
desk /desk/ Schreibtisch I
◦ desperate /ˈdesp(ə)rət/ verzweifelt 2O2
detail /ˈdiːteɪl/ Detail, Einzelheit 4A5
determined /dɪˈtɜːmɪnd/ entschlossen 6C9
dialogue /ˈdaɪəlɒg/ Gespräch, Dialog I
diary /ˈdaɪəri/ Tagebuch I
dictionary /ˈdɪkʃən(ə)ri/ Wörterbuch 3B5
to **die (of)** /ˈdaɪ‿əv/ sterben (an) 2C7
different /ˈdɪfrənt/ anders, andere(r, s); verschieden 1B10
different /ˈdɪfrənt/ einzeln 6C4
difficult /ˈdɪfɪk(ə)lt/ schwierig, schwer I
◦ dining room /ˈdaɪnɪŋ ˌruːm/ Esszimmer, Speisesaal 2O2
dinner /ˈdɪnə/ Abendessen, Mittagessen I
direct speech /dɪˌrekt ˈspiːtʃ/ direkte Rede 1B10

direction /dɪˈrekʃ(ə)n/ Richtung 1B7
directions *(only pl)* /dɪˈrekʃ(ə)nz/ Anweisungen, Instruktionen; Wegbeschreibung 3C2
dirty /ˈdɜːti/ dreckig, schmutzig 5C6
to **disagree** /ˌdɪsəˈgriː/ nicht übereinstimmen, nicht einverstanden sein 1C6
disappointed /ˌdɪsəˈpɔɪntɪd/ enttäuscht I
to **discuss** /dɪˈskʌs/ besprechen, diskutieren I
◦ discussion /dɪˈskʌʃ(ə)n/ Diskussion, Erörterung 5P1
dishwasher /ˈdɪʃˌwɒʃə/ Geschirrspülmaschine I
to **load the dishwasher** /ˌləʊd ðə ˈdɪʃˌwɒʃə/ die Spülmaschine einräumen I
to **dislike** /dɪsˈlaɪk/ nicht mögen 6C1
◦ to dissolve into giggles and laughter /dɪˌzɒlv‿ˌɪntʊ ˌgɪg(ə)lz‿ən ˈlɑːftə/ loskichern und loslachen 2O4
to divide into /dɪˈvaɪd‿ˌɪntʊ/ (auf)teilen in 5A2
Diwali /dɪˈwɑːli/ *hinduistisches Lichterfest* 2A2
to **do** *(irr)* /duː/ machen, tun I
to do one's best /ˌduː wʌnz ˈbest/ sein Bestes tun/versuchen 6C4
to **do research** /ˌduː ˈriːsɜːtʃ/ (er)forschen, recherchieren 4B1
to **do sightseeing** /ˌduː ˈsaɪtˌsiːɪŋ/ eine Besichtigungstour machen I
to do the washing up /ˌduː ðə ˌwɒʃɪŋˈʌp/ abspülen, abwaschen 5B4
◦ to do karate /ˌduː kəˈrɑːti/ Karate betreiben 6P14
dog /dɒg/ Hund I
to donate /dəʊˈneɪt/ spenden 5A2
door /dɔː/ Tür I
doorbell /ˈdɔːbel/ Türklingel 2C7
double-decker /ˌdʌb(ə)l ˈdekə/ Doppeldecker 3B7
◦ doubtful /ˈdaʊtf(ə)l/ zweifelnd, skeptisch 2O4
down /daʊn/ hinunter, herunter I
dragon /ˈdrægən/ Drache 2A2
◦ drama /ˈdrɑːmə/ Theater-, Schauspiel- 5P1
drama group /ˈdrɑːmə ˌgruːp/ Theatergruppe, Schauspielgruppe 4C7
dramatic /drəˈmætɪk/ dramatisch, theatralisch 6C4
to **draw** *(irr)* /drɔː/ zeichnen I
◦ dream /driːm/ Traum 1P4
to dream (of) /ˈdriːm‿əv/ träumen (von) 4B4

◦ dress /dres/ Kleid 6P15
drink /drɪŋk/ Getränk 4A1
drink *(no pl)* /drɪŋk/ Trinken I
to **drink** *(irr)* /drɪŋk/ trinken I
◦ drive /draɪv/ Einfahrt 2O2
to **drive** *(irr)* /draɪv/ fahren I
◦ to drop /drɒp/ fallen lassen 2O4
◦ druid /ˈdruːɪd/ Druide *(keltischer Priester)* 1PP
duck /dʌk/ Ente I
dummy /ˈdʌmi/ Puppe 2A2
dumpling /ˈdʌmplɪŋ/ Teigtasche 2A2
during /ˈdjʊərɪŋ/ während 6B2

E

each /iːtʃ/ jede(r, s) I
each other /ˌiːtʃ‿ˈʌðə/ einander, gegenseitig 2A2
ear /ɪə/ Ohr I
early /ˈɜːli/ früh, zeitig 5C6
◦ earnestly /ˈɜːnɪstli/ ernsthaft 2O2
◦ east /iːst/ Osten, östlich, Ost- 1PP
easy /ˈiːzi/ leicht, einfach I
to **eat** *(irr)* /iːt/ essen, fressen I
eerie /ˈɪəri/ unheimlich 4B11
e.g. /ˌiː ˈdʒiː/ z. B. (zum Beispiel) 1B9
egg /eg/ Ei I
eight /eɪt/ acht I
◦ either ... or /ˌaɪðə ˈɔː/ entweder ... oder ... 2O5
elbow /ˈelbəʊ/ Ell(en)bogen 6B2
elephant /ˈelɪfənt/ Elefant I
eleven /ɪˈlev(ə)n/ elf I
else /els/ sonst (noch) 2B3
to email /ˈiːmeɪl/ e-mailen, eine E-Mail schreiben 3B3
embarrassed /ɪmˈbærəst/ verlegen, peinlich berührt 2C2
embarrassing /ɪmˈbærəsɪŋ/ peinlich, unangenehm 2C2
emotion /ɪˈməʊʃ(ə)n/ Gefühl, Emotion 4C1
emotional /ɪˈməʊʃ(ə)nəl/ emotional, gefühlvoll 6C9
end /end/ Ende I, Schluss 2C8
in the end /ˌɪn ðɪ‿ˈend/ letzten Endes, schließlich, zum Schluss I
to **end** /end/ beenden, zu Ende bringen; enden 6B1
ending /ˈendɪŋ/ Ende, Schluss 4A5
energy *(no pl)* /ˈenədʒi/ Energie, Kraft 5A2
English /ˈɪŋglɪʃ/ Englisch; englisch I
English-speaking /ˈɪŋglɪʃˌspiːkɪŋ/ englischsprachig 2A3
to **enjoy** /ɪnˈdʒɔɪ/ genießen I
enough /ɪˈnʌf/ genügend, ausreichend, genug I
entertaining /ˌentəˈteɪnɪŋ/ unterhaltsam 5A4

entertainment / ˌentəˈteɪnmənt / Unterhaltung 5A2
enthusiastic / ɪnˌθjuːziˈæstɪk / enthusiastisch, begeistert 6C4
envelope / ˈenvələʊp / Briefumschlag 2A2
environment *(no pl)* / ɪnˈvaɪrənmənt / Umwelt 5A2
especially / ɪˈspeʃ(ə)li / besonders, insbesondere 3B1
even / ˈiːv(ə)n / selbst, sogar I
even if / ˈiːv(ə)n‿ɪf / selbst wenn 3B7
evening / ˈiːvnɪŋ / Abend I
in the evening / ˌɪn ðiˈiːvnɪŋ / am Abend I
event / ɪˈvent / Ereignis, Veranstaltung, Event 6C2
ever / ˈevə / jemals 3B7
every / ˈevri / jede(r, s) I
everybody / ˈevriˌbɒdi / alle, jede/r I
everyone / ˈevriˌwʌn / jede/r 1B7; alle zusammen 2C7
everyone else / ˌevriˌwʌn‿ˈels / jede/r andere 4C5
everything / ˈevriθɪŋ / alles I
everywhere / ˈevriˌweə / überall I
exactly / ɪgˈzæktli / genau I
exam / ɪgˈzæm / Prüfung I
example / ɪgˈzɑːmp(ə)l / Beispiel I
excellent / ˈeksələnt / ausgezeichnet 4A3
except / ɪkˈsept / außer 1B7
excited / ɪkˈsaɪtɪd / aufgeregt I
exciting / ɪkˈsaɪtɪŋ / aufregend I, spannend 1A3
exercise / ˈeksəsaɪz / Übung, Aufgabe 5A2
exercise book / ˈeksəsaɪz ˌbʊk / Heft I
to **expect** / ɪkˈspekt / erwarten, rechnen 2C2
expensive / ɪkˈspensɪv / teuer I
experience *(no pl)* / ɪkˈspɪəriəns / Erfahrung, Erlebnis I
to **explain (sth to sb)** / ɪkˈspleɪn / (jdm etw) erklären I
to **explore** / ɪkˈsplɔː / erforschen, untersuchen 3A4
to express / ɪkˈspres / ausdrücken, aussprechen 1C3
eye / aɪ / Auge I
to roll one's eyes / ˌrəʊl wʌnz‿ˈaɪz / die Augen verdrehen 4C1

F

fabulous / ˈfæbjʊləs / fabelhaft, sagenhaft 2B2
face / feɪs / Gesicht I
to pull a face / ˌpʊl‿ə ˈfeɪs / das Gesicht verziehen 4C1
fact / fækt / Wirklichkeit, Tatsache 6B2
to **fall** *(irr)* / fɔːl / (um)fallen, stürzen I
to **fall down** / ˌfɔːl ˈdaʊn / hin(unter) fallen, (ein)stürzen 6B2, zusammenfallen 5C6
to fall off / ˌfɔːl‿ˈɒf / (hinunter) fallen 1B1
◦ false / fɔːls / falsch 1P15
◦ fame / feɪm / Ruhm 2O
family / ˈfæm(ə)li / Familie I
famous / ˈfeɪməs / berühmt 2A2
fantastic *(informal)* / fænˈtæstɪk / fantastisch I
fantasy / ˈfæntəsi / Vorstellung, Fantasie 2C6
farm / fɑːm / Bauernhof I
◦ farmer / ˈfɑːmə / Bauer/Bäuerin 1O1
fascinating / ˈfæsɪneɪtɪŋ / faszinierend I
fashion / ˈfæʃ(ə)n / Mode 5A2
fast / fɑːst / schnell 1B1
father / ˈfɑːðə / Vater I
fault / fɔːlt / Schuld, Fehler 1C2
favourite / ˈfeɪv(ə)rət / Lieblings- I
favourite / ˈfeɪv(ə)rət / Liebling, Favorit/in 1C7
February / ˈfebruəri / Februar I
to **feed** *(irr)* / fiːd / (zu) essen geben, füttern I
to **feel** *(irr)* / fiːl / (sich) fühlen 1C3; halten von 2B9
to feel sorry / ˌfiːl ˈsɒri / bedauern, leidtun 1C3
◦ to feel that ... / ˈfiːl ðæt / der Meinung sein, dass ... 1O1
feeling / ˈfiːlɪŋ / Gefühl I
festival / ˈfestɪv(ə)l / Fest 2A2
as fit as a fiddle *(informal)* / æz ˌfɪt‿æz‿ə ˈfɪd(ə)l / fit wie ein Turnschuh sein 6A2
field / fiːld / Wiese, Feld; Spielfeld 6C4
field study / ˈfiːld ˌstʌdi / Feldstudie *(systematische wissenschaftliche Beobachtung außerhalb des Labors)* 5A2
fieldwork / ˈfiːldˌwɜːk / Feldarbeit, Feldforschung 5A2
◦ fighter / ˈfaɪtə / Kämpfer/in 1O1
to **fight** *(irr)* / faɪt / (be)kämpfen 6C4
to **fill in** / ˌfɪl‿ˈɪn / (aus)füllen, eintragen 1B4
◦ film / fɪlm / Film 1PP
◦ to film / fɪlm / filmen, drehen 1PP
finally / ˈfaɪn(ə)li / schließlich, endlich I
to **find** *(irr)* / faɪnd / finden I
to **find out** / ˌfaɪnd‿ˈaʊt / herausfinden 1A3
to **finish** / ˈfɪnɪʃ / (be)enden, aufhören I; abschließen 5B4
finishing line / ˈfɪnɪʃɪŋ laɪn / Ziellinie 6C4
fireworks *(only pl)* / ˈfaɪəˌwɜːks / Feuerwerk 2A2
first / fɜːst / erste(r, s) I; zuerst; als Erstes 1B2
◦ first of all / ˌfɜːst‿əv‿ˈɔːl / zu(aller) erst 2O4
first night / ˌfɜːst ˈnaɪt / Premiere 4C5
fish *(pl* **fish** *or* **fishes)** / fɪʃ, fɪʃ, fɪʃɪz / Fisch I
to **fit** / fɪt / passen I
five / faɪv / fünf I
flag / flæg / Fahne, Flagge 6B4
flexible / ˈfleksəb(ə)l / flexibel, biegsam, gelenkig 6A2
◦ to flicker / ˈflɪkə / flackern 2O2
floor / flɔː / Boden I; Stock(werk) 3A4
to **sweep the floor** / ˌswiːp ðə ˈflɔː / den Boden fegen I
flower / ˈflaʊə / Blume I
to **fly** *(irr)* / flaɪ / fliegen I
foggy / ˈfɒgi / neblig 1A3
to **follow** / ˈfɒləʊ / folgen I
to follow sb around / ˌfɒləʊ ˌsʌmbədi‿əˈraʊnd / jdm überallhin folgen 2C2
following / ˈfɒləʊɪŋ / folgende(r, s) 2P8
food *(no pl)* / fuːd / Essen, Nahrung, Futter I
to make a fool of sb/oneself / ˌmeɪk‿ə ˈfuːl‿əv / jdn/sich lächerlich machen 5B8
foot *(pl* **feet)** / fʊt, fiːt / Fuß I
football / ˈfʊtˌbɔːl / Fußball I
for / fɔː / für I; seit 4B1
for a while / fər‿ə ˈwaɪl / eine ganze Weile; schon länger 4B1
for ages *(informal)* / fər‿ˈeɪdʒɪz / eine Ewigkeit, ewig 4B1
for example / fər‿ɪgˈzɑːmp(ə)l / zum Beispiel I
for free *(informal)* / fə ˈfriː / gratis, umsonst 3A4
for help / fə ˈhelp / als Hilfe 6A6
for how long / fə ˈhaʊ ˌlɒŋ / wie lange (schon) 4B4
◦ for a long time / fər‿ə ˈlɒŋ ˌtaɪm / lange Zeit 6P15
forest / ˈfɒrɪst / Wald 5A2
forever / fərˈevə / ewig, ständig 4C1
to **forget** *(irr)* / fəˈget / vergessen I
fork / fɔːk / Gabel 5C2
to **form** / fɔːm / formen, bilden 2B6
◦ form / fɔːm / Form 6P11
four / fɔː / vier I
◦ fragrance / ˈfreɪgrəns / Duft, Parfüm 4P4
free time / ˌfriː ˈtaɪm / Freizeit I

◦ to freeze *(irr)* /friːz/ gefrieren; erstarren 2O2
French /frentʃ/ Französisch I
Friday /ˈfraɪdeɪ/ Freitag I
fridge *(informal)* /frɪdʒ/ Kühlschrank I
friend /frend/ Freund/in I
friendly /ˈfrendli/ freundlich I
frightened /ˈfraɪt(ə)nd/ verängstigt 3C1
from /frɒm/ von, aus I
front *(no pl)* /frʌnt/ vorderer Bereich 5C5
fruit *(no pl)* /fruːt/ Frucht, Obst I
frustrated /frʌˈstreɪtɪd/ frustriert 6C9
full /fʊl/ voll; überfüllt 3C2
fun *(no pl)* /fʌn/ Spaß I
to **be fun** /ˌbiː ˈfʌn/ Spaß machen I
fundraising /ˈfʌndreɪzɪŋ/ Geldbeschaffung, Wohltätigkeits-/Benefiz- 4A1
funny /ˈfʌni/ lustig, witzig, komisch I
furniture *(no pl)* /ˈfɜːnɪtʃə/ Möbel I
future /ˈfjuːtʃə/ Zukunft 2B6
◦ futuristic /ˌfjuːtʃəˈrɪstɪk/ futuristisch 1PP

G

to gain /geɪn/ bekommen, erreichen, gewinnen 6C2
gallery /ˈgæləri/ Galerie 3C5
game /geɪm/ Spiel I
garden /ˈgɑːd(ə)n/ Garten I
◦ gardener /ˈgɑːd(ə)nə/ Gärtner/in 6P10
gaslight /ˈgæsˌlaɪt/ Gaslampe 3C5
◦ gently /ˈdʒentli/ sanft, behutsam 2O2
geography /dʒiːˈɒgrəfi/ Erdkunde, Geografie I
German /ˈdʒɜːmən/ Deutsche/r; Deutsch(unterricht); deutsch I
◦ to gesture /ˈdʒestʃə/ deuten 2O4
to **get** *(irr)* /get/ erhalten, bekommen; holen I; werden 2C7; geraten 6A2
to **get away** /ˌget‿əˈweɪ/ fortkommen, flüchten I
to **get back** /ˌget ˈbæk/ zurückkommen I
to **get dressed** /ˌget‿ˈdrest/ sich anziehen I
to get home /ˌget ˈhəʊm/ nach Hause kommen 3C5
to **get into** /ˈget‿ˌɪntʊ/ einsteigen in 3A4
to get into trouble /ˌget‿ˌɪntʊ ˈtrʌb(ə)l/ in Schwierigkeiten geraten 1C1
to **get lost** /ˌget ˈlɒst/ sich verirren, sich verlaufen 3C2
to **get off** /ˌget‿ˈɒf/ aussteigen 3C2; runterkommen 6A2
Get off! /ˌget‿ˈɒf/ Geh weg! 5C6
to **get scared** /ˌget ˈskeərd/ sich (anfangen zu) fürchten 2C5
to get set /ˌget ˈset/ vorbereiten, bereit machen 6B1
to get sth started /ˌget ˌsʌmθɪŋ ˈstɑːtɪd/ etw ins Laufen bringen 2A1
to **get to** /ˈget‿tʊ/ erreichen I
to **get up** /ˌget‿ˈʌp/ aufstehen I
to **get used** to /ˌget ˈjuːst‿tʊ/ sich gewöhnen an I
◦ to get back /ˌget ˈbæk/ zurückholen 6P15
◦ to get there /ˈget ðeə/ hinkommen 1PP
◦ to get up /ˌget‿ˈʌp/ verkleiden 2O2
ghost /gəʊst/ Geist, Gespenst I
ghostly /ˈgəʊstli/ geisterhaft 4B11
girl /gɜːl/ Mädchen I
◦ girlfriend /ˈgɜːlˌfrend/ Freundin 6P3
girly /ˈgɜːli/ mädchenhaft 4B1
to **give** *(irr)* /gɪv/ geben I
to give away /ˌgɪv‿əˈweɪ/ verschenken, hergeben 5C5
to give in /ˌgɪv‿ˈɪn/ nachgeben, aufgeben 6C4
to give sb a scare /ˌgɪv ˌsʌmbədi‿ə ˈskeə/ jdm einen Schreck einjagen 4B11
to give sb the thumbs down /ˌgɪv ˌsʌmbədi ðə ˌθʌmz ˈdaʊn/ *jemandem den Daumen nach unten zeigen* 4C1
to **give up** /ˌgɪv‿ˈʌp/ aufgeben, resignieren 6C4
◦ to give a little jump /ˌgɪv‿ə ˌlɪt(ə)l ˈdʒʌmp/ einen Hüpfer machen 2O2
◦ to give sth to sb: jdm etw geben 4P5
◦ gladiator fighting *(no pl)* /ˈglædiˌeɪtə ˌfaɪtɪŋ/ Gladiatorenkämpfe 1O1
glass *(no pl)* /glɑːs/ Glas 5B8
gloomy /ˈgluːmi/ trostlos, düster; betrübt 4C5
◦ glow /gləʊ/ Leuchten, Scheinen 2O2
glue *(no pl)* /gluː/ Klebstoff I
to **go** *(irr)* /gəʊ/ gehen, fahren I
to **go to bed** /ˌgəʊ tə ˈbed/ ins Bett gehen I
to **go camping** /ˌgəʊ ˈkæmpɪŋ/ zelten gehen I
to go for a ride /ˌgəʊ fər‿ə raɪd/ eine Fahrt machen; ausreiten 1B1
◦ to go horse-riding /ˌgəʊ ˈhɔːsˌraɪdɪŋ/ reiten gehen 1B6
to go mad /ˌgəʊ ˈmæd/ verrückt werden; ausflippen 5C5
to go off /ˌgəʊ‿ˈɒf/ hochgehen, explodieren 2C7
to **go on a tour** /ˌgəʊ‿ɒn‿ə ˈtʊə/ eine Tour machen 3B1
to **go on a trip** /ˌgəʊ‿ɒn‿ə ˈtrɪp/ einen Ausflug / eine Reise machen 3B9
to **go on holiday** /ˌgəʊ‿ɒn ˈhɒlədeɪ/ in Urlaub gehen/fahren I
to **go on** /ˌgəʊ‿ˈɒn/ weitergehen; passieren; weitermachen I
to go red /ˌgəʊ ˈred/ rot werden 5C6
to **go shopping** /ˌgəʊ ˈʃɒpɪŋ/ einkaufen gehen I
to **go surfing** /ˌgəʊ ˈsɜːfɪŋ/ surfen gehen I
to **go swimming** /ˌgəʊ ˈswɪmɪŋ/ schwimmen gehen I
to **go to the seaside** /ˌgəʊ tə ðə ˈsiːˌsaɪd/ ans Meer fahren I
to **go walking** /ˌgəʊ ˈwɔːkɪŋ/ wandern, spazieren gehen I
◦ to go online /ˌgəʊ‿ˌɒnˈlaɪn/ online gehen 1P12
◦ to go whale spotting /ˌgəʊ ˈweɪl ˌspɒtɪŋ/ Wale beobachten gehen 1PP
goal /gəʊl/ Ziel, Tor 6B1
◦ gobsmacked *(informal)* /ˈgɒbˌsmækt/ baff, platt 2O4
goddess /ˈgɒdes/ Göttin 2A2
Going green /ˌgəʊɪŋ‿ˈgriːn/ sich immer umweltbewusster verhalten 5A1
good /gʊd/ gut I
to **be good at** /ˌbiː ˈgʊd‿ət/ gut in … sein I
◦ goods *(only pl)* /gʊdz/ Waren, Güter 1O2
grandfather /ˈgrænˌfɑːðə/ Großvater I
◦ Grandma *(informal)* /ˈgrænˌmɑː/ Oma, Omi 1P5
grandmother /ˈgrænˌmʌðə/ Großmutter I
grandparents *(only pl)* /ˈgrænˌpeərənts/ Großeltern I
◦ gravel *(no pl)* /ˈgræv(ə)l/ Kies, Schotter 2O2
great /greɪt/ groß, riesig, großartig, wunderbar I
◦ Great Britain /ˌgreɪt ˈbrɪt(ə)n/ Großbritannien 1PP
Greek /griːk/ Grieche/Griechin, griechisch 2B3
green /griːn/ grün I
◦ to greet /griːt/ grüßen 2O2
grey /greɪ/ grau I
grid /grɪd/ Gitter(netz), Tabelle 1A2
◦ to grin /grɪn/ grinsen 2O2

ground /graʊnd/ (Erd)boden, Erde; Platz 6B1
group /gruːp/ Gruppe I
to **guess** /ges/ (er)raten I; annehmen 1C2
◦ to guess /ges/ vermuten 6P5
Guess what! /ˌges ˈwɒt/ Stell dir vor!, Rate mal! 2B5
guest /gest/ Gast I
guidebook /ˈgaɪdˌbʊk/ Reiseführer 3C8
guy /gaɪ/ Kerl, Typ; Guy-Fawkes-Puppe 2C7
gym /dʒɪm/ Turnhalle I

H

hair *(no pl)* /heə/ Haare I
◦ hairdresser /ˈheəˌdresə/ Friseur/in 6P10
half /hɑːf/ halb; dreißig Minuten I
half an hour /ˌhɑːf‿ən‿ˈaʊə/ eine halbe Stunde I
half past (seven) /ˌhɑːf pɑːst ˈsev(ə)n/ halb (acht) I
half *(pl* halves) /hɑːf, hɑːvz/ Hälfte 4A3
◦ halfway down /ˌhɑːfˌweɪ ˈdaʊn/ in der Mitte 2O2
ham /hæm/ Schinken I
hand /hænd/ Hand I
handprint /ˈhændˌprɪnt/ Handabdruck 5A2
to hang out with sb /ˌhæŋ‿ˈaʊt wɪð/ Zeit mit jdm verbringen 4B11
to **happen** /ˈhæpən/ geschehen, passieren I
happy /ˈhæpi/ glücklich, zufrieden, fröhlich I
hard /hɑːd/ hart, schwer, schwierig 4A3
hardly /ˈhɑːdli/ kaum 6A2
hat /hæt/ Hut I
to **hate** /heɪt/ hassen, verabscheuen I
to **hate to do** /ˌheɪt‿tə ˈduː/ äußerst ungern tun 4A1
to **have** *(irr)* /hæv/ haben; essen I
to have a crush on /ˌhæv‿ə ˈkrʌʃ‿ɒn/ verknallt sein in 2C2
to **have a look** /ˌhæv‿ə ˈlʊk/ nachsehen, nachschauen 3C5
to **have a party** /ˌhæv‿ə ˈpɑːti/ eine Party geben I
to have a vote /ˌhæv‿ə ˈvəʊt/ abstimmen 5B4
to **have breakfast** /ˌhæv ˈbrekfəst/ frühstücken I
to **have got** /ˌhæv ˈgɒt/ haben I
to **have lunch** /ˌhæv ˈlʌntʃ/ zu Mittag essen I
◦ to have tea /ˌhæv ˈtiː/ Tee trinken 3P8
have to /ˈhæv tə/ müssen I
to **have/take a shower** /ˌhæv/ˌteɪk‿ə ˈʃaʊə/ sich duschen 5C6
he /hiː/ er I
head /hed/ Kopf I
head teacher /ˌhed‿ˈtiːtʃə/ Schulleiter/in, Direktor/in 1C2
heading /ˈhedɪŋ/ Überschrift, Titel 3B4
headline /ˈhedˌlaɪn/ Schlagzeile 5A4
health *(no pl)* /helθ/ Gesundheit 6A2
◦ heart /hɑːt/ Herz 2O2
to **hear** *(irr)* /hɪə/ hören I
hello /həˈləʊ/ hallo! I
help /help/ Hilfe 1C6
to **help** /help/ helfen I
her /hɜː/ ihr(e, r) I, ihr; sie I
here /hɪə/ hier I
here /hɪə/ hierher 3C2
here you are /ˌhɪə ju‿ˈɑː/ Hier, bitte!, Bitte schön! I
here you go /ˌhɪə ju ˈgəʊ/ Hier, bitte!, Bitte schön! 1B7
hers /hɜːz/ ihre(r, s), ihrs 5C5
to **hide** *(irr)* /haɪd/ (sich) verstecken I
high /haɪ/ hoch I
high jump *(no pl)* /ˈhaɪ dʒʌmp/ Hochsprung 6C2
hill /hɪl/ Hügel, Berg 1B7
him /hɪm/ ihm, ihn I
himself /hɪmˈself/ sich, selbst; persönlich 2B2
Hindu /ˈhɪnduː/ Hindu, hinduistisch, Hindu- 2A2
his /hɪz/ sein(e, r) I; seine(r, s), seins 5C5
history /ˈhɪst(ə)ri/ Geschichte *(als Schulfach)* I
to **hit** *(irr)* /hɪt/ schlagen, treffen, stoßen (gegen) 6B2
Hogmanay /ˈhɒgməneɪ/ *traditionelles schottisches Neujahrsfest* 2A3
to **hold** *(irr)* /həʊld/ halten 6B4
to hold up /ˌhəʊld‿ˈʌp/ hochhalten 5C6
◦ to hold out /ˌhəʊld‿ˈaʊt/ ausstrecken 2O2
holiday /ˈhɒlədeɪ/ Urlaub, Ferien I
on holiday /ɒn ˈhɒlədeɪ/ im Urlaub, in den Ferien I
to **go on holiday** /ˌgəʊ‿ɒn ˈhɒlədeɪ/ in Urlaub gehen/fahren I
home /həʊm/ zu Hause; nach Hause 6B2
at home /æt ˈhəʊm/ zu Hause I
to get home /ˌget ˈhəʊm/ nach Hause kommen 3C5
home town /ˈhəʊm ˌtaʊn/ Heimatstadt 1A3
homework *(no pl)* /ˈhəʊmwɜːk/ Hausaufgabe(n) I
honest /ˈɒnɪst/ ehrlich 3B1
◦ honestly /ˈɒnɪstli/ (ganz) ehrlich 2O2
to **hoover** /ˈhuːvə/ staubsaugen I
to hop off /ˌhɒp‿ˈɒf/ schnell aussteigen 3B7
to hop on /ˌhɒp‿ˈɒn/ schnell einsteigen 3B7
to **hope** /həʊp/ hoffen I
horrible /ˈhɒrəb(ə)l/ schrecklich 3C5
horse /hɔːs/ Pferd I
to go horse-riding /ˌgəʊ ˈhɔːsˌraɪdɪŋ/ reiten gehen 1B6
hospital /ˈhɒspɪt(ə)l/ Krankenhaus 3C3
◦ host family /ˈhəʊst ˌfæm(ə)li/ Gastfamilie 6P5
hot /hɒt/ heiß I
hour /ˈaʊə/ Stunde I
house /haʊs/ Haus I
Houses of Parliament /ˌhaʊzɪz‿əv ˈpɑː(r)ləmənt/ das Parlament (von Großbritannien) 2A2
◦ housewife /ˈhaʊsˌwaɪf/ Hausfrau 6P10
how /haʊ/ wie I
How are you? /ˌhaʊ‿ˈɑː juː/ Wie geht es dir/Ihnen/euch? I
How many ...? /haʊ ˈmeni/ Wie viele ...? I
How much is/are ...? /ˈhaʊ ˌmʌtʃ‿ɪz/ɑː/ Was kostet/kosten ...? I
How much ...? /ˌhaʊ ˈmʌtʃ/ Wie viel ...? I
How old are you?: Wie alt bist du? I
how to /ˈhaʊ tə/ wie man 1C6
however /haʊˈevə/ jedoch 1B7
to hug /hʌg/ umarmen 6C4
huge /hjuːdʒ/ riesig, riesengroß 3C2
hungry /ˈhʌŋgri/ hungrig I
◦ hurdles *(only pl)* /ˈhɜːd(ə)lz/ Hürdenlauf 6P11
◦ to hurry /ˈhʌri/ sich beeilen 2O2; schnell gehen 2O4
Hurry up! /ˌhʌri‿ˈʌp/ Beeil dich!, Beeilt euch! 5C6
hurt /hɜːt/ verletzt, verwundet I
to **hurt** (sb) /ˈhɜːt/ (jdm) wehtun, (jdn) verletzen 6B5
husband /ˈhʌzbənd/ (Ehe)mann I

I

I /aɪ/ ich I
I don't think so /aɪ ˌdəʊnt ˈθɪŋk səʊ/ Das glaube ich nicht 1C2
I guess ... /aɪ ˈges/ Ich

schätze ... I
I took the team on whole. /aɪ ˌtʊk ðə ˌtiːm‿ɒn ˈhəʊl/ Ich nahm es mit der ganzen Mannschaft auf. 6B1
I'd (= I would) /aɪd, aɪ ˈwʊd/ ich würde 3B1
I'd like to (= I would like to) /aɪd ˈlaɪk tʊ, aɪ ˌwʊd ˈlaɪk tʊ/ ich würde gern 3A3
I'm afraid /ˌaɪm‿əˈfreɪd/ leider I
I'm fine /aɪm ˈfaɪn/ Es geht mir gut. I
I'm from ... Ich komme aus ... I
(I'm) sorry. /ˌaɪm ˈsɒri/ Entschuldigung!, Tut mir leid. I
I'm ten. Ich bin zehn (Jahre alt). I
I'm ... years old. Ich bin ... Jahre alt. I
∘ I'd love to (= I would love to) /aɪd ˈlʌv tʊ, aɪ ˌwʊd ˈlʌv tʊ/ ich würde sehr gern 3P5
∘ I'd rather (= I would rather) /aɪd ˈrɑːðə, aɪ ˌwʊd ˈrɑːðə/ ich würde lieber 3P5
ice cream /ˌaɪs ˈkriːm/ Eiscreme, Eis I
idea /aɪˈdɪə/ Idee, Einfall I
∘ ideal /aɪˈdɪəl/ ideal 1PP
if /ɪf/ wenn, falls, ob 1B7
ill /ɪl/ krank I
to **imagine** /ɪˈmædʒɪn/ sich vorstellen 2A2
immediately /ɪˈmiːdiətli/ sofort, gleich, direkt 5C2
impatient /ɪmˈpeɪʃ(ə)nt/ ungeduldig 6C4
important /ɪmˈpɔːt(ə)nt/ wichtig, wesentlich, bedeutend 2C2
to **improve** /ɪmˈpruːv/ (sich) verbessern, besser werden 6C8
in /ɪn/ in; auf I
in English /ɪn‿ˈɪŋglɪʃ/ auf Englisch I
in front of /ɪn ˈfrʌnt‿əv/ vor I
in style /ɪn ˈstaɪl/ stilvoll 2B2
in the afternoon /ˌɪn ðiˌ‿ɑːftəˌnuːn/ am Nachmittag I
in the end /ˌɪn ði‿ˈend/ letzten Endes, schließlich, zum Schluss I
in the evening /ˌɪn ði‿ˈiːvnɪŋ/ am Abend I
in the morning /ˌɪn ðə ˈmɔːnɪŋ/ am Morgen I
in winter /ɪn ˈwɪntə/ im Winter I
∘ in fact /ɪn ˈfækt/ genaugenommen 2O2
∘ in order to do sth /ɪn‿ˌɔːdə tʊ ˈduː/ um etw zu tun 1O2
∘ in the countryside /ˌɪn ðə ˈkʌntriˌsaɪd/ auf dem Land 1PP
to **include** /ɪnˈkluːd/ beinhalten; mit einschließen 2A3; aufnehmen 4A2
included /ɪnˈkluːdɪd/ inklusive 4A1
∘ including /ɪnˈkluːdɪŋ/ einschließlich 2O2
∘ incomplete /ˌɪnkəmˈpliːt/ unvollständig, unfertig 6P3
∘ India /ˈɪndiə/ Indien 4P10
∘ indoors /ɪnˈdɔː(r)z/ hinein, nach drinnen 2O2
infinitive /ɪnˈfɪnətɪv/ Infinitiv (Grundform des Verbs) 6B3
∘ informal /ɪnˈfɔːm(ə)l/ informell 6P3
information *(no pl)* /ˌɪnfəˈmeɪʃ(ə)n/ Information(en), Auskunft I
informative /ɪnˈfɔː(r)mətɪv/ informativ 1A3
inside /ˈɪnˌsaɪd/ innen, drinnen; nach drinnen 2C7
instructor /ɪnˈstrʌktə/ Betreuer/in 1B7
interest /ˈɪntrəst/ Interesse I
to **be interested (in)** /ˌbi‿ˈɪntrəstɪd‿ɪn/ sich interessieren (für), interessiert sein (an) I
interesting /ˈɪntrəstɪŋ/ interessant I
∘ to search the Internet /ˌsɜːtʃ ði‿ˈɪntəˌnet/ im Internet recherchieren 1PP
to **interview** /ˈɪntəˌvjuː/ interviewen, befragen 5B4
into /ˈɪntuː/ in 2A2
to introduce /ˌɪntrəˈdjuːs/ vorstellen; einleiten 2B6
introduction /ˌɪntrəˈdʌkʃ(ə)n/ Vorstellung; Einleitung 4A5
∘ to invade /ɪnˈveɪd/ einfallen, einmarschieren 1O1
invasion /ɪnˈveɪʒ(ə)n/ Invasion, Eindringen 4B1
invitation /ˌɪnvɪˈteɪʃ(ə)n/ Einladung I
to **invite** /ɪnˈvaɪt/ einladen I
∘ irregular /ɪˈregjʊlə/ unregelmäßig 6P7
island /ˈaɪlənd/ Insel I
it /ɪt/ es, er/sie/es I
it says /ɪt ˈsez/ darauf steht 3C2
it says so /ɪt ˈsez‿səʊ/ es steht da 3C5
It won't happen again.: Es wird nicht wieder vorkommen.
it's (= it is) /ɪts, ˈɪt‿ɪz/ es ist I; es kostet I
it's (= it is) /ɪts, ˈɪt‿ɪz/ hier spricht 2B5
it's OK *(informal)* /ɪts‿əʊˈkeɪ/ es geht schon 1B7
IT *(no pl)* (= **information technology**) /ˌaɪ ˈtiː, ˌɪnfəˈmeɪʃ(ə)n tekˌnɒlədʒi/ Informationstechnologie I
its /ɪts/ sein(e), ihr(e) I

J

jacket /ˈdʒækɪt/ Jacke I
January /ˈdʒænjuəri/ Januar I
jealous /ˈdʒeləs/ eifersüchtig, neidisch 6C9
∘ job /dʒɒb/ Stelle, Job 6P10
to jog /dʒɒg/ joggen 6B5
∘ to **join** /dʒɔɪn/ verbinden; sich gesellen 6C4
juice /dʒuːs/ Saft I
July /dʒʊˈlaɪ/ Juli I
jumble sale /ˈdʒʌmb(ə)l seɪl/ Flohmarkt, Wohltätigkeitsbasar 4A1
jump /dʒʌmp/ Sprung, Satz 6C4
to **jump (up)** /ˌdʒʌmp‿ˈʌp/ (auf) springen, (hoch)springen I
June /dʒuːn/ Juni I
∘ jungle /ˈdʒʌŋg(ə)l/ Dschungel, Urwald 1PP
just /dʒʌst/ nur; bloß; einfach I; gerade 2B5; genau 4C1

K

to **keep** *(irr)* /kiːp/ behalten, aufbewahren; halten I
to keep away /ˌkiːp‿əˈweɪ/ fernhalten 2A2
to keep cool /ˌkiːp ˈkuːl/ ruhig bleiben, cool bleiben 4C6
∘ to keep hold of /ˌkiːp‿ˈhəʊld‿əv/ festhalten 2O4
∘ to keep up with sb /ˌkiːp‿ˈʌp wɪð/ mit jdm Schritt halten 2O2
to keep up /ˌkiːp‿ˈʌp/ hochhalten; weiterhin tun 6A2; dranbleiben 6C4
to keep warm /ˌkiːp ˈwɔːm/ warm halten, nicht frieren 5B9
to kick /kɪk/ treten, schießen 6B1
to **kill** /kɪl/ töten, umbringen 2A2
kind /kaɪnd/ nett, freundlich, liebenswürdig 4C1
kind /kaɪnd/ Art, Sorte 1C9
king /kɪŋ/ König 2A2
∘ kitchen /ˈkɪtʃən/ Küche 2P7
knife *(pl* **knives***)* /naɪf, naɪvz/ Messer 5C2
to **know** *(irr)* /nəʊ/ wissen, kennen I

L

∘ to label /ˈleɪb(ə)l/ etikettieren, beschriften 6P13
lady /ˈleɪdi/ Frau, Dame I
lamp /læmp/ Lampe I
to land /lænd/ landen 2C7

° land *(no pl)* /lænd/ Land, Boden 1O1
language /ˈlæŋgwɪdʒ/ Sprache 1C9
° lantern /ˈlæntən/ Laterne 2O2
last /lɑːst/ letzte(r, s) I
late /leɪt/ (zu) spät I
later /leɪtə/ später I
° Latin /ˈlætɪn/ Latein(-), lateinisch, Latino(-) 5P1
to **laugh** /lɑːf/ lachen I
° laugh *(no pl)* /lɑːf/ Lachen 2O2
° lawyer /ˈlɔːjə/ Rechtsanwalt/-anwältin 6P10
to **lay the table** /ˌleɪ ðə ˈteɪb(ə)l/ den Tisch decken I
lazy /ˈleɪzi/ faul, träge 5B4
lead /liːd/ Leine, Führung 6C2
to be in the lead /ˌbi‿ɪn ðə ˈliːd/ in Führung sein 6C2
° to lead *(irr)* /li/ führen 2O4
° to lead the way /ˌliːd ðə ˈweɪ/ vorangehen 2O2
leading role /ˌliːdɪŋ ˈrəʊl/ Hauptrolle 4C1
leaflet /ˈliːflət/ Flyer, Prospekt I
to **learn** *(irr)* /lɜːn/ lernen I
to leave for /ˈliːv‿fɔː/ gehen nach; gehen auf 4A1
to leave on standby /ˌliːv‿ɒn ˈstændbaɪ/ im Stand-by-Betrieb lassen 5B3
to leave sb alone /ˌliːv ˌsʌmbədi‿əˈləʊn/ jdn in Ruhe lassen 5C6
° to leave out /ˌliːv‿ˈaʊt/ auslassen, weglassen 5C8
to **leave** *(irr)* /liːv/ verlassen, weggehen; zurücklassen I; lassen 6B1
left /left/ (nach) links I
left /left/ linke Seite 6C4
leg /leg/ Bein I
less /les/ weniger 5B8
lesson /ˈles(ə)n/ (Unterrichts)stunde I
let me see /ˌlet mi ˈsiː/ Moment (mal), also 4B1
let's (= **let us**) /lets, ˈlet‿ʌs/ Lass(t) uns I
letter /ˈletə/ Brief I
letter /ˈletə/ Buchstabe 3B4
to **let** *(irr)* /let/ lassen I
library /ˈlaɪbrəri/ Bibliothek, Bücherei I
to **lie** *(irr)* /laɪ/ liegen, sich hinlegen I
life (*pl* **lives**) /laɪf, laɪvz/ Leben I
light /laɪt/ Licht, Lichtquelle, Lampe 3C5
to light *(irr)* /laɪt/ anzünden 2A2
like /laɪk/ wie I
like this /ˌlaɪk ˈðɪs/ so, auf diese Weise 3B8
° like that /ˌlaɪk ˈðæt/ so, auf diese Weise 2O2
to **like** /laɪk/ mögen I
° line /laɪn/ Linie; Zeile 2O3
° to link /lɪŋk/ verbinden 1P6
lion /ˈlaɪən/ Löwe I
to **listen** to /ˈlɪs(ə)n tə/ zuhören, (an)hören I
little /ˈlɪt(ə)l/ klein(e, er, es) I
little /ˈlɪt(ə)l/ wenig 6C6
to **live** /lɪv/ leben; wohnen I
living room /ˈlɪvɪŋ ˌruːm/ Wohnzimmer I
to **load the dishwasher** /ˌləʊd ðə ˈdɪʃˌwɒʃə/ die Spülmaschine einräumen I
to **lock** /lɒk/ (ab)schließen, einschließen 6B10
° London Dungeon /ˌlʌndən ˈdʌndʒ(ə)n/ *Londoner Gruselmuseum* 3C5
long /lɒŋ/ lang I
long jump *(no pl)* /ˈlɒŋ dʒʌmp/ Weitsprung 6C2
to **look** /lʊk/ aussehen, sehen, schauen I
to **look after** /ˌlʊk‿ˈɑːftə/ sich kümmern um I
to **look around** /ˌlʊk‿əˈraʊnd/ sich umsehen I
to **look at** /ˈlʊk‿æt/ (sich) ansehen, anschauen I
to **look for** /ˈlʊk fɔː/ suchen nach I
to **look forward** to **doing sth** /ˌlʊk ˌfɔːwəd‿tə ˈduːɪŋ/ sich darauf freuen, etw zu tun I
to **look forward** to **sth** /ˌlʊk ˈfɔːwəd‿tə/ sich auf etw freuen I
to **look up sth** /ˌlʊk‿ˈʌp/ etw nachschlagen, etw heraussuchen 3B3
to **lose** *(irr)* /luːz/ verlieren; aus den Augen verlieren 3C2
to **lose one's way** /ˌluːz wʌnz ˈweɪ/ sich verirren 3C1
to lose sight of /ˌluːz‿ˈsaɪt‿əv/ aus den Augen verlieren 3C1
loser /ˈluːzə/ Verlierer/in 4C6
a lot (of) /ə ˈlɒt‿əv/ viel(e), eine Menge I
lots of *(informal)* /ˈlɒts‿əv/ viel(e), eine Menge I
loud /laʊd/ laut I
° loudly /ˈlaʊdli/ laut 2O4
loudspeaker /ˈlaʊdˌspiːkə/ Lautsprecher 6C4
love /lʌv/ Liebe; alles Liebe (Briefschlussformel) 1B2
to **love** /lʌv/ lieben, sehr mögen I
lovely /ˈlʌvli/ schön, hübsch, nett I
to bring good/bad luck /ˌbrɪŋ‿ˌgʊd/ˌbæd ˈlʌk/ Glück bringen/Unglück bringen 2A2
luck *(no pl)* /lʌk/ Glück 2A2
lucky /ˈlʌki/ glücklich *(Glück habend; Glück bringend)* I
to **be lucky** /ˈlʌki/ Glück haben I
lunch /lʌntʃ/ Mittagessen I
lunch break /ˈlʌntʃ breɪk/ Mittagspause 5B8
to lurk /lɜːk/ lauern, sich verborgen halten 4B11
lyrics *(only pl)* /ˈlɪrɪks/ (Lied)text 4B10

M

mad /mæd/ wahnsinnig, verrückt 6C4
magic /ˈmædʒɪk/ magisch, zauberhaft, wundervoll 5A2
magic *(no pl)* /ˈmædʒɪk/ Magie, Zauber 5A2
° magnifying glass /ˈmægnɪfaɪɪŋ‿glɑːs/ Lupe 3C5
main /meɪn/ Haupt- 3C2
° main /meɪn/ der/das/die wichtigste(n) ... 2P14
main hall /ˌmeɪn ˈhɔːl/ Hauptsaal 4A1
to **make** *(irr)* /meɪk/ machen; erstellen I; ausmachen 2C1
to make a fool of sb/oneself /ˌmeɪk‿ə ˈfuːl‿əv/ jdn/sich lächerlich machen 5B8
to make a pledge /ˌmeɪk‿ə ˈpledʒ/ geloben 5A2
to make sb angry /ˌmeɪk ˌsʌmbədi‿ˈæŋgri/ jdn wütend machen 1C1
to make sb do sth /ˌmeɪk ˌsʌmbədi ˈduː ˌsʌmθɪŋ/ jdn zu etwas bringen, jdn etwas tun lassen 3A3
to **make sure (that)** /ˌmeɪk ˈʃɔː ðæt/ darauf achten, (dass) 5C2
to make up /ˌmeɪk‿ˈʌp/ erfinden, (sich) ausdenken 6B10
° to make one's way /ˌmeɪk wʌnz ˈweɪ/ sich auf den Weg machen 2O2
man (*pl* **men**) /mæn, men/ Mann I
° man-made /ˌmænˈmeɪd/ künstlich 1PP
° Mandarin /ˈmændərɪn/ Mandarin (Hochchinesisch) 5P1
many /ˈmeni/ viele I
map /mæp/ (Land)karte, (Stadt)plan I
March /mɑːtʃ/ März I
mark /mɑːk/ Fleck, (Kenn)zeichen, Markierung 1B7
° mark /mɑːk/ (Schul)note 6P11
to mark /mɑːk/ markieren, kennzeichnen 1C6

market /ˈmɑːkɪt/ Markt I
to **match sth to sth** /ˈmætʃ‿ˌsʌmθɪŋ tʊ ˌsʌmθɪŋ/ etw auf etw abstimmen; etw zuordnen 2C7
material /məˈtɪəriəl/ Material 1C7, Stoff 5B8
maths *(informal, only pl)* /mæθs/ Mathe(unterricht) I
May /meɪ/ Mai I
may /meɪ/ können, dürfen 5B5
may /meɪ/ vielleicht 5C6
maybe /ˈmeɪbi/ vielleicht, möglicherweise 1C2
me /miː/ mir, mich I
meal /miːl/ Mahlzeit, Essen 5C2
meaning /ˈmiːnɪŋ/ Bedeutung 3B5
to **mean** *(irr)* /miːn/ bedeuten, meinen I
medical bag /ˈmedɪk(ə)l ˌbæg/ Arztkoffer 3C5
medicine *(no pl)* /ˈmed(ə)s(ə)n/ Medizin, Medikamente 5C2
° medieval /ˌmediˈiːv(ə)l/ mittelalterlich 1PP
to **meet** *(irr)* /miːt/ (sich) treffen I
melody /ˈmelədi/ Melodie 4B10
member /ˈmembə/ Mitglied 2A2
to **mention** /ˈmenʃ(ə)n/ erwähnen 5B8
mess *(no pl)* /mes/ Unordnung, Durcheinander 2B5
message /ˈmesɪdʒ/ Nachricht, Botschaft 2B2
metre /ˈmiːtə/ Meter 5C6
microphone /ˈmaɪkrəˌfəʊn/ Mikrofon 4C5
middle /ˈmɪd(ə)l/ Mitte 3B4
might /maɪt/ vielleicht 2C7
° mile /maɪl/ Meile (= 1,609 km) 1PP
mill /mɪl/ Mühle 5A
mine /maɪn/ meine(r, s), meins 5C5
minute /ˈmɪnɪt/ Minute I
Miss /mɪs/ Frau Lehrerin (Anrede) 4C1
to **miss** /mɪs/ vermissen 1B1; verfehlen, versäumen, verpassen 6B10
° missing /ˈmɪsɪŋ/ verschwunden, fehlend 2P5
mistake /mɪˈsteɪk/ Fehler, Irrtum, Versehen 1C2
to **mix** /mɪks/ (miteinander) (ver)mischen I
mobile (= **mobile phone**) /ˈməʊbaɪl, ˌməʊbaɪl ˈfəʊn/ Mobiltelefon, Handy I
moment /ˈməʊmənt/ Moment, Augenblick I
Monday /ˈmʌndeɪ/ Montag I
money *(no pl)* /ˈmʌni/ Geld I
to save money /ˌseɪv ˈmʌni/ Geld sparen 1C9
month /mʌnθ/ Monat I
more /mɔː/ (noch) mehr, weitere(r, s) I
° more or less /ˌmɔːr‿ɔː ˈles/ mehr oder weniger, ungefähr 1P10
morning /ˈmɔːnɪŋ/ Morgen I
in the morning am Morgen I
most /məʊst/ (die) meisten 1A1
most /məʊst/ am meisten 6C1
mostly /ˈməʊstli/ meistens, größtenteils, hauptsächlich 6A2
mother /ˈmʌðə/ Mutter I
motorway /ˈməʊtəˌweɪ/ Autobahn 5A2
mountain /ˈmaʊntɪn/ Berg I
mouse (*pl* **mice**) /maʊs, maɪs/ Maus I
mouth /maʊθ/ Mund I
to **move** /muːv/ (sich) bewegen 4C4
Mr (= **Mister**) /ˈmɪstə/ Herr *(Anrede)* I
Mrs /ˈmɪsɪz/ Frau *(Anrede)* I
Ms /məz/ Fr., Frau *(Alternativbezeichnung zu Mrs und Miss, die sowohl für verheiratete wie unverheiratete Frauen zutrifft)* 4B1
much /mʌtʃ/ viel I
to muck sth up *(informal)* /ˌmʌk ˌsʌmθɪŋ‿ˈʌp/ etw vermasseln 4C1
mum *(informal)* /mʌm/ Mama, Mutti I
music /ˈmjuːzɪk/ Musik *(als Schulfach)* I
musician /mjuˈzɪʃ(ə)n/ Musiker/in 3A4
must /mʌst/ müssen I
mustn't (= **must not**) /ˈmʌsnt, mʌst ˈnɒt/ nicht dürfen I
my /maɪ/ mein(e) I
My favourite ... is /maɪ ˈfeɪv(ə)rət ... ɪz/ Mein Lieblings... ist I
My name is /ˈmaɪ neɪm‿ɪz/ Ich heiße I
mystery /ˈmɪst(ə)ri/ Geheimnis, Rätsel; mysteriöse Geschichte 6B10

N

name /neɪm/ Name I
narrow /ˈnærəʊ/ eng, schmal 3C5
national /ˈnæʃ(ə)nəl/ national I
natural history *(no pl)* /ˌnætʃ(ə)rəl ˈhɪst(ə)ri/ Naturkunde 3B1
near /nɪə/ nahe, in der Nähe I
nearby /ˌnɪəˈbaɪ/ in der Nähe gelegen, nahe gelegen 5A2
neat /niːt/ ordentlich, sauber 1A3
necessary /ˈnesəs(ə)ri/ nötig, notwendig, erforderlich 2B9
neck and neck /ˌnek‿ən‿ˈnek/ Kopf an Kopf 6C2
need /niːd/ müssen, brauchen I
negative /ˈnegətɪv/ negativ, ablehnend, verneinend 2B6
nervous /ˈnɜːvəs/ nervös 1B7
net /net/ Netz 6B1
never /ˈnevə/ nie(mals) I
never ever /ˌnevə(r)‿ˈevə/ nie im Leben, niemals 6C8
never-ending /ˌnevərˈendɪŋ/ endlos, unaufhörlich 4A3
new /njuː/ neu I
New Year /ˌnjuː ˈjɪə/ Neujahr 2A2
° New Zealand /nju ˈziːlənd/ Neuseeland 6P5
news *(only pl)* /njuːz/ Neuigkeit 2B5; Nachricht; Nachrichtensendung 5B4
next /nekst/ nächste(r, s), als Nächste(r, s) I
next to /ˈnekst‿tə/ neben I
nice /naɪs/ schön, angenehm, nett, freundlich I
night /naɪt/ Nacht, Abend I
at night: nachts I
nightmare /ˈnaɪtˌmeə/ Albtraum 4C5
nine /naɪn/ neun I
no /nəʊ/ nein; kein/e I
No way! *(informal)* /ˌnəʊ ˈweɪ/ Ausgeschlossen!; Jetzt echt, oder? 1B1
noise /nɔɪz/ Geräusch I; Lärm, Krach 2A2
noisy /ˈnɔɪzi/ laut 2B3
° nonsense *(no pl)* /ˈnɒns(ə)ns/ Unsinn, Quatsch 1P10
normal /ˈnɔːm(ə)l/ normal, üblich 2A1
° normally /ˈnɔːm(ə)li/ normalerweise 6P14
north /nɔːθ/ Norden, nördlich, Nord- I
nose /nəʊz/ Nase I
nosy /ˈnəʊzi/ neugierig 2B4
not /nɒt/ nicht I
not ... anymore /nɒt‿ˌeniˈmɔː/ nicht mehr 3C2
not ... anything else /nɒt ˌeniθɪŋ‿ˈels/ gar nichts anderes 3B1
not that high on my list: nicht so weit oben auf meiner Liste 3B7
° not ... either /nɒt‿ˈaɪðə/ auch nicht 6P11
note /nəʊt/ Notiz, Mitteilung 1C6
to **note down** /ˌnəʊt‿ˈdaʊn/ (sich) notieren 1B1
nothing /ˈnʌθɪŋ/ nichts 6C4

to **notice** / ˈnəʊtɪs / bemerken, beachten I
November / nəʊˈvembə / November I
now / naʊ / jetzt, nun I
number / ˈnʌmbə / Zahl, Ziffer, Nummer I
° nurse / nɜːs / (Kranken)schwester 6P10

O

(one) o'clock / ˌwʌn‿əˈklɒk / (ein) Uhr I
October / ɒkˈtəʊbə / Oktober I
of / əv / von I
of course / əv ˈkɔːs / natürlich I
to **offer** / ˈɒfə / anbieten, bieten I
often / ˈɒf(ə)n / oft I
Oh dear! *(informal)* / əʊ ˈdɪə / Du meine Güte! 6A2
° Oh no! / əʊ ˈnəʊ / Oh nein! 2O2
old / əʊld / alt I
on / ɒn / auf I; zu; über 1C2
on holiday / ɒn ˈhɒlədeɪ / im Urlaub, in den Ferien I
° on one's own / ˌɒn wʌnz‿ˈəʊn / (ganz) allein(e) 2O2
on the left / ˌɒn ðə ˈleft / links, auf der linken Seite I
on the right / ˌɒn ðə ˈraɪt / rechts, auf der rechten Seite I
on the Romans: über die Römer 1C2
On your marks, get set, go! / ˌɒn jə ˈmɑːks, ˌget ˈset, ˈgəʊ / Auf die Plätze, fertig, los! 6C4
once / wʌns / früher, einst 3A4
one / wʌn / eins, ein(e, er, es) I
(one) o'clock / ˌwʌn‿əˈklɒk / (ein) Uhr I
a small one / ə ˈsmɔːl ˌwʌn / ein(e) kleine(s, r) 1B1 (Box *one/ones* S. 156)
only / ˈəʊnli / nur; einzige(r, s); erst 3C2
to **open** / ˈəʊpən / öffnen I
open / ˈəʊpən / offen, geöffnet I
open (from … to …) / ˈəʊpən frəm tʊ / offen, geöffnet (von … bis …) I
opinion / əˈpɪnjən / Meinung, Ansicht, Standpunkt 6C9
opposite / ˈɒpəzɪt / gegenüberliegend 1B7
optimistic / ˌɒptɪˈmɪstɪk / optimistisch I
or / ɔː / oder I
orange / ˈɒrɪndʒ / orange, orange(farben) I
order / ˈɔːdə / Ordnung, Reihenfolge 3A2
organic waste / ɔːˌgænɪk ˈweɪst / Biomüll 5B8
to **organize** / ˈɔːgənaɪz / organisieren, ordnen 1A1
orienteering *(no pl)* / ˌɔːriənˈtɪərɪŋ / Orientierungslauf I
other / ˈʌðə / andere(r, s) I
others *(only pl)* / ˈʌðəz / andere I
our / aʊə / unser(e) I
out / aʊt / außen, draußen I
outside / ˌaʊtˈsaɪd / außen, außerhalb; nach draußen 4C1
outstanding / aʊtˈstændɪŋ / außergewöhnlich, bemerkenswert, hervorragend 6C2
over / ˈəʊvə / über 1C8
° over: hinüber, drüben; auf, herüben, herüber 2O2
° over here: hierher 2O4
over there: dort drüben I
to **overtake** / ˌəʊvəˈteɪk / überholen, einholen 6C2
own / əʊn / eigene(r, s) I
owner / ˈəʊnə / Besitzer/in, Eigentümer/in 5C6

P

PA (= public address) system / ˌpiː‿ˈeɪ ˌsɪstəm, ˌpʌblɪk‿əˈdres‿ˌsɪstəm / Lautsprecheranlage 1C8
to **pack one's bags** / ˌpæk wʌnz ˈbægz / die Koffer packen 3B3
packaging *(no pl)* / ˈpækɪdʒɪŋ / Verpackungsmaterial 5B8
page / peɪdʒ / Seite 3A3
to pair / peə / ein Paar bilden 6C1
° palace / ˈpæləs / Palast 1PP, Palais 3P1
pale / peɪl / blass, bleich 6C4
solar panel / ˌsəʊlə ˈpæn(ə)l / Sonnenkollektor 5A2
paper *(no pl)* / ˈpeɪpə / Papier I
° paradise / ˈpærədaɪs / Paradies 1PP
paragraph / ˈpærəˌgrɑːf / Absatz, Abschnitt 3C8
parents *(only pl)* / ˈpeərənts / Eltern I
part / pɑːt / Teil 2B8
anyone in particular / ˌeniˌwʌn‿ɪn pəˈtɪkjʊlə / jemand Bestimmtes 2B3
to **have a party** / ˌhæv‿ə ˈpɑːti / eine Party geben I
past / pɑːst / Vergangenheit 2A2
past / pɑːst / nach I; an … vorbei; hinter 3C2
ten past one: zehn nach eins
° path / pɑːθ / Weg, Pfad, Bahn 2O2
to pay *(irr)* / peɪ / (be)zahlen 3B1
PE (= physical education) / ˌpiː‿ˈiː, ˌfɪzɪk(ə)l‿ˌedjʊˈkeɪʃ(ə)n / Sport *(als Schulfach)* I
pen / pen / Stift I
pencil / ˈpensl / Bleistift I
pencil case / ˈpensl ˌkeɪs / Federmäppchen I
penny / ˈpeni / Penny *(Untereinheit des brit. Pfunds)* 2A2
people *(no pl)* / ˈpiːp(ə)l / Leute, Menschen I
pepper *(no pl)* / ˈpepə / Pfeffer I
perfect / ˈpɜːfɪkt / perfekt I
to **perform** / pəˈfɔːm / vorführen, aufführen 2A2; auftreten 4A3
perhaps / pəˈhæps / vielleicht I
person / ˌpɜːs(ə)n / Person I
to **persuade** / pəˈsweɪd / überreden, überzeugen 4B1
pet / pet / Haustier I
phone (= telephone) / ˈfəʊn, ˈtelɪˌfəʊn / Telefon I
to answer the phone / ˌɑːnsə ðə ˈfəʊn / ans Telefon gehen I
phone call (= telephone call) / ˈfəʊn ˌkɔːl, ˈtelɪˌfəʊn ˌkɔːl / Anruf, Telefongespräch 3B7
° phone number / ˈfəʊn‿ˌnʌmbə / Telefonnummer 1B6
to **phone** / fəʊn / anrufen, telefonieren 1C2
to **take photos** / ˌteɪk ˈfəʊtəʊz / fotografieren, Fotos machen I
phrase / freɪz / Satz, Ausdruck 1B2
to **pick up** / ˌpɪk‿ˈʌp / aufheben; abholen 5C2
pickpocket / ˈpɪkˌpɒkɪt / Taschendieb/in I
picture / ˈpɪktʃə / Bild I
piece / piːs / Stück 4A3
piece of paper / ˌpiːs‿əv ˈpeɪpə / Blatt Papier I
pig / pɪg / Schwein I
pile / paɪl / Stapel, Haufen 4C4
to pinch / pɪntʃ / kneifen; klauen 5C5
pink / pɪŋk / rosa, pink I
° pipe / paɪp / Pfeife 3C5
place / pleɪs / Ort, Platz, Stelle I
to **plan** / plæn / planen 1C9
planet / ˈplænɪt / Planet 5A2
planner / ˈplænə / Planer/in 2B1
plant / plɑːnt / Pflanze 5A2
to plant / plɑːnt / pflanzen 5B9
plastic / ˈplæstɪk / Plastik(-), Kunststoff(-) 5B2
plate / pleɪt / Teller 5C2
play / pleɪ / Spiel; (Theater)stück 4B1
to **play** / pleɪ / spielen I
to play a trick on sb / ˌpleɪ‿ə ˈtrɪk‿ɒn / jdm einen Streich spielen 5C6
player / pleɪə / Spieler/in 4C4
° playwright / ˈpleɪˌraɪt / Dramatiker/in 1PP
please / pliːz / bitte I

pleased /pli:zd/ froh, zufrieden I
to make a pledge /ˌmeɪk‿ə 'pledʒ/ geloben 5A2
° plenty of /'plenti‿əv/ viel 2O2
pm (= **post meridiem**) /ˌpi:‿'em, ˌpəʊst mə'rɪdiəm/ nachmittags, abends *(nur hinter Uhrzeit zwischen 12 Uhr mittags und Mitternacht)* I
pocket /'pɒkɪt/ Tasche *(an Kleidungsstücken)* I
pocket knife /'pɒkɪt ˌnaɪf/ Taschenmesser 5C2
pocket money /'pɒkɪt ˌmʌni/ Taschengeld 5C2
poem /'pəʊɪm/ Gedicht I
point of view /ˌpɔɪnt‿əv‿'vju:/ Ansicht, Einstellung, Perspektive 6C9
pointy /'pɔɪnti/ spitz 4B11
policeman (*pl* **policemen**) /pə'li:smən/ Polizist I
polite /pə'laɪt/ höflich 1C9
pony camp /'pəʊni ˌkæmp/ Reiterferienlager 1B1
poor /pɔ:/ arm 3C5
popular /'pɒpjʊlə/ beliebt, populär 4A1
positive /'pɒzətɪv/ positiv; bejahend 2B6
possible /'pɒsəb(ə)l/ möglich I
postcard /'pəʊstˌkɑ:d/ Postkarte I
to postpone /pəʊs'pəʊn/ verschieben 4C5
baked potato /ˌbeɪkt pə'teɪtəʊ/ Ofenkartoffel 2A2
power station /'paʊə ˌsteɪʃ(ə)n/ Kraftwerk 3A4
° practice *(no pl)* /'præktɪs/ Übung 1P11
to **practise** /'præktɪs/ üben I
to praise /preɪz/ loben 4A3
praise *(no pl)* /preɪz/ Lob 4A3
pre- /pri:/ Vor- 4A1
preparation /ˌprepə'reɪʃ(ə)n/ Vorbereitung, Zubereitung 2C5
to **prepare** /prɪ'peə/ vorbereiten, erstellen 1A3
present /'prez(ə)nt/ Geschenk I
to **present (sth to sb)** /prɪ'zent/ (jdm etw) präsentieren; vortragen I
presentation /ˌprez(ə)n'teɪʃ(ə)n/ Präsentation 1A3
press-up /'presʌp/ Liegestütz 6A2
to **pretend** /prɪ'tend/ vorgeben, vortäuschen 4C5
pretty /'prɪti/ hübsch, nett 1B1
price /praɪs/ Preis I
prize /praɪz/ (Sieg)preis, Gewinn 4A1
probably /'prɒbəbli/ wahrscheinlich 2B8
to **produce** /prə'dju:s/ herstellen, produzieren 5B8
product /'prɒdʌkt/ Produkt, Erzeugnis 5B8
profile /'prəʊfaɪl/ Profil, Porträt 4B12
programme /'prəʊgræm/ Programm, Sendung 3A4
to **promise** /'prɒmɪs/ versprechen 6C3
prompter /'prɒmptə/ Souffleur/ Souffleuse *(jd, der den Text flüsternd vorspricht)* 4C5
to **pronounce** /prə'naʊns/ aussprechen 6C5
prop /prɒp/ Requisite 3A4
proper /'prɒpə/ echt, richtig 4B1
to **protect** /prə'tekt/ (be)schützen 5B1
to **pull** /pʊl/ ziehen 6B1
to pull a face /ˌpʊl‿ə 'feɪs/ das Gesicht verziehen 4C1
° pumpkin /'pʌmpkɪn/ Kürbis 2O4
° punchbag /'pʌntʃˌbæg/ Sandsack 6P14
to punish /'pʌnɪʃ/ (be)strafen 1C9
pupil /'pju:p(ə)l/ Schüler/in I
purple /'pɜ:pl/ violett, lila I
to **push** /pʊʃ/ stoßen, schieben 6B2
to **put up** /ˌpʊt‿'ʌp/ aufhängen, hochheben; aufstellen 5C6
to **put** *(irr)* /pʊt/ setzen, legen, stellen I; bringen 6C2
° to puzzle out /ˌpʌz(ə)l‿'aʊt/ herausfinden, entschlüsseln 2P5

Q

quarter (past/to) /'kwɔ:tə/ Viertel (nach/vor) I
quarter of an hour /ˌkwɔ:tər‿əv‿ən‿'aʊə/ Viertelstunde I
queen /kwi:n/ Königin 3B9
question /'kwestʃ(ə)n/ Frage I
queue /kju:/ Schlange, Reihe 3C2
quick /kwɪk/ schnell I
quickly /'kwɪkli/ schnell *(Adverb)* I
quiet /'kwaɪət/ leise, ruhig I
quietly /'kwaɪətli/ leise, still *(Adverb)* 4C2
quite /kwaɪt/ ziemlich, ganz 2B3
° quiz (*pl* quizzes) /kwɪz, kwɪzɪz/ Quiz, Ratespiel 1P1

R

race /reɪs/ Rennen 1B1
to race /reɪs/ rennen; rasen 3A4
rain *(no pl)* /reɪn/ Regen I
to **rain** /reɪn/ regnen I
rainy /'reɪni/ regnerisch 1A3
rather /'rɑ:ðə/ ziemlich, recht 6C4
RE (= **religious education**) /ˌɑ:r‿'i:, rəˌlɪdʒəs‿ˌedjʊ'keɪʃ(ə)n/ Religionslehre I
to **react (to sb/sth)** /ri'ækt‿tə/ (auf jdn/etw) reagieren 2B5
to **read** *(irr)* /ri:d/ lesen I
° to read on /ˌri:d‿'ɒn/ weiterlesen 2O4
° reading *(no pl)* /'ri:dɪŋ/ Lesen 2P5
ready /'redi/ fertig, bereit I
real /rɪəl/ wirklich, echt I
really /'rɪəli/ wirklich I
reason /'ri:z(ə)n/ Grund 2A2
° to reassure sb /ˌri:ə'ʃʊə/ jdn (wieder) beruhigen 2O4
to **receive** /rɪ'si:v/ erhalten, bekommen 4A3
recipe /'resəpi/ Rezept I
° to recognize /'rekəgnaɪz/ (wieder) erkennen, anerkennen 6P15
record /'rekɔ:d/ Rekord 6C2
to record /rɪ'kɔ:d/ aufzeichnen, aufnehmen 1C2
to **recycle** /ri:'saɪk(ə)l/ wiederverwenden 5B3
red /red/ rot I
to go red /ˌgəʊ 'red/ rot werden 5C6
to refer (back) to /rɪˌfɜ: 'bæk tʊ/ (zurück)verweisen auf, sich beziehen auf 5A4
° to relax /rɪ'læks/ entspannen 1PP
relaxed /rɪ'lækst/ entspannt, locker 6C9
relay (race) /'ri:leɪ reɪs/ Staffellauf 6C2
° religion *(no pl)* /rɪ'lɪdʒ(ə)n/ Religion, Glaube 1O2
° religious studies *(only pl)* /rə'lɪdʒəs 'stʌdiz/ Religionswissenschaft 5P1
to **remember** /rɪ'membə/ sich erinnern 1B7; daran denken 4C2
to **repeat** /rɪ'pi:t/ wiederholen; nachsprechen 6C8
report /rɪ'pɔ:t/ (Zeitungs-)Bericht, (Zeitungs-)Meldung 5A2
reporter /rɪ'pɔ:tə/ Reporter/in 5B4
to represent sb/sth /ˌreprɪ'zent/ jdn/etw repräsentieren 4A3, jdn vertreten 5B4
to **do research** /ˌdu: 'ri:sɜ:tʃ/ (er)forschen, recherchieren 4B1
restaurant /'restrɒnt/ Restaurant, Gaststätte I
result /rɪ'zʌlt/ Folge; Ergebnis I
° revision *(no pl)* /rɪ'vɪʒ(ə)n/ Wiederholung (des Stoffs) 1P3
reward /rɪ'wɔ:d/ Belohnung, Anerkennung 4A3
rhyming /'raɪmɪŋ/ Reim- 6C8
rice pudding /ˌraɪs 'pʊdɪŋ/ Milchreis 2A2

ride /raɪd/ Fahrt 1B1
to go for a ride /ˌɡəʊ fər‿ə raɪd/ eine Fahrt machen; ausreiten 1B1
to **ride** *(irr)* /raɪd/ fahren (mit), reiten I
right /raɪt/ richtig; (nach) rechts I
right /raɪt/ gleich, direkt 3A4
to **be right** /ˌbiː ˈraɪt/ recht haben I
right *(informal)* /raɪt/ also 3B7
to **ring (up)** *(irr)* /ˌrɪŋ‿ˈʌp/ anrufen, klingeln, läuten 2C9
rival /ˈraɪv(ə)l/ Rivale/Rivalin, Konkurrent/in 6C4
river /ˈrɪvə/ Fluss 1B7
road /rəʊd/ Straße 3C2
roar *(no pl)* /rɔː/ Brüllen, Dröhnen; Tosen 6B1
◦ Rock Department /ˈrɒk dɪˌpɑːtmənt/ *Abteilung für Rockmusik* 2O2
rocket /ˈrɒkɪt/ Rakete 2B3
role /rəʊl/ Rolle 1C9
◦ to roll in /ˌrəʊl‿ˈɪn/ hineinrollen, hereinrollen 1PP
to roll one's eyes /ˌrəʊl wʌnz‿ˈaɪz/ die Augen verdrehen 4C1
Roman /ˈrəʊmən/ Römer/in 1C6, römisch 1C7
room /ruːm/ Zimmer, Raum I
◦ round /raʊnd/ rund 1O1
rowing *(no pl)* /ˈrəʊɪŋ/ Rudern 6A2
rubbish *(no pl)* /ˈrʌbɪʃ/ Müll I
to ruin /ˈruːɪn/ zerstören, verderben, kaputtmachen 4C5
rule /ruːl/ Regel I
ruler /ˈruːlə/ Lineal I
to **run (away)** /ˌrʌn‿əˈweɪ/ (weg) rennen I; laufen 6A2

S

sad /sæd/ traurig I
safe /seɪf/ sicher I
salt *(no pl)* /sɔːlt/ Salz I
samosa /səˈməʊsə/ *indische Teigtasche* 2C7
◦ sandy /ˈsændi/ sandig 1PP
Saturday /ˈsætədeɪ/ Samstag I
to **save** /seɪv/ retten, schützen, (be)wahren 5A2
to **save money** /ˌseɪv ˈmʌni/ Geld sparen 1C9
to **say** *(irr)* /seɪ/ sagen I
to **say sorry** /ˌseɪ ˈsɒri/ sich entschuldigen I
to **scare** /skeə/ Angst machen, erschrecken I
scared /ˈskeərd/ verängstigt I
to **get scared** /ˌɡet ˈskeərd/ sich (anfangen zu) fürchten 2C5
scarf /skɑːf/ Schal 1B5
scary /ˈskeəri/ furchterregend I
◦ scenery *(no pl)* /ˈsiːnəri/ Landschaft 1PP
school /skuːl/ Schule I
school bag, schoolbag /ˈskuːl ˌbæɡ/ Schultasche I
science /ˈsaɪəns/ (Natur)wissenschaft I
scissors *(only pl)* /ˈsɪzəz/ Schere I
to **score** (a goal) /ˌskɔːr‿ə ˈɡəʊl/ (ein Tor) schießen 6B1, erzielen 6C2
Scotland /ˈskɒtlənd/ Schottland I
◦ Scottish /ˈskɒtɪʃ/ schottisch 1PP
to **scream** /skriːm/ schreien, kreischen I
script /skrɪpt/ Drehbuch, Skript, Regiebuch 4B8
sea *(no pl)* /siː/ Meer, (die) See I
◦ seal /siːl/ Seehund, Robbe 1PP
search /sɜːtʃ/ Suche, Durchsuchung; Suchaufgabe 3B6
◦ to search (for sb/sth) /ˈsɜːtʃ fə/ (nach jdm/etw) suchen 1PP
◦ to search the Internet /ˌsɜːtʃ ði‿ˈɪntəˌnet/ im Internet recherchieren 1PP
seaside *(no pl)* /ˈsiːˌsaɪd/ (Meeres)küste I
to **go to the seaside**: ans Meer fahren I
season /ˈsiːz(ə)n/ Jahreszeit I
seat /siːt/ (Sitz)platz 6C4
second /ˈsekənd/ zweite(r, s) I
second /ˈsekənd/ Sekunde 6A2
secretary /ˈsekrətri/ Sekretär/in 4B8
See you soon! *(informal)* /ˌsiː jʊ ˈsuːn/ bis bald! I
to **seem** /siːm/ scheinen I
to **see** *(irr)* /siː/ sehen I; verstehen 2C2
selection /sɪˈlekʃ(ə)n/ Auswahl 4A1
to **sell** *(irr)* /sel/ verkaufen I
to **send** *(irr)* /send/ (zu)schicken I
sensible /ˈsensəb(ə)l/ vernünftig, angemessen 5C3
September /sepˈtembə/ September I
serious /ˈsɪəriəs/ ernst 6C2
seven /ˈsevn/ sieben I
◦ several /ˈsev(ə)rəl/ einige, ein paar 2O4
shadow /ˈʃædəʊ/ Schatten 4B11
to share /ʃeə/ teilen 6A2
she /ʃiː/ sie I
sheep *(pl* **sheep)** /ʃiːp/ Schaf I
shelf *(pl* **shelves)** /ʃelf, ʃelvz/ (Regal)brett, Bord I
ship /ʃɪp/ Schiff I
shirt /ʃɜːt/ Hemd 5B6
shocked /ʃɒkt/ schockiert, entsetzt I
shoe /ʃuː/ Schuh I
to **shoot** *(irr)* /ʃuːt/ schießen 6B1
to shoot sb /ʃuːt/ jdn anschießen, jdn erschießen 3C5
shop /ʃɒp/ Geschäft, Laden I
shop assistant /ˈʃɒp‿əˌsɪst(ə)nt/ Verkäufer/in I
shopping *(no pl)* /ˈʃɒpɪŋ/ Einkaufen I
to **go shopping** /ˌɡəʊ ˈʃɒpɪŋ/ einkaufen gehen I
short /ʃɔːt/ kurz I
should /ʃʊd/ sollen I
to **shout (at)** /ˈʃaʊt‿æt/ (an)schreien I
to **show sb (a)round** /ʃəʊ ˌsʌmbədi‿əˈraʊnd/ jdn herumführen 3B1
to **have/take a shower** /ˌhæv/ˌteɪk‿ə ˈʃaʊə/ sich duschen 5C6
to **show** *(irr)* /ʃəʊ/ zeigen 1C6
◦ to show *(irr)* verraten 2O3
sick /sɪk/ krank I
sight /saɪt/ Sehenswürdigkeit 3A2
sightseeing *(no pl)* /ˈsaɪtˌsiːɪŋ/ Besichtigungen, Sightseeing I
to **do sightseeing**: eine Besichtigungstour machen I
sign /saɪn/ Zeichen, (Straßen-/Verkehrs)schild 3C2
silent /ˈsaɪlənt/ still, ruhig, schweigsam 5B9
silly /ˈsɪli/ Dussel, Dummerchen 4B1
silly /ˈsɪli/ albern, dumm I
similar /ˈsɪmɪlə/ ähnlich 3B5
since /sɪns/ seitdem; seit, seither 3B1
singer /ˈsɪŋə/ Sänger/in I
to **sing** *(irr)* /sɪŋ/ singen I
Sir /sɜː/ *engl. Adelstitel* 3C5
sister /ˈsɪstə/ Schwester I
to **sit** *(irr)* /sɪt/ sitzen I
to **sit down** /ˌsɪt‿ˈdaʊn/ sich (hin) setzen I
six /sɪks/ sechs I
size /saɪz/ Größe I
◦ skill /skɪl/ Geschick; Fähigkeit, Fertigkeit 6P12
skin *(no pl)* /skɪn/ Haut 4B11
skirt /skɜːt/ Rock I
to **sleep** *(irr)* /sliːp/ schlafen I
to **sleep late** /ˌsliːp ˈleɪt/ lange schlafen, ausschlafen I
sleeping bag /ˈsliːpɪŋ ˌbæɡ/ Schlafsack 5C2
slow /sləʊ/ langsam 4B10
small /smɔːl/ klein I
to **smell** *(irr)* /smel/ riechen, duften I
◦ smile /smaɪl/ Lächeln 2O2
to **smile** /smaɪl/ lächeln 4C4
to **smile (at)** /ˈsmaɪl‿æt/ (an)lächeln 4C1

snake /sneɪk/ Schlange I
snow *(no pl)* /snəʊ/ Schnee 1B1
snowy /ˈsnəʊi/ schneereich 1A3
so /səʊ/ also, deshalb I; so, sehr 2C7
° so-so *(informal)* /ˈsəʊ səʊ/ so lala, einigermaßen 1P2
soap /səʊp/ Seife 5C2
solar /ˈsəʊlə/ Solar-, Sonnen- 5A2
to solve /sɒlv/ lösen; aufklären 6B10
some /sʌm/ einige, etwas I
somebody /ˈsʌmbədi/ (irgend) jemand, irgendwer I
someone /ˈsʌmwʌn/ (irgend) jemand, irgendwer 1C3
someone else /ˌsʌmwʌn‿ˈels/ jemand anders 4C5
something /ˈsʌmθɪŋ/ etwas I
something else /ˌsʌmθɪŋ‿ˈels/ etwas anderes 6B3
sometimes /ˈsʌmtaɪmz/ manchmal I
° somewhere /ˈsʌmweə/ irgendwo 2O2
son /sʌn/ Sohn I
soon /suːn/ bald 2B8
sorry /ˈsɒri/ Entschuldigung!, Tut mir leid. I
to **say sorry**: sich entschuldigen I
° to sort /sɔːt/ sortieren 6P2
° sort of /ˈsɔːt‿əv/ so ungefähr, sozusagen 2O4
to sort out /ˌsɔːt‿ˈaʊt/ klären/ regeln 2B5
sound /saʊnd/ Geräusch, Klang, Laut I
to **sound** /saʊnd/ klingen I
° south /saʊθ/ Süden, südlich 1PP, Süd- 1O1
souvenir /ˌsuːvəˈnɪə/ Andenken, Souvenir 1A1
sparkler /ˈspɑːklə/ Wunderkerze 2B3
to **speak** *(irr)* /spiːk/ sprechen I
to **speak** to **sb** /ˈspiːk tʊ/ mit jdm reden 2C2
to speak up /ˌspiːk‿ˈʌp/ lauter sprechen 1A3
speaking /ˈspiːkɪŋ/ sprechend; am Apparat 2B5
special /ˈspeʃ(ə)l/ besondere(r, s) 2A1
spectacular /spekˈtækjʊlə/ atemberaubend, fantastisch 3A4
to **speculate (on)** /ˈspekjuleɪt‿ɒn/ spekulieren, Vermutungen anstellen (über) 2C10
speech bubble /ˈspiːtʃ ˌbʌb(ə)l/ Sprechblase 2C10
spelling *(no pl)* /ˈspelɪŋ/ Rechtschreibung; Schreibweise 4C3
to **spend** *(irr)* /spend/ verbringen *(Zeit)*, ausgeben *(Geld)* I
to spoil *(irr)* /spɔɪl/ verderben, ruinieren 2C7

spoon /spuːn/ Löffel 5C2
sports *(only pl)* /spɔːts/ Sport; Sportart 6A6
sports ground /ˈspɔːts ˌgraʊnd/ Sportplatz I
° to spot /spɒt/ entdecken 2O2
spring /sprɪŋ/ Frühling I
sprint /sprɪnt/ Sprint; Lauf 6C2
squirrel /ˈskwɪrəl/ Eichhörnchen 3B9
St Patrick's Day /sənt ˈpætrɪks ˌdeɪ/ *irischer Nationalfeiertag* 2A3
stable /ˈsteɪb(ə)l/ Stall, Box 1B1
stadium /ˈsteɪdiəm/ Stadion 3A4
stage /steɪdʒ/ Bühne 4A3
stairs *(only pl)* /steəz/ Treppe I; Treppenstufen 6A2
to stammer /ˈstæmə/ stottern, stammeln 4C1
to **stand** *(irr)* /stænd/ ertragen, aushalten 5B4; stehen 6B1
I can't stand ... Ich kann ... nicht ertragen/nicht aushalten
to **stand up** /ˌstænd‿ˈʌp/ aufstehen 5C6
to star in a film/play /ˌstɑːr‿ɪn‿ə ˈfɪlm, ˈpleɪ/ in einem Film/ Theaterstück die Hauptrolle spielen 3C5
start /stɑːt/ Anfang, Beginn 1B1
to **start** /stɑːt/ anfangen I
to start a business /ˌstɑːt‿ə ˈbɪznəs/ ein Unternehmen gründen; Handel treiben 1C9
° to start off /ˌstɑːt‿ˈɒf/ anfangen; loslaufen 6P11
starting line /ˈstɑːtɪŋ laɪn/ Startlinie 6C4
° statement /ˈsteɪtmənt/ Äußerung, Aussage 1P15
station /ˈsteɪʃ(ə)n/ Bahnhof, Haltestelle, Station 3C2
to **stay** /steɪ/ bleiben; sich aufhalten, untergebracht sein I
stay /steɪ/ Aufenthalt 5A2
to **steal** *(irr)* /stiːl/ stehlen I
step /step/ Schritt; (Treppen)stufe 3B9
to take a step /ˌteɪk‿ə ˈstep/ einen Schritt machen 5A2
to stick out *(irr)* /ˌstɪk‿ˈaʊt/ ausstrecken; herausstrecken 6B4
still /stɪl/ (immer) noch, trotzdem, noch immer 2C2
stone /stəʊn/ Stein I
to **stop** /stɒp/ aufhören; stoppen, (an)halten; beenden; aufhalten I
Stop it! *(informal)* /ˈstɒp‿ɪt/ Hör auf!, Hört auf! 2B3
store /stɔː/ Laden, Geschäft, Kaufhaus 3B1

story /ˈstɔːri/ Geschichte, Erzählung I
straight /streɪt/ gerade(aus), direkt 5C6
strange /streɪndʒ/ sonderbar, merkwürdig; unheimlich I
street /ˈstriːt/ Straße I
stress /stres/ Betonung 6C5
° to stretch /stretʃ/ (sich) dehnen, strecken 6P14
stretching exercise /ˈstretʃɪŋ‿ˌeksəsaɪz/ Dehnungsübung 6A2
strict /strɪkt/ streng, strikt, genau 5C3
striped /straɪpt/ gestreift 5B6
strong /strɒŋ/ stark, kräftig, fest 3C5
to **structure** /ˈstrʌktʃə/ strukturieren 1B2
structure /ˈstrʌktʃə/ Struktur, Aufbau 1B9
to **study** /ˈstʌdi/ studieren, sich befassen mit, erforschen 5A2
study /ˈstʌdi/ Arbeitszimmer 3C5
stuff *(no pl, informal)* /stʌf/ Zeug, Sachen 4B1
stunning /ˈstʌnɪŋ/ toll, fantastisch, umwerfend 3A4
stupid /ˈstjuːpɪd/ dumm, blöd I
in style /ɪn ˈstaɪl/ stilvoll 2B2
subject /ˈsʌbdʒɪkt/ (Schul)fach I
success *(no pl)* /səkˈses/ Erfolg 4A3
successful /səkˈsesf(ə)l/ erfolgreich 6C2
such /sʌtʃ/ solch(er/es) I; so 4B11
suddenly /ˈsʌd(ə)nli/ plötzlich 1B1
sugar /ˈʃʊgə/ Zucker I
to **suggest** /səˈdʒest/ vorschlagen 4B1
suggestion /səˈdʒestʃ(ə)n/ Vorschlag 3B1
° suitable /ˈsuːtəb(ə)l/ geeignet, passend, angemessen 2O2
suitcase /ˈsuːtˌkeɪs/ Koffer I
summer /ˈsʌmə/ Sommer I
all summer /ˌɔːl ˈsʌmə/ den ganzen Sommer I
sun /sʌn/ Sonne I
Sunday /ˈsʌndeɪ/ Sonntag I
sunglasses *(only pl)* /ˈsʌnˌglɑːsɪz/ Sonnenbrille I
sunny /ˈsʌni/ sonnig I
super *(informal)* /ˈsuːpə/ besonders 5B7
support /səˈpɔːt/ Unterstützung; Hilfestellung 1B5
sure /ʃɔː/ sicher I
to **be sure**: sicher sein I
to **go surfing** /ˌgəʊ ˈsɜːfɪŋ/ surfen gehen I
surprise /səˈpraɪz/ Überraschung I

to **surprise** /səˈpraɪz/ überraschen I
surprised /səˈpraɪzd/ überrascht, erstaunt I
◦ to surround /səˈraʊnd/ einkreisen 2O4
◦ to survive /səˈvaɪv/ überleben 5P2
to **sweep** /swiːp/ kehren, fegen I
to **sweep the floor** /ˌswiːp ðə ˈflɔː/ den Boden fegen I
sweetly /ˈswiːtli/ süß(lich) 4C5
sweets *(only pl)* /swiːts/ Süßigkeiten I
swimming /ˈswɪmɪŋ/ Schwimmen I
to **go swimming** /ˌɡəʊ ˈswɪmɪŋ/ schwimmen gehen I
to swim *(irr)* /swɪm/ **schwimmen** 6C7
symphony orchestra /ˈsɪmfəni‿ˌɔːkɪstrə/ Sinfonieorchester 4A1

T

table /ˈteɪb(ə)l/ Tisch I
to **lay the table** /ˌleɪ ðə ˈteɪb(ə)l/ den Tisch decken I
to **take** *(irr)* /teɪk/ (mit)nehmen; bringen; wegnehmen I
to **take ... for a walk** /ˌteɪk fər‿ə ˈwɔːk/ ... spazieren führen; Gassi gehen mit ... I
to take a break /ˌteɪk‿ə ˈbreɪk/ eine Pause machen 5B4
to take a step /ˌteɪk‿ə ˈstep/ einen Schritt machen 5A2
to take notes /ˌteɪk ˈnəʊts/ (sich) Notizen machen 6C3
to **take out the rubbish** /ˌteɪk‿ˌaʊt ðə ˈrʌbɪʃ/ den Müll hinausbringen I
to **take out** /ˌteɪk‿ˈaʊt/ herausnehmen, hinausbringen I
to take over /ˌteɪk‿ˈəʊvə/ übernehmen 4C7
to **take part (in)** /ˌteɪk ˈpɑːt‿ɪn/ teilnehmen (an) I
to **take photos** /ˌteɪk ˈfəʊtəʊz/ fotografieren, Fotos machen I
to **take place** /ˌteɪk ˈpleɪs/ stattfinden I
talent /ˈtælənt/ Talent, Begabung 4B1
to **talk (about)** /ˈtɔːk‿əˌbaʊt/ sprechen (über); reden (über) I
to **talk (to)** /tɔːk/ sprechen, reden (mit) I
tall /tɔːl/ groß, hoch (gewachsen) I
◦ talon /ˈtælən/ Klaue, Kralle 2O2
◦ tea (no pl) /tiː/ Tee; Zwischenmahlzeit 2O2
teacher /ˈtiːtʃə/ Lehrer/in I
technology /tekˈnɒlədʒi/ Technologie, Technik I
telephone /ˈtelɪˌfəʊn/ Telefon I
to **tell** *(irr)* /tel/ erzählen, sagen I
to tell a sob story *(informal)* /ˌtel‿ə ˈsɒb ˌstɔːri/ mit einer Mitleid heischenden Ausrede daherkommen 4C5
◦ temperature /ˈtemprɪtʃə/ Temperatur 1P14
◦ temple /ˈtemp(ə)l/ Tempel 1O1
ten /ten/ zehn I
tense /tens/ Zeitform, Tempus 2B6
tense /tens/ angespannt 4C5
tent /tent/ Zelt I
terrible /ˈterəb(ə)l/ schrecklich, furchtbar I
◦ terrific /təˈrɪfɪk/ großartig, fantastisch 6P2
◦ to test /test/ prüfen, testen 1PP
text message /ˈtekst ˌmesɪdʒ/ SMS 4B9
to **text (sb)** /tekst/ (jdm) eine SMS senden 2B3
than /ðæn/ als 1B1
than ever /ðæn‿ˈevə/ als jemals zuvor 6C4
thank you /ˈθæŋk ju/ Danke I
thanks /θæŋks/ Danke I
that /ðæt/ das; der/die/das I, dass 1C2
that day: an diesem Tag 5B2
That would be great. /ˌðæt wəd bi ˈɡreɪt/ Das wäre toll. I
that's why /ˈðæts ˌwaɪ/ deshalb, darum, deswegen 3C2
◦ that's it! *(informal)* /ˌðæts‿ˈɪt/ genau! 6P15
the /ðə/ der/die/das I
the ... the /ðə ðə/ je ..., desto ... 2B3
the BBC (= British Broadcasting Corporation) /ðə ˌbiː biː ˈsiː, ˌbrɪtɪʃ ˈbrɔːdkɑːstɪŋ ˌkɔːpəˌreɪʃ(ə)n/ *britische Rundfunkanstalt* 1C7
the best thing (about) /ðə ˈbest ˌθɪŋ‿əˌbaʊt/ das Beste (an) 2A2
the Celts /ðə ˈkelts/ die Kelten 1C2
the furthest /ðə ˈfɜːðɪst/ am weitesten 6C2
the next day /ðə ˈnekst‿deɪ/ am nächsten Tag 1B7
the one /ðə ˈwʌn/ der-/die-/dasjenige 4C9
the only one /ði‿ˈəʊnli ˌwʌn/ der/die/das Einzige 1B1
the other one /ði‿ˈʌðə wʌn/ der/die andere I
the others /ði‿ˈʌðəz/ die anderen 1B7
the police *(no pl)* /ðə pəˈliːs/ die Polizei I
the real thing /ðə ˈrɪəl ˌθɪŋ/ das Echte, das Wahre 3B7
the Romans /ðə ˈrəʊmənz/ die Römer 1C2
the same /ðə ˈseɪm/ der-/die-/dasselbe 2B3
the Underground *(no pl)* /ði‿ˈʌndəˌɡraʊnd/ U-Bahn 3C2
the universe /ðə ˈjuːnɪˌvɜːs/ das Universum 3A4
◦ the Atlantic /ði‿ətˈlæntɪk/ der Atlantik 1PP
◦ the British Isles /ðə ˌbrɪtɪʃ‿ˈaɪlz/ die Britischen Inseln 1PP
◦ the odd one out /ði‿ˌɒd wʌn‿ˈaʊt/ *das, was nicht dazugehört* 6P1
◦ the Shetland Islands /ðə ˈʃetlənd‿ˌaɪləndz/ *die Shetlandinseln* 1PP
their /ðeə/ ihr(e) I
theirs /ðeəz/ ihre(r, s), ihrs 5C5
them /ðem/ sie, ihnen I
then /ðen/ dann, da nach, darauf I
there /ðeə/ dort, da I
there /ðeə/ dahin, dorthin 3B1
◦ to get there /ˈɡet ðeə/ hinkommen 1PP
there is/are /ðeər‿ˈɪz, ˈɑː/ es gibt, da ist; da sind I
◦ thermal spa /ˌθɜːm(ə)l ˈspɑː/ Thermal(heil)bad 1PP
these (= *pl of* **this**) /ðiːz/ diese I
they /ðeɪ/ sie I
thing /θɪŋ/ Ding, Gegenstand, Sache I
the real thing /ðə ˈrɪəl ˌθɪŋ/ das Echte, das Wahre 3B7
to **think** *(irr)* /θɪŋk/ denken, glauben, meinen I
to **think about sb/sth** /ˈθɪŋk‿əˌbaʊt/ an jdn/etw denken, über jdn/etw nachdenken 1C9
to think about sb/sth /ˈθɪŋk‿əˌbaʊt/ sich etw überlegen 4B3
to **think of** /ˈθɪŋk‿əv/ denken an, sich ausdenken I
third /θɜːd/ dritte(r, s) I
this /ðɪs/ diese(r, s), das I
This is my brother/sister. Das ist mein Bruder/meine Schwester. I
◦ This is ... /ˈðɪs‿ɪz/ Hier spricht ... 6B7
◦ this time /ˈðɪs ˌtaɪm/ diesmal 1O1
those (= *pl of* **that**) /ðəʊz/ diese I
though /ðəʊ/ trotzdem; aber 3B1
◦ though /ðəʊ/ obwohl 2O4
thought /θɔːt/ Gedanke 6C9
three /θriː/ drei I
through /θruː/ durch 1B7
to **throw (away)** *(irr)* /ˌθrəʊ‿əˈweɪ/ (weg)werfen 5B3

to give sb the thumbs down /ˌɡɪv ˌsʌmbədi ðə ˌθʌmz ˈdaʊn/ *jemandem den Daumen nach unten zeigen* 4C1
Thursday /ˈθɜːzdeɪ/ Donnerstag I
° ticket /ˈtɪkɪt/ Fahrkarte, (Eintritts)karte 4P6
tidy /ˈtaɪdi/ ordentlich 1A3
to **tidy (up)** /ˌtaɪdi‿ˈʌp/ aufräumen I
till (= **until**) /tɪl, ʌnˈtɪl/ bis 3C3
time /taɪm/ Zeit, Uhrzeit I
all the time /ˌɔːl ðə ˈtaɪm/ die ganze Zeit I
° time /taɪm/ Mal 6P14
for the first time /fɔː ðə ˌfɜːst‿ˈtaɪm/ zum ersten Mal 6C4
° timeline /ˈtaɪmˌlaɪn/ Zeitachse 1O2
timetable /ˈtaɪmˌteɪb(ə)l/ Stundenplan I
tired /ˈtaɪəd/ müde I
title /ˈtaɪt(ə)l/ Titel 4A5
to /tʊ/ in, nach, zu, an, vor, bis I
today /təˈdeɪ/ heute I
toffee apple /ˈtɒfi‿ˌæp(ə)l/ *kandierter Apfel* 2A2
together /təˈɡeðə/ zusammen I
toilet /ˈtɔɪlət/ Toilette, Klo I
tomato /təˈmɑːtəʊ/ Tomate I
tomorrow /təˈmɒrəʊ/ morgen I
tongue /tʌŋ/ Zunge 6B4
tonight /təˈnaɪt/ heute Abend I
too /tuː/ auch; zu I
(too) bad /tuː ˈbæd/ (zu) schade 1A3
too loud /ˌtuː ˈlaʊd/ zu laut I
tooth (*pl* **teeth**) /tuːθ, tiːθ/ Zahn I
toothbrush /ˈtuːθˌbrʌʃ/ Zahnbürste 5C2
top /tɒp/ oberes Ende, Spitze 3B4
° top /tɒp/ oberste(r, s) 1PP; Spitzen- 3C8
topic /ˈtɒpɪk/ Thema 5B8
totally /ˈtəʊt(ə)li/ völlig, total 4B1
to **touch** /tʌtʃ/ berühren 6A2
toward(s) /təˈwɔːdz/ in Richtung I; gegenüber 2C7
tower /ˈtaʊə/ Turm I
toy /tɔɪ/ Spielzeug(-) 4A1
track /træk/ Weg, Pfad, (Lauf)bahn 6C4
° trade (*no pl*) /treɪd/ Handel 1O1
traffic (*no pl*) /ˈtræfɪk/ Verkehr 5A2
train /treɪn/ Zug 3B3
to **train** /treɪn/ trainieren 6C3
trainer /ˈtreɪnə/ Trainer/in, Turnschuh I
transport (*no pl*) /ˈtrænspɔːt/ Transport, Beförderung 5B8
trapdoor /ˈtræpˌdɔː/ Falltür 3C5
to travel /ˈtræv(ə)l/ reisen 2C6
treasure (*no pl*) /ˈtreʒə/ Schatz 1B7
° treat /triːt/ (Extra)vergnügen 2O2
tree /triː/ Baum I
° tribe /traɪb/ Stamm, Sippe 1O1
to play a trick on sb /ˌpleɪ‿ə ˈtrɪk‿ɒn ˌsʌmbədi/ jdm einen Streich spielen 5C9
° trick /trɪk/ Trick; Streich 5C9
° trick or treat /ˌtrɪk‿ɔː ˈtriːt/ *Halloween-Spruch* 2O1
to trick sb (out of sth) /ˌtrɪk ˌsʌmbədi‿ˈaʊt‿ɒv ˌsʌmθɪŋ/ jdn (um etw) betrügen 4C5
to **make a trip** /ˌmeɪk‿ə ˈtrɪp/ einen Ausflug machen 3B9
° triumphant /traɪˈʌmfənt/ triumphierend 2O2
° tropical /ˈtrɒpɪk(ə)l/ Tropen-, tropisch 1PP
to get into trouble /ˌɡet‿ˌɪntʊ ˈtrʌb(ə)l/ in Schwierigkeiten geraten 1C1
trouble (*no pl*) /ˈtrʌb(ə)l/ Schwierigkeiten, Ärger 1C1
trousers (*only pl*) /ˈtraʊzəz/ Hose I
true /truː/ wahr I
° to trust /trʌst/ vertrauen 2O2
to **try** /traɪ/ versuchen, probieren I
to **try on** /ˌtraɪ‿ˈɒn/ anprobieren I
Tube /tjuːb/ *die (Londoner) U-Bahn* 3C2
Tuesday /ˈtjuːzdeɪ/ Dienstag I
to turn /tɜːn/ (sich) umdrehen; werden 3B1
to turn (a)round /ˌtɜːn‿əˈraʊnd/ sich umdrehen 1B7
to **turn off** /ˌtɜːn‿ˈɒf/ abschalten, ausmachen 5B1
to turn out /ˌtɜːn‿ˈaʊt/ sich herausstellen 5A2
to **turn right/left** /ˌtɜːn ˈraɪt/ˈleft/ rechts/links abbiegen 3C2
to turn sth upside down /ˌtɜːn ˌsʌmθɪŋ‿ˌʌpsaɪd‿ˈdaʊn/ etw auf den Kopf stellen; umdrehen 4C4
° to turn back /ˌtɜːn ˈbæk/ umkehren, zurückgehen 2O2
° to turn up /ˌtɜːn‿ˈʌp/ erscheinen, auftauchen 2O2
TV station /ˌtiː ˈviː ˌsteɪʃ(ə)n/ Fernsehsender 5B4
twelve /twelv/ zwölf I
twice /twaɪs/ zweimal 4C2
twilight /ˈtwaɪlaɪt/ Dämmerung, Zwielicht 4B1
two /tuː/ zwei I
typical (of) /ˈtɪpɪk(ə)l‿əv/ typisch (für) 2A2
Typical! (*informal*) /ˈtɪpɪk(ə)l/ Typisch! 6C4

U

UK (= **the United Kingdom**) /ˌjuːˈkeɪ, ðə juːˌnaɪtɪd ˈkɪŋdəm/ Vereinigtes Königreich I
umbrella /ʌmˈbrelə/ (Regen)schirm I
unacceptable /ˌʌnəkˈseptəb(ə)l/ inakzeptabel, nicht hinnehmbar 1C2
° uncertain /ʌnˈsɜː(r)t(ə)n/ unsicher 2O2
uncle /ˈʌŋk(ə)l/ Onkel I
unconscious /ʌnˈkɒnʃəs/ bewusstlos 6B10
under /ˈʌndə/ unter I
to **understand** (*irr*) /ˌʌndəˈstænd/ verstehen I
° unfriendly /ʌnˈfrendli/ unfreundlich 6P2
unhappy /ʌnˈhæpi/ unglücklich I
uniform /ˈjuːnɪfɔːm/ Uniform I
university /ˌjuːnɪˈvɜːsəti/ Universität(s-) 3C3
until /ʌnˈtɪl/ bis 1B7
up /ʌp/ nach oben, hoch I
up and down /ˌʌp‿ən ˈdaʊn/ auf und ab 6A2
upset /ʌpˈset/ aufgeregt, aufgebracht, bestürzt I
upstairs /ʌpˈsteəz/ (nach) oben 3C5
us /ʌs/ uns I
us (*informal*) wir 2B5
to **use** /juːz/ benutzen I
° used to (do sth) /ˈjuːst‿tuː duː/ *drückt aus, was man früher (gewohnheitsmäßig) gemacht hat oder war* 1PP
usually /ˈjuːʒʊəli/ gewöhnlich, normalerweise I

V

° Valentine's Day /ˈvæləntaɪnz ˌdeɪ/ Valentinstag 2P13
vampire /ˈvæmpaɪə/ Vampir/in 4B1
vegetable /ˈvedʒtəb(ə)l/ Gemüse 3A4
verse /vɜːs/ Strophe 4B11
very /ˈveri/ sehr, außerordentlich I
° vet /vet/ Tierarzt/Tierärztin 6P10
victim /ˈvɪktɪm/ Opfer 6B10
victory /ˈvɪkt(ə)ri/ Sieg 6C4
view /vjuː/ (Aus)sicht, (Aus)blick 3A4
° viewing (*no pl*) /ˈvjuːɪŋ/ Anschauen 5P13
village /ˈvɪlɪdʒ/ Dorf 5C2
virtual /ˈvɜːtʃʊəl/ virtuell 3A4
to **visit** /ˈvɪzɪt/ besuchen, anschauen I
visit /ˈvɪzɪt/ Besuch 3A3
visitor /ˈvɪzɪtə/ Besucher/in, Gast I
voice /vɔɪs/ Stimme 4C5
to have a vote /ˌhæv‿ə ˈvəʊt/ abstimmen 5B4
to vote for sb/sth /ˈvəʊt fə/ für jdn/etw stimmen 5B7

W

to **wait** /weɪt/ warten I; erwarten 3B1
to **wait for** /ˈweɪt fɔː/ warten auf I
waiting room /ˈweɪtɪŋ ˌruːm/ Wartezimmer 6B5
to **wake up** *(irr)* /ˌweɪk‿ˈʌp/ aufwecken, aufwachen 5C6
to **take … for a walk** /ˌteɪk fər‿ə ˈwɔːk/ … spazieren führen, Gassi gehen mit … I
walk /wɔːk/ Spaziergang 5A2
to **walk** /wɔːk/ zu Fuß gehen, laufen I
to **walk on** /ˌwɔːk‿ˈɒn/ weiterlaufen 3C2
to **walk straight on** /ˌwɔːk ˌstreɪt‿ˈɒn/ immer geradeaus weiterlaufen 3C2
to **walk the dog** /ˌwɔːk ðə ˈdɒg/ den Hund ausführen I
to walk up to sb /ˌwɔːk‿ˈʌp tə/ auf jdn zugehen 5C6
to **go walking** /ˌgəʊ ˈwɔːkɪŋ/ wandern, spazieren gehen I
wall /wɔːl/ Wand I
to **want** /wɒnt/ wünschen, wollen I
to **want sb** to **do sth** /ˌwɒnt ˌsʌmbədi tə ˈduː ˌsʌmθɪŋ/ wollen, dass jd etw tut 2C3
warm /wɔːm/ warm I
◦ warm-up /ˈwɔːmˌʌp/ (sich) aufwärmen, Warm-up 6P14
◦ to waste /weɪst/ verschwenden, vergeuden 5P9
waste *(no pl)* /weɪst/ Verschwendung, Vergeudung; Abfall 5B8
to **watch** /wɒtʃ/ beobachten, zuschauen, anschauen I
to watch out (for) /ˌwɒtʃ‿ˈaʊt fɔː/ aufpassen (auf) 3A4
to **watch TV** /ˌwɒtʃ ˌtiː ˈviː/ fernsehen I
water *(no pl)* /ˈwɔːtə/ Wasser I
◦ water sport /ˈwɔːtə spɔːt/ Wassersport(art) 1PP
◦ wave /weɪv/ Welle 1PP
way /weɪ/ Weg; Art und Weise I; Möglichkeit 6C4
◦ to lead the way /ˌliːd ðə ˈweɪ/ vorangehen 2O2
◦ to make one's way /ˌmeɪk wʌnz ˈweɪ/ sich auf den Weg machen 2O2
we /wiː/ wir I
We're just looking. Wir schauen uns nur um. I
We're twelve. Wir sind zwölf (Jahre alt). I
wealth /welθ/ Reichtum, Vermögen, Fülle 2A2
weapon /ˈwepən/ Waffe 3C5
to **wear** *(irr)* /weə/ tragen, anhaben I
weather /ˈweðə/ Wetter I
Wednesday /ˈwenzdeɪ/ Mittwoch I
week /wiːk/ Woche I
weekend /ˌwiːkˈend/ Wochenende I
well /wel/ nun (ja), tja I
Well done! /ˌwel ˈdʌn/ gut gemacht!, super! I
well-organized /ˌwel‿ˈɔːgənaɪzd/ gut organisiert 3C2
◦ west /west/ Westen, westlich, West- 1PP
wet /wet/ nass 5C6
◦ to go whale spotting /ˌgəʊ ˈweɪl ˌspɒtɪŋ/ Wale beobachten gehen 1PP
◦ whale /weɪl/ Wal 1PP
what /wɒt/ was I; welche(r, s) 1C9
What a mess! /ˌwɒt‿ə ˈmes/ Was für ein Durcheinander! 2B5
What a/an …! /ˈwɒt‿ə/ Was für ein(e) …! 2C7
What about …? *(informal)* /ˈwɒt‿əˌbaʊt/ Was ist mit …?, Wie wäre es mit …? I
What is … about? /ˌwɒt‿ɪz əˈbaʊt/ Worum geht es in/bei …? 2B2
What time is it? /ˌwɒt‿ˈtaɪm‿ɪz‿ɪt/ Wie spät/Wie viel Uhr ist es? I
What's the time? /ˌwɒts ðə ˈtaɪm/ Wie spät/Wie viel Uhr ist es? I
What's wrong with …? /ˌwɒts‿ˈrɒŋ wɪð …/ Was stimmt nicht mit …?, Was fehlt …? I
What's wrong? /ˌwɒts‿ˈrɒŋ/ Was ist los? 4C1
What's your name? /ˌwɒts jə ˈneɪm/ Wie heißt du? I
What's … in English? /ˌwɒts ɪn‿ˈɪŋglɪʃ/ Was bedeutet … auf Englisch? I
whatever /wɒtˈevə/ was auch immer, egal was 2B3
when /wen/ wann; als; wenn I
where /weə/ wo; wohin I
Where are you from? /ˌweər‿ə jʊ ˈfrɒm/ Woher kommst du? I
which /wɪtʃ/ welche(r, s) 1A2; der/die/das 3C5
which one /ˈwɪtʃ wʌn/ welche(r, s) 1B10
while /waɪl/ während 1B7, als 6B3
to **whisper** /ˈwɪspə/ flüstern 4C1
white /waɪt/ weiß I
who /huː/ wer I; der/die/das 3C5
whole /həʊl/ ganz, gesamt 6B1
whose /huːz/ wessen 1A2
why /waɪ/ warum I
◦ why's that? /ˌwaɪz ˈðæt/ wieso das (denn)? 2O2
wife /waɪf/ (Ehe)frau I
wild /waɪld/ wild; in freier Wildbahn lebend I
wildlife *(no pl)* /ˈwaɪldˌlaɪf/ *die (natürliche) Tier- und Pflanzenwelt* 5A2
will /wɪl/ werden 2B5
window /ˈwɪndəʊ/ Fenster I
◦ wine /waɪn/ Wein 1O1
winner /ˈwɪnə/ Gewinner/in, Sieger/in 3B9
winning team /ˌwɪnɪŋ ˈtiːm/ Siegermannschaft 4A1
winter /ˈwɪntə/ Winter I
in winter /ɪn ˈwɪntə/ im Winter I
to **win** *(irr)* /wɪn/ gewinnen I
to **wish** /wɪʃ/ wünschen I
◦ witch /wɪtʃ/ Hexe 2O2
with /wɪð/ mit I
without /wɪðˈaʊt/ ohne 1C7
witness /ˈwɪtnəs/ Zeuge/ Zeugin 6B10
woman (*pl* **women**) /ˈwʊmən, ˈwɪmɪn/ Frau I
won't (= will not) /ˈwəʊnt, wɪl ˈnɒt/ nicht werden 2B5
It won't happen again.: Es wird nicht wieder vorkommen.
wonderful /ˈwʌndəf(ə)l/ wunderbar, wundervoll I
woods *(only pl)* /wʊdz/ Wald 1B7
word /wɜːd/ Wort I
word web /ˈwɜːd ˌweb/ Wortnetz 6A3
to **work** /wɜːk/ arbeiten; funktionieren I
work /wɜːk/ Arbeit I
world /wɜːld/ Welt I
worried /ˈwʌrid/ beunruhigt, besorgt I
◦ worriedly /ˈwʌridli/ besorgt 4P13, beunruhigt 4P7
to **worry (about)** /ˈwʌri‿əˌbaʊt/ sich Sorgen machen (um) I
would /wʊd/ würde(n/st/t) 2A2
would like to /wʊd ˈlaɪk tʊ/ würde(n/st/t) gern 2B2
wouldn't (= **would not**) /ˈwʊd(ə)nt, wʊd ˈnɒt/ würde(n/st/t) nicht 2B3
to **write** *(irr)* /raɪt/ schreiben I
to **write down**: aufschreiben, niederschreiben I
writer /ˈraɪtə/ Verfasser/in, Autor/in 3C5
◦ writing *(no pl)* /ˈraɪtɪŋ/ Schreiben 5P1
wrong /rɒŋ/ falsch I

Y

yard /jɑːd/ *Längenmaß (91,44 cm)* 6B1
year /jɪə/ Jahr I; (Schul-)Jahrgang 4A3
◦ to yell /jel/ (gellend) schreien 2O4
yellow /ˈjeləʊ/ gelb I
yes /jes/ ja I
yesterday /ˈjestədeɪ/ gestern I
yet /jet/ bis jetzt, schon, noch 3B1
you /juː/ du, dich, dir, Sie, Ihnen, ihr, euch I
You must be joking! *(informal)* /juː məs bi ˈdʒəʊkɪŋ/ Das meinst du doch nicht im Ernst! 3B1
◦ you'd (= you would) /juːd, ˈjuː wʊd/ du würdest, ihr würdet, Sie würden 2O4
◦ you'll (= you will) /juːl, ˈjuː wɪl/ du wirst, Sie werden, ihr werdet 2O2
◦ You'll have to do better than that. /juːl ˌhæv tə duː ˈbetə ðən ˌðæt/ da wirst du dich schon mehr anstrengen müssen 2O2
young /jʌŋ/ jung I
your /jɔː/ dein(e), euer/eure, Ihr(e) I
yours /jɔːz/ deine(r, s), eure(r, s), Ihre(r, s) 5C5
Yours sincerely /jɔːz‿sɪnˈsɪəli/ Mit freundlichen Grüßen 5C2
yourself (*pl* yourselves) /jəˈself, jəˈselvz/ dich, dir, selbst 3A4

Z

zip wire /ˈzɪp ˌwaɪə/ Seilrutsche 1B7

German-English dictionary

A

Abend evening, night
Abendessen dinner
abends *(nur hinter Uhrzeit zwischen 12 Uhr mittags und Mitternacht)* pm (= post meridiem)
Abenteuer adventure
aber but, though
Abfall waste *(no pl)*
abholen to pick up
ablehnend negative
abschalten to turn off
abschließen to finish
abschreiben to copy
Adresse address
ähnlich similar
Aktivität activity
albern silly
Albtraum nightmare
alle everybody
alle zusammen everyone
allein alone
alle(s) all
alles everything
alles Liebe *(Briefschlussformel)* love
als when, than, as, when
als Erstes first
als Nächste(r, s) next
also so
alt old
Alter age
am Abend in the evening
am liebsten/am meisten best
am Morgen in the morning
am Nachmittag in the afternoon
an at, about, to
an ... vorbei past
anbieten to offer
andere others *(only pl)*
andere(r, s) other, different
ändern to change
anders different
es sich anders überlegen to change one's mind
Anfang start, beginning
anfangen to start, to begin *(irr)*
angemessen sensible
angenehm nice
Angst haben (vor) to be afraid (of)
Angst machen to scare
anhaben to wear *(irr)*
anhalten to stop
anhören to listen to
ankommen to arrive
(an)lächeln to smile (at)
annehmen to guess
anprobieren to try on
Anruf phone call (= telephone call)
anrufen to phone, to ring (up) *(irr)*
ans Meer fahren to go to the seaside
ans Telefon gehen to answer the phone
anschauen to visit, to look at, to watch
(an)schreien to shout (at)
Anschrift address
(sich) ansehen to look at
Antwort answer
antworten to answer
sich anziehen to get dressed
Apfel apple
April April
Arbeit work
arbeiten to work
arbeitsreich busy
sich über jdn ärgern to be angry with sb
Argument argument
Arm arm
arm poor
arrogant arrogant
Art und Weise way
atemberaubend spectacular
attraktiv attractive
auch too, also
auf on, at, on, in
auf der linken Seite on the left
auf der rechten Seite on the right
auf Englisch in English
aufbewahren to keep *(irr)*
aufführen to perform
aufgebracht upset
aufgeregt excited, upset
aufhalten to stop
sich aufhalten to stay
aufhängen to put up *(irr)*
aufheben to pick up, to collect
aufhören to stop, to finish
aufmuntern to cheer up
aufnehmen to include
aufräumen to tidy (up)
aufregend exciting
aufschreiben to write down *(irr)*
(auf)springen to jump (up)
aufstehen to get up *(irr)*, to stand up *(irr)*
aufstellen to put up *(irr)*
auftreten to perform
aufwachen to wake up *(irr)*
aufwecken to wake up *(irr)*
Auge eye
Augenblick moment
August August
aus from
aus den Augen verlieren to lose *(irr)*
Ausblick view
sich ausdenken to think of *(irr)*
Ausdruck phrase
einen Ausflug machen to go on a trip
Auseinandersetzung argument
ausfüllen to fill in
ausfüllen to complete
ausgeben *(Geld)* to spend *(irr)*
ausgezeichnet excellent
aushalten to stand *(irr)*
Auskunft information *(no pl)*
ausmachen to turn off, to make *(irr)*
ausreichend enough
ausschlafen to sleep late
aussehen to look
Aussicht view
aussprechen to pronounce
aussteigen to get off *(irr)*
auswählen to choose *(irr)*
auswendig by heart
Auto car
Autor/in writer
außen out, outside
außergewöhnlich outstanding
außerhalb outside
außerordentlich very, very
äußerst ungern tun to hate to do

B

backen to bake
Bad(ezimmer) bathroom
Bahnhof station
bald soon
Banane banana
Batterie battery
Bauernhof farm
Baum tree
beachten to notice
beantworten to answer
Becher cup
bedeuten to mean *(irr)*
bedeutend important
Beeil dich!, Beeilt euch! Hurry up!
beenden to stop, to finish
sich befassen mit to study
Beförderung transport *(no pl)*
befragen to interview
begeistert delighted, enthusiastic
Beginn beginning, start
beginnen to begin *(irr)*
behalten to keep *(irr)*
bei at
beide both
Bein leg
beinahe almost
beinhalten to include
Beispiel example
beißen to bite *(irr)*
bejahend positive
bekommen to receive, to get *(irr)*
beliebt popular
bemerken to notice
bemerkenswert outstanding
Benehmen behaviour *(no pl)*
benutzen to use
beobachten to watch
bereit ready
bereits already

Berg mountain, hill
Bericht report
sich beruhigen to calm down
berühmt famous
beschäftigt busy
beschreiben to describe
beschützen to protect
Besichtigungen sightseeing *(no pl)*
eine Besichtigungstour machen to do sightseeing
besondere(r, s) special
besorgt worried
besprechen to discuss
besser better
besteigen to climb (up)
beste(r, s) best
bestimmen to decide
bestimmt certain
bestürzt upset
besuchen to visit
die Besucher the audience
Besucher/in visitor
Betragen behaviour *(no pl)*
Bett bed
beunruhigt worried
bevor before
bewahren to save
(sich) bewegen to move
bezahlen to pay *(irr)*
bieten to offer
Bild picture
bilden to form
billig cheap
Biologie biology *(no pl)*
bis till (= until), to
bis bald! See you soon! *(informal)*
bis jetzt yet
bitte please
Bitte schön! here you are
(um etw) bitten to ask (for sth)
Blatt Papier piece of paper
blau blue
bleiben to stay
Bleistift pencil
blöd stupid
blond blond(e)
bloß just
Blume flower
Boden floor
Boot boat
Bord shelf (*pl* shelves)
Botschaft message
brauchen need
braun brown
Brett board
Brief letter
bringen to take *(irr)*
britisch British
Broschüre brochure
Bruder brother
Buch book
buchen to book
Bücherei library
Bühne stage
mit dem Bus by bus
Butter butter

C

Chips crisps *(only pl)*
Cousin cousin
Cousine cousin

D

da there, as, because
da sein to arrive
Dame lady
danach after that, then
Danke thanks, thank you
dann then
daran denken to remember
darauf then
darauf achten, (dass) to make sure (that)
darum that's why
das the
das ist that's (= that is)
das ist nicht that's not (= that is not)
Das wäre toll. That would be great.
dass that
Datum date
dein(e) your
deine(r, s) yours
dekorieren to decorate
denken to think *(irr)*
denken an to think of *(irr)*
an jdn/etw denken to think about sb/sth
der the
der-/die-/dasjenige the one
der-/die-/dasselbe the same
der/die andere the other one
deshalb that's why, so
deswegen that's why
Detail detail
deutlich clear
Deutsche/r; deutsch German
Deutsch(unterricht) German
Dezember December
Dialog dialogue
dich you
die the
Dienstag Tuesday
diese(r, s) this
Ding thing
dir you
direkt immediately
diskutieren to discuss
Donnerstag Thursday
Dorf village
dort there
dort drüben over there
draußen out
dreckig dirty
drinnen inside
dritte(r, s) third
du you
duften to smell *(irr)*
dumm stupid, silly
dunkel dark
durch through
etw tun dürfen be allowed to do sth
sich duschen to have/take a shower

E

echt proper, real
Ecke corner
ehe before
Ehefrau wife
Ehemann husband
ehrgeizig ambitious
ehrlich honest
Ei egg
eifersüchtig jealous
eigene(r, s) own
ein(e) a/an
ein(e) andere(r) another
ein bisschen a bit
ein wenig a bit
einander each other
eindeutig clear
einfach easy, just
Einfall idea
einige some, a few
sich einigen (auf) to agree (on)
Einkaufen shopping *(no pl)*
einkaufen gehen to go shopping
einladen to invite
Einladung invitation
einsammeln to collect
mit einschließen to include
einsteigen in to get into
eintragen to fill in
Einzelheit detail
einzige(r, s) only
Eis(creme) ice cream
Elefant elephant
Eltern parents *(only pl)*
Emotion emotion
emotional emotional
Ende end
enden to finish
endlich finally
Energie energy *(no pl)*
eng narrow
Englisch; englisch English
englischsprachig English-speaking
Ente duck
enthusiastisch enthusiastic
entlang along
entscheiden to decide
entschlossen determined
sich entschuldigen to say sorry
Entschuldigung! (I'm) sorry.
entsetzt shocked
entspannt relaxed

Wordbanks p. 149 | Word lists p. 154 | English-German dictionary p. 186

enttäuscht disappointed
er he
Erdkunde geography
ereignisreich busy
Erfahrung experience *(no pl)*
Erfolg success *(no pl)*
erforschen to explore, to do research, to study
Ergebnis result
erhalten to get *(irr)*, to receive
sich erinnern to remember
(jdm etw) erklären to explain (sth to sb)
Erlebnis adventure, experience *(no pl)*
erraten to guess
erreichen to get to
erschrecken to scare
erst only
erstaunlich amazing
erstaunt surprised
erstellen to make *(irr)*, to prepare
erste(r, s) first
ertragen to stand *(irr)*
Erwachsene/r adult
erwähnen to mention
erwarten to wait
erzählen to tell *(irr)*
Erzählung story
Erzeugnis product
es it
Es geht mir gut. I'm fine
essen to eat *(irr)*
Essen food *(no pl)*, meal
etwas something, some
euch you
euer/eure your
eure(r, s) yours
ewig forever

F

fabelhaft fabulous
fahren to drive *(irr)*, to go *(irr)*
fahren (mit) to ride *(irr)*
Fahrrad bike *(informal)*
mit dem Fahrrad by bike
falls if
falsch wrong
Familie family
fangen to catch *(irr)*
fantastisch fantastic *(informal)*, spectacular, stunning
Farbe colour
fast almost
faszinierend fascinating
faul lazy
Februar February
Federmäppchen pencil case
(den Boden) fegen to sweep (the floor)
fehlen to be missing
Fehler mistake
Feier celebration
feiern to celebrate
Fenster window
Ferien holiday
in den Ferien on holiday
fernsehen to watch TV
fertig ready
Fest festival
fest strong
Feuerwerk fireworks *(only pl)*
finden to find *(irr)*
Fisch fish (*pl* fish *or* fishes)
Flasche bottle
fliegen to fly *(irr)*
flüchten to get away *(irr)*
Fluss river
flüstern to whisper
Flyer leaflet
Folge result
folgen to follow
formen to form
forschen to do research
fortkommen to get away *(irr)*
Fotoapparat camera
fotografieren to take photos
Frage question
fragen to ask
Französisch French
Frau woman (*pl* women), lady
Frau *(Anrede)* Mrs, Ms
frei haben/sein to be free
Freitag Friday
Freizeit free time
fressen to eat *(irr)*
sich auf etw freuen to look forward to sth
sich darauf freuen, etw zu tun to look forward to doing sth
Freund/in friend
freundlich friendly, kind, nice
froh pleased
fröhlich cheerful, happy
Frucht fruit *(no pl)*
früh early
Frühling spring
Frühstück breakfast
frühstücken to have breakfast
frustriert frustrated
(sich) fühlen to feel *(irr)*
funktionieren to work
für for
furchtbar awful, terrible
sich fürchten (vor) to be afraid (of)
sich (anfangen zu) fürchten to get scared
furchterregend scary
Futter food *(no pl)*
füttern to feed *(irr)*
Fuß foot (*pl* feet)
Fußball football

G

Gabel fork
ganz quite
den ganzen Sommer all summer
Garten garden
Gassi gehen mit ... to take ... for a walk
Gast guest, visitor
Gaststätte restaurant
Gebäude building
geben to give *(irr)*
Gebiet area
Geburtstag birthday
Gedicht poem
gefährlich dangerous
Gefühl feeling, emotion
gefühlvoll emotional
gegen against
Gegend area
gegenseitig each other
Gegenstand thing
gegenüber toward(s)
gegenüberliegend opposite, across
gehen to go *(irr)*
jdm gehören to belong to sb
Geist ghost
gelangweilt bored
gelb yellow
Geld money *(no pl)*
Geld sparen to save money
Gemüse vegetable
genannt werden to be called
genau exactly
genießen to enjoy
genug, genügend enough
geöffnet (von ... bis ...) open (from ... to ...)
Geografie geography
gerade just
Geräusch noise, sound
Geschäft shop, store
geschehen to happen
Geschenk present
Geschichte story
Geschichte *(als Schulfach)* history
Geschirrspülmaschine dishwasher
Gesicht face
Gespenst ghost
Gespräch dialogue, conversation
gestern yesterday
Getränk drink
gewinnen to win *(irr)*
Gewinner/in winner
gewiss certain
sich gewöhnen an to get used to
gewöhnlich usually
Gitter(netz) grid
Glas glass *(no pl)*
glauben to believe, to think *(irr)*
gleich immediately
Glück luck *(no pl)*

Glück haben to be lucky
glücklich happy
glücklich *(Glück habend)* lucky
Glückwunsch! Congratulations!
gratis for free *(informal)*
Gratuliere! Congratulations!
grau grey
Grill; Grillparty barbecue
groß great, big, tall
großartig great
Großbritannien (Great) Britain
Größe size
Großeltern grandparents *(only pl)*
Großmutter grandmother
(Groß)stadt city
Großvater grandfather
grün green
Grund reason
Gruppe group
gut good
gut gemacht! Well done!
gut in … sein to be good at

H

Haare hair *(no pl)*
haben to have *(irr)*, to have got *(irr)*
halb half
halb (acht) half past (seven)
eine halbe Stunde half an hour
hallo! hello
Hallo, ich heiße … Hello, I'm …
halten to keep *(irr)*
halten von to feel *(irr)*
Haltestelle station
Hand hand
handeln to act
Handlung action
Handy mobile (= mobile phone)
hart hard
hassen to hate
Haupt- main
Haus house
Hausaufgabe(n) homework *(no pl)*
Haustier pet
Haut skin *(no pl)*
Heft exercise book
heiter cheerful
heiß hot
heißen to be called
helfen to help
Hemd shirt
herausfinden to find out *(irr)*
herausnehmen to take out *(irr)*
etw heraussuchen to look up sth
Herbst autumn
Herr *(Anrede)* Mr (= Mister)
herrisch bossy
herrschsüchtig bossy
herstellen to produce
jdn herumführen to show sb (a)round
herunter down
hervorragend oustanding
heute today
heute Abend tonight
hier here
Hier, bitte! here you are
Hilfe help
Hilfestellung support
(hinauf)steigen to climb (up)
hinausbringen to take out *(irr)*
sich hinlegen to lie *(irr)*
sich hinsetzen to sit down *(irr)*
hinter behind, past
hinunter down
(etw etw) hinzufügen to add (sth to sth)
hoch high, up
hoch (gewachsen) tall
hocherfreut delighted
hochheben to put up *(irr)*
(hoch)springen to jump (up)
hoffen to hope
höflich polite
holen to get *(irr)*
hören to hear *(irr)*
Hose trousers *(only pl)*
hübsch pretty, lovely
Hügel hill
Huhn chicken
Hund dog
den Hund ausführen to walk the dog
hungrig hungry
Hut hat

I

ich I
ich bin I'm (= I am)
Ich bin … Jahre alt. I'm … years old.
Ich heiße My name is
Ich komme aus … I'm from …
Ich mag I like
Ich mag … nicht. I don't like …
Ich schätze … I guess …
Idee idea
ihm, ihn him
ihnen them
Ihnen you
ihr you
ihr(e) their
Ihr(e) your
ihr(e, r) her
ihre(r, s) their, hers
Ihre(r, s) yours
ihrs her, theirs
im Moment at the moment
im Urlaub on holiday
im Winter in winter
immer always
immer geradeaus weiterlaufen to walk straight on
(immer) noch still
in in, to, into, at
in der Nähe near
Information(en) information *(no pl)*
Informationstechnologie IT *(no pl)* (= information technology)
innen inside
ins Bett gehen to go to bed
Insel island
interessant interesting
Interesse interest
sich interessieren (für) to be interested (in)
interessiert sein (an) to be interested (in)
interviewen to interview
(irgend)ein(e) any
(irgend)etwas anything
(irgend)jemand somebody, anyone, someone
(irgend)was anything
irgendwer someone, somebody
sich irren to be wrong
Irrtum mistake

J

ja yes
Jacke jacket
Jahr year
Jahreszeit season
Jahrhundert century
Januar January
je …, desto … the … the
jede/r everyone, everybody
jeden all
jedenfalls anyway
jede(r, s) every, each, any
jemals ever
jenseits across
jetzt now
jubeln to cheer
Juli July
jung young
Junge boy
Juni June

K

Käfig cage
Kalender calendar
kalt cold
Kamera camera
Karte card
Käse cheese
Katalog brochure
Katze cat
kaufen to buy *(irr)*
Kaufhaus store
kehren to sweep
kein/e no
Keller basement
kennen to know *(irr)*
Kerze candle
Kind child *(pl* children)

Wordbanks p. 149 | Word lists p. 154 | English-German dictionary p. 186

Kino cinema
Kirche church
Kiste box
Klang sound
klar clear
Klassenkamerad/in classmate
Klassenzimmer classroom
Klebstoff glue *(no pl)*
Kleidung clothes *(only pl)*
klein small
klein(e, er, es) little
ein(e) kleine(s, r) a small one
klettern (auf) to climb (up)
klingeln to ring (up) *(irr)*
klingen to sound
Klo toilet
kochen to cook
Kochen cooking
Koffer suitcase
die Koffer packen to pack one's bags
komisch funny
kommen to come *(irr)*
kommentieren to comment (on)
Komm(t) jetzt! Come on! *(informal)*
König king
Königin queen
können can
etw tun können be able to do sth
Konkurrent/in rival
Konzert concert
Kopf head
kopieren to copy
es kostet it's (= it is)
köstlich delicious
Kostüm costume
Krach noise *(no pl)*
Kraft energy *(no pl)*
kräftig strong
krank sick, ill
Krankenhaus hospital
kreischen to scream
Kuchen cake
Kuh cow
Kühlschrank fridge *(informal)*
sich kümmern um to look after
Kunde/Kundin customer
Kunststoff plastic
Kunst(unterricht) art
kurz short
Küste coast

L

lächeln to smile
lachen to laugh
Laden store, shop
Lampe lamp, light
Land country
(Land)karte map
lang long
lange schlafen to sleep late
langsam slow
langweilig boring
Lärm noise *(no pl)*
lassen to let *(irr)*
Lass(t) uns let's (= let us)
laufen to walk
laut loud, noisy
Laut sound
läuten to ring (up) *(irr)*
leben to live
Leben life (*pl* lives)
lecker delicious
legen to put *(irr)*
Lehrer/in teacher
leicht easy
leider I'm afraid
leise quiet
lernen to learn *(irr)*
lesen to read *(irr)*
letzten Endes in the end
letzte(r, s) last
Leute people *(no pl)*
Licht light
Lichtquelle light
Liebe love
lieben to love
liebenswürdig kind
Liebe(r, s) ... Dear ...,
Lieblings- favourite
(Lied)text lyrics *(only pl)*
liegen to lie *(irr)*
lila purple
Lineal ruler
links on the left
(nach) links left
Löffel spoon
Löwe lion
locker relaxed
lustig funny

M

machen to do *(irr)*, to make *(irr)*
sich etw machen (aus) to care (about)
Mach(t) schon! Come on! *(informal)*
Mädchen girl
magisch magic
Mahlzeit meal
Mai May
Mama mum *(informal)*
manchmal sometimes
Mann man (*pl* men)
Mantel coat
Markt market
März March
Mathe(unterricht) maths *(informal, only pl)*
Maus mouse (*pl* mice)
Medikamente medicine *(no pl)*
Medizin medicine *(no pl)*
(noch) mehr more
Meer sea *(no pl)*
(Meeres)küste seaside *(no pl)*
Mein Lieblings... ist My favourite ... is
mein(e) my
meine(r, s) mine
meinen to mean *(irr)*, to think *(irr)*
meins mine
(die) meisten most
Melodie melody
eine Menge lots of *(informal)*, a lot (of)
Menschen people *(no pl)*
merkwürdig strange
Messer knife (*pl* knives)
mich me
Mikrofon microphone
mindestens at least
Minute minute
mir me
mit with
(mit)bringen to bring *(irr)*
(miteinander) (ver)mischen to mix
Mitglied member
mitnehmen to take *(irr)*
Mitschüler/in classmate
Mittagessen lunch, dinner
Mitte middle, centre
Mitteilung note
Mittwoch Wednesday
mobben to bully
Möbel furniture *(no pl)*
Mobiltelefon mobile (= mobile phone)
mögen to like
möglich possible
möglicherweise maybe
Moment moment
im Moment at the moment
Monat month
Montag Monday
Morgen morning
morgen tomorrow
morgens am (= ante meridiem)
müde tired
Müll rubbish *(no pl)*
den Müll hinausbringen to take out the rubbish
Mülleimer bin
Mülltonne bin
Mund mouth
Musik *(als Schulfach)* music
müssen must, have to *(irr)*
Mutter mother
Mutti mum *(informal)*

N

nach after, past, to
nach draußen outside
nach drinnen inside
nach oben up
Nachmittag afternoon
nachmittags pm (= post meridiem)
Nachricht message, news *(only pl)*

Nachrichtensendung news *(only pl)*
nachschauen to have a look
etw nachschlagen to look up sth
nachsehen to have a look
nachsprechen to repeat
nächste(r, s) next
Nacht night
nachts at night
in der Nähe near
nahe near
Nahrung food *(no pl)*
Name name
Nase nose
nass wet
national national
natürlich of course
(Natur)wissenschaft science
neben next to
neidisch jealous
negativ negative
nehmen to take *(irr)*
nein no
nennen to call
nervös nervous
nett kind, pretty, lovely, nice
neu new
neugierig nosy
Neuigkeit news *(only pl)*
Neujahr New Year
nicht not
nicht einverstanden sein to disagree
nicht mehr not ... anymore
nicht mögen to dislike
nicht stimmen to be wrong
nicht übereinstimmen to disagree
niederschreiben to write down *(irr)*
nie(mals) never
noch yet
noch eine(r, s) another
noch einmal again
noch immer still
(noch) mehr more
Nord-, Norden, nördlich north
normal normal
normalerweise usually
(sich) notieren to note down
Notiz note
(sich) Notizen machen to take notes
November November
Nummer number
nun now
nun (ja) well
nur just, only

O

ob if
oberes Ende top
Obst fruit *(no pl)*
obwohl although
oder or
offen open
öffnen to open
oft often
ohne without
ohnehin anyway
Ohr ear
Oktober October
(Omni)bus coach
Onkel uncle
optimistisch optimistic
orange(farben) orange
ordnen to organize
organisieren to organize
Orientierungslauf orienteering *(no pl)*
Ort place

P

Papa dad *(informal)*
Papier paper *(no pl)*
eine Party geben to have a party
passen to fit
passieren to go on *(irr)*, to happen
peinlich embarrassing
peinlich berührt embarrassed
perfekt perfect
Person person
Pfeffer pepper *(no pl)*
Pferd horse
Pflanze plant
pink pink
planen to plan
Planet planet
Plastik plastic
Platz place
plötzlich suddenly
die Polizei the police *(no pl)*
Polizist policeman (*pl* policemen)
populär popular
positiv positive
Postkarte postcard
Präsentation presentation
(jdm etw) präsentieren to present (sth to sb)
Preis price
preiswert cheap
probieren to try
Produkt product
produzieren to produce
Prospekt leaflet
Prüfung exam
Publikum audience
putzen to clean

R

Fahrrad bike *(informal)*
mit dem Fahrrad by bike
Rakete rocket
Rat advice *(no pl)*
raten to guess
Raum room
(auf jdn/etw) reagieren to react (to sb/sth)
recherchieren to do research
recht haben to be right
rechts on the right
(nach) rechts right
rechts/links abbiegen to turn right/left
reden (mit) to talk (to)
mit jdm reden to speak to sb
reden (über) to talk (about)
Regal shelf (*pl* shelves)
Regel rule
Regen rain *(no pl)*
Regenschirm umbrella
Region area
regnen to rain
reinigen to clean
eine Reise machen to go on a trip
Reisebus coach
reiten to ride *(irr)*
Religionslehre RE (= religious education)
Rennen race
(weg)rennen to run (away) *(irr)*
Reporter/in reporter
reservieren to book
Restaurant restaurant
retten to save
Rezept recipe
richtig right, proper
Richtung direction
in Richtung toward(s)
riechen to smell *(irr)*
riesengroß huge
riesig huge, great
Rivale/Rivalin rival
Rock skirt
Rolle role
rosa pink
rot red
Rücken back
Rückseite back
rufen to call
ruhig quiet
rund um around

S

Sache thing
Saft juice
sagen to say *(irr)*, to tell *(irr)*
sagenhaft fabulous
Salz salt *(no pl)*
sammeln to collect
Samstag Saturday
Sänger/in singer
Satz phrase
sauber machen to clean
Schachtel box
Schaf sheep (*pl* sheep)
Schal scarf
Schatten shadow
schauen to look
Schauspieler actor
Schauspielerin actress
schauspielern to act

scheinen to seem
Schere scissors *(only pl)*
schicken to send *(irr)*
Schiff ship, boat
Schinken ham
schlafen to sleep *(irr)*, to be asleep
Schlafzimmer bedroom
Schlagzeile headline
Schlange snake
schlecht bad
schließen to close
schließlich finally, after all, in the end
schlimm bad
Schluss end
schmal narrow
schmutzig dirty
Schnee snow *(no pl)*
schneiden to cut *(irr)*
schnell quick, fast
schockiert shocked
Schokolade chocolate *(no pl)*
schon already
schon yet
schön nice, beautiful, lovely
Schottland Scotland
Schrank cupboard
schrecklich terrible, horrible, awful
schreiben to write *(irr)*
Schreibtisch desk
schreien to shout, to scream, to cry
Schritt step
Schuh shoe
(Schul-)Jahrgang year
Schule school
Schüler/in pupil
Schulfach subject
Schulklasse class
Schultasche school bag
schützen to save, to protect
schwarz black
Schwein pig
schwer hard, difficult
Schwester sister
schwierig difficult, hard
Schwimmen swimming
schwimmen gehen to go swimming
(die) See sea *(no pl)*
sehen to see *(irr)*, to look
Sehenswürdigkeit sight
sehr very, so
Sehr geehrte(r) ... Dear ...,
sehr mögen to love
Seife soap
sein to be *(irr)*
seine Meinung ändern to change one's mind
sein(e) its
sein(e, r) his
seins his
seit since, for
seitdem since
Seite page
seither since
selbst even
selbstbewusst confident
selbstsicher confident
September September
setzen to put *(irr)*
sicher sure, safe, certain
sicher sein to be sure
sie she, they, her, them
Sie you
Sieger/in winner
Sightseeing sightseeing *(no pl)*
singen to sing *(irr)*
sitzen to sit *(irr)*
SMS text message
(jdm) eine SMS senden to text (sb)
so so, such
so ... wie as ... as
sofort immediately
sogar even
Sohn son
solch(er/es) such
sollen should
Sommer summer
sonderbar strange
Sonne sun
Sonnenbrille sunglasses *(only pl)*
sonnig sunny
Sonntag Sunday
sonst (noch) else
sich Sorgen machen (um) to worry (about)
sowieso anyway
spannend exciting
spät late
später later
spazieren gehen to go walking
Spaß fun *(no pl)*
Spaß machen to be fun
... spazieren führen to take ... for a walk
spekulieren to speculate (on)
Spiel game, play
spielen to play
Spielzeug toy
Spitze top
Sport *(als Schulfach)* PE (= physical education)
Sportplatz sports ground
Sprache language
sprechen to speak *(irr)*, to talk (to)
sprechen (über) to talk (about)
springen to jump
die Spülmaschine einräumen to load the dishwasher
Stadion stadium
städtisch city
(Stadt)plan map
ständig forever
stark strong
Station station
stattfinden to take place
staubsaugen to hoover
stehen to stand *(irr)*
stehlen to steal *(irr)*
Stein stone
Stelle place
stellen to put *(irr)*
sterben (an) to die (of)
Stiefel boot
Stift pen
Stimme voice
Stock(werk) floor
stoppen to stop
Strand beach
Straße street, road
Straßenschild sign
streng strict
strikt strict
Strophe verse
strukturieren to structure
Stück bit
studieren to study
Stuhl chair
Stunde hour
Stundenplan timetable
stürzen to fall *(irr)*
suchen nach to look for
super! Well done!
surfen gehen to go surfing
Süßigkeiten sweets *(only pl)*

T

Tabelle grid
Tafel board
Tag day
Tagebuch diary
Tante aunt
Tanz dance *(no pl)*
tanzen to dance
Tasche bag
Tasche *(an Kleidungsstücken)* pocket
Taschendieb/in pickpocket
Taschengeld pocket money
Taschenmesser pocket knife
Tasse cup
Tat action
Tätigkeit activity
Technik technology
Technologie technology
Teil part, bit
teilen to share
teilnehmen (an) to take part (in)
Telefon phone (= telephone)
Telefongespräch phone call (= telephone call)
telefonieren to phone
Teller plate
Tempus tense
Teppich carpet
teuer expensive
Theaterstück play
Thema topic
Tier animal

Tipp advice *(no pl)*
Tisch table
den Tisch decken to lay the table
Titel title, heading
tja well
Tochter daughter
Toilette toilet
toll stunning, amazing
toll, klasse brilliant *(informal)*
Tomate tomato
tot dead
töten to kill
eine Tour machen to go on a tour
(Touristen)attraktion attraction
träge lazy
tragen to wear *(irr) (Kleidung)*, to carry
Trainer/in coach, trainer
trainieren to train
Transport transport *(no pl)*
traurig sad
(sich) treffen to meet *(irr)*
(Treppen)stufe step
trinken to drink *(irr)*
Trinken drink *(no pl)*
trotzdem still, though
tschüss bye *(informal)*/goodbye
etw tun dürfen be allowed to do sth
etw tun können to be able to do sth
Tür door
Turm tower
Turnhalle gym
Turnschuh trainer
Tut mir leid. (I'm) sorry.
Tüte bag
tyrannisieren to bully

U

U-Bahn the Underground *(no pl)*
üben to practise
über about, across, over
(über etw) traurig/aufgebracht sein to be upset (about sth)
über jdn/etw nachdenken to think about sb/sth
überall everywhere
überfüllt full
überhaupt at all
überqueren to cross
überraschen to surprise
überrascht surprised
Überraschung surprise
überreden to persuade
Überschrift heading
überzeugen to convince, to persuade
überzeugend convincing
üblich normal
Uhr clock
(ein) Uhr (one) o'clock
Uhrzeit time
um at, around
um ... herum around
umbringen to kill
(um)fallen to fall *(irr)*
umher around
sich umsehen to look around
umsonst for free *(informal)*
Umwelt environment *(no pl)*
umwerfend stunning
unangenehm embarrassing
und and
unglücklich unhappy
unheimlich eerie, strange
Uniform uniform
Universität(s-) university
uns us
unser(e) our
unter under, below
untergebracht sein to stay
Untergeschoss basement
unterhalb below
unterhaltsam entertaining
Unterhaltung entertainment, conversation
Unterrichtsstunde lesson
Unterstützung support
untersuchen to explore
Urlaub holiday
im Urlaub on holiday
in Urlaub gehen/fahren to go on holiday

V

Vampir/in vampire
Vater father
Vati dad *(informal)*
verabscheuen to hate
verändern to change
verängstigt scared, frightened
verärgert angry, annoyed
verbringen *(Zeit)* to spend *(irr)*
Vereinigtes Königreich UK (= the United Kingdom)
Verfasser/in writer
Vergangenheit past
vergessen to forget *(irr)*
Vergeudung waste *(no pl)*
vergleichen to compare
vergnügt cheerful
Verhalten behaviour *(no pl)*
sich verirren to lose one's way, to get lost
verkaufen to sell *(irr)*
Verkäufer/in shop assistant
Verkehr traffic *(no pl)*
Verkehrsschild sign
verlassen to leave *(irr)*
sich verlaufen to get lost
verlegen embarrassed
verletzt hurt
verlieren to lose *(irr)*
Verlierer/in loser
verlockend attractive
vermischen to mix
vermissen to miss
Vermutungen anstellen (über) to speculate (on)
verneinend negative
vernünftig sensible
verrückt crazy
verschieden different
Verschwendung waste *(no pl)*
Versehen mistake
(sich) verstecken to hide *(irr)*
verstehen to understand *(irr)*, to see *(irr)*
verstoßen gegen to break *(irr)*
versuchen to try
vervollständigen to complete
verwundet hurt
viel much
viel(e) lots of *(informal)*, a lot (of)
viele many
vielleicht perhaps, maybe
Viertel (nach/vor) quarter (past/to)
Viertelstunde quarter of an hour
violett purple
Vogel bird
voll full
von from, of, by, about
vor in front of, before, ago, to
vorbei sein to be over
vorbereiten to prepare
Vorbereitung preparation
vorführen to perform
vorgeben to pretend
vorgehen to act
vorher before
vormittags *(nur hinter Uhrzeit zwischen Mitternacht und 12 Uhr mittags)* am (= ante meridiem)
Vorschlag suggestion
vorschlagen to suggest
vorsichtig careful
sich vorstellen to imagine
vortäuschen to pretend
vortragen to present (sth to sb)

W

wahr true
während while
wahrscheinlich probably
Wald forest
Wand wall
wandern to go walking
wann when
warm warm
warten (auf) to wait (for)
warum why
was what
Was bedeutet ... auf Englisch? What's ... in English?
Was fehlt ...? What's wrong with ...?

Was ist mit ...? What about ...? *(informal)*
Was ist mit dir? What about you?
Was kostet/kosten ...? How much is/are ...?
Was magst du? What do you like?
Was magst du nicht? What don't you like?
Was stimmt nicht mit ...? What's wrong with ...?
Wasser water *(no pl)*
Weg way
weg away
wegen about
weggehen to leave *(irr)*
wegnehmen to take *(irr)*
(weg)rennen to run (away) *(irr)*
(weg)werfen to throw (away) *(irr)*
Weihnachten Christmas
weil because, as
weinen to cry
weitere(r, s) more
weitergehen to go on *(irr)*
weiterlaufen to walk on
weitermachen to go on *(irr)*
weiß white
welche(r, s) which, what
Welt world
wenige a few
weniger less
wenigstens at least
wenn if, when
wer who
werden to become *(irr)*, to get *(irr)*
(weg)werfen to throw (away) *(irr)*
wesentlich important
wessen whose
Wettbewerb competition
Wetter weather
wichtig important
wie how, like, as
Wie alt bist du? How old are you?
Wie geht es dir/Ihnen/euch? How are you?
Wie heißt du? What's your name?
Wie spät/Wie viel Uhr ist es? What's the time?, What time is it?
Wie viel ...? How much ...?
Wie viele ...? How many ...?
Wie wäre es mit ...? What about ...? *(informal)*
wieder again
(wieder) zurück back
wiederholen to repeat
wiederverwenden to recycle
wild wild
Winter winter
im Winter in winter
wir we
Wir schauen uns nur um. We're just looking.
wirklich really, real
wissen to know *(irr)*
witzig funny
wo where
Wo ist ...? / Wo sind ...? Where is ...? / Where are ...?
Woche week
Wochenende weekend
Woher kommst du? Where are you from?
wohin where
wohnen to live
Wohnzimmer living room
Wolke cloud
wollen to want
wollen, dass jd etw tut to want sb to do sth
Wort word
Wörterbuch dictionary
Worum geht es in/bei ...? What is ... about?
wunderbar wonderful, great
wundervoll wonderful, magic
wünschen to want, to wish
würde(n/st/t) would
würde(n/st/t) gern would like to
würde(n/st/t) nicht wouldn't (= would not)
wütend angry

Z

z. B. *(zum Beispiel)* e.g.
Zahl number
zahlen to pay *(irr)*
Zahn tooth (*pl* teeth)
Zahnbürste toothbrush
zauberhaft magic
zehn ten
Zeichen sign
zeichnen to draw *(irr)*
zeigen to show *(irr)*
Zeit time
Zeit für etw haben to be free
die ganze Zeit all the time
Zeitform tense
zeitig early
Zeitungsbericht report
Zeitungsmeldung report
Zelt tent
zelten gehen to go camping
Zentrum centre
(zer)brechen to break *(irr)*
ziemlich quite
Ziffer number
Zimmer room
Zirkus circus
zornig angry
zu too, on, to
(zu) essen geben to feed *(irr)*
zu Fuß gehen to walk
zu Hause at home
zu laut too loud
zu Mittag essen to have lunch
(zu) spät late
Zubereitung preparation
Zucker sugar
zuerst at first, first
zufrieden pleased, happy
Zug train
zugeben to admit
zuhören to listen to
Zukunft future
zum Beispiel for example
zum Schluss in the end
zumachen to close
zumindest after all, at least
Zunge tongue
zurückkommen to get back *(irr)*
zurücklassen to leave *(irr)*
zusammen together
zuschauen to watch
Zuschauer audience
(zu)schicken to send *(irr)*
(wieder) zurück back
zustimmen to agree (on)
zuversichtlich confident
zuvor before
zwischen between
zwölf twelve

Names

Girls / women
Alex /ˈælɪks/
Alexandra /ˌælɪɡˈzɑːndrə/
Amber /ˈæmbə/
Anastasia /ˌænəˈsteɪziə/
Anna /ˈænə/
Becky /ˈbeki/
Boudicca /ˈbuːdɪkə/
Caro /ˈkærəʊ/
Caroline /ˈkærəlaɪn/
Che Chon /ˌtʃe ˈtʃɒn/
Cherry /ˈtʃeri/
Chloe /ˈkləʊi/
Claire /kleə/
Daisy /ˈdeɪzi/
Dana /ˈdɑːnə/
Denah /ˈdiːnə/
Emma /emə/
Georgia /ˈdʒɔːdʒə/
Gill /dʒɪl/
Gillian /ˈdʒɪliən/
Gloria /ˈɡlɔːriə/
Hamida /həˈmiːdə/
Harriet /ˈhæriət/
Helen /ˈhelən/
Jessica /ˈdʒesɪkə/
Joanna /dʒəʊˈænə/
Juliet /ˈdʒuːliət/
Kadhija /kədˈhiːdʒə/
Karen /ˈkærən/
Katrina /kəˈtriːnə/
Lakshmi /ˈlʌkʃmi/
Leanne /liˈæn/
Lisa /ˈliːsə/
Meredith /ˈmerədɪθ/
Moira /ˈmɔɪrə/
Myra /ˈmaɪrə/
Nadine /nəˈdiːn/
Natalie /ˈnætəli/
Navina /nəˈviːnə/
Olivia /əˈlɪviə/
Princess /ˌprɪnˈses/
Rachel /ˈreɪtʃəl/
Rebecca /riˈbekə/
Rihanna /riˈænə/
Roberta /rəˈbɜːtə/
Ronke /ˈrɒŋki/
Sarah /ˈsɑːrə/
Sheree /ˈʃeri/
Sophie /ˈsəʊfi/
Spud /spʌd/
Thomasina /ˌtɒməˈsiːnə/

Boys / men
Alex /ˈælɪks/
Arthur /ˈɑːθə/
Ben /ben/
Brady /brædi/
Charles /tʃɑːlz/
Charlie /ˈtʃɑːli/
Colin /ˈkɒlɪn/
Conan /ˈkəʊnən/
Daniel /ˈdænjəl/
Danny /ˈdæni/
Darvesh /ˈdɑːveʃ/
David /ˈdeɪvɪd/
Dennis /ˈdenis/
Donald /ˈdɒn(ə)ld/
Dylan /ˈdɪlən/
Evan /ˈev(ə)n/
Gareth /ˈɡærəθ/
George /dʒɔːdʒ/
Guy /ɡaɪ/
Harry /ˈhæri/
Holden /ˈhəʊldən/
Hugo /ˈhjuːɡəʊ/
Jack /dʒæk/
James /dʒeɪmz/
Jason /ˈdʒeɪs(ə)n/
Jeremy /ˈdʒerəmɪ/
John /dʒɒn/
Jude /dʒuːd/
Leo /ˈliːəʊ/
Lewis /ˈluːɪs/
Lionel /ˈlaɪən(ə)l/
Manish /məˈnɪʃ/
Marty /ˈmɑːtɪ/
Matt /mæt/
Michael /ˈmaɪk(ə)l/
Nathan /ˈneɪθ(ə)n/
Oliver /ˈɒlɪvə/
Oscar /ˈɒskə/
Peter /ˈpiːtə/
Phil /fɪl/
Rajiv /rɑːˈdʒiːv/
Rick /rɪk/
Rob /rɒb/
Robin /ˈrɒbɪn/
Salman /ˈsælmən/
Sam /sæm/
Stephen /ˈstiːv(ə)n/
Vaughan /vɔːn/
William /ˈwɪljəm/

Families
Amin /ɑːˈmiːn/
Baker /ˈbeɪkə/
Basildon /ˈbæz(ə)ld(ə)n/
Batson /ˈbæts(ə)n/
Beckham /ˈbekəm/
Brogden /ˈbrɒɡd(ə)n/
Butler /ˈbʌtlə/
Carson /ˈkɑːs(ə)n/
Cousins /ˈkʌz(ə)nz/
Cullen /ˈkʌlən/
de Falla /də ˈfælə/
Dickens /ˈdɪkɪnz/
Doyle /dɔɪ(ə)l/
Dupuy /duˈpwiː/
Eastman /ˈiːstmən/
Edwards /ˈedwədz/
Fawkes /fɔːks/
Fowler /ˈfaʊlə/
Gibson /ˈɡɪbs(ə)n/
Glover /ˈɡlʌvə/
Grey /ɡreɪ/
Hawtrey /ˈhɔːtri/
Hickman /ˈhɪkmən/
Hood /hʊd/
Jackson /ˈdʒæks(ə)n/
Jones /dʒəʊnz/
Khan /kɑːn/
Lambert /ˈlæmbət/
Lambraki /ˌlæmˈbrɑːki/
Law /lɔː/
Malik /ˈmælɪk/
Mumbanga /mumˈbæŋə/
Murphy /ˈmɜːfɪ/
Perry /ˈperi/
Potter /ˈpɒtə/
Purcell /ˈpɜːs(ə)l/
Rogers /ˈrɒdʒəz/
Scott /skɒt/
Shakespeare /ˈʃeɪkˌspɪə/
Shimmin /ˈʃɪmɪn/
Stravinsky /strəˈvɪnski/
Walsh /wɔːlʃ/
Watson /ˈwɒtsən/
Williams /ˈwɪljəmz/
Wilson /ˈwɪls(ə)n/
Young /jʌŋ/
Yussuf /ˈjʊsʊf/

Wordbanks p. 149 | Word lists p. 154 | English-German dictionary p. 186

Other names

A Christmas Carol /ə ˈkrɪsməsˈkæral/
Acland Burghley /ˌæklənd ˈbɜːli/
Alexandra Palace /ˌælɪgˈzaːndrə ˌpæləs/
Arsenal /ˈɑːs(ə)n(ə)l/
Bad Romance /ˌbæd rəʊˈmæns/
Beam House /ˈbiːm ˌhaʊs/
The Believe Foundation /bɪˈliːv‿faʊnˌdeɪʃ(ə)n/
Big Ben /ˌbɪg ˈben/
Blues /bluːz/
Buckingham Palace /ˌbʌkɪŋəm ˈpæləs/
Camden School for Girls /ˌkæmdən ˌskuːl fə ˈgɜːlz/
CamdenTV /ˈkæmdənˌtiːˌviː/
Cats /kæts/
Cha cha slide /ˈtʃɑː tʃɑː ˌslaɪd/
Christchurch /ˈkraɪstʃɜːtʃ/
Come Ye Sons of Art /ˌkʌm ji ˌsʌnz‿əv‿ˈɑːt/
CSG /ˌsiː‿ˌes ˈdʒiː/
Dance Company /ˈdɑːns ˌkʌmp(ə)ni/
Disturbia /dɪˈstɜːbiə/
Eden Project /ˈiːd(ə)n ˌprɒdʒekt/
Electric Girls /ɪˌlektrɪk‿ˈgɜːlz/
Emirates Stadium /ˌemərəts‿ˈsteɪdiəm/
The Film Museum /ˈfɪlm‿mjuːˌziːəm/
Good Girl Gone Bad /ˌgʊd gɜːl gɒn ˈbæd/
Grammy /ˈgræmi/
Green Week /ˌgriːn ˈwiːk/
Gucci /ˈguːtʃi/
Guy Fawkes /ˌgaɪ ˈfɔːks/
Hampton Court /ˌhæmt(ə)n ˈkɔːt/
Haverstock School /ˈhævəstɒk skuːl/
The HMS Belfast /ˌeɪtʃ‿em‿ˌes ˈbelˌfɑːst/
Horrible Histories /ˌhɒrəb(ə)l ˈhɪst(ə)riz/
The Houses of Parliament /ˌhaʊzɪz‿əv ˈpɑː(r)ləmənt/
The Imperial War Museum /ɪmˌpɪəriəl ˈwɔː mjuːˌziːəm/
Invasion from Planet Zorgon /ɪnˌveɪʒ(ə)n frəm ˌplænɪt ˈzɔːgən/
Jay-Z /ˌdʒeɪ ˈziː/
Julius Caesar /ˌdʒuːliəs ˈsiːzə/
King James I /kɪŋ ˌdʒeɪmz ðə ˈfɜːst/
Lionheart /ˈlaɪənˌhɑːt/
Liverpool F. C. /ˌlɪvəpuːl ˌef ˈsiː/
London Bridge /ˌlʌndən ˈbrɪdʒ/
The London Dungeon /ˌlʌndən ˈdʌndʒ(ə)n/
The London Eye /ˌlʌndən‿ˈaɪ/
The London Film Museum /ˌlʌndən ˈfɪlm‿mjuːˌziːəm/
London Zoo /ˌlʌndən ˈzuː/
Madame Tussauds /məˌdɑːm təˈsɔːdz/
Madonna /məˈdɒnə/
Mamma Mia /ˌmɑːmə ˈmiːə/
Manchester United /ˌmænˌtʃestə juːˈnaɪtɪd/
Marmalade /ˈmɑː(r)məleɪd/
Mickey Mouse /ˌmɪki ˈmaʊs/
Muse /mjuːz/
Music of the Sun /ˌmjuːzɪk‿əv ðə ˈsʌn/
The Natural History Museum /ˌnætʃ(ə)rəl ˈhɪst(ə)ri mjuːˌziːəm/
New Moon /ˌnjuː ˈmuːn/
Notting Hill Carnival /ˈnɒtɪŋ ˌhɪl ˌkɑːnɪv(ə)l/
Pon de Replay /ˌpɒn də ˈriːpleɪ/
Popsicles /ˈpɒpsɪk(ə)lz/
Portobello Road Market /ˌpɔːtəʊˌbeləʊ ˈrəʊd ˌmɑːkɪt/
Reb'l Fleur /ˌrebl ˈflɜː/
Red House /red ˈhaʊs/
Reds /redz/
Romeo and Juliet /ˌrəʊmiəʊ‿ən ˈdʒuːliət/
Royal Opera House /ˌrɔɪəl‿ˈɒp(ə)rə haʊs/
Sadler's Wells Theatre /ˈsædləz ˌwelz ˌθɪətə/
Sadler's Wells /ˌsædləz ˈwelz/
The Science Museum /ˈsaɪəns mjuːˌziːəm/
Shakespeare's Globe /ˌʃeɪkˌspɪəz ˈgləʊb/
Sherlock Holmes /ˌʃɜːlɒk ˈhəʊmz
Socks /sɒks/
SOS /ˌes‿əʊ‿ˈes/
Sports Day /ˈspɔːts deɪ/
Starlight Express /ˈstɑːlaɪt‿ɪkˌspres/
Step Live! /ˌstep ˈlaɪv/
Tate Modern /ˌteɪt ˈmɒdən/
The Age of Stupid /ðiˌ‿eɪdʒ‿əv ˈstjuːpɪd/
the BBC (= British Broadcasting Corporation) /ðə ˌbiː biː ˈsiː, ˌbrɪtɪʃ ˈbrɔːdkɑːstɪŋ ˌkɔːpəˌreɪʃ(ə)n/
The Firebird /ðə ˈfaɪəbɜːd/
The Lark Ascending /ðə ˌlɑːk‿əˈsendɪŋ/
The Lion King /ðə ˈlaɪən kɪŋ/
the Mill /ðə ˈmɪl/
Twilight /ˈtwaɪlaɪt/
Umbrella /ʌmˈbrelə/
Wembley Stadium /ˌwembli ˈsteɪdiəm/
William Ellis School /ˌwɪljəm‿ˈelɪs‿ˌskuːl/
Yellows /ˈjeləʊz/

Geographical names

Africa /ˈæfrɪkə/
Albert Street /ˈælbət ˌstriːt/
Arundel /ˈærənd(ə)l/
the Atlantic /ði‿ətˈlæntɪk/
Auckland /ˈɔːklənd/
Australia /ɒˈstreɪliə/
The Avenue /ði‿ˈævəˌnjuː/
Baker Street /ˈbeɪkə ˌstriːt/
Barbados /bɑːˈbeɪdɒs/
Bath /bɑːθ/
Blenheim Palace /ˌblenɪm ˈpæləs/
Birmingham /ˈbɜːmɪŋəm/
Bond Street /ˈbɒnd ˌstriːt/
the British Isles /ðə ˌbrɪtɪʃ‿ˈaɪlz/
Camden /ˈkæmdən/
Camden High Street /ˌkæmdən ˈhaɪ ˌstriːt/
Camden Lock Market /ˌkæmdən ˈlɒk ˌmɑːkɪt/
Camden Market /ˌkæmdən ˈmɑːkɪt/
Camden Town /ˌkæmdən ˈtaʊn/
Church Street /ˈtʃɜːtʃ striːt/
Cornwall /ˈkɔːnwɔːl/
Covent Garden /ˌkɒvənt ˈgɑːd(ə)n/
Croatia /krəʊˈeɪʃə/
Crooklets Beach /ˌkrʊkləts ˈbiːtʃ/
Finsbury Park /ˌfɪnzbəri ˈpɑːk/
Forest Green /ˌfɒrɪst ˈgriːn/
George Street /ˈdʒɔːdʒ striːt/
Germany /ˈdʒɜːməni/
Great Britain /ˌgreɪt ˈbrɪt(ə)n/
Green Park /ˌgriːn ˈpɑːk/
Hawaii /həˈwaɪi/
High Street /ˈhaɪ striːt/
Highgate Road /ˈhaɪˌgeɪt rəʊd/
India /ˈɪndiə/
Isle of Lewis /ˌaɪl‿əv ˈluːɪs/
Italy /ˈɪtəli/
Kynance Cove /ˌkaɪnænts ˈkəʊv/
Liverpool/ lɪvəpuːl/
London /ˈlʌndən/
Madagascar /ˌmædəˈgæskə/
Manchester /ˈmænˌtʃestə/
Marylebone High Street /ˌmærələbən ˈhaɪ striːt/

Marylebone Road /ˈmærələbən ˌrəʊd/
Maudlin Street School /ˈmɔːdlɪn striːt skuːl/
Munich /ˈmjuːnɪk/
New York /njuː ˈjɔːk/
New Zealand /nju ˈziːlənd/
the North Pole /ðə ˌnɔːθ ˈpəʊl/
Notting Hill /ˌnɒtɪŋ ˈhɪl/
Nottingham /ˈnɒtɪŋəm/
Nottingham Street /ˈnɒtɪŋəm striːt/
Oxford /ˈɒksfəd/
Oxfordshire /ˈɒksfədʃə/
Oxford Street /ˈɒksfəd striːt/
Paris /ˈpærɪs/
Park Avenue /ˌpɑːk‿ˈævəˌnjuː/
Parkway /ˈpɑːkweɪ/
Piccadilly Circus /ˌpɪkəˌdɪli ˈsɜːkəs/
Rome /rəʊm/
Shetland /ˈʃetlənd/
the Shetland Islands /ðə ˈʃetlənd‿ˌaɪləndz/
Spain /speɪn/
Station Lane /ˈsteɪʃ(ə)n ˌleɪn/
Stonehenge /ˌstəʊnˈhendʒ/
Stratford-upon-Avon /ˌstrætfəd‿əˌpɒn‿ˈeɪv(ə)n/
Surrey /sʌrɪ/
Sussex /ˈsʌsɪks/
Texas /ˈteksəs/
The Thames /temz/
Thorpe Park /ˌθɔːp‿ˈpɑːk/
Tower Bridge /ˌtaʊə ˈbrɪdʒ/
Trafalgar Square /trəˌfælgə ˈskweə/
Victoria Road /vɪkˈtɔːriə ˌrəʊd/
Wales /weɪlz/
Westfield /ˈwestfiːld/
Wood Lane /ˈwʊd ˌleɪn/

The English alphabet

a	/eɪ/	h	/eɪtʃ/	o	/əʊ/	v	/viː/
b	/biː/	i	/aɪ/	p	/piː/	w	/ˈdʌbljuː/
c	/siː/	j	/dʒeɪ/	q	/kjuː/	x	/eks/
d	/diː/	k	/keɪ/	r	/ɑː/	y	/waɪ/
e	/iː/	l	/el/	s	/es/	z	/zed/
f	/ef/	m	/em/	t	/tiː/		
g	/dʒiː/	n	/en/	u	/juː/		

English sounds

Im Englischen spricht man Wörter oft anders aus, als man sie schreibt.
Deshalb ist die Lautschrift sehr nützlich: Sie gibt an, wie ein Wort ausgesprochen wird.
Hier ist eine Liste der Lautschriftzeichen zusammen mit Beispielwörtern:

Vokale

/ɑː/	arm
/ʌ/	but
/e/	desk
/ə/	a, an
/ɜː/	girl, bird
/æ/	apple
/ɪ/	in, it
/i/	every
/iː/	easy, eat
/ɒ/	orange
/ɔː/	all, story
/ʊ/	look
/u/	February
/uː/	food

Doppellaute

/aɪ/	eye, buy
/aʊ/	house
/eə/	there
/eɪ/	take, they
/ɪə/	here
/ɔɪ/	boy
/əʊ/	go, old
/ʊə/	you're

Konsonanten

/b/	bag, club
/d/	duck, card
/f/	fish, laugh
/g/	get, dog
/h/	hot
/j/	you
/k/	can, duck
/l/	lot, small
/m/	more, mum
/n/	now, sun
/ŋ/	song, long
/p/	present, top
/r/	red, right
/s/	sister, class (scharfes s)
/t/	time, cat
/z/	nose, dogs (weiches s)
/ʒ/	television
/dʒ/	orange
/ʃ/	sure, English
/tʃ/	child, cheese
/ð/	these, mother (weicher Laut)
/θ/	mouth, think (harter Laut)
/v/	very, have
/w/	what, word

Betonungszeichen für die folgende Silbe

/ˈ/	Hauptbetonung
/ˌ/	Nebenbetonung

Wörter, die im Deutschen und Englischen ähnlich sind

Es gibt viele Wörter, die im Englischen und im Deutschen gleich sind. Sie unterscheiden sich oft nur darin, wie sie geschrieben werden. Viele dieser Wörter sprechen wir gleich aus.
Diese Wörter stehen nicht in den Wortlisten, weil sie dir ja nicht neu sind. Bei denen, die ein bisschen anders ausgesprochen werden als im Deutschen, ist die Lautschrift farbig hervorgehoben.

action / 'ækʃ(ə)n /
active / 'æktɪv /
album / 'ælbəm /
alien / 'eɪliən /
argument / 'ɑ:gjʊmənt /
audio guide / 'ɔ:diəʊ ˌgaɪd /
backstage / 'bækˌsteɪdʒ /
balance / bæləns /
band / bænd /
banker / 'bæŋkə /
basketball / 'bɑ:skɪtˌbɔ:l /
buffet / 'bʊfeɪ /
bus / bʌs /
business *(no pl)* / 'bɪznəs /
café / 'kæfeɪ /
cafeteria / ˌkæfə'tɪəriə /
cartoon / kɑ:'tu:n /
CD / ˌsi: 'di: /
chance / tʃɑ:ns /
chat / tʃæt /
to check / tʃek /
checklist / 'tʃeklɪst /
city / 'sɪti /
clever / 'klevə /
clip / klɪp /
clown / klaʊn /
coke / kəʊk /
collage / 'kɒlɑ:ʒ /
comic / 'kɒmɪk /
computer / kəm'pju:tə /
cool / ku:l /
coordination / kəʊˌɔ:dɪ'neɪʃ(ə)n /
correct / kə'rekt /
couch / kaʊtʃ /
definition / defə'nɪʃ(ə)n /
to design / dɪ'zaɪn /
detail / 'di:teɪl /
detective / dɪ'tektɪv /
doctor / 'dɒktə /
DVD / ˌdi:vi:'di: /
email / 'i:meɪl /
England / 'ɪŋglənd /
euro / 'jʊərəʊ /
event / ɪ'vent /
extra / 'ekstrə /
fair / feə /
fan / fæn /
fast food *(no pl)* / 'fɑ:st ˌfu:d /
feedback / 'fi:dbæk /
film / fɪlm /
finger / 'fɪŋgə /
fit / fɪt /
fitness *(no pl)* / 'fɪtnəs /
flyer / 'flaɪə /
form / fɔ:m /
gold / gəʊld /
golf / gɒlf /
gorilla / gə'rɪlə /
Halloween / ˌhæləʊ'i:n /
hamburger / 'hæmˌbɜ:gə /
highlight / 'haɪˌlaɪt /
hip hop / 'hɪp hɒp /
hit / hɪt /
hobby / hɒbi /
hockey / 'hɒki /
hot dog / ˌhɒt 'dɒg /
hotel / həʊ'tel /
ideal / aɪ'dɪəl /
Internet / 'ɪntə(r)ˌnet /
jazz / dʒæz /
job / dʒɒb /
jury / 'dʒʊəri /
karate *(no pl)* / kə'rɑ:ti /
kid / kɪd /
kilometre / kɪ'lɒmɪtə /
limit / 'lɪmɪt /
list / lɪst /
live / laɪv /
marshmallow / ˌmɑ:ʃ'mæləʊ /
meeting / 'mi:tɪŋ /
million / 'mɪljən /
mindmap / 'maɪndˌmæp /
model / 'mɒd(ə)l /
monster / 'mɒnstə /
motorsport / 'məʊtəˌspɔ:t /
motto / 'mɒtəʊ /
MP3 player / ˌem pi: 'θri: ˌpleɪə /
museum / mju:'zi:əm /
musical / 'mju:zɪk(ə)l /
normal / 'nɔ:m(ə)l /
OK (= okay) *(informal)* / əʊ'keɪ /
online / ˌɒn'laɪn /
open-air / ˌəʊpən‿'eə /
park / pɑ:k /
partner / 'pɑ:tnə /
patient / 'peɪʃ(ə)nt /
performance / pə'fɔ:məns /
photo / 'fəʊtəʊ /
pizza / 'pi:tsə /
plan / plæn /
player / pleɪə /
plus / plʌs /
podcast / 'pɒdˌkɑ:st /
pony / 'pəʊni /
pop / pɒp /
poster / 'pəʊstə /
problem / 'prɒbləm /
programme / 'prəʊgræm /
project / 'prɒdʒekt /
pullover / 'pʊləʊvə /
quad bike / 'kwɒd ˌbaɪk /
quiz (*pl* quizzes) / kwɪz, kwɪzɪz /
quizmaster / 'kwɪzˌmɑ:stə /
radio / 'reɪdiəʊ /
recycling *(no pl)* / ri:'saɪklɪŋ /
to relax / rɪ'læks /
rest / rest /
rock / 'rɒk /
rucksack / 'rʌkˌsæk /
sandwich / 'sænwɪdʒ /
second-hand / ˌsekənd'hænd /
set / set /
show / ʃəʊ /
show time *(no pl)* / 'ʃəʊ taɪm /
single / 'sɪŋg(ə)l /
situation / ˌsɪtʃu'eɪʃ(ə)n /
smoothie / 'smu:ði /
snack / snæk /
song / sɒŋ /
souflaki / su'flɑ:ki /
spaghetti bolognaise / spəˌgeti ˌbɒlə'neɪz /
sport / spɔ:t /
star / stɑ: /
statement / 'steɪtmənt /
stewardess / ˌstju:ə'des /
stop / stɒp /
studio / 'stju:diəʊ /
supermarket / 'su:pəˌmɑ:kɪt /
surfing / 'sɜ:fɪŋ /
swimming pool / 'swɪmɪŋ pu:l /
symbol / 'sɪmb(ə)l /
tattoo / tæ'tu: /
team / ti:m /
teamwork *(no pl)* / 'ti:mˌwɜ:k /
teenager / 'ti:nˌeɪdʒə /
tennis / 'tenɪs /
test / test /
text / tekst /
theatre / 'θɪətə /
ticket / 'tɪkɪt /
tip / tɪp /
top / tɒp /
tour / tʊə /
tourist / tʊərɪst /
training / 'treɪnɪŋ /
trick / trɪk /
trip / trɪp /
T-shirt / 'ti: ʃɜ:t /
TV / ˌti: 'vi: /
unfair / ʌn'feə /
version / 'vɜ:ʃ(ə)n /
video / 'vɪdiəʊ /
video clip / 'vɪdiəʊ klɪp /
volleyball / 'vɒliˌbɔ:l /
website / 'webˌsaɪt /
wind / wɪnd /
zoo / zu: /

Class instructions

Hier kannst du die häufigsten Arbeitsanweisungen in deinem Buch nachschlagen.

Add information about ...	**Füge** Informationen über ... **hinzu.**
Ask and answer questions.	**Stelle und beantworte Fragen.**
Can you solve this puzzle?	**Kannst du dieses Rätsel lösen?**
Check your results.	**Überprüft** eure Ergebnisse.
Check LiF 17 on page 148.	**Sieh** bei LiF 17 auf Seite 148 **nach.**
Choose the best title for the story.	**Wählt** den besten Titel für die Geschichte **aus.**
Close your books and listen.	**Schließt eure Bücher und hört zu.**
Collect ideas in class.	**Sammelt Ideen im Unterricht.**
Collect words and **phrases.**	**Sammelt Wörter** und **Ausdrücke.**
Compare your results.	**Vergleicht** eure Ergebnisse.
Complete the **grid.**	**Vervollständige** die **Tabelle.**
Copy the text.	**Schreibe** den Text **ab.**
Correct the wrong sentences.	**Korrigiere** die falschen Sätze.
Describe the broschure.	**Beschreibe** die Broschüre.
Design a page for a calendar.	**Gestalte** eine Seite für einen Kalender.
Fill in the words.	**Setze** die Wörter **ein.**
Find out more about ...	**Finde** mehr **heraus** über ...
Find phrases to talk about ...	**Finde Ausdrücke, mit denen man** über ... sprechen kann.
Finish the story.	**Beende** die Geschichte.
Imagine you are Rajiv.	**Stell dir vor,** du wärest Rajiv.
Listen to ...	**Hör** dir ... an.
Look at the picture/the text/the dialogue.	**Sieh dir** das Bild/den Text/den Dialog **an.**
Make notes on ...	**Macht euch Notizen zu ...**
Match the photos **to** the words.	**Ordne** die Fotos den Wörtern **zu.**
Need help? Look at p. 40.	**Brauchst du Hilfe? Sieh auf** S. 40 **nach.**
Note down information in a grid.	**Notiere** Informationen in einer Tabelle.
Practise your dialogue.	**Übt** euren Dialog.
Present the story to the class.	**Präsentiert** der Klasse die Geschichte.
Read the dialogue.	**Lies** den Dialog.
Speculate on what happens next.	**Stelle Vermutungen darüber an,** was als Nächstes passiert.
Start a grammar card.	**Beginne** eine *grammar card.*
Take notes (on ...).	**Mach dir Notizen (zu ...).**
Use your phrases/ideas/notes to ...	**Benutze** deine Ausdrücke/Ideen/Notizen um ...
Watch the clip again.	**Sieh dir den Clip** noch einmal **an.**
What is ... about?	**Worum geht es in/bei ...?**
Work in groups./Work in groups of four.	**Arbeitet in Gruppen./Arbeitet in Vierergruppen.**
Work with a partner.	**Arbeite mit einem Partner/einer Partnerin.**
Write a dialogue./Write about your feelings.	**Schreibe einen Dialog./Schreibe über** deine Gefühle.
Write down ...	**Schreibe** ... **auf.**

Irregular verbs

infinitive	simple past	participle	German
to be /biː/	was/were /wɒz/wɜː/	been /biːn/	sein
to beat /biːt/	beat /biːt/	beaten /ˈbiːtən/	schlagen
to become /bɪˈkʌm/	became /bɪˈkeɪm/	become /bɪˈkʌm/	werden
to begin /bɪˈgɪn/	began /bɪˈgæn/	begun /bɪˈgʌn/	anfangen
to bite /baɪt/	bit /bɪt/	bitten /bɪt(ə)n/	beißen
to bleed /bliːd/	bled /bled/	bled /bled/	bluten
to blow up /ˌbləʊ‿ˈʌp/	blew up /ˌbluː‿ˈʌp/	blown up /ˌbləʊn‿ˈʌp/	in die Luft sprengen
to break /breɪk/	broke /brəʊk/	broken /ˈbrəʊkən/	brechen
to bring /brɪŋ/	brought /brɔːt/	brought /brɔːt/	(mit)bringen
to buy /baɪ/	bought /bɔːt/	bought /bɔːt/	kaufen
to catch /kætʃ/	caught /kɔːt/	caught /kɔːt/	fangen
to choose /tʃuːz/	chose /tʃəʊz/	chosen /ˈtʃəʊzən/	(aus)wählen
to come /kʌm/	came /keɪm/	come /kʌm/	kommen
to cost /kɒst/	cost /kɒst/	cost /kɒst/	kosten
to creep /kriːp/	crept /krept/	crept /krept/	kriechen
to cut /kʌt/	cut /kʌt/	cut /kʌt/	schneiden
to do /duː/	did /dɪd/	done /dʌn/	machen, tun
to draw /drɔː/	drew /druː/	drawn /drɔːn/	zeichnen
to dream /driːm/	dreamt/dreamed /dremt, driːmd/	dreamt/dreamed /dremt, driːmd/	träumen (von)
to drink /drɪŋk/	drank /dræŋk/	drunk /drʌŋk/	trinken
to drive /draɪv/	drove /drəʊv/	driven /ˈdrɪvn/	fahren
to eat /iːt/	ate /et/	eaten /ˈiːt(ə)n/	essen; fressen
to fall /fɔːl/	fell /fel/	fallen /ˈfɔːlən/	(um)fallen
to feed /fiːd/	fed /fed/	fed /fed/	füttern
to feel /fiːl/	felt /felt/	felt /felt/	(sich) fühlen
to fight /faɪt/	fought /fɔːt/	fought /fɔːt/	(be)kämpfen
to find /faɪnd/	found /faʊnd/	found /faʊnd/	finden
to fly /flaɪ/	flew /fluː/	flown /fləʊn/	fliegen
to forget /fəˈget/	forgot /fəˈgɒt/	forgotten /fəˈgɒtən/	vergessen
to get /get/	got /gɒt/	got/gotten /gɒt/ˈgɒtən/	bekommen
to give /gɪv/	gave /geɪv/	given /ˈgɪvən/	geben
to go /gəʊ/	went /went/	gone /gɒn/	gehen; fahren
to hang /hæŋ/	hung /hʌŋ/	hung /hʌŋ/	hängen
to have /hæv/	had /hæd/	had /hæd/	haben
to hear /hɪə/	heard /hɜːd/	heard /hɜːd/	hören
to hide /haɪd/	hid /hɪd/	hidden /ˈhɪd(ə)n/	(sich) verstecken
to hit /hɪt/	hit /hɪt/	hit /hɪt/	schlagen
to hold /həʊld/	held /held/	held /held/	halten
to hurt /hɜːt/	hurt /hɜːt/	hurt /hɜːt/	schmerzen
to keep /kiːp/	kept /kept/	kept /kept/	aufbewahren
to know /nəʊ/	knew /njuː/	known /nəʊn/	wissen; kennen
to learn /lɜːn/	learnt/learned /lɜːnt, lɜːnd/	learnt/learned /lɜːnt, lɜːnd/	lernen
to leave /liːv/	left /left/	left /left/	verlassen
to let /let/	let /let/	let /let/	lassen
to lie /laɪ/	lay /leɪ/	lain /leɪn/	liegen
to light /laɪt/	lit /lɪt/	lit /lɪt/	anzünden
to lose /luːz/	lost /lɒst/	lost /lɒst/	verlieren

infinitive	simple past	participle	German
to make /meɪk/	made /meɪd/	made /meɪd/	machen
to mean /miːn/	meant /ment/	meant /ment/	bedeuten
to meet /miːt/	met /met/	met /met/	(sich) treffen
to overtake /ˌəʊvəˈteɪk/	overtook /ˌəʊvəˈtʊk/	overtaken /ˌəʊvəˌteɪkən/	überholen
to pay /peɪ/	paid /peɪd/	paid /peɪd/	(be)zahlen
to put /pʊt/	put /pʊt/	put /pʊt/	setzen, legen, stellen
to read /riːd/	read /red/	read /red/	lesen
to ride /raɪd/	rode /rəʊd/	ridden /ˈrɪd(ə)n/	fahren (mit); reiten
to ring (up) /ˌrɪŋ‿ˈʌp/	rang (up) /ˌræŋ‿ˈʌp/	rung (up) /ˌrʌŋ‿ˈʌp/	anrufen
to run /rʌn/	ran /ræn/	run /rʌn/	rennen
to say /seɪ/	said /sed/	said /sed/	sagen
to see /siː/	saw /sɔː/	seen /siːn/	sehen
to sell /sel/	sold /səʊld/	sold /səʊld/	verkaufen
to send /send/	sent /sent/	sent /sent/	(zu)schicken
to shoot /ʃuːt/	shot /ʃɒt/	shot /ʃɒt/	schießen
to show /ʃəʊ/	showed /ʃəʊd/	shown /ʃəʊn/	zeigen
to sing /sɪŋ/	sang /sæŋ/	sung /sʌŋ/	singen
to sit /sɪt/	sat /sæt/	sat /sæt/	sitzen
to sleep /sliːp/	slept /slept/	slept /slept/	schlafen
to smell /smel/	smelt/smelled /smelt, smeld/	smelt/smelled /smelt, smeld/	duften; riechen
to speak /spiːk/	spoke /spəʊk/	spoken /ˈspəʊkən/	sprechen
to spend /spend/	spent /spent/	spent /spent/	ausgeben *(Geld)*; verbringen *(Zeit)*
to spoil /spɔɪl/	spoilt/spoiled /spɔɪlt, spɔɪld/	spoilt/spoiled /spɔɪlt, spɔɪld/	ruinieren
to stand /stænd/	stood /stʊd/	stood /stʊd/	stehen
to steal /stiːl/	stole /stəʊl/	stolen /ˈstəʊlən/	stehlen
to stick out /ˌstɪk‿ˈaʊt/	stuck out /ˌstʌk‿ˈaʊt/	stuck out /ˌstʌk‿ˈaʊt/	ausstrecken
to swim /swɪm/	swam /swæm/	swum /swʌm/	schwimmen
to take /teɪk/	took /tʊk/	taken /ˈteɪkən/	(mit)nehmen
to tell /tel/	told /təʊld/	told /təʊld/	erzählen; sagen
to think /θɪŋk/	thought /θɔːt/	thought /θɔːt/	denken, glauben, meinen
to throw /θrəʊ/	threw /θruː/	thrown /θrəʊn/	werfen
to understand /ˌʌndəˈstænd/	understood /ˌʌndəˈstʊd/	understood /ˌʌndəˈstʊd/	verstehen
to wake up /ˌweɪk‿ˈʌp/	woke up /ˌwəʊk‿ˈʌp/	woken up /ˌwəʊkən‿ˈʌp/	aufwachen; aufwecken
to wear /weə/	wore /wɔː/	worn /wɔːn/	tragen *(Kleidung)*
to win /wɪn/	won /wʌn/	won /wʌn/	gewinnen
to write /raɪt/	wrote /rəʊt/	written /ˈrɪtən/	schreiben

Wordbanks p. 149 | Word lists p. 154 | English-German dictionary p. 186

Quellenverzeichnis · Lösungen

Bildquellen:
(c) Arsenal/SammlungRichter, Wetzlar: 56, 125 (beide); 123RF.com, Hong Kong: 10 (aninata); alamy images, Abingdon/Oxfordshire: 23.1 (CW Images), 23.2 (mambo), 23.3 (The Photolibrary Wales), 23.4 (Stuart Pearce), 27.2 (David Levenson), 27.3 (Nik Taylor Sport), 27.4 (Jon Arnold Images Ltd.), 27.6 (Jon Arnold Images Ltd), 27.7 (David Cole), 27.8 (BL Images Ltd), 30.1 (Asiaselects), 30.2 (Paul Brown), 30.3 (Kate Rose), 48.3 (Michael Kemp), 48.4 (one-image photography (Emirates Stadium)), 49.10 (imagebroker), 49.9 (Alex Segre), 64 (Mike Booth), 64.1 (Alex Segre), 64.3 (Alex Segre), 65.2 (Alex Segre), 65.4 (imagebroker/Helmut Meyer zur Capellen), 65.6 (Jon Arnold Images Ltd), 65.7 (Steve Vidler), 67.2 (kpzfoto), 86.1 (i love images/recycling), 87.1 (AB9EGT), 121.2 (Patrick Ward), 121.6 (Sloop/LOOP IMAGES); BIS Department for Business, Innovation & Skills: 45.1 (Crown Copyright. Pub 8898/20k/08/09/AR. URN 08/1108); Camden School for Girls, London: 69.1, 110.1, 110.2; David Fickling Books, Oxford: 66.1 (Cover illustrated by David Dean); dreamstime.com, Brentwood: 48.5 (Peter Lovás); dsphotos.de, Hamburg: Titel (Dirk Schmidt); F1online digitale Bildagentur GmbH, Frankfurt/M.: 10.1 (RFJohner); Fischer, Knoblauch & Co. Medienproduktionsgesellschaft mbH, München: 44.1, 44.2, 44.3, 118; Focus Photo- u. Presseagentur GmbH, Hamburg: 31.2 (Focus Network Photographers, Homer Skyes); fotolia.com, New York: 11.4 (Zu & Zu), 49.8 (steffenw); Getty Images, München: 10.4 (ABPL/Photolibrary), 11.1, 30.4 (Fuse), 79.1 (Gregg DeGuire/Kontributor/FilmMagic), 114 (Christopher Lee); Hammersen, Bettina, Braunschweig: 20.1; Harper Collins Publishers, London: 122.1; http://russiancyprus.com/london/slides/dsc05144.html: 49, 63.1; iStockphoto.com, Calgary: 11.2 (© stocknshares), 27 (Joris Van Ostaeyen), 49 (Issaurinko), 51 (Dmitrii Kharchenko); London 2012 Head Office, London: 121.3, 121.5; mauritius images GmbH, Mittenwald: 48.1 (Steve Vidler); Monk, Jonathan: 67.1; Penguin Books (UK) Ltd, Essex: 84.1 (Jill McDonald/Puffin Books Cover illustrated by Martin Simpson), 102.1; Picture-Alliance GmbH, Frankfurt/M.: 48.2 (dpa/Rousseau), 121.4 (EMPICS Sport/Stephen Pond (Cricket)); Shutterstock.com, New York: 11 (Akif Oztoprak), 27 (Mark A. Rice), 51 (pinta.t.s), 51 (astudio), 121.1, 121.1 (Padmayogini), 121.5, 121.7 (Lucy Clark), 121.8 (Sportphotographer.eu); The Travel Library, Berlin: 31.1 (Andy Williams); ullstein bild, Berlin: 63.2 (The Granger Collection); Usborne Publishing Ltd., London: 46.1; Wefringhaus, Klaus, Braunschweig: 104 (alle), 104.2, 104.3, 104.4, 104.5; Zwick, Joachim, Gießen: 2.

Textquellen
46/47 "Fame School: Trick or Treat"
© Cindy Jeffries, 2010, Usborne Publishing Ltd., London
66 "The London Eye Mystery"
© Siobhan Dowd, 2007, David Fickling Books, Oxford
84/85 "Monstroso" © Charlie Higson, 2010, Puffin Books, London
102/103 "The Legend of Spud Murphy" © Eoin Colfer, 2004, Puffin Books, London
122/123 "The Boy in the Dress" © David Walliams, 2008, HarperCollins, London

Lösungen zu *Can you do it?* im Personal Trainer:

Theme 1
P12 (S. 24): When did you see Mr Jackson? • Why did you have a meeting with the head teacher?

Theme 2
P12 (S. 43): If Rick and Holden don't come to the party, Emma will be really upset. • Rajiv will bring some more food to the party if Caroline asks him.

Theme 3
P3 (S. 58): George has wanted to visit the London Dungeon for a long time. • Most of his friends have been there.
P7 (S. 60): A film star is an actor who/that is famous. • Covent Garden is a place which/that was once a fruit market.

Theme 4
P11 (S. 81): Caroline can read very quickly. • She is a quick reader.

Theme 5
P6 (S. 98): Matt and Michael are the boys who are bullying Jason. *(Weglassen von „who" nicht möglich)* • George has seen the knife Matt and Michael put in Jason's tent.

Theme 6
P11 (S. 117): Emma can run two kilometres quite easily. But Caroline can run two kilometres faster. • Charlie is a terrible dancer, but George dances more terribly.

London
0 mile 1/4 1/2
0 km 0.5 1
HENDON
CAMDEN TOWN
Primrose Hill
London Zoo
MAIDA VALE
Regent's Park
Mme. Tussauds
PADDINGTON
BLOOMSBURY
University
British Museum
FINSBURY
CLERKENWELL
MARYLEBONE
HOLBORN
NOTTING HILL
SOHO
Covent Garden
St. Paul's Cathedral
CITY
Tower of London
MAYFAIR
Piccadilly Circus
River Thames
Kensington Gardens
Hyde Park
KENSINGTON
Buckingham Palace
WESTMINSTER
Westminster Bridge
Big Ben
Westminster Hall
Holland Park
Royal Albert Hall
Museums
National History Museum
SOUTHWARK
CHELSEA
Wellington Rd
Park Road
Maida Vale
Edgware Road
Marylebone Road
Westway A 40 (M)
Baker Street
Camden High St.
High Holborn
Oxford Street
Fleet Street
Cannon Street
City Road
Moorgate
Bishopsgate
Notting Hill Gate
Bayswater Road
Park Lane
Piccadilly
Whitehall
Waterloo Road
London Bridge
Tower Bridge
Borough High Street
Kensington Road
Grosvenor Place
Victoria Street
Brompton Road
Cromwell Road
William Ellis School
Highgate Road
Gordon Ho. Road
Mansfield Rd.
Grafton Rd.
Maiden Rd.
Rhyl St.
Athlone St.
Talacre Rd.
Marsden St.
Prince Of Wales Rd.
Haverstock Hill
Belsize Park
Belsize
Lancaster Grove
Lambolle Rd.
Belsize Park Gdns.
England's La.
Steele's Rd.
Eton Avenue
Fellows Road
Eton Rd.
Eton College Rd.
Chalk Farm
Chalk Farm Rd.
Finchley Road
Adelaide Road
King Henry's Road
Elsworthy Road
Primrose Hill Rd.
Oppidans Rd.
Regent's Park Rd.
Ainger Road
Gloucester Avenue
Chalcot Rd.
Fitzroy Rd.
Princess Road
Mark's Cl.
Regents Park Rd.
Grand Union
Stables Market
Lock
PRIMROSE HILL
Primrose Hill
Avenue Road
Grove
Queen's Grove
Ordnance Hill
Acacia Road
Allitsen Road
St. John's Wood High St.
Wellington Road
Prince Albert Road
Outer Circle
London Zoo
Regent's Park
Ave./Av. Avenue
Cl. Close
Gdns. Gardens
La. Lane
Pl. Place
Rd. Road
St. Street
Terr. Terrace
Station (Railway)
Station (Underground)
Park / open space
0 mile 1/8 1/4
0 m 250 500

Classroom phrases

Was die Lehrerin oder der Lehrer sagt

Open your books at page …	Öffnet eure Bücher auf Seite …
Turn to page …	Blättert zu Seite …
Look at line …	Seht euch Zeile … an.
Read the text on page …	Lest den Text auf Seite …
Work with a partner.	Arbeite mit einem Partner/einer Partnerin.
Work in groups of four.	Arbeitet zu viert.
Sit in a circle.	Bildet einen Sitzkreis.
Listen to the CD.	Hört die CD an.
Write about …	Schreibt über …
Talk about …	Sprecht über …
Ask questions about …	Stellt Fragen zu …
Answer the question, please.	Beantworte bitte die Frage.
Match the sentences.	Ordnet die Sätze zu.
Who wants to read the text?	Wer möchte den Text vorlesen?
Write down the answers.	Schreibt die Antworten auf.
Act out the dialogue.	Spielt den Dialog vor.
Change roles.	Tauscht die Rollen.
Make your own dialogue.	Denkt euch einen Dialog aus.
Take a card.	Nehmt eine Karte.
Come to the board, please.	Komm/Kommt bitte zur Tafel.
Collect the exercise books, please.	Sammelt bitte die Hefte ein.
Do this exercise at home, please.	Macht diese Aufgabe bitte zu Hause.
Please be quiet.	Sei/Seid bitte ruhig.
Please sit down.	Setz dich bitte. / Setzt euch bitte.
Please speak up.	Sprich bitte lauter.
You can do better.	Das kannst du besser.
Try again.	Versuch es noch einmal.
That's correct.	Das ist richtig.
Well done.	Gut gemacht.

Diesterweg
westermann

937.752 aus Camden Town 2 (ISBN 978-3-425-73402-6)

Classroom phrases

Wenn man ankommt oder geht

Good morning.	Guten Morgen.
Sorry I'm late.	Tut mir leid, dass ich zu spät komme.
Sorry, I don't have my exercise book with me.	Tut mir leid, ich habe mein Heft nicht dabei.
What's our homework?	Was haben wir als Hausaufgabe auf?
See you tomorrow.	Bis morgen.

Wenn es ein Problem gibt

What's the matter with you?	Was ist mit dir los?
I'm fine. / I feel sick.	Mir geht's gut. / Mir ist schlecht.
Can I go to the toilet, please?	Kann ich bitte zur Toilette gehen?

Wenn man Hilfe braucht

Can you help me, please?	Können Sie/Kannst du mir bitte helfen?
I don't understand this.	Ich verstehe das hier nicht.
What's … in English/German?	Was heißt … auf Englisch/Deutsch?
What does … mean?	Was bedeutet …?
Can you say that again, please?	Können Sie/Kannst du das bitte noch einmal sagen?
Sorry, I don't know.	Tut mir leid, das weiß ich nicht.
Which page, please?	Auf welcher Seite bitte?

Wenn man mit dem Computer arbeitet

You can click on this link.	Du kannst auf diesen Link klicken.
Can I print it out/download it?	Kann ich es ausdrucken/herunterladen?
I saved it.	Ich habe es gespeichert.
My computer has crashed.	Mein Computer ist abgestürzt.

Wenn man zusammen arbeitet oder spielt

Whose turn is it?	Wer ist dran?
Do you want to work with me?	Möchtest du mit mir arbeiten?
How would you do it?	Wie würdest du das machen?
Who is doing the presentation?	Wer übernimmt die Präsentation?
Who is writing down the results?	Wer notiert die Ergebnisse?

Diesterweg
westermann
937.752 aus Camden Town 2 (ISBN 978-3-425-73402-6)